REASON, WILL, AND SENSATION

Reason, Will, and Sensation

Studies in Descartes's Metaphysics

Edited by
JOHN COTTINGHAM

CLARENDON PRESS · OXFORD
1994

*This book has been printed digitally and produced in a standard design
in order to ensure its continuing availability*

OXFORD
UNIVERSITY PRESS

Great Clarendon Street, Oxford OX2 6DP

Oxford University Press is a department of the University of Oxford.
It furthers the University's objective of excellence in research, scholarship,
and education by publishing worldwide in

Oxford New York

Athens Auckland Bangkok Bogotá Buenos Aires Cape Town
Chennai Dar es Salaam Delhi Florence Hong Kong Istanbul Karachi
Kolkata Kuala Lumpur Madrid Melbourne Mexico City Mumbai Nairobi
Paris São Paulo Shanghai Singapore Taipei Tokyo Toronto Warsaw

with associated companies in Berlin Ibadan

Published in the United States
by Oxford University Press Inc., New York
10047 26426
© John Cottingham

ISBN 0-19-824083-X

Contents

List of Contributors   vii

Abbreviations   x

Introduction: *Plus una vice agendum*: Cartesian
Metaphysics Three and a Half Centuries On   1
John Cottingham

PART ONE:
REASON, HISTORY, AND METHOD

1. Descartes and the Historiography of Philosophy   19
   Bernard Williams

2. Descartes's Modernity   29
   Tom Sorell

3. The Sources of Descartes's Procedure of Deductive
   Demonstration in Metaphysics and Natural Philosophy   47
   Stephen Gaukroger

PART TWO: REASON, BEING, AND TRUTH

4. Descartes's Concepts of Substance   63
   Peter Markie

5. God without Cause   89
   Carol Rovane

6. Descartes's Denial of the Autonomy of Reason   111
   Howard Wickes

7. Truth, Error, and the Order of Reasons:
   Descartes's Puzzling Synopsis of the Fourth
   Meditation   141
   Donald A. Cress

PART THREE: THE WILL

8. Human Nature, Reason, and Will in the Argument of
Descartes's *Meditations*   159
  Peter Schouls

9. Descartes's Compatibilism   177
  Vere Chappell

10. Descartes's Doctrine of Freedom: Differences between
the French and Latin Texts of the Fourth Meditation   191
  Michelle Beyssade

PART FOUR: THE SENSES AND THE BODY

11. Descartes on Sense and 'Resemblance'   209
  Margaret D. Wilson

12. Sensory Ideas, Objective Reality, and Material Falsity   229
  Lilli Alanen

13. The Reconfiguration of Sensory Experience   251
  Ann Wilbur MacKenzie

14. Descartes: The End of Anthropology   273
  Stephen Voss

Bibliography   307
Table of Citations from Descartes's Works   317
Index   325

List of Contributors

LILLI ALANEN is Research Fellow of the Academy of Finland and teaches philosophy at the University of Helsinki. Her work on Descartes written in English includes *Studies in Cartesian Epistemology and Philosophy of Mind* (1982), 'Descartes, Omnipotence and Kinds of Modality' (1988), 'Descartes's Dualism and the Philosophy of Mind' (1989), and 'Thought-Talk: Descartes and Sellars on Intentionality' (1992).

MICHELLE BEYSSADE is Maître de conférences at the University of Paris I. She is the author of *Descartes* (1972), and of an edition of Descartes's *Meditations* which juxtaposes her own modern French translation with the original Latin text and the first French translation by Luynes. Her essays on Descartes include 'La Problématique du cercle et la métaphysique du *Discours de la méthode*' and 'System and Training in Descartes' *Meditations*' (1990).

VERE CHAPPELL is Professor of Philosophy at the University of Massachusetts. He is the author, with Willis Doney, of *Twenty-Five Years of Descartes Scholarship* (1987), editor of the twelve-volume *Essays on Early Modern Philosophers* (1992), and editor of *The Cambridge Companion to Locke* (1994). He also edited the modern library *Hume* and the Hume volume in the Anchor Collections of Critical Essays series.

JOHN COTTINGHAM is Professor of Philosophy at the University of Reading and editor of the journal *Ratio*. He is co-translator of *The Philosophical Writings of Descartes* (1985–91), author of *Rationalism* (1984), *Descartes* (1986), *The Rationalists* (Oxford History of Western Philosophy series, 1988), and *A Descartes Dictionary* (1993), and editor of *Descartes' Conversation with Burman* (1976) and *The Cambridge Companion to Descartes* (1992).

DONALD CRESS is Associate Professor of Philosophy and Associate Dean of Liberal Arts and Sciences at Northern Illinois University. He is translator of *Rousseau: The Basic Political Writings* (1987), editor of *Aristotle: Greek Commentaries in Latin Translation* (1982), and co-editor of *A Guide to Rare & Out-of-Print Books in the Vatican Film Library* (1986).

STEPHEN GAUKROGER is Reader in Philosophy at the University of Sydney. He is author of *Explanatory Structures* (1987) and *Cartesian Logic* (1989), editor of *Descartes: Philosophy, Mathematics and Physics* (1980) and *The Uses of Antiquity* (1991), and translator of *Arnauld: On True and False Ideas* (1990).

ANN WILBUR MACKENZIE is Associate Professor of Philosophy and Multidisciplinary Studies at Glendon College, York University, Ontario, and is currently (1993–4) President of the Canadian Philosophical Association. Her research in cognitive science focuses on intentionality, representation, subjectivity, and telelology, and she is the author of a number of articles on Descartes relating his scientific work to his metaphysics, philosophy of mind, and epistemology.

PETER MARKIE is Professor of Philosophy at the University of Missouri-Columbia and author of *Descartes's Gambit* (1986) and of various articles on Descartes, ethics, and intentionality.

CAROL ROVANE is Assistant Professor of Philosophy at Yale University. She has published numerous articles in the philosophy of language and mind and in metaphysics. Her forthcoming book is *The Bounds of Agency: An Essay in Revisionary Metaphysics*.

PETER SCHOULS is Professor of Philosophy at the University of Alberta, where he has chaired the departments of Philosophy, of Religious Studies, and of East Asian Studies. He is the author of *The Imposition of Method: A Study of Descartes and Locke* (1980) and *Reasoned Freedom: John Locke and the Enlightenment* (1992).

TOM SORELL is Reader in Philosophy and Head of Department at the University of Essex. He is the author of *Hobbes* (1986), *Descartes* (1987), and *Scientism* (1991), and is editor of *The Rise of Modern Philosophy* (1993).

STEPHEN VOSS is Professor of Philosophy at Boğaziçi University, Istanbul. He is editor of Descartes, *Passions of the Soul* (1989), and of *Essays on the Philosophy and Science of René Descartes* (1993), and has written on metaphysics and morals and their reflections in seventeenth-century philosophy.

HOWARD WICKES is Senior Lecturer in Philosophy and the History of Ideas at the University of Northumbria at Newcastle upon Tyne.

BERNARD WILLIAMS is White's Professor of Moral Philosophy at Oxford University and Deutsch Professor of Philosophy at the University of California, Berkeley. His writings include *Descartes: the Project of*

Pure Enquiry (1978) and *Ethics and the Limits of Philosophy* (1985). His most recent book is *Shame and Necessity* (1993).

MARGARET D. WILSON is Professor of Philosophy at Princeton University. She is the author of *Descartes* (1978), and of many articles on seventeenth- and eighteenth-century philosophy.

Abbreviations

THROUGHOUT this book, references to Descartes's works are made in parentheses in the main body of the text, by volume and page number of the standard Franco-Latin and English editions of Descartes (AT and CSM or CSMK respectively). In the cases of Descartes's *Principles of Philosophy* and *Passions of the Soul*, parenthetical references are sometimes given simply by the original part and article numbers (which are reproduced in all editions). The Bibliography contains full details of all other editions of Descartes, and other books and articles cited in footnotes.

AT *Œuvres de Descartes*, ed. C. Adam and P. Tannery (rev. edn., 12 vols., Paris: Vrin/CNRS, 1964–76)

CSM *The Philosophical Writings of Descartes*, i–ii, ed. J. Cottingham, R. Stoothoff, and D. Murdoch (Cambridge: Cambridge University Press, 1985)

CSMK *The Philosophical Writings of Descartes*, iii, ed. J. Cottingham, R. Stoothoff, D. Murdoch, and A. Kenny (Cambridge: Cambridge University Press, 1991)

Introduction: Plus una vice agendum: Cartesian Metaphysics Three and a Half Centuries On

JOHN COTTINGHAM

It has often been observed that the relationship of philosophy to its history is uniquely problematic. Some subjects, notably the scientific disciplines, are what could be termed 'progress driven'; they regard the systems of the past largely as curiosities. The ideas of previous ages, however great and original, are thought of as having held pride of place only until they were refuted or superseded, and the original texts in which they appeared are certainly not regarded as essential reading for modern practitioners. In the arts and letters, by contrast, the great works of the past are indeed assiduously and meticulously studied, but this is a simple function of the fact that those works, and the tradition into which they fit, constitute the very subject-matter of the relevant academic disciplines; the accurate study of that subject-matter is a large part of their *raison d'être*. Only in philosophy do we find that the driving force for the subject arises from a curious synergy of the demands of present and past: on the one hand, there is a commitment to the quasi-scientific ideal of a modern 'progressive' discipline, with advances to make and past errors to refute, while on the other there is an inescapable felt need to refer to earlier theories, and to engage in a continuing dialogue with their authors. Each philosophical generation has to come to terms with what Plato or Aristotle or Hume or Kant said; our very philosophical identity is shaped by how we interpret the ideas of these great canonical thinkers, and by how we locate our own philosophical beliefs and attitudes against the conceptual reference-grid they helped create.

Nowhere is philosophy's preoccupation with its past more apparent than in the study of Descartes. The importance of the Cartesian system in the academic structures of our university courses today can scarcely be exaggerated: countless undergraduate students are taught to cut their philosophical teeth on the ideas and arguments of the *Discourse on the Method* and the *Meditations*. At one level this could, of course, be a dreary institutional fact—indicating nothing more than the habits of the classroom passed down from one pedagogue to the next; but it seems hard to deny that it has a deeper significance for our contemporary philosophical culture, reflecting the special place of Descartes's ideas in our own time. Cartesianism today has become the ultimate philosophical *bête noire*: both in the theory of knowledge and the philosophy of mind, late-twentieth-century philosophers tend to define their position in stark opposition to what are seen as deeply flawed Cartesian paradigms, whether of 'foundationalist' epistemology or of 'dualist' philosophical psychology. Descartes, the 'father of modern philosophy', has been comprehensively disowned by his putative offspring. Yet the effects of this filial revolt have been at least partially mitigated by a surprising resurgence of interest in what Descartes actually wrote. The vigorous expansion in Cartesian scholarship over the last two decades or so has revealed a philosophy of extraordinary richness and complexity, often far more nuanced and more challenging than the caricature Cartesianism which has provided such an easy target for modern detractors.

The present volume of essays, all appearing here for the first time, should give some indication of the fruits of that scholarship as applied to some of the central concepts of Cartesian metaphysics—reason, will, and sensation. The metaphysical focus of many of the contributions is to some extent a reflection of the recent move away from a study of Descartes based exclusively on his epistemology. The Descartes who has often been portrayed in standard first-year courses is in some respects a rather silly thinker, chiefly preoccupied with the kinds of far-fetched questions that get philosophy a bad name— questions such as 'Do I really know if I am awake?' or 'Does the "external world" really exist?' Certainly it is true that Descartes was interested in uncovering new and reliable foundations for human knowledge; certainly, too, the way in which he presented his arguments was influenced by the revival of classical scepticism in the late sixteenth and early seventeenth centuries. But a proper grasp of his enquiries into what can be doubted requires us to go far deeper than the stock debates about bent sticks and dreaming. Descartes himself brusquely observed that the value of his arguments was 'not that they prove that there really is a world and that human beings have bodies, and so on, since no sane person has ever doubted such things' (AT VII 16; CSM II 11). To understand the underlying philosophical motivations at work, we need to appreciate the scope of Descartes's scientific ambitions, and this in turn requires us to unravel the structure of the metaphysical system which he devised to underpin those ambitions. As will be clear from the volume's table of contents, the chapters in the central sections of the book are concerned with key notions of Cartesian metaphysics—God, substance, reason, and truth, and the relationship between the intellect and the will; in the final section, the scope is widened to embrace the transition from metaphysics to science, and in particular the role of the senses and the body in the Cartesian system. The questions arising here are in many cases ones which have always been at the forefront of philosophical enquiry. Not only is there an inherent satisfaction in analysing and evaluating Descartes's intricate answers, but it is also true that the questions and the answers often interconnect with problems that remain philosophically perplexing even today.

By way of a prologue to these enquiries, the initial section of the volume is devoted to clarifying Descartes's place in the history of thought, and how the study of his ideas relates to the philosophical enterprise itself. In his opening study of 'Descartes and the Historiography of Philosophy', Bernard Williams reflects on the complex and problematic distinction between 'history of ideas' and 'history of philosophy', and argues that the chief point of the latter activity, with its essential commitment to a diachronic approach, is to 'give a philosophical point to writing historically about philosophy'. What this involves is not merely the uncovering of a tradition, and the examining of how that tradition relates to our own philosophical concerns, but a characteristic deepening of our philosophical understanding: at its best, the philosophical study of the 'father of modern philosophy' will generate what Nietzsche called an 'untimely perspective', making the familiar seem strange and vice versa. Seen in this light, the history of philosophy in general, and the philosophical study of Cartesianism in particular, finds its meaning and purpose in the challenge it offers to entrenched patterns of interpretation, its power to free us from anodyne received models of our philosophical past and our relationship to that past.

Just as the philosophy of our own day has found it necessary to reassess its relationship to the Cartesianism of the early modern period, so Descartes himself found it imperative to define what he was doing by reference to the errors of earlier philosophical dogmas. In his chapter on 'Descartes's Modernity', Tom Sorell unravels some of the complexities involved in Descartes's attitude to traditional systems of thought, and examines the extent to which Descartes qualifies as a genuine innovator. He argues that recent challenges to the standard conception of Descartes as breaking new ground have been overdone, and that the evidence for 'traditionalist' elements in his philosophy has been exaggerated. He concludes that in two respects at least Descartes can appropriately be called 'modern'—namely in his championing of an 'anti-eruditionist' model of science, and in his anticipation of the now familiar 'pro-scientific' stance which relegates subjects such as history and poetry to a lower level of importance than physics and mathematics. An uncovering of these strands in the thinking of the historical Descartes suggests that there may after all be something illuminating in the long-standing label which dubs him the father of our modern age.

Turning more specifically to Descartes's metaphysics, Stephen Gaukroger in his chapter 'The Sources of Descartes's Procedure of Deductive Demonstration' argues that here at least the structure of Cartesian thought is deeply indebted to traditional elements. He suggests, however, that it is far from easy to identify the precise model which influenced the way in which Descartes's metaphysical arguments were set out. It has often been supposed that Descartes was following a mathematical, or more specifically geometrical prototype, but Gaukroger shows that the model of deduction from axioms was rejected by Descartes even as an account of how truths could be discovered in geometry, let alone metaphysics. Gaukroger also examines, but rejects, an alternative proposal, namely that Descartes might have been attracted by the model of an 'art of discovery' developed in the sixteenth century by humanist writers like Agrippa, on the basis of much earlier work by Raymond Lull; again, Descartes's own recorded critique of the Lullian project rules out his own allegiance to such a model. The eventual solution which Gaukroger presents relies on a distinction (much emphasized by Descartes himself) between discovery and exposition: whatever his views on the method of discovery, Descartes was concerned to find a convincing way of presenting the metaphysical results he had achieved, and the education he had received at La Flèche provided him with a readily available paradigm for such a presentation—the *disputatio* model of the Jesuit commentators, which aimed to 'restructure already developed material in such a way as to draw from it conclusions which might have been obscured or even denied if the material had been presented in a different way'. Two interesting results follow from Gaukroger's interpretation: first, that considerations of presentation are of great importance in determining the structure of Descartes's metaphysical writings, not just in part I of the *Principles of Philosophy* (as Descartes himself affirms), but also, despite the marked differences of style, in his metaphysical masterpiece, the *Meditations*; and, secondly, that Descartes's own official account of what he was doing in the *Meditations* (in terms of a supposed 'method of analysis') does not after all do much to illuminate the true rationale behind the argumentative structure of the work. But, as Gaukroger implicitly allows at the end of his paper, debates over the debt Descartes owed to his predecessors are likely to continue; what remains true is that, however strongly his ideas were shaped by the culture of his time, he was able to remould them in such a way as to construct a system genuinely distinct from anything that had gone before.

As noted earlier, Descartes was for many years studied in the anglophone world almost exclusively for his views on knowledge—an orientation retrojected and legitimized by the historiographical cliché that Descartes founded modern philosophy by assigning a special priority to questions about what we can know. In his contribution, Peter Markie criticizes the imbalance which has led commentators to concentrate on Cartesian epistemology at the expense of the metaphysics, and aims to redress it by a detailed examination of Descartes's use of that quintessentially metaphysical notion—the concept of substance. Or rather, concepts, in the plural; for Markie argues that three different notions of substance are deployed by Descartes, the first deriving from the idea of (causally or grammatically) independent existence, the second invoking the idea of a subject on which other things depend, and the third, and most metaphysically significant, implying 'mereological' independence. 'Pure' substances, in this third sense, do not depend for their existence on having any substantial parts, and this, for Descartes, explains their immunity to destruction (except by divine annihilation). This distinction throws considerable light on the vexed ontological status within the Cartesian system of human beings, constituted by what Descartes called the 'substantial union' of mind and body. While a mind united to a body can count

as a substance in the sense of being an independent subject, it does
not count as a substance in the 'pure' sense of existing without any
necessary parts.

At the centre of Cartesian metaphysics dwells the supreme substance, God. In Descartes's programme for establishing secure metaphysical foundations for his system, no firm progress can be made until
the mediator can prove the existence of 'a substance that is infinite,
eternal, immutable, independent, supremely intelligent, supremely
powerful and the creator of myself and everything else (if anything else
there be)' (AT VII 45; CSM II 31). Yet few of Descartes's arguments
have been subjected to such devastating attacks as that whereby
Descartes seeks to establish, in the Third Meditation, that the
supreme substance, so defined, 'necessarily exists'. As Carol Rovane
notes in her chapter, the chief stumbling block has always been the
first premiss which Descartes needs for his argument—the highly
complex causal principle that 'there must be at least as much in the
cause as in the effect'—a principle which he not only unquestioningly
accepts as 'manifest by the natural light', but also proceeds to apply,
highly controversially, to the representative content of his ideas.
Rovane does not attempt to rescue Descartes's argument as presented,
but instead ingeniously constructs an analogous argument which is in
many respects faithful to the spirit, if not the letter, of the Third
Meditation. In the actual text, the meditator reasons from his possession, notwithstanding his own imperfection, of the idea of perfection,
to the perfect cause which placed that idea in his mind. In the parallel
argument constructed by Rovane, the doubting, enquiring meditator
comes to see that his concept of perfect unlimited knowledge presupposes something which transcends the possible capacity (however
amplified) of a temporally bounded being. And hence 'we must
acknowledge that the idea of . . . a being [with such perfect knowledge]
is not just an indefinite extension of our ideas of ourselves; it is the
positive idea of a being that is essentially unlike us [and hence not]
constructible by amplifying or extending our ideas of ourselves and
our actual states of knowledge.' This conceptual analogue of Descartes's
causal argument uncovers what is a central theme of the reasoning he
actually offers in the Third Meditation—the notion of God as
perfection which I can approach in my thought and of which I can
even form a positive conception, but which, in virtue of my finite
nature, I can never fully encompass in terms of my own resources.
This still, of course, falls short of a demonstration that the being so

conceived actually exists; but Rovane suggests that the best hope for making this last move may come from what Descartes has to say in the Third Meditation about the logical interconnections between the divine attributes; if omnipotence implies independence, and independence implies total self-sufficiency, then it may not be too great a step to conclude such an entirely self-sufficient being must exist by its very nature. Though Rovane explicitly avoids addressing the issue of whether this final inference is valid, the fact that the seeds of such reasoning are, if she is right, contained in the reflections offered by Descartes in the Third Meditation suggests that there is perhaps not quite so vast a gulf as is often supposed between the 'cosmological' reasoning of the Third Meditation and the 'ontological' argument of the Fifth.

The proofs of God's existence are one instance of what is often taken to be a general feature of Cartesian metaphysics—its attempt to derive substantive conclusions about the nature of reality from rational reflection on the concepts or ideas found within us. Descartes's supposed ascription to the human intellect of the power to derive conclusions of this sort—his alleged insistence that the unaided natural light will guide us along a 'royal road' to absolute knowledge—this is the doctrine which Howard Wickes in his chapter dubs the doctrine of the 'autonomy of reason'. Wickes makes out a strong case for thinking that Descartes was not after all committed to such a doctrine. In the first place, Descartes's thesis that the 'eternal verities' of logic and mathematics are contingent on the sovereign power of God forecloses any possibility that human reason could discern ultimate necessary truths; and, in the second place, the account Descartes gives of the mind's spontaneous and irresistible assent to the truths of the natural light (when it is in a state of what Wickes aptly calls 'epistemic enthusiasm') seems to ground Cartesian metaphysics on the foundation of unshakeable and unconditional psychological certainty rather than any aspiration to absolute knowledge. Such a deflationary, or at least epistemically modest, interpretation of the Cartesian programme has to explain the precise import of Descartes's frequent appeals to the Deity as the source of all truth; on Wickes's account, the proofs of the existence of God 'offer us permanent certainty' by 'removing retrospective doubts about the reliability of the natural light', but they cannot 'change those certainties into absolute knowledge'. The Descartes who emerges from this analysis is in many respects a more 'modern' thinker than is suggested by the traditional portraits of him as a 'rationalist' metaphysician—a result which underlines the conclusions of earlier chapters about how often his ideas fail to slot neatly into the standard categories of historiographers of philosophy.

In unfolding his metaphysical system and developing his validation of knowledge, Descartes sets great store by the precise order in which the argument of the *Meditations* is constructed; as the great French commentator Martial Gueroult famously demonstrated, a proper understanding of the *Meditations* requires us to attend to the 'order of reasons' which its author purports to follow. In his chapter 'Truth, Error, and the Order of Reasons' Donald Cress focuses on a little studied aspect of the overall structure of the *Meditations*, namely the role of the Fourth Meditation. Descartes himself explicitly claimed, in the Synopsis, that the results of the Fourth Meditation need to be known 'to confirm what has gone before, and also to make intelligible what follows' (AT VII 15; CSM II 11); yet many expositors have been content to see the argument of the Fourth Meditation as a kind of interlude, offering a series of reflections on the relationship between divine goodness and the fact of human error, but not providing any new justification for the earlier account of truth, clarity, and distinctness, nor in any significant way preparing the ground for the argument of the last two Meditations. Cress implicitly acknowledges that the 'interlude' interpretation could gain support from much of the content of the Fourth Meditation: the project of theodicy which Descartes outlines turns out to be derived in large part from Augustinian ideas, and relies on theological presuppositions which are often presented unsystematically and with precious little in the way of supporting proof. But in two respects at least, Cress contends, the argument of the Fourth Meditation connects up in a more systematic and methodical way with the project of the *Meditations* as a whole. In the first place, the reflections on divine goodness and human error generate a kind of retrospective 'pragmatic' rationale for the stance taken in the earlier Meditations: they reveal the point of the sceptical doubts of the First Meditation, and the reason behind the procedures adopted in the Second and Third Meditations. And, in the second place, the discussion of the criterion of clarity and distinctness in the final paragraph of the Fourth Meditation illuminates the general strategy of the *Meditations* by providing a far more tightly organized and explicit exposition of that criterion than anything that has gone before. That said, it remains a source of disquiet, given Descartes's express claim to be 'starting afresh', that the way in which he expresses himself remains so closely indebted to the rhetorical and, more importantly, theological apparatus of Augustine. If the results of Wickes's analysis reveal the unexpectedly 'modern' orientation of some aspects of Cartesian thought, Cress's chapter reminds us of the extent to which other aspects were structured and informed by traditional ideas: 'the chief components of Augustine's mature theodicy flow from Descartes's pen as truths of the natural light of reason, the sole source of knowledge.'

Any attempt to understand the structure of argument in the *Meditations* must come to grips with one of the most complex issues in Cartesian metaphysics—the relationship between the intellect and the will. Although this relationship comes explicitly to the fore only in the Fourth Meditation, it has a pervasive importance in much of the rest of the work. Peter Schouls, in his chapter 'Human Nature, Reason, and Will in the argument of Descartes's *Meditations*', under- lines the close 'co-operation' of intellect and will in Descartes's system: the argument of the *Meditations* is 'structured by the funda- mental need to prove the existence of the *res cogitans* as an autonomous, reasoning, and willing being'. But, while the intellect is concerned with the passive reception of the truth, true action is possible only through the deliberate operations of the will; there is thus, Schouls argues, a 'primacy of free will over reason', in so far as our self-realization as thinking beings, capable of pursuing the truth, depends throughout on the exercise of the will. Both in the testing of reason, through the willed supposition of the omnipotent deceiver, and in the subsequent grasp of those truths which survive the test, the will is paramount.

Before the full powers of reason have been validated . . . we already know that the will is autonomous, that we really are active when we experience ourselves to be so, and that we won't have such experiences unless we will to have them. . . . Autonomous human nature dictates, for both theoretical work and practical experience, that activity precede passivity.

Descartes's frequent stress on the freedom of the will is complicated by his professed determinism—his insistence that both material and mental created things are causally dependent on an all powerful God. These two aspects of Cartesian thought make it natural to suppose that Descartes may have favoured a 'compatibilist' account of freedom (holding that the existence of free human action was not threatened by the truth of determinism). In his chapter 'Descartes's Compatibilism'

Vere Chappell provides a detailed analysis of Descartes's account of volitions and their causes, and shows both that Descartes is logically committed to compatibilism and that he explicitly affirms it. It is another question, however, whether the constraints of the Cartesian system enable such a compatibilist account to be presented as plausible and convincing. To begin with, Descartes's insistence on the total causal dependency on God of everything, including the workings of the human mind, does not seem easy to reconcile with genuinely free action of the will; though Chappell intriguingly suggests that, despite his theocratic rhetoric, Descartes may have been attracted to the view that the contribution of divine power to the determination of human action was necessary rather than sufficient. Theology aside, there remains an interesting tension between Descartes's affirmation of the freedom of our will and his doctrine that clear perception compels our assent. There is a curious kind of interdependence between will and intellect here, for, on the one hand, the will cannot act except in response to an exercise of the intellect ('no volition without representation', as Chappell puts it), while, on the other hand, when a perception of the intellect is sufficiently clear, the will is irresistibly moved to affirm its truth. In the latter case, it seems that Descartes must do more than assert that such determination of the will does not threaten our freedom; he must provide an acceptable account of what our freedom in such cases could amount to.

This last issue is taken up by Michelle Beyssade in her chapter 'Descartes's Doctrine of Freedom'. Beyssade focuses on a vexed passage in the Fourth Meditation where Descartes appears to stress that a two-way power is not necessary for true freedom. Having initially defined freedom as the power to affirm or deny, pursue or avoid, he proceeds apparently to correct himself, and substitute as the essence of freedom mere spontaneous action unconstrained by any external force. There is no need, he goes on to explain, for me to be able to go both ways in order to be free; rather, the more I incline in one direction because of my intellectual perception of truth or goodness, the freer is my choice (AT VII 58). This, at any rate, appears to be the position as set out in the original Latin text of the *Meditations*, published in 1641 (though, as Beyssade indicates, that text raises philosophically interesting issues of translation and interpretation). But the later French version of his work (authorized by Descartes and published in 1647) differs significantly from the Latin version, and a painstaking examination of these discrepancies leads Beyssade to the conclusion that Descartes's views on the nature of freedom had undergone an important shift. Having originally dissociated freedom from a two-way power, he now, in the French edition, reformulated the passage in question so as to leave it open whether such a power was required for freedom. Beyssade argues that this shift was partly the result of correspondence in 1645 between Descartes and the Jesuit priest Denis Mesland, as a result of which 'Descartes became more and more aware of the importance of the two-way power in freedom'. If this is right, then the Cartesian prospects for a compatibilist solution to the problem of freedom are gloomy indeed; for the pro-Jesuit conception of freedom, to which Descartes was (if Beyssade is correct) increasingly attracted, requires a 'real and positive power of deter- mining oneself to one or the other of two contraries'—something conspicuously lacking, it seems, in a mind divinely disposed to assent automatically to the deliverances of the natural light. If this introduces further tensions into the Cartesian account of freedom, they only compound what was acknowledged by Descartes himself to be a philosophical puzzle of daunting proportions (*Principles*, pt. I, art. 41).

The world of Cartesian metaphysics can in some respects appear a curiously closed world—an 'interior' universe formed and structured by content of the ideas found within the mind of the meditator. Yet this picture cannot entirely correspond to what Descartes intended, if only because one chief aim of the Cartesian project is clearly to establish a reliable account of the external physical universe. Even when the existence of that universe is established, however, its true description turns out to depend, in all general and essential aspects, not on our empirical contact with the world via the senses, but on the mathematical concepts innately implanted in the mind by God. This generates a major difficulty about the role of the senses in the Cartesian system. Though not exactly left out in the cold (Descartes acknowledges their utility to embodied creatures for survival purposes), their importance for metaphysical and scientific understanding appears to be minimal. As Margaret Wilson puts it in her chapter 'Descartes on Sense and "Resemblance"', what comes across at least in the *Meditations* is 'a largely *negative* and *purgative* approach to sense experience'. Indeed, if the 'real' world is characterized only in terms of mathematical extension, then the phenomenal world as depicted by our sensory ideas turns out to be something of a systematic illusion: the ideas of sense constitute a 'veil of perception' (in Jonathan Bennett's suggestive phrase) interposed between us and reality. Now when writing as a physiologist (for example in the *Optics*), Descartes was, as Wilson acknowledges, highly suspicious of theories of sense perception that posited intermediate entities requiring some kind of inference from an 'image' to its external cause. But she argues, nevertheless, that the account given in the *Meditations* (where the aims and concerns are very different from those in the scientific works) inescapably commits Descartes to the view that 'knowledge of physical existence is secondary to, and inferentially derivative from, knowledge of mental ideas'. There is a link here with the general mechanistic programme of Cartesian science; for, in so far as there is a systematic contrast, in the mechanist's account, between bodies 'as they really are' and bodies as they appear to us (in terms of colour, taste, smell and so on), this tends (Wilson argues) to push the mechanist towards 'a denial that sensory awarensss of bodies is "direct"'. One classic objection to construing sense perception as an indirect process (an objection pioneered by Berkeley) is that it makes no sense to talk of ideas resembling, or failing to resemble, external things. In the final section of her chapter, Wilson suggests that Cartesian talk of sensory ideas failing to resemble external things should be understood as partly metaphorical—as a way of conveying that such ideas fail to provide a basis for an intelligible conception of the physical objects that give rise to them. If she is correct, then, despite the fact that 'veil-of-perception' accounts are generally taken to be deeply suspect from a philosophical point of view, Descartes's implicit espousal of such an account, and his associated discussion of whether ideas resemble external objects, can 'at least be placed in a philosophically serious context'.

The status of sensory ideas is further examined by Lilli Alanen in her chapter 'Sensory Ideas, Objective Reality, and Material Falsity'. In the Third Meditation Descartes ascribes to sensory ideas a special, intrinsic kind of falsity, 'which occurs in ideas when they represent non-things as things' (AT VII 43; CSM II 30). Alanen argues that it is a general feature of Cartesian ideas that 'they are representative, that is they have a certain kind of objective being [what we should now call intentionality or representative content] by their very nature; as such they are always about something even when, as is the case with sensory ideas, there is no telling what thing they are of or about'. Now sensory awareness, on Descartes's account, is not a species of clear and distinct perception; rather it is an obscure and confused kind of perception, not proper to the mind as a pure thinking thing, but arising from the 'union' of mind and body. The 'material falsity' of sensory ideas is thus, Alanen suggests, connected with this obscurity and confusion. A complication here is that Descartes himself notes that, if ideas are considered 'simply in themselves, without being referred to anything outside, they can scarcely provide any subject-matter for error'. Scarcely, but not absolutely: he insists there is a kind of falsity that can arise, but what exactly does it consist in, and how is it connected with obscurity? Alanen's solution is that material falsity pertains not to the simple sensations as such, but rather to 'unanalysed, confused, complex sensory ideas, the components of which turn out, on closer scrutiny, to be incompatible and contradictory'. In other words, our sensory awareness is often, for Descartes, linked to a background of habitual beliefs or attitudes in terms of which they are automatically interpreted: 'an essential part of Descartes's method of clarification consists in rendering the unnoticed, habitual and mostly precipitate beliefs involved in sensory perception explicit, and thereby subject to critical evaluation.' In one respect the moral Alanen draws from this is close to Wilson's conclusion that the unsatisfactoriness of sensory ideas, from Descartes's point of view, is that they cannot provide a distinctly intelligible conception of external objects; as Alanen puts it, beyond pointing to *something* (whatever it is in the external world whose impinging on our sensory organs gave rise to their occurrence), they have 'no determinate, distinctly conceivable content that could be further analysed or specified'. Although the terms of this discussion are constrained by the need to make sense of Descartes's often confusing terminology, it should be clear that the underlying issues involved, concerning the analysis of sensory qualities and the relation between our subjective perceptions and the objective world of physics, are still very much on the contemporary philosophical agenda.

These themes also figure in Ann MacKenzie's chapter, 'The Reconfiguration of Sensory Experience', which begins by underlining the 'deeply negative assessment of the cognitive role of the senses in the search for truth' found in Descartes's metaphysical writings. She suggests, however, that Descartes's underlying aim is to get us to 'pare apart' the primary- and the secondary-quality components of our sensory experience, which in our unreflective lives we tend to jumble together fairly indiscriminately: 'Descartes's conceptual work constitutes a transformation—or reconfiguration—of this common sense understanding because it emphasizes the fundamental difference between these two components within sensory experience.' MacKenzie then provides a detailed survey of the more positive role which Descartes ends up assigning to sensory perception both in his metaphysical and in his scientific writings. In science, sensory experience may indeed be used as a basis for judgements about the primary properties of the ordinary middle-sized objects we find around us; while in metaphysics it has a key function first in establishing with certainty that the external world exists, and secondly in alerting us to the closeness and intimacy of the union between mind and body (an intimacy which sharp distinction between the two substances made by the intellect might have led us to overlook).

The vexed problem of the 'union' between mind and body in Cartesian metaphysics is taken up in the volume's concluding chapter by Stephen Voss, provocatively entitled 'Descartes: The End of Anthropology'. Any systematic philosophy, Voss begins by observing, should surely be able to offer some answer to the question 'What is a human being?' What Descartes says in the *Meditations* about the 'intermingling' of mind and body, and his later discussion in the letters to Regius of the 'substantial union' between the two substances, have led some commentators to believe that he managed with increasing success to find a genuine place in his writings for embodied creatures of flesh and blood, capable of abstract thought and reflection, but also subject to the more mundane earthly cycle of pleasure and pain, feeling, sensation and passion—in short, a place for human beings. Voss argues, however, that Descartes ultimately failed to incorporate human beings into his new universe; his thinking evolved from a moderate Platonism (where soul and body were regarded as components of a man), via a scholastic phase (where he toyed with various stock formulae, such as that man was an *ens per se*, or 'entity in itself'), through to a final stage of 'extreme Platonism' or 'angelism' (in which soul and body cease to compose a man). In carefully charting the course through these various phases, Voss suggests that the ultimate extreme position is prefigured in the metaphysics of the *Meditations*, but is fully developed only in later works such as the *Principles of Philosophy* and the *Passions of the Soul*. Once the foundations of Descartes's metaphysical system are firmly established, and their implications fully worked out, no room is left for a Cartesian anthropology. On Voss's deflationary account, Descartes's scattered suggestions about a soul–body union engendering a capacity for sensations tell us nothing about human nature, only something about soul and body, and how they are related. Reflecting this, the taxonomy of the *Principles* is, Voss claims, 'wholly silent on the question of [essential attributes] for *man*, or of a procedure for determining what characteristics man can possess, once characteristics have been parcelled out to mind and body'. In short, the framework of Descartes's mature philosophy is, in the end, 'deeply inhospitable to the thesis that man exists at all'. If this is indeed the logical end-point of Cartesian metaphysics, it is hard to imagine a more counter-intuitive consequence, or one which exposes Descartes more dangerously to the standard modern jibe that his theory boils down to the bizarre assertion that each of us is a 'ghost in the machine'.[1] That said, it has to be admitted that the philosophers and scientists of our own day are still far from being able to provide a systematic and comprehensive account of human nature—if by that is meant an account explaining how our physiological make-up is related to our intellectual and volitional abilities, and, most puzzling of all, how to fit in those 'obscure and confused' yet vividly intrusive feelings of hunger, thirst, pleasure, and pain which Descartes cited as evidence of our mysterious and intimate involvement with the body. Part of the enduring appeal of Cartesian metaphysics is that it grapples with that most perennial and challenging of philosophical tasks—the task of seeing how far our conception of ourselves connects up with our conception of the rest of reality.

The chapters in this volume are all versions (in many cases substantially revised) of papers originally given at the British Society for the History of Philosophy conference held at the University of Reading in September 1991 to mark the 350th anniversary of the publication of Descartes's *Meditations*. The conference was made possible by generous support from the British Academy and the Mind Association, which I am glad to acknowledge here. As the original organizer of the conference, and the present Chairman of the BSHP, I should like to thank all those who participated; the countries represented at the conference included Australia, Canada, Britain, Finland, France, Greece, Holland, Ireland, Italy, Mexico, and the United States. Over forty papers were delivered, and by common consent the general standard was extremely high; my one regret is that the constraints of space, and the need to preserve a reasonable degree of thematic unity,

---

[1] Phrase first coined in Ryle, *The Concept of Mind*.

have meant that only a small proportion of the papers given could be included in the present volume. In preparing the volume for the press, I was greatly assisted by Enrique Chávez-Arvizo, who compiled the Table of Citations and the Index and did most of the work for the Bibliography.

Descartes himself declared in the Preface to the *Meditations* that the problems of metaphysics were of sufficient importance to deserve treatment 'more than once'.[2] Whether he would have been happy to see the close attention still accorded to his views over 350 years after the publication of his metaphysical masterpiece, it is impossible to say. Ever impatient with critics and commentators, he is reported to have told one eager student that it was a mistake to dig any deeper into these matters than he himself had done.[3] However that may be, the chapters presented here should prove at least one thing: despite the fiercely anti-Cartesian philosophical orthodoxy of our own times, Descartes's metaphysical writings have still not lost their power to fascinate, to challenge, and to illuminate.

---

[2] 'Tanti ... momenti mihi visae sunt, ut plus una vice de ipsis agendum esse judicarem' (*Meditations*, Preface to Reader: AT VII 7; CSM II 6).

[3] 'Non adeo incumbendum esse meditationibus, nec rebus metaphysics, nec eas commentariis et similibus elaborandas; multo minus altius repetendas quam author fecit' (*Conversation with Burman*: AT V 165; CSMK 346).

PART ONE

Reason, History, and Method

I

Descartes and the Historiography of Philosophy

BERNARD WILLIAMS

Discussing, some years ago, different ways of approaching the thought of Descartes, I made a broad distinction between two activities that I labelled 'the history of ideas' and 'the history of philosophy'.[1] The two are distinguished in the first place by their product. The history of ideas yields something that is history before it is philosophy, while with the history of philosophy it is the other way round. In particular, the product of the history of philosophy, being in the first place philosophy, admits more systematic regimentation of the thought under discussion. The two activities can be distinguished also by having rather different directions of attention. The history of ideas, as I intended the distinction, naturally looks sideways to the context of a philosopher's ideas, in order to realize what their author might be doing in making those assertions in that situation. The history of philosophy, on the other hand, is more concerned to relate a philosopher's conception to present problems, and is likely to look at his influence on the course of philosophy from his time to the present.

It is obvious that these two activities cannot be totally separated from one another, and each needs to some extent the skills of the other. It would be a mistake, however, to suppose that the distinction is simply baseless, or that the best possible historical approach to a philosopher would consist in an ideal fusion of these two activities. There is more than one reason why this cannot be so. One is that the best possible history of ideas is likely to show that the philosophy did not in fact mean in contemporary terms what subsequent philosophy has most

[1] B. Williams, *Descartes: The Project of Pure Enquiry*, preface.

made of it. But, apart from that, the kinds of sensibility needed for the two activities are bound to yield partly incompatible products, in rather the way that Impressionism, by exploring as intensely as possible the surface effects of light, was thereby debarred from giving as much information about structure as was accessible to some other styles of painting.

I have said that the approach associated with what I called 'the' history of philosophy' is marked out both by a concern that its product should be in good part philosophy, and also by an interest in diachronic influence (a dimension which the phrase itself, of course, particularly suggests). It is important, however, that these two points do not simply, or always easily, go together. One way of putting the philosophy of the past to use in present terms is to neglect or overlook, to some extent, the history that lies between that philosophy and the present day, and to reconsider the philosophy in partial independence from its actual influence. It has been a particular speciality, in fact, of the analytic history of philosophy to approach the philosophy of the past in this way. At its extreme, this activity could take the form of triumphant anachronism, as when it used to be said, in the heyday of analytic confidence, that we should approach the works of Plato as though they had appeared in last month's issue of *Mind*. The claim that it did actually proceed in this way is now one of the standard charges associated with the demonized image of analytical history of philosophy.

Other charges against analytical history of philosophy are that it suffers from the limitations of analytic philosophy itself, in considering only a narrow range of philosophical interests; and that it neglects the literary dimension of philosophical works, so that—in the case of some of them, at least—it misses a good deal of what can be got from them even philosophically. Finally, there is the charge of its obtrusive cockiness, the condescension with which earlier writers are treated to instruction by current philosophical methods, and are reproved for their errors—errors to which they have been committed, typically, by the way in which analytical philosophy interprets them. All these charges are certainly true, in the sense that there are very many works in this style to which one or more, and often all, of the charges can justly be applied. I shall not discuss all the charges here.[2]

The first of the charges, however (and, to some extent, the last),

---

[2] I have said something about the literary character of some philosophical works in B. Williams, *Shame and Necessity*, 13–14.

raises the question not only of how such activities should be conducted, but of why. The idea of treating philosophical writings from the past as though they were contemporary is, at the limit, simply unintelligible. If one abstracts entirely from their history—including in this both the history of their context and the history of their influence—one has an obvious problem of what object one is even supposed to be considering. One seems to be left simply with a set of words in some modern language (which, in many cases, have been generated by a translator), and one associates with these words whatever philosophical notions they may carry with them today. This activity has no title to being history of any sort. But even when the activity is less arbitrary than this suggests, there remains a question of its point. The point of any history, one might suppose, is to achieve some distance from the present, which can help one to understand the present. The more extreme forms of analytical history of philosophy addressed themselves to removing that distance altogether, and in doing so lost the title to being any pointful form of historical activity. In these extreme forms, they owed their existence only to the fact that something called 'the history of philosophy' appeared in the syllabus, and they provided a philosophical activity to fill this place.

However it may have been in earlier years, these very extreme forms of the analytical history of philosophy do now belong to the demonology of the subject, and are rarely to be found in inhabited places in the daylight. There is a good deal of history of philosophy that uses analytical techniques, and yet is genuinely and non-arbitrarily historical; it is still history of philosophy in my terms, which is to say that its product is to an important extent philosophy. To justify its existence, it must maintain a historical distance from the present, and it must do this in terms that sustain its identity as philosophy. It is just to this extent that it can indeed be useful, because it is just to this extent that it can help us to deploy ideas of the past in order to understand our own. We can adapt to the history of philosophy a remark that Nietzsche made about classical philology: 'I cannot imagine what [its] meaning would be in our own age, if it is not to be untimely—that is, to act against the age, and by so doing to have an effect on the age, and, let us hope, to the benefit of a future age.'[3] One way in which the history of philosophy can help to serve this purpose is the basic and familiar one of making the familiar seem strange, and

[3] F. Nietzsche, 'History in the Service or Disservice of Life', in *Unmodern Observations*, 88.

conversely, but it needs to learn how better to do this. We should bear in mind this well-known aim of history—and specifically of a history that aims in some part to be philosophy—in turning, now, to some more specific questions about Descartes.

It used to be true (and may still be so) that the guide to the Panthéon in Paris would say at one point of the tour: '*Ici, mesdames et messieurs, vous voyez le tombeau du plus grand philosophe français, Jean-Jacques Rousseau.*' One wonders what he would say if, as very nearly happened, Descartes's body had also ended up in the Panthéon. Indeed, there are rather more similarities between the two than the usual descriptions allow. Both are marvellous writers, both are extremely self-consciously original, both have been massively influential, and, despite having very different attitudes towards antiquity, they have both centrally contributed to a distinctively modern consciousness. In these last respects, moreover, each of them presents problems to the history of ideas and to the history of philosophy: each of them has had an influence that owes a great deal to gigantic misunderstandings, and each has been made use of in ways neither of them could, needless to say, either have foreseen or have tolerated. Going back to their original context, and to the influences on them, may indeed help to remove those misunderstandings, but at the same time it raises the question, in each case, of the thinker's originality.

In neither case is the originality to be denied—it is a question rather of its nature. With both of them, it is a matter of conscious self-presentation; it is not the more nearly naïve originality of Frege or of C. S. Peirce. In Descartes's case, this raises two questions. The first is where the idea of such a self-presentation came from. Descartes's methodological and metaphysical turn towards himself has been associated often enough with such influences as Augustine and Montaigne, but they do not provide enough to explain his presentation of his project as a way of life. The modes of 'self-fashioning' that Stephen Greenblatt has discussed in relation to the Renaissance consciousness[4] are perhaps relevant to the idea that Descartes had formed of what he was to do, an idea formed, of course, while he was pursuing the life of a soldier. In the words of Ausonius which he recalled, '*Quod vitae sectabor iter?*', it is important that the word is *iter*, not *via*: there is a journey to be made.

The second question concerns what we might find in Descartes if

4 S. Greenblatt, *Renaissance Self-Fashioning*.

we removed the 'misunderstandings' that have so immeasurably contributed to and formed his influence. In asking this question, I am not looking for an understanding of Descartes that is free of later presuppositions, which benefits from no hindsight. Clearly, there could be no such thing. It is a question, rather, of its not benefiting from *this* hindsight, or the presuppositions peculiarly associated with our inherited history of philosophy. (This is one way in which we can aim to make the familiar strange again.) As things are, the history of ideas and the history of philosophy, applied to Descartes, are likely to yield, respectively, one of two types of understanding, one purely historical, and the other largely anachronistic. The history of ideas quite properly invites us to learn about late scholastic influences and the syllabus at La Flèche, or introduces us to problems that were encountered in developing an adequate mechanics of inertia. The history of philosophy, on the other hand, speaks in terms of how one can develop a non-transcendental epistemology starting from scepticism. The first of these two activities, the history of ideas, certainly has nothing wrong with it, but, in itself, it does not yield much philosophy that can help us in reviving a sense of strangeness or questionability about our own philosophical assumptions. It may be, simply and quietly, what it seeks to be, about the past. The history of philosophy, very often, does no more to release us from our preconceptions, for the different reason that it is merely constructed out of our preconceptions. The important thing about these two approaches is not that one is historical in relation to Descartes, while the other is anachronistic. The point, rather, is that neither of them, as things are, helps us to use Descartes to gain what Nietzsche called an 'untimely' perspective on our philosophical concerns. The first fails to do so because it does not, in itself, yield philosophy; the second yields philosophy, but only too much of the time it yields *our* philosophy.

Any philosopher who is likely to be of interest now to the history of philosophy is going to raise questions of this kind. But such questions are specially raised by Descartes, because he makes a unique claim to the suspect title 'the founder of modern philosophy'. At least two difficulties attach to this title, and to Descartes's relation to it. One of them is closely connected to the matter I mentioned before, of Descartes's self-presentation. A difficulty in getting behind this title is that Descartes seems to have arranged things, in particular his presentation of himself, in order to invite such a title; to a greater extent than many philosophers, Descartes is the architect of his own reputation and, by the same token, responsible for some of the misunderstandings that have attached themselves to that reputation.

A more general difficulty lies in the shifting content of the idea of 'modern philosophy' and of what could count as being its founder. 'Modern philosophy' used to mean *our* philosophy, but perhaps that is no longer true: some would say that 'modern' now signified only a period in the history of philosophy, a period that is closed or is closing. Perhaps it makes less difference than one might suppose to the present discussion whether one accepts that description or not. Even if the 'modern philosophy' that Descartes founded is taken to be the philosophy to which our discussions still contribute, Descartes's relation to it has for a long time been problematical or contested. The view which takes the philosophy of language rather than epistemology as the heart of philosophy has already for a long time relegated Descartes to the role of anti-hero, and has replaced him with Frege in the position of the founder of legitimate modern philosophical activity. This view itself, of course, has various ways of using Descartes, with the result that he remains part of the discourse of philosophy. One important use is indeed in the role of anti-hero: his works (or a few of them) are read (or partly read) as the most challenging and informatively misleading example of what is to be rejected.

Even in this role, however, he is rather paradoxically used. Those who have wanted to displace epistemology, and in particular a concern with scepticism, from a central place in philosophy have in many cases claimed to be interested in diagnosing the apparent attractions of the problem; they have wanted to replace attempts to answer it with an understanding of why we are tempted into it. Descartes is typically wheeled out as an example of one who indulged himself in trying to answer the problem of scepticism, but not so much, it seems, as someone from whom we can learn about the temptations to get into it. He is typically presented, in his brief appearance at the beginning of philosophy courses, as one who simply had a weakness for scepticism, or perhaps for mathematical certainty; or a brief expedition is made into the history of ideas to bring back an externalist explanation in terms of seventeenth-century Christian apologetics.

This obviously does little good for the understanding of Descartes or of scepticism, and it is fairly damaging to a sense of philosophy itself and of its history. If one presents Descartes as the founder of modern philosophy, and as seized by the problem of scepticism; if the problem of scepticism is said to be interesting not for its solution, but for the motives that lead to it; and if Descartes is not represented as displaying any interesting motive for it, but is diagnosed as being trapped in history, or (as it is more usually explained) in whatever misconception particularly impresses the teacher as providing the source of scepticism: a student will reasonably conclude, not only that Descartes is a fool, or at least that he has been overtaken by history, but, more damagingly, that a subject which not only has him as its founder but thinks it important that one should now read the works of such a founder cannot be a very serious subject. Descartes's own approach to his problems had better be presented as adequate to our own interest both in them and in him.

Not every view of Descartes as part of present philosophy need treat him as an anti-hero. He can be taken to be the founder of a modern philosophy to which we still belong in virtue of more general characteristics of his work that we strive to share: that it claims to persuade by argument and the fact that its starting-point (unlike its conclusions) is not religious. This view of Descartes depends, like the anti-hero view, on interpreting it so as to make a particular kind of sense as philosophy. It depends, that is to say, on the activity that I called 'the history of philosophy'. But, equally, those who wish to detach themselves from 'modern philosophy', leaving Descartes as the founder of a certain period in philosophy's history, cannot do without the activity of interpreting him in ways that result in a set of philosophical claims. Their style of doing this is likely to lean more heavily in the direction of interpreting his philosophy in terms of a set of supposed influences. The need to separate the activities the writers would like us to pursue from something now delimited as having been 'modern philosophy' requires them to identify a set of recent philosophical activities, the activities of 'modern philosophy', precisely as having been influenced by Descartes.

This post-modern approach, as it may be called, typically runs the risk of a split consciousness. On the one hand, it has to take the history of philosophy seriously enough to constitute a tradition; it has to detect enough continuity of concerns and assumptions to support the claims of influence. On the other hand, if it looks closely enough, it will, of course, find that the influence has worked, and the tradition been constituted, through misunderstanding. The writers it invokes will, at the very least, have made partial and selective use of earlier writers,

since that is what creative writers, philosophers or not, of course do
with the writers they read. Now the recognition of these facts need
not destroy the image of the tradition; it may merely constitute it as a
tradition of misunderstanding. But it has a damaging effect on the use
that the post-modern critic can make of the tradition. The better its
writers are understood, the less it looks as though they necessarily
hang together as the 'modernity' that the critic wants to get beyond.
Ironically enough, his own typical emphasis on contingency should
make him less contented with the Hegelian classifications that define
his own historical position.

He may say that he need not, after all, take his own historical
position too seriously. The constitution of the 'modern' tradition,
with Descartes as its founder, may figure simply as a ludic trope,
which gains a certain edge from the fact that its members, including Descartes himself, usually do not seem, when they are more
closely examined, to be doing quite what the story of the tradition
requires them to be doing. But the only point of the ludic, at least
as deployed in the history of philosophy, is to disturb and unsettle,
and the effect of taking the tradition of modernity as given, with
Descartes as its founder, can only be deeply settling and undisturbing,
since it confronts us exactly with what we thought we had already.
Our sense of our situation will be unsettled only when we come to
see Descartes and the other supposed contributors as stranger than
they seem while they are still regarded as the constituents of that
tradition.

What was called in the original distinction 'the history of philosophy'
is essential to any activity that is going to give a philosophical point to
writing historically about philosophy. That point is going principally
to be found in the possibility of the past philosophy's being untimely,
and helping to make strange what is familiar in our own assumptions.
In order to do this, the history of philosophy must be separated from
two tendencies with which it has often been associated. On the one
hand, it cannot treat its object as though it were merely contemporary,
without losing the point of historical distance altogether. On the other
hand, it cannot be identified with the history of influence, the
progressive exploitation of original writing in one or more philosophical traditions; this, again, destroys strangeness, by following a
path which necessarily lands us at precisely the place we are at. What
we must do is to use the philosophical materials that we now have to

hand, together with historical understanding, in order to find in, or make from, the philosophy of the past a philosophical structure that will be strange enough to help us to question our present situation and the received picture of the tradition, including those materials themselves.

2

Descartes's Modernity

TOM SORELL

This chapter can be understood as a defence of the cliché that Descartes is the father of modern philosophy. The cliché needs defending, because a growing body of revisionist commentary on seventeenth-century philosophy and science in general, and on Descartes in particular, suggests that the sharp break with the past conveyed by the phrase 'modern philosophy' is probably not to be found in seventeenth-century thought, and that Descartes, notwithstanding his modernist rhetoric, was significantly influenced by traditional philosophy, that is, significantly influenced by Aristotle, by Augustine, and by the authors of scholastic textbooks, particularly those used at La Flèche.

The thesis that traditional philosophy survived well into the so-called modern period has been put forward by, among others, Charles Schmitt.[1] In recent Descartes studies Daniel Garber[2] has been sympathetic to Schmitt's thesis, and there have been other commentators, from Étienne Gilson[3] in 1930 to Desmond Clarke[4] in 1982, who have argued independently of Schmitt that Descartes is deeply enmeshed in scholasticism and Aristotelianism. In defending the cliché that Descartes is the father of modern philosophy, I do not want to repudiate everything that Clarke, Gilson, and others have maintained; for one thing, quite a lot of their work suggests that Descartes did start something new, but that he did not start from scratch. Again, I do not

---

[1] C. Schmitt, *Aristotle and the Renaissance*; also relevant is his 'Toward an Assessment of Renaissance Aristotelianism'.

[2] D. Garber, 'Descartes, the Aristotelians, and the Revolution that did not Happen in 1637', 486 n.

[3] E. H. Gilson, *Études sur le rôle de la pensée médiévale dans la formation du système cartésien*. [4] D. M. Clarke, *Descartes' Philosophy of Science*.

want to depart totally from Schmitt; for, while I believe that it is possible to identify aspects of Descartes's thought that make it modern, I do not believe that the whole range of philosophies classified as early modern are close enough to one another or far enough away from ancient and scholastic philosophy to constitute a coherent modern movement in philosophy. If the saying that Descartes is the father of modern philosophy implies that a single doctrinal path was followed by Hobbes, Gassendi, Leibniz, Locke, and Spinoza, and that Descartes blazed this path, then I do not want to defend the saying.

On the other hand, I do not think that this is the only interpretation of the saying that can be given. Another interpretation, and one which makes the saying defensible, is to the effect that Descartes broke in a number of ways, and broke self-consciously, with traditional philosophy, and that other supposed early moderns registered this fact, and, at least partly under Descartes's influence, enacted their own greater or lesser breaks from tradition, so that making the break, rather than the precise form that the break took, became, thanks to Descartes, a mark of modernity. Of course, it is also true that the precise form of Descartes's break from tradition was influential. In a number of European countries in the late seventeenth and early eighteenth centuries there were avowed followers of Descartes, people who wished to complete the programme for the new science partly executed in the *Principles*. And a number of important seventeenth-century philosophers who were not Cartesian defined their own positions by reference to their disagreements with Descartes. Locke and Gassendi, and, to a lesser extent, Hobbes, are examples, and the list of names could be extended. In bequeathing to subsequent philosophy a set of metaphysical and scientific theories that attracted both strong support and strong opposition, Descartes differs from Francis Bacon, who is also said to have started the fashion in the 1600s for fresh starts or big departures from tradition.

This chapter falls roughly into three parts. In the first I consider critically some of the textual evidence that has been thought to put Descartes's modernity in doubt. Next, I try to spell out some grounds for supposing that Descartes *is* modern; finally, I ask whether the label 'modern', the distinction between ancient and modern, and the cliché that Descartes is the father of modern philosophy might not have a value that the revisionist history of philosophy makes us overlook.

I

To what extent do Descartes's own published works encourage the idea that his thought breaks decisively from that of his predecessors? I think that the answer is: to a limited extent.[5] It is true that in the *Discourse* and the *Meditations* he writes of starting afresh and building from new foundations: but this may be a way of saying that he will be speaking for himself and not on behalf of the ancients; it may be a way of saying that he will present his conclusions—novel or not—on his own authority or that of his method of reasoning, and not on the authority of a Plato or an Aristotle. Interpreted in this way, Descartes's rhetoric expresses a declaration of intellectual independence or autonomy, not a declaration of innovation. If his findings happen to agree with those of the ancients, that is not necessarily a blemish on them; what matters is that they are genuine findings, arrived at by Descartes *in propria persona*.

The rhetoric of starting afresh and building anew, then, is ambiguous, and there are well-known passages in which Descartes seems to be friendly to traditional philosophy. For instance, in part VI of the *Discourse* he counts the best known of the ancient philosophers as among the finest minds of their time, praising Aristotle in particular for a knowledge of nature far greater than any of his later followers, and comparing the later followers to the ivy that can never grow taller than the trees it fastens on (AT VI 70). In the preface to the French edition of the *Principles* he is prepared to use the honorific term 'wisdom' to describe the results of conversing with the writings of the ancients (AT IXB 5; CSM I 181). It is true that the level of wisdom attained in this way is not supposed to be the highest; it is true that Descartes thinks that his own philosophy is a better attempt at achieving the highest level of wisdom than some traditional philosophy. Nevertheless, Descartes is prepared to regard conversation with the tradition as a source of wisdom. In the Letter to Father Dinet he denies that his own philosophy and traditional philosophy are really at odds over fundamentals. 'As far as principles are concerned,' Descartes says, 'I only accept those which in the past have always been common ground among all philosophers without exception, and which are therefore the most ancient of all' (AT VII 580; CSM II 392). He

---

[5] Here I am in disagreement with John Cottingham, who thinks that Descartes himself encouraged the idea that he was a radical innovator. See his 'A New Start?'.

goes on to suggest a sense in which principles that are distinctively Aristotelian are new and not ancient, but without retracting the point that his philosophy has something in common with every other, even including the Aristotelian. And the point is repeated with some force in part IV of the *Principles* (AT IXB 323; CSM I 286).

In the *Passions of the Soul*, and in his correspondence, there are indications of robust hostility to both the ancients and the schools (see esp. AT XI 327–8; CSM I 327); but the relevant passages have to be taken together with others, especially in his letters, in which he is prepared to praise or at least not criticize the traditional philosophers. These are among the passages seized upon by commentators who doubt or deny Descartes's modernity, or who think that it is at least unclear in what sense Descartes is modern.

One such passage comes in a reply to Jean-Baptiste Morin, a schoolman who submitted objections to the *Essais*. Morin reported that he had been forewarned of Descartes's scorn for scholastic terms, only to find, when he read the *Discourse* and *Essais*, that Descartes was not 'as much of an enemy of the schools as you are made out to be' (AT I 541). On the contrary, in Morin's view, Descartes's hostility to the schools did not go beyond that of Morin himself, who complained that the schoolmen were overconcerned with the search for terminology and not concerned enough with the search for truth in nature (ibid.). Did Descartes, in his reply to Morin, do nothing to disturb the impression that he and Morin had similar attitudes to the schools? Certainly Descartes denied being scornful of scholastic language. 'It could only have been imagined', he says, 'by those who know neither my ways nor my temperament. And even though in my essays I have scarcely used these terms, which are only known by the learned, this is not to say that I disapprove of them, but only that I desired to make myself understood by others as well' (AT II 201–2; CSMK 108). Taken on its own, this passage may indeed encourage second thoughts about Descartes's hostility to the schools.[6] Yet it is a short aside in a long letter that is devoted to rebutting in detail a great number of Morin's scholastic criticisms of the Cartesian theory of light. After he has answered a good many of these objections, even Descartes's professed tolerance of scholastic terminology begins to wear thin. 'As for what you add about *a relative being, a potential being, and an absolute*

---

[6] See Garber, 'Descartes, the Aristotelians, and the Revolution that did not Happen in 1637', 477 ff.

act or form, I know very well that I will be told by the Schools that Light is a more real being than action or movement; but I would deserve to be sent to school . . . if I swore that it could be proved' (AT II 210).

It is not only that the exchange with Morin is overwhelmingly taken up with rebuttals of scholastic objections; it is that the gap between scholastic and Cartesian physics is fully acknowledged on both sides. Morin does not take Descartes to be putting forward a notational variant of a traditional theory of light, nor more generally a mere variation on traditional physics. He refers at least three times in his letter to Descartes's 'new physics' or 'new doctrine' (AT I 537, 539, 557), never with any discernible irony. There is very little evidence that Morin mistook Descartes for a kindred spirit, or that Descartes did much to foster the impression that Morin and he agreed about any matter of substance.

Libert Froidmont is another critic of the *Essais* who has been taken to have doubted Descartes's hostility to tradition.[7] A letter of September 1637 to Plempius compares Descartes in passing to Democritus and Pythagoras, and suggests that in physics Descartes falls back on a crude Epicureanism (AT I 402). Whether or not these comments are reasonable, do they show that Froidmont doubted Descartes's claims to be outlining a new sort of philosophy in the *Essais*? I do not think they do. Unlike Morin, Froidmont never acknowledges Descartes's pretensions to novelty, and the status of the doctrines in the *Essais* as either 'new' or 'traditional' does not appear to be at issue in his objections to them. Froidmont does compare Descartes, the willing visitor to foreign parts and investigator of nature, with Democritus and Pythagoras, but there is no sign that Descartes is identified as a follower of either Democritus or Pythagoras. It is different with Epicurus. Froidmont does take Descartes to revive Epicurean doctrines, but what seems important in the imputation of Epicureanism is not Epicurus' being an ancient or traditional philosopher, but Epicurus' having put forward a crude and crass physics: Descartes is held to be crass in similar ways, and is compared unfavourably with Aristotle.

In his reply to Froidmont (AT I 413 ff.; CSMK 61 ff.) Descartes protests at objections that he says are apt when directed at a Democritus or an Epicurus but that misunderstand his own doctrine.

---

[7] Ibid. 473 ff.

In dissociating his own views from those of Epicurus and Democritus, however, Descartes is not, as I read him, asserting his modernity and rebutting an insinuation that he has borrowed from tradition. It is not because they are traditional that he repudiates Epicurus and Democritus, but because they believe in atoms and the void. As for his own views, he is quite prepared to say that they are mechanical, that mechanics is not original with him, and that mechanics has survived in the body of learning under the protection of mathematics rather than philosophy:

I am surprised that [Froidmont] does not realize that the mechanics now current is nothing but a part of the true physics which, not being welcomed by the supporters of the common sort of philosophy, took refuge with the mathematicians. This part of philosophy has in fact remained truer and less corrupt than others ... (AT I 421; CSMK 62)

The reason Descartes feels comfortable in locating the old mechanics in the true physics is that claims about the old and the new are not at issue in his correspondence with Froidmont. What *is* at issue is the difference between the 'common', i.e. Aristotelian, philosophy and the crass but true philosophy, where the true philosophy, as the passage just quoted makes clear, is not wholly new.

II

So far it has emerged that Descartes does not unequivocally advertise his own modernity, and that he sometimes goes to some lengths to point out affinities between his thought and tradition. It does not follow that he is, after all, a traditional philosopher. It is possible to hold instead that he is genuinely modern but that he found it advisable to give his doctrine a traditional façade. According to this interpretation, a scholastic vocabulary is employed at times, and warmth is expressed in some personal communications with individual school-men, but this is for display only and signals no commitment to the substance of scholasticism. It seems to me that this interpretation is not far from the truth, but, as we shall now see, it exaggerates the degree to which Descartes had freed himself from tradition.

Étienne Gilson has shown that errors in Descartes's theory of the movement of the heart, discussed in part V of the *Discourse*, and the *Description of the Human Body*, proceed from the acceptance of the scholastic idea that the heart is the seat of a very intense heat.[8] Gilson also shows that a number of difficulties with Descartes's explanations in meteorology proceed from his acceptance of the scholastic distinction between exhalations and vapours.[9] These points of agreement with the tradition, however, do not show that either Descartes's theory of the heart or his meteorology was traditional overall, and Gilson never suggests as much himself. On the contrary, he thinks that certain other, more characteristic, features of Descartes's accounts—their hostility to the usual scholastic proliferation of natural powers and virtues, and their tendency to be single-mindedly mechanical—make them into specimens of the new science. The assumption about the intense heat of the heart and the distinction between exhalations and vapours are regarded as uncharacteristic lapses.

Is Gilson too confident of Descartes's modernity? Desmond Clarke has given an account of Cartesian science which suggests that it was geared, like its scholastic competition, to common experience—that is, to what was widely and commonly observed—rather than to what was revealed by controlled experiment.[10] There is reason to think that some descriptions of what was commonly observed, or some ways of classifying and distinguishing the phenomena, were borrowed uncritically by Descartes from scholastic sources.[11] The *Essai* on the meteors, for example, goes through a long list of phenomena, and the order, arrangement, and description of these phenomena seem to have been modelled in many (but not all) cases on material in scholastic textbooks on the subject, textbooks with which Descartes hoped his essay would be favourably compared. If it was in this way that the offending scholastic assumptions of his meteorology and theory of the heart intruded, then it is unclear that their intrusion can be put down to an uncharacteristic lapse, for, to the extent that Descartes and the scholastics relied on common observations, understood in the same way, some use of common observations from traditional sources was probably as much a feature of Cartesian practice as anything called for by his official method. But, even if it is in this sense no accident that traditional observations and distinctions made their way into Descartes's scientific writings, it cannot be said that this by itself makes Descartes's science traditional or strikingly Aristotelian, as

---

[8] Gilson, *Études sur le rôle de la pensée médiévale*, 82. [9] Ibid. 126.
[10] Ibid. 204; see D. Clarke, *Descartes' Philosophy of Science*, ch. 8.
[11] Ibid. 105 ff.

Clarke has insisted. It also matters how what is commonly observed
is explained, and, even on Clarke's showing, the use of mechanical
models makes Descartes's explanations untraditional. Again, as Garber
has shown in a recent paper on Descartes's attitude towards experiment,[12] it cannot be said that Descartes is definitely a believer in
common observation as *opposed* to an experimentalist practitioner of
the new science: sometimes he is the one thing, and sometimes the
other.

Not all commentators who are sensitive to the presence of traditional
and untraditional elements in Descartes's writings agree about the
proportions. Gilson thinks that the untraditional is dominant,[13] Clarke
that the traditional is. Clarke calls Descartes an innovative Aristotelian,[14]
implying by his use of the label that Descartes extends rather than
abandons an ancient approach to science and its method. Clarke's
proposal is certainly correct up to a point: Descartes, like Aristotle,
explains the certainty of scientific knowledge by reference to the
certainty of first principles; Descartes, like Aristotle, has a remarkable
regard for common observations; finally, Descartes, like Aristotle, is
prepared to relax the demand for perfect certainty in the actual
practice of science. These are parallels, but they are parallels at a very
high level of generality, and they are compatible with major disagreement over matters of great importance. For instance, they are compatible with major disagreements over the objectivity of the sensible
qualities and over the categories to be used in scientific explanation.
Substance; attribute; genus and species; these are all extensively recast
in Descartes even if not entirely abandoned.[15]

---

[12] D. Garber, 'Descartes and Experiment in the *Discourse* and *Essays*'.
[13] Gilson, *Études sur le rôle de la pensée médiévale*, 99.
[14] Clarke, *Descartes' Philosophy of Science*, ch. 8.
[15] Clarke's is not the only argument for regarding Descartes as a methodological
traditionalist that fails by being overly general. In a recent paper ('A Forest of Trees:
Descartes and the Classification of the Sciences', unpublished), Roger Ariew considers
Descartes's ambition of putting the sciences on a mathematical footing, and shows that
this project was already being advocated by scholastic predecessors of Descartes, notably
Christopher Clavius. Ariew notes that, in the scholastic classification of learning,
sciences were divided into high, middle, and low, according to the nobility of the
subject-matter. Physics was high, mathematics low, and the sciences of astronomy,
astrology, and optics were in the middle. According to the orthodoxy, the principles of
the low sciences were not transferable to the high. Mathematics dealt with quantified
being, physics with natural being. Clavius argued against the segregation of mathematics
and the middle sciences from physics, and for Ariew Descartes falls into place as a
holder of Clavian views. Although one can see what Ariew means—Clavius' and
Descartes's views undoubtedly have something in common—Ariew does not show that

I have been concentrating on real and supposed accretions of traditional thought in Descartes's science and his philosophy of science. What about his metaphysics? Descartes himself concedes that the Cogito is not his own invention but that it is to be found in Augustine. There are suspiciously scholastic-sounding principles about causality in the Third Meditation. Even Descartes's use of the idea of natural light may be borrowed from Eustachius a Sancto Paulo,[16] and a number of the lines of thought that lead to the doctrine of God-created eternal truth probably only make sense against the background of Suarez.[17] Is not Descartes utterly entangled, then, in traditional metaphysics? There is considerable room for doubt. Robert Adams has shown that there even the scholastic principles Descartes uses in the Third Meditation depart from Aristotelian orthodoxy in their implications about the causes of ideas,[18] while Marion is the latest in a long line of French commentators who have insisted on the absolute novelty of Descartes's line on the creation of the eternal truths.[19] Certain traditional-looking elements of Descartes's metaphysics, then, may not be traditional after all. Then there is Descartes's overall use of his metaphysics to consider. It is widely agreed that the doubt, and the emergence from it via the proof of God's existence and perfection, contribute to a would-be demolition of the principles of Aristotelian physics and the vindication of the principles of a physics geared to a conception of matter as extension. Descartes claims as much in correspondence with Mersenne (AT III 279–8; CSMK 172–3), and a coherent, even a compelling, reading of the *Meditations* emerges if one takes the claim seriously. Surely this use of metaphysics is not only untraditional but anti-traditional, notwithstanding the

---

Descartes's project of mathematizing the sciences is conceived against the background of a scheme of high, middle, and low sciences. That at least would have to be shown for Descartes to appear party to a scholastic reform of the sciences. The division of high, middle and low apart, it is clear that Descartes believed that mathematics itself needed reform, and that this reform would complement the reform of physics. Again, Descartes was no mere advocate of the reform of the sciences and of the extension of mathematics to the realm of physics: he was actively involved in carrying out the reform. Ariew does not show that Clavius was, or that they saw eye to eye on the nature of the reform beyond the introduction of mathematics. For these reasons it is as hard to agree that Descartes is a thoroughgoing Clavian as it is to agree that he is a thoroughgoing Aristotelian.

[16] F. Van de Pitte, 'Some of Descartes' Debts to Eustachius a Sancto Paulo'.
[17] J.-L. Marion, *Sur la théologie blanche de Descartes*, 110 ff.
[18] R. M. Adams, 'Where do our Ideas Come from?'.
[19] Marion, *Sur la théologie blanche de Descartes*.

official billing of the first philosophy as a demonstration of truths about the soul, in particular the truth that the soul is immortal (AT VII 3; CSM II 4).

III

On the evidence so far reviewed, only a weak case exists for reconsidering Descartes's status as the father of modern philosophy. But this conclusion is only as valuable as the positive account given of Descartes's modernity, and of modernity as it is applied to this period of philosophy. Is it possible to say what makes Descartes modern? I shall not try to give an exhaustive account, but I think that the elements of what is required already exist in the literature and that they have only to be satisfactorily assembled. Many of these elements are entirely familiar from stock expositions of Descartes's views. Thus, his attack on real qualities and substantial forms through the medium of the Doubt, and his defence and application of the geometrical conception of matter—these are modern elements of his natural philosophy; then, and equally central, there are the modern elements of his metaphilosophy—that is, of his conception of the nature, organization, and method of science. Foremost among these modern elements, I think, is his distinction between science and history.

In the *Regulae* Descartes writes that it is not enough to become a philosopher to know all the arguments of Plato and Aristotle: 'we shall never become philosophers', he says, 'if we are unable to make a sound judgement on matters which come up for discussion; in this case what we would have seemed to have learnt would be not science but history' (AT X 367; CSM I 13). The message is that science is not merely different from history but superior to it. Elsewhere the message is the same. In the *Recherche* he writes, 'But to give you a more distinct conception of the sort of doctrine I propose to teach, I should like you to notice how the sciences differ from those simple forms of knowledge which can be acquired without any process of reasoning, such as languages, history, geography and in general any subject which rests on experience alone' (AT X 502–3; CSM II 403). Here, as in the *Regulae*, the intellectual basis for science is more elevated than the basis for history. According to the *Regulae*, the basis for science is intuition or deduction; in the *Recherche* it is reason. A letter of 1640 stresses the difference between taking in a record of invention and having within one the means to extend invention. Descartes distinguishes history, which is 'everything that has already been invented and that is contained in books', from science, 'which is the ability to solve all problems, and, through that, to discover by one's own ingenuity everything in this science which cannot be discovered by the human mind' (letter to Hogeland of 8 February 1640: AT III 722; CSMK 144). It is clear that the ranking of science over history was a ranking of science over civil as well as natural history,[20] but the branch of history of which Descartes took the dimmest view was the branch that recirculated the views of the ancient authorities. He dreamed of a treatise against erudition (letter to Elizabeth of 31 January 1648: AT V 111; CSMK 329), and, despite the conciliatory words in the preface to the French edition of the *Principles*, he did not think that one could get the best sort of knowledge from books, or from the intellectual tradition. On the contrary, he thought that those who immersed themselves in the tradition and who tried to find answers to every question in the writings of the ancient authorities were worse off than if they had never studied. The appeal to the texts of the authorities, Descartes writes,

is very convenient for those with mediocre minds, for the obscurity of the distinctions and principles they use makes it possible for them to speak about everything as confidently as if they knew it, and to defend all they say against the most subtle and clever thinkers without anyone having the means to convince them that they are wrong. In this way they seem to resemble a blind man who, in order to fight without disadvantage against someone who can see, lures him into the depths of a very dark cellar. (AT VI 70–1; CSM I 147)

On the one hand, the followers of the ancient authorities add nothing to the knowledge they appropriate; and, on the other hand, the techniques of disputation and analysis that they use obscure and thereby diminish the knowledge that they appropriate.

If, for Descartes, knowledge of the tradition is vicarious knowledge obscurely expressed, knowledge that is unable to increase and unable to be criticized, then science is the very opposite of knowledge of tradition. Founded on metaphysics, the principles of which have to be taught so as to enable the receiver of them to make them his own, science is through and through the product of active and personal enquiry. It results from method, which, unlike a corpus of writing or

---

[20] Or at least the accounts of civil historians (AT VI 7). For natural history, see J. Laporte, *Le Rationalisme de Descartes*, 386–90.

a text, in Descartes's view, can be applied to an open-ended range of problems. And, partly because of the content of the method, science can be both luminously grasped and easily subjected to critical reflection, again by contrast with knowledge of tradition. To see Cartesian science as a kind of anti-erudition is to see why Descartes's philosophy of science is individualist rather than communitarian. The more that science is regarded as the scattered possession of a community, the more each individual in the community possesses it vicariously, without really making it his own. The individual's share of the knowledge may enable him to speak plausibly on a range of subjects as a spokesman for an Aristotle or an Aquinas, but it does not enable him to take over where Aristotle or Aquinas leaves off, or to defend Aristotle or Aquinas to those who are not yet converts. At best, members of the community enable Aristotle or Aquinas or some other authority to speak through them. To see Cartesian science as a kind of anti-erudition is also to see why it is a necessary stage in the acquisition of science to detach oneself from opinions that have been infected by tradition. As Descartes revealingly points out in the preface to the French edition of the *Principles*, 'those who have not followed Aristotle (and this group includes many of the best minds) have nevertheless been saturated with his opinions in their youth (since these are the only opinions taught in the Schools) and this has so dominated their outlook that they have been unable to arrive at knowledge of true principles' (AT IXB 7–8; CSM I 182). The method of doubt is not the only means Descartes uses of purging this influence; in chapter 5 of *Le Monde* he resorts to a non-Aristotelian description of the elements of an imaginary universe. But, whatever means he employs, it is evident that for him a true science, including a true science of nature, has to begin with the clearing of the preconceptions we inherit from the intellectual tradition. To see Cartesian science as a kind of anti-erudition, then, is for some of the familiar features of Cartesian science—its individualism and its begin-nings in an emptying of the intellect—to assume a kind of unity. Finally, to see Cartesian science as a kind of anti-erudition is to see it as a self-consciously modern intellectual production, not necessarily free of all traces of the past, but insistent on the need to conduct enquiry with the influence of the past firmly under control.

More signs of modernity are evident in Descartes's theory of the structure of the sciences, and in his implicit valuations of science relative to the arts. Descartes does away with Aristotle's idea that science as a whole is composed of three distinct types of science: theoretical, practical, and productive. For him sciences that are practical and productive in Aristotle's sense grow out of the theoretical sciences, not merely alongside them. Thus ethics, morals, and mechanics grow out of physics and metaphysics (AT IXB 14; CSM I 186). And there is no prior grounding of metaphysics in theology, as Aristotle held. What is more, the same three sciences that grow out of metaphysics and physics are supposed to be more valuable than physics and metaphysics, for apparently sciences are to be valued according to the degree to which they are applicable for human benefit (AT IXB 15; CSM I 186); in this respect Descartes seems to accept the Baconian idea of what science is for.

The impression of modernity is further reinforced when the content of the derivative Cartesian sciences is taken into account, for the problems that these sciences take up—namely the problems of securing human health and blessedness—are all tailored to a distinctively Cartesian and surely modern metaphysical conception of the human being as a composite of mental and material substances. Descartes's metaphysics, then, lends modern content to Descartes's morals. And it is not just the metaphysics. The acquisition of moral science depends, according to Descartes, on a grasp of all of the other sciences: it is not the autonomous practical wisdom described by Aristotle, or even, despite its affinities with stoicism, a rearrangement of any other ancient doctrine. For one thing it is all to do with the control of passions, and therefore with the causes of the passions, and Descartes thinks that these causes were very badly understood by traditional philosophy. As he writes at the beginning of the *Passions of the Soul*, 'the defects of the sciences we have from the ancients are nowhere more apparent than in their writings on the passions' (AT XI 327; CSM I 328). In a number of respects, then, Descartes's moral science is modern. As for medicine, its parallelism with Cartesian morals,[21] described very well by Gueroult,[22] seems to make it untraditional as well. It, too, inherits some modern content from the modern metaphysical conception of the human being that informs it, not to mention what it draws from Cartesian physics.

I claimed a moment ago that Descartes was modern not only in his view of the structure of science, but in his valuation of the sciences

---

[21] For more detail, see T. Sorell, 'Morals and Modernity in Descartes'.
[22] M. Gueroult, *Descartes selon l'ordre de raisons*, ch. 19.

relative to the arts or non-sciences, or most of the departments of
'letters'. We have already seen something of his view of the inferiority
of history to science. The *Discourse* is a source of his views about the
other arts. In Part I he writes that he was once persuaded that by
means of letters one could acquire a clear and certain knowledge of
all that was useful in life (AT VI 4; CSM I 113). But, he says, as soon
as his schooldays ended, 'I completely changed my opinion'. Not that
in the end he believed that letters had no value at all, but those
branches of it that did have value did not have to be pursued by formal
study. Poetry and rhetoric and their benefits were the product of innate
ability rather than learning, and theology imparted things that could
also be known by those without learning (AT VI 7; CSM I 114). The
benefits of some branches of the traditional world of letters, then, did
not depend on the advancement of learning at all, while the certain
knowledge of all that was useful in life did not depend on the
advancement of traditional learning, but rather on the advancement of
science. This seems to be the moral of Descartes's story of how he
fell out of love with letters, and it is of a piece with his saying that the
best fruits of the tree of science come from morals, which presupposes
a complete knowledge of the other sciences (AT IXB 14;
CSM I 186). The other sciences, Descartes says, not the rest of
learning or letters.

Descartes was not alone in his period in revaluing the scientific
branches of learning upwards, and in regarding as unscientific branches
of learning such subjects as history and poetry and theology. Bacon's
Advancement of Learning contains similar revaluations, though it is less
thoroughgoing in its detachment of the science of well-being from
religion. Though they are different, Bacon's and Descartes's revaluations do seem to belong in a pro-science tradition of philosophy that
starts in the early seventeenth century and continues to our own day.
Or, to put it another way, these revaluations seem to be distinctively
modern.

IV

I have been trying to identify some points of doctrine in Descartes that
count in favour of classifying him as a modern or anti-traditional
philosopher. But of course the historiographical concept of modernity
in philosophy is never applied to Descartes alone. It is applied to a

range of philosophers from the seventeenth and eighteenth centuries. A proper defence of its application to Descartes must include a defence of the idea that this whole range of philosophers is anti-traditional as well. And reasons have to be given why classifying them as anti-traditional illuminates the views of these philosophers more than it distorts them. These are much bigger tasks than I can discharge, let alone discharge briefly,[23] but I should like to make a small start on them by making some concluding suggestions about what would be lost if we dropped talk of modernity in connection with seventeenth-century philosophy.

I gather that some historians of philosophy believe that little would be lost if one ceased to refer to an early modern period, or if one ceased to regard Descartes as the one who initiates this period. They believe that talk of modernity is more misleading than helpful because it exaggerates the discontinuity between Descartes and the schoolmen or Descartes and Aristotle. I agree that stock accounts of Descartes's contribution to philosophy do exaggerate his departure from tradition and so probably are open to the charge of distortion, but I do not believe that the distortion is inevitable, and I deny that even in the stock accounts it is acute enough to discredit the distinction between traditional and modern philosophy altogether.

In defending the use of the traditional/modern distinction I want to say something about its utility relative to other stock historiographical distinctions, and something about the use of historiographical concepts in philosophy in general. To begin with stock historiographical distinctions, it is instructive to compare the dichotomy between traditional and modern with the dichotomy between rationalism and empiricism, or, even worse, the distinction between British empiricism and continental rationalism. Neither the unqualified rationalist/empiricist distinction nor the version of it which accords significance to the two sides of the English Channel is easy to ground in the writings of the philosophers whom it is supposed to classify. Descartes did not deny the importance of observation or experiment, or, more generally, experience, to a complete physics; on the contrary, he called attention to it. Berkeley did not think that self-knowledge derived from sense experience. Both of these aspects of their thought make trouble for the stock application of the rationalist/empiricist distinction. It is not just that there are aspects of their thought that are missed by this

---

[23] A start is made, however, in T. Sorell (ed.), *The Rise of Modern Philosophy*.

distinction, but that important aspects of their thought are distorted by it. What is more, one knows that the rationalist/empiricist distinction belongs to a story that culminates in a Kantian synthesis. Its attraction is not so much the light it sheds on the philosophy of the seventeenth and eighteenth centuries but the light in which it puts the response to the philosophy of those centuries. The distinction between traditional and modern is different in several respects; first, it is known that in the sixteenth and seventeenth centuries people wrote and spoke extensively about the relative intellectual merits of the ancients and moderns. There is no question of *foisting* such a preoccupation on the period; it is already there. Secondly, although it is not true that all of the philosophers classified as 'moderns' in stock accounts agree in their attitudes to traditional philosophy—Gassendi and Leibniz, for example, are far more sympathetic to the history of philosophy than Descartes—all rejected explanation by substantial forms in physics, and all had philosophies of science that implied that important sections of Aristotelian and other ancient natural philosophy were either not science or bad science. Virtually all of the figures classified as modern in the stock accounts admire Galileo, Harvey, and Copernicus.

Now it is true that not all of the 'moderns' mentioned in the stock accounts were thoroughgoing in their rejection of tradition even when they thought they were: Descartes is a good case in point. It is also true that there were many figures who were contemporaries of the stock moderns, who were influential in their day, and who are in a clear sense just as representative of, say, seventeenth-century thought, perhaps more so, but who were either intellectually reactionary, like Morin or Fromondus, or too eclectic, like Thomas White or Kenelm Digby, to classify as either traditional or modern.[24] These things are true, but they do not seem to me to show that we should dispense with the traditional/modern distinction; they show only that we need more historiographical apparatus besides. It is not as if we have so much such apparatus that it is burdensome. It is not that the apparatus that we do have gives us no illumination. Those who dismiss the traditional/modern distinction as mere caricature and who crave greater fidelity to the thought of the seventeenth century sometimes

---

[24] For the case of English thinkers in the seventeenth century, see R. F. Jones, *Ancients and Moderns*. More recent literature concerning earlier periods and the situation on the Continent is extensively cited in Sorell (ed.), *The Rise of Modern Philosophy*.

seem to me to forget that historiographical distinctions at their best can only contribute to an intellectual map, and that every map results from decisions about what to omit and what to emphasize and what to make prominent. This is not to say that every map is as good as any other; but even a rough map can give important guidance.

3

The Sources of Descartes's Procedure of Deductive Demonstration in Metaphysics and Natural Philosophy

STEPHEN GAUKROGER

It is often assumed that the deduction of truths from first principles that one finds in the *Meditations* and the *Principles of Philosophy* derives from an attempt to model metaphysical and natural philosophical reasoning on a mathematical, and more specifically geometrical, prototype. In the first section of this chapter I shall show that, if this is taken to mean that these truths are to be discovered deductively, then the axiomatic arguments of geometry cannot be the model, for Descartes explicitly rejects the idea that one can discover truths in geometry by deduction from first principles. I shall then look briefly at another possible model, a humanist–Aristotelian approach to the deduction of truths from basic principles. This model, as we shall see, is even less promising than the geometrical one. In the third section I shall argue that Descartes never in fact used deduction from first principles as a method of discovery, or even suggested that it should be used as such, but he did use it as a method of presentation. Consequently, what we need is a model for a method of presentation. In the final section I suggest a model for the use of deduction as a method of reconstructing and systematizing metaphysical doctrines and natural-philosophical results, namely the scholastic *disputationes* of Toletus, Fonseca, and the Coimbra commentators, which aimed at reconstructing Aristotle from first principles.

I

The view that the procedure of deduction from first principles found in the *Meditations* and the *Principles* is in some way modelled upon geometrical demonstration is by far the most obvious way of construing what Descartes is doing in these texts. After all, his explicit aim was to show how the kind of certainty that can be achieved in mathematics can also be achieved in other areas, provided one proceeds in the right way. In both the *Meditations* and the *Principles* the procedure appears to consist of clearing our minds of anything we can doubt, fixing on an indubitable truth—the Cogito—and then proceeding to build up knowledge in some way on the basis of this truth.[1] There is a very close parallel here with the procedure followed in famous mathematical texts of antiquity. In Euclid's *Elements*, for example, we are presented with very basic and apparently indubitable axioms and definitions, from which we gradually build up complex systems of theorems. It is true that, if one places the *Elements* against the *Meditations*, for example, then there will be very significant differences: the former lists definitions, axioms, theorems, etc., whereas the latter does not do this, approaching the material in a much more discursive way. But one can find some less strict form of one-to-one correspondence, between the definitions and the sceptical ground-clearing, the axioms and the Cogito, and the deductive proof of geometrical theorems and the establishment of metaphysical results about the nature of God, mind, and body. Moreover, the key notion in the establishment of these metaphysical results is that of clear and distinct ideas, something which Descartes is explicit finds its paradigmatic manifestation in the case of mathematics.

But if the *Elements* and the *Meditations* are placed against Descartes's only systematic writing on mathematics, the *Geometry*, the case for a mathematical model for the deductive structure of the *Meditations* begins to look much harder to defend, for what is striking about the *Geometry* is that it does *not* proceed in the classical fashion of deductive proof from axioms and definitions. It looks not only quite unlike the *Elements* but also quite unlike the *Meditations*. After a few pages of introduction on the ways in which arithmetical operations can be represented geometrically, we are immediately thrown into a complex

[1] This is, at least, the standard reading of Descartes's project. I believe it can be challenged, but to do so would take us too far afield. I offer a different reading in my forthcoming biography of Descartes.

and advanced problem, Pappus' locus-problem for four or more lines. The concern is not deductive demonstration, but problem-solving and the elaboration of new techniques for problem-solving. In short, when he is doing mathematics, even in the context of a reasonably systematic treatise, Descartes does not use a deductive procedure, and first principles play no role in his solution of mathematical problems. And the text is certainly not organized in such a way that we start from something indubitable and deduce other truths from this.

Indeed, the problem is deeper than this, for not only does Descartes not use such a procedure as a matter of fact in his mathematical problem-solving, he does not use it *as a matter of principle*. It is antithetical to his whole enterprise in mathematics. This is made clear as early as the *Regulae*, where in rule 4 the ancients are accused of duplicity in presenting their mathematics in a synthetic fashion, deducing their results from first principles. That they cannot have discovered their results in this way is clear to Descartes, and it is also clear that the rationale for such a mode of presentation of results is to cover up their real method of discovery:

I have come to think that these writers themselves, with a kind of low cunning, later suppressed this mathematics as, notoriously, many inventors are known to have done where their own discoveries were concerned. They may have feared that their method, just because it was so easy and simple, would be depreciated if it were divulged; so to gain our admiration, they may have shown us, as the fruits of their method, some barren truths proved by clever arguments, instead of teaching us the method itself, which might have dispelled our admiration. (AT X 376–7; CSM I 19)

Deduction of truths from first principles is here described as showing us barren truths proved by clever arguments, where the context indicates that 'clever' should be taken as 'merely clever'. Clearly such a procedure is being rejected as a source of the discovery of truth. Given this, it could scarcely be employed as a model for the discovery of truth.

II

A mathematical model was certainly not the only one available for the exercise of building knowledge deductively on first principles, and there was a long medieval tradition of construing dialectic as a kind of master science which enabled one to proceed from first principles to other truths. Following Aristotle (*Topics*, 101^{b}3), dialectic had been defined in the works of Peter of Spain and Lambert of Auxerre as 'the art of arts, the science of sciences, possessing the path to the principles of all methods'.[2] Not only did the scholastic tradition thrive on this definition, but, when Agricola took it up in his *De inventione dialectica libri tres* (1515), it also became a basic premiss for an important strand of humanist thought.[3] As we shall see, such a conception need not necessarily be thought of as suggesting a method of discovery, but there can be little doubt that it was widely thought of in these terms. The details of how the procedure was to be effected were generally left vague, however, and, if one takes this 'dialectic' to be something conducted in a systematic way, starting from first principles, then it is hard to see what it could be other than syllogistic. And if something along these lines was intended, then there can be little doubt that it would not have suggested itself as a model for Descartes, for he decisively rejects syllogistic on a number of occasions; in rule 10 of the *Regulae*, for example, he tells us that logicians 'are unable to devise by their rules any syllogism with a true conclusion unless they already have the whole syllogism, i.e. unless they have already ascertained in advance the very truth deduced in that syllogism' (AT X 406; CSM I 36). Syllogistic cannot, any more than synthesis, act as a method of discovery.

One version of this kind of project which does not rely on syllogistic or geometry was proposed by Lull (1233–1315), which in his earlier writings he called 'the art of finding the truth' (*ars inveniendi veritatem*) and in later writings simply the 'general art' (*ars generalis*).[4] Lull's aim was to develop a kind of universal language which, by using an axiomatic system, could be used to generate truths from basic premisses. Lull saw the specific purpose of the system in terms of convincing Muslims and Jews of the truth of the Christian doctrines of the Trinity and the Incarnation. Largely forgotten from shortly after his death, Lull's project, stripped of its evangelical purpose, was revived in Agrippa's very popular *De incertitudine et vanitate de scientarium et artum* (1527). Agrippa's work, with its endorsement of the

---

[2] Peter of Spain in *Petri Hispani summulae logicales*, ed. I. M. Bochenski (Turin, 1947), 1. Lambert of Auxerre in Martin Grabmann, 'Handschriftliche Forschungen und Funde zu den philosophischen Schriften des Petrus Hispanus, des späten Papstes Johannes XXI (†1277)', Sitzungsberichte, Bayerische Akademie der Wissenschaft, Jahrgang 1936, Heft 9, 46.   [3] See S. Gaukroger, *Cartesian Logic*, 33–8.
[4] e.g. the *Ars generalis ultima*, Palma de Mallorca, 1645.

writings of Hermes Trismegistus, supposedly demonstrating a marvellous anticipation of Christianity by the ancient magus, and its talk
of a secret key to the whole of knowledge based on Lull's *Ars brevis*,
subsequently came to form part of the basis for the mysterious
'Brotherhood of the Rosy Cross'. Now, in contrast to his later
dismissive attitude, Descartes took an interest in Rosicrucianism in
1619 and 1620 and had some contact with the Rosicrucian mathe-
matician Johannes Faulhaber in the second half of 1619.[5] The Lullian
art in the version of Agrippa had two fundamental characteristics
which mirror those that Descartes ascribes to his 'method'. These are,
first, that it is a general and universal science, starting from absolutely
certain principles, and establishing a secure criterion of knowledge;
and, secondly, that it is the science of all sciences, offering a key to
the ordering of all knowledge.[6] But whatever doubts one might have
about Descartes's attitude to Lull in 1619, there can be no doubt at
all that he had completely rejected it by the late 1620s, and there is
no question of it playing a role in, for example, the *Meditations*. The
closest he ever comes to considering such an enterprise is in his
discussion of a project for a universal language in a letter to Mersenne
of 20 November 1629, and he makes it very clear there that such a
language could in no way act as a means of discovering anything, but
would provide a way of representing matters clearly to one's judgement, provided one had already established the 'true philosophy' (AT
I 81; CSMK 13).

Consequently, it is hard to understand how either the more general
Aristotelian doctrine of dialectic as a procedure for getting one from
first principles to other truths, or the specifically Lullian 'art of
discovery' could have served as a model for Descartes, since he rejects
them both. And if, as I have indicated, the geometrical model is also
to be ruled out, then we have reached an impasse with this line of
interpretation.

III

But in fact we have been seeking the wrong thing up to now. What we
have been concerned with is deduction from first principles as a

[5] For a discussion of Descartes and Rosicrucianism, see W. R. Shea, 'Descartes and
the Rosicrucian Enlightenment'.
[6] See P. Rossi, 'The Legacy of Ramon Lull in Sixteenth-Century Thought'.

method of discovery. Many commentators have treated the procedure in the *Meditations* and the *Principles* in these terms, as if Descartes believed, for example, that quite specific natural–philosophical truths could somehow be discovered from the Cogito, by simple deduction with the help of a divinely guaranteed criterion of clear and distinct ideas. Since I have shown in some detail elsewhere that such an insane idea cannot be attributed to Descartes,[7] I shall not go over this ground again here. What is important is that we grasp the significance, for an understanding of Descartes, of the difference between an effective method for discovering new truths, and an effective method of presenting already discovered truths in a systematically revealing way. And we will be helped in our understanding of this by reflecting on what Descartes himself says about the question of discovery.

In a letter to Antoine Vatier of 22 February 1638 Descartes writes:

I must say that my purpose was not to teach the whole of my Method in the Discourse in which I propound it, but only to say enough to show that the new views in the *Dioptrics* and the *Meteors* were not random notions, and were perhaps worth the trouble of examining. I could not demonstrate the use of this Method in the three treatises which I gave, because it prescribes an order of research which is quite different from the one I thought proper for exposition. I have however given a brief sample of it in my account of the rainbow, and if you take the trouble to re-read it, I hope it will satisfy you more than it did the first time. (AT I 559–60; CSMK 85)

Like the *Geometry*, the *Meteors* starts not from first principles—first principles simply do not come into it—but from specific problems to be solved. The problem that Descartes picks out as being illustrative of his method of discovery is that of explaining why the bows of the rainbow appear in the sky at certain fixed angles (book 8 of the *Meteors*). Starting from the empirical observation that rainbows are found not only in the sky but also in fountains, etc., he sets out to test the hypothesis that the phenomenon is caused by light reacting on drops of water by constructing a glass sphere filled with rain-water, to act as a model of a raindrop. Standing with his back to the sun, he holds up the sphere and moves it up and down so that colours are produced, noting the exact angles at which particular colours are formed. The sphere is then covered except at the exact points at which rays entering and leaving result in colour dispersion, and Descartes is able to deduce that two refractions and one or two internal reflections

---

[7] See S. Gaukroger, 'Descartes: Methodology'.

are involved in the production of the rainbow in this case. Then, asking whether something similar to this must always be the case in the production of the rainbow, he experiments with a prism, and finds that he can produce colour dispersion with a plane surface, with no internal reflection at all, and with only one refraction, and moreover the angle of incidence does not seem to be a determining factor. Finally, he calculates from the refractive index of rain-water what an observer would see when light strikes a drop of water at varying angles of incidence, and calculates that the optimum difference for visibility between incident and refracted rays is in line with what his hypothesis predicts.

The procedure being followed here, involving experiment, observation, the construction of physical models, even some elements of inductive reasoning (in the first step), is clearly different from the procedure followed in the *Meditations* and the *Principles*. I do not believe that the two procedures are at odds with one another, however, and this is particularly clear in the case of the *Principles*, where one appears to get a deduction from first principles of very specific physical results. They are not at odds because they occupy different stages of a general process, which I believe should be reconstructed along the following lines. Descartes's procedure is to start from problem-solving. The problems have to be posed in quantitative terms and there are a number of constraints on what form an acceptable solution takes (some of these admittedly being rather specific and contentious). The solution is then tested experimentally to determine how well it holds up compared with other possible explanations, meeting the same constraints, which also appear to account for the facts. Finally, the solution, which may take the form of anything from a relatively isolated empirical result to a body of experimentally verified theory, is incorporated into a system of natural philosophy, and the principal aim of a work like the *Principles* is to set out this natural philosophy in detail.

The *Meditations* and the *Principles* are not so much an account of how one discovers the truths they defend, but a particular kind of systematic presentation of these truths which reveals an order and coherence in them. In so far as we are concerned with the question of deduction from first principles, then, we are concerned not with the issue of discovery but with the issue of presentation, and the question now becomes that of asking whether we can find a model for the deductive schema as a method of presentation. This being the case, we can return to the two candidates that we have already looked at, and ask whether they could have served Descartes as a model for methods of presentation.

IV

Let us take the geometrical model first. Does Descartes's deductive method of presentation derive from synthetic proofs in mathematics? It might seem that his strong rejection of synthetic demonstration rules it out as having any use. But in fact Descartes does give the odd synthetic proof in the *Geometry*, even if grudgingly. Note, however, that he does not do this for every problem, and he only gives a synthetic proof once he has already provided an analytic solution to the problem, which, in his terminology, means once he has solved the problem by genuine problem-solving techniques. Unless he had done this, he would be subject to his own strictures about the dishonest ancient mathematicians who kept their analytic techniques, i.e. their real problem-solving techniques, hidden, and who presented us with 'sterile' truths deduced from first principles. It is crucial to his whole approach that these 'sterile truths', sterile because of the way one has come by them, namely by having them deduced from first principles, be avoided by first presenting the procedure by which they were discovered. Because of this, it is unlikely that mathematical synthetic proof formed the basis for Descartes's use of the method of presentation that we find in the *Meditations* and the *Principles*. Synthetic demonstration has no legitimacy in its own right for Descartes; it must always be preceded by an analysis, in which genuine problem-solving techniques are brought to bear on a problem. Even though synthetic proof is a form of deduction from first principles, it surely cannot be the model for the metaphysical and natural–philosophical deductions from first principles.

When we turn to the non-mathematical traditions, one stands out as especially promising. This is neither Lullian, nor something one would associate with humanism, but a rearguard form of presentation of Aristotle to be found in Jesuit textbooks of the second half of the sixteenth century. While it owes a good deal to medieval tradition of construing dialectic as the 'art of all arts, the science of all sciences', it has some very distinctive features which are worth our attention.

In his final year at the Jesuit college of La Flèche, Descartes studied metaphysics and ethics. Such courses, especially metaphysics, could only be given by those who had attended advanced courses in theology, and who showed evidence of orthodoxy. Metaphysics had become an extremely contentious subject by the sixteenth century, not so much because of the proliferation of Platonist and other rivals to Aristotelian philosophy, but because of the proliferation of different and unorthodox interpretations of Aristotle. Of particular concern were various naturalist readings of Aristotle. There had always been naturalist readings of Aristotle—not surprisingly, since Aristotle was in all probability himself a naturalist—and Aquinas had countered various naturalist readings when attempting to provide Christianity with a foundation in Aristotelian philosophy. But in the latter part of the fifteenth century there was a revival of naturalist readings of Aristotle, mainly deriving from the University of Padua, where a concern with medicine rather than theology had led to readings of the *De anima*, in particular, which stressed naturalistic elements in Aristotelian psychology. At stake was the doctrine of the personal immortality of the soul. The Averroistic reading of Aristotle, offered in part by commentators like Nifo,[8] allowed immortality but disallowed personal immortality, on the grounds that once the soul is disembodied it cannot be individuated, and so becomes part of the one single soul which includes God. The Alexandrian reading of Aristotle, defended above all by Pomponazzi,[9] refused to allow any immortality on philosophical grounds, stressing the functionalist conception of the mind or soul as the form of the body, as its 'organizing principle', and refusing to allow, on good Aristotelian grounds, that forms can exist separately from matter, so that the soul or mind must be essentially embodied. Such naturalist readings accepted the theological doctrine of personal immortality, but undermined philosophical support for the doctrine.

The Lateran Council condemned such interpretations in 1513, instructing philosophers and theologians to seek a philosophical defence of the doctrine of personal immortality.[10] Descartes tells us at the beginning of the *Meditations* that the account he is to provide does just this (AT VII 3; CSM II 4). My suggestion is that the general

[8] Agostino Nifo, *In librum Destructio destructionum Averrois commentarii* (Lyons, 1529).
[9] Pietro Pomponazzi, *Tractatus de immortalitate animae* (1516; ed. G. Morra, Bologna, 1954).
[10] Bulla, 'Apostolici regiminis' (1513), of Pope Leo X. For details of the controversies, see E. H. Gilson, 'Autour de Pomponazzi'.

structure of the argument, deduction from first principles, mirrors the way in which the Jesuit commentators had undertaken the same task. As Charles Lohr, in particular, has shown in some detail, the response of the Jesuit Collegio Romano to the instruction of the Lateran Council was not simply to restrict themselves to piecemeal attacks on naturalistic readings, but more importantly to seek to avoid naturalistic doctrines by reconstructing Aristotle's thought from first principles, thereby cutting off any logical route to naturalistic conclusions, and allowing the straightforward derivation of orthodox conclusions. Aristotle was to be rewritten in such a way that those Christian truths demonstrable in natural theology could be derived from first principles. This, and a number of related developments, resulted in a new kind of commentary in the late sixteenth century. In contrast to many medieval Aristotle commentaries, such as those of Aquinas, which followed through the arguments in the order they were given in the text, the Jesuit commentaries (called *disputationes*, after this tradition of commentary) completely rearranged the material, presenting it in a way that purported to move from true first principles outwards to specific doctrines.[11] These new commentaries, by Suárez, Fonseca, Toletus, and the Coimbra commentators of the 1590s, were not designed to supplement Aristotle but rather were considered to supplant him.[12] It is from these commentaries that Descartes learnt his metaphysics, and he does not seem to have been particularly familiar with the commentaries of Aquinas until much later, around 1628.[13]

What the *disputationes* do is to restructure already developed material in such a way as to draw from it conclusions which may be obscured, or even denied, if the material were presented in a different way (which includes the original presentation). That this approach was developed explicitly to counter aberrant metaphysics, especially with respect to the question of the personal immortality of the soul, and that it was not only the standard mode of presentation in the textbooks from

[11] On the Jesuit commentaries on the *Metaphysics*, I am indebted to the writings of Charles Lohr, especially his 'Jesuit Aristotelianism and Sixteenth-Century Metaphysics'; 'The Sixteenth-Century Transformation of the Aristotelian Division of the Speculative Sciences'; and 'Metaphysics', esp. 605 ff. See, in particular, his comparison in the latter (p. 612) of the ordering of the contents of Aristotle's *Metaphysics*, with those of Cobos' *Expositio in libros Metaphysicae* (1583), Mas' *Disputatio Metaphysica* (1587), Zúñiga's *Philosophiae prima pars* (1597), and Suárez's *Disputationes metaphysicae* (1597).
[12] See J. Gómez, 'Pedro da Fonseca'.
[13] See J. Sirven, *Les Années d'apprentissage de Descartes*, 15.

which Descartes learnt his metaphysics but also remained the orthodox mode of presentation throughout his career, both suggest that here
we have a suitable model that Descartes was certainly familiar with
and which he could have followed.

Unfortunately the matter is not so straightforward. The idea that
the *disputationes* provide the model for Descartes's two mature systematic works, the *Mediations* and the *Principles*, turns on the claim that
the structure of the texts is dictated by considerations of presentation.
This is relatively unproblematic in the case of the *Principles*, but the
Meditations do present problems in this respect.

It is not too difficult to see that the structure of the *Principles* is
dictated by considerations of presentation because Descartes provides
us elsewhere—in the *Discourse* and in the letter to Vatier—with an
explicit independent account of the question of the discovery of
empirical results in natural philosophy, an account which leaves us in
no doubt that the derivation from first principles presented there
cannot be an account of how the results were discovered. Moreover,
the *Principles* reads very much like a textbook, which is indeed what it
was designed to be, and one only has to consider what, as a textbook,
it would be likely to be in competition with to realize that its very close
similarities with contemporary Jesuit textbooks are not superficial. Of
course, Jesuit textbooks were not the only ones in the tradition of
Aristotelian natural philosophy that Descartes would have been familiar
with, and the genre was a thriving one in the first half of the
seventeenth century.[14] Nevertheless, they were not only a very
important part of this genre, but Descartes was very familiar with
them, and they were the epitome of orthodoxy.

The *Meditations* are quite a different matter, however. In the first
place, the *Meditations* do not read like a textbook at all: they read like
an account of a spiritual journey in which the truth is only to be
discovered by a purging, followed by a kind of rebirth. Certainly the
precedents for this do not come from late scholastic textbooks, but
from writers such as Ignatius Loyola, and more generally from the
manuals of devotional exercises. But this should not worry us unduly,
for, whatever structural considerations this style of presentation brings
with it, it is quite compatible with the *disputationes* model: the sense
of purging that one gets in the First Meditation can, after all, be seen
simply as a means of forcing the reader to take the procedure of

[14] See e.g. P. Reif, 'The Textbook Tradition in Natural Philosophy, 1600–1650'.

deduction from first principles seriously by endowing scepticism with
a quasi-religious imperative. But even these structural parallels may
be questionable, for the main point of calling the *Meditations* by that
name seems to have been simply to focus the mind on the nature of
the subject-matter and to remind Descartes's audience that what he
is doing is strictly within the bounds of orthodoxy: they certainly do
not draw in any way on the genre of devotional meditations for their
content, or indeed in any precise way.[15]

A second problem is that, whereas we can compare an explicit
account of how, for example, Descartes developed aspects of his
theory of light empirically and experimentally with the deductive
presentation in the *Principles*, we cannot do this in the case of the
Meditations: we get no explicit independent account of how we are to
discover such doctrines as mind–body dualism. So in what sense can
we say that the *Meditations* restructure material already developed but
in a different form? Short of a full reconstruction of the early
development of Descartes's metaphysics—for which we do not have
sufficient materials—we cannot compare his early arguments with his
later presentation of the issues in the *Meditations*, so we will never be
in a position to carry out the kind of comparison possible in the case
of the *Principles*. But we can certainly point out that, since Descartes
is very explicit elsewhere that we cannot discover new truths by
deductive means, then, by his own arguments, we cannot allow that
the deductive procedure of the *Meditations* yields the mind–body
doctrine. And we do not have to reconstruct the arguments by which
Descartes came to his final position to establish that.

The most serious problem for the *disputationes* model interpretation
is that Descartes himself tells us us that what he is doing is an exercise
in analysis! In the Reply to the Second Set of Objections to the
Meditations, Descartes maintains that the *Meditations* are an example
of analytic demonstration, and he presents a synthetic version of some
of the arguments to show the difference. The latter (AT VII 160–70)
comprises 'arguments drawn up in a geometrical fashion'. But this is
both misleading and confusing. It is misleading because Descartes also
tells us that he has tried to follow the 'order of proof'—that is, what
is effectively the synthetic mode—in the *Meditations*: this, he says, is
why he has presented the fundamental doctrine of mind–body dualism
in the last of the Meditations, and not in the second, as one might

---

[15] See B. Rubidge, 'Descartes' *Meditations* and Devotional Meditations'.

have expected, given its fundamental role. It is confusing because the procedure in the *Meditations* does not look at all like analysis in the mathematical sense, which seems to be what Descartes is maintaining. Now, if what I have said above about analysis and synthesis in the mathematical sense is correct, it is exceedingly hard to understand how what is going on in the *Meditations* is either analysis or synthesis. Descartes seems intent upon construing the discussion in these terms, even though there is no way in which they can be made appropriate. The reason for this seems to be that he believes that, unless what he is doing can be modelled in some way upon mathematical procedures, it cannot be legitimated.

In sum, Descartes's problem is that he cannot construe the *Meditations* as synthetic, because this would, by his own account of synthesis, render them 'sterile'. But nor can he construe them as analytic, because they are deductive in form. Indeed, the terms 'analytic' and 'synthetic', taken in the sense which he gives them in a mathematical context, seem peculiarly inappropriate, even though it is clearly in this sense that he wants to use the terms, for it is only in this sense that the requisite legitimation can be provided. Yet what Descartes has actually done in the *Meditations* does not seem to be vitiated by this problem: the problem seems to be very much extraneous to the *Meditations* themselves. I suggest it is indeed extraneous. Despite what Descartes suggests, I can find no evidence that considerations of analysis and synthesis motivate either the substantive argument of the *Meditations* or its structure. This is not to say that such considerations are merely an afterthought, for they figure deeply in Descartes's project of legitimating his metaphysics. The trouble is that they provide little purchase on his way of actually proceeding.

The *disputationes*, on the other hand, do seem to have such a purchase, and in quite a precise way. They explicitly enable one to provide a defence of doctrines whose truth one is already certain of, by showing how such doctrines can be deduced from shared premises. And they do this in a way that makes no reference at all to mathematical demonstration, but which, on the contrary, is designed *specifically* for metaphysical, theological, and natural–philosophical arguments.

Yet I believe it would be going too far to maintain that the *Meditations* simply follow a *disputationes* model. The evidence is just too circumstantial to establish this and, in any case, it would have been surprising indeed if Descartes had simply based his procedure on what was effectively a rearguard defence of an Aristotle-based theology by the Jesuit commentators of the late sixteenth century. But what I do wish to maintain is that: (i) the source of Descartes's deductive procedure in the *Meditations* and the *Principles* does not derive from a model of synthetic geometrical demonstration; (ii) it does not derive from the fantasies about method current in Rosicrucian circles; and (iii) it has sufficient parallels with the *disputationes* model, both in what it seeks to achieve and in how it seeks to achieve it, to entitle this model to serious consideration as an important influence on Descartes's procedure, albeit one which he would have felt free to reshape to his own purposes.

PART TWO

Reason, Being, and Truth

4

Descartes's Concepts of Substance

PETER MARKIE

Substance is a central concept in Descartes's metaphysics, just as certainty is a central concept in his epistemology, and Descartes's remarks about substance are often obscure and confusing, just as his remarks about certainty are, yet his views on substance have not received the same critical attention as his views on certainty. The imbalance is part of a general tendency, especially among Anglo-American commentators, to concentrate on Descartes's epistemology at the expense of his metaphysics. To help correct it, I shall examine Descartes's conception of substance in three well-known passages: *Principles*, pt. I, arts. 51-2, the Second Replies' definition of substance, and the Synopsis of the *Meditations*.

I shall argue that these passages contain three different conceptions of substance. *Principles*, pt. I, arts. 51-2, defines substance in terms of independence, the Second Replies in terms of dependence, and the Synopsis in terms of a kind of independence not found in the *Principles* passage. The definitions of substance contained in *Principles*, pt. I, arts. 51-2, and the Second Replies are co-extensive; both are satisfied by individual minds, bodies, and even the substantial unions of minds and bodies. The Synopsis conception of substance is not satisfied by bodies or the substantial unions of minds and bodies, but only by minds and matter in general. Descartes thus has at least three ways of making an inventory of the world, two of which produce the same list and one of which produces a more restricted one.

In examining Descartes's concepts of substance, I shall consider in passing some related parts of his epistemology, including his view of how we can know that something is a substance and his claim to know that he himself is one. Old habits die hard.

I. The *Principles*

Let us start with *Principles*, pt. I, arts. 51–2:

By substance we can understand nothing other than a thing which exists in
such a way as to depend on no other thing for its existence. And there is only
one substance which can be understood to depend on no other thing
whatsoever, namely God. In the case of all other substances, we perceive that
they can exist only with the help of God's concurrence. Hence, the term
'substance' does not apply *univocally*, as they say in the Schools, to God and
to other things; that is, there is no distinctly intelligible meaning of the term
which is common to God and his creatures. . . . {In the case of created things,
some are of such a nature that they cannot exist without other things, while
some need only the concurrence of God in order to exist. We make this
distinction by calling the latter 'substances' and the former 'qualities' or
'attributes' of those substances.}

But as for corporeal substance and mind (or created thinking substance)
these can be understood to fall under this common concept: things that need
only the concurrence of God in order to exist. (AT VIIIA 24; CSM I 210;
the section in curved brackets is added in the French edition (AT IXB 47))[1]

Descartes defines the concept of substance as an independent existent,
what I shall call substance₁. God alone satisfies the definition
of substance as what exists independently of all other things; created
minds and bodies satisfy a weaker definition as what exists independently
of everything other than God. Qualities do not satisfy either definition.

It is important to see that Descartes thinks particular bodies and
minds are substances₁. He writes vaguely of corporeal substance
and mind, but he proceeds to define real distinctness as a relation
unique to substances₁—'Strictly speaking, a real distinction exists only
between two or more substances . . .' (*Principles*, pt. I, art. 60: AT
VIIIA 28; CSM I 213)—and to claim that particular chunks and bits
of matter are really distinct from each other and from him.

For example, even though we may not yet know for certain that any extended
or corporeal substance exists in reality, the mere fact that we have an idea of
such a substance enables us to be certain that it is capable of existing. And
we can also be certain that, if it exists, each and every part of it, as delimited
by us in our thought, is really distinct from the other parts of the same
substance. Similarly, from the mere fact that each of us understands himself

---

[1] I follow Cottingham's translation (in CSM) throughout; note that the translation
distinguishes between Descartes's use of the Latin or French for 'substance' and his
use of related terms for 'thing', 'subject', and the like.

to be a thinking thing and is capable, in thought, of excluding from himself every other substance, whether thinking or extended, it is certain that each of us, regarded in this way, is really distinct from every other thinking substance and from every corporeal substance. And even if we suppose that God has joined some corporeal substance to such a thinking substance so closely that they cannot be more closely conjoined, thus compounding them into a unity, they nonetheless remain really distinct. (*Principles*, pt. I, art. 60: AT VIIIA 28–9; CSM I 213)[2]

Descartes gives several apparent examples of substances$_1$ throughout his works. In the Third Meditation he instances both a stone and himself: 'For example, I think that a stone is a substance or a thing capable of existing independently, and I also think that I am a substance' (AT VII 44; CSM II 30). He presents the concept of a substance$_1$ in the Fourth Replies ('the notion of substance is just this— that it can exist by itself, that is without the aid of any other substance' (AT VII 226; CSM II 159)), and he treats a person's arm as one, as well as the union of a mind and body.

Now someone who says that a man's arm is a substance that is really distinct from the rest of his body does not thereby deny that the arm belongs to the nature of the whole man. And saying that the arm belongs to the nature of the whole man does not give rise to the suspicion that it cannot subsist in its own right. In the same way, I do not think I proved too much in showing that the mind can exist apart from the body. (AT VII 228; CSM II 160)

Thus a hand is an incomplete substance when it is referred to the whole body of which it is a part; but it is a complete substance when it is considered on its own. And in just the same way the mind and the body are incomplete substances when they are referred to a human being which together they make up. But if they are considered on their own they are complete. (AT VII 222; CSM II 157)

Just as a hand is both a substance$_1$ and part of another substance$_1$ which is the body, so too a particular human being's mind and body

---

[2] Two substances are really distinct just when each can exist without the other, as Descartes puts it in the Second Replies: 'Two substances are said to be really distinct, when each of them can exist apart from the other' (AT VII 162; CSM II 114). Descartes states his position on real distinctness too strongly at *Principles*, pt. I, art. 60, when he says he is 'really distinct from every other thinking substance and from every corporeal substance'. He is not, strictly speaking, really distinct from God, for example, since he cannot exist without God. Some commentators seem to understand the concept of a real distinction differently. E. M. Curley (*Descartes against the Skeptics*, 197–9) seems to equate it with numerical distinctness; B. Williams (*The Project of Pure Enquiry*, 117) seems to equate it with necessary numerical distinctness. For a criticism of Curley's and Williams's positions, see P. J. Markie, *Descartes' Gambit*, 239–43.

are both substances$_1$ and part of another substance$_1$ which is the human being.

How are we to understand Descartes's concept of a substance$_1$? Let us begin with some inadequate interpretations.

D1 *x* is a primary substance$_1$ =df. *x* depends on no other thing for its existence.

D2 *x* is a secondary substance$_1$ =df. *x* needs only the concurrence of God in order to exist.

These definitions stay so close to the text as to be vague and confusing just where it is. The first definition uses the concept of a thing. Is this the same concept as that of a substance$_1$? If so, the definition is circular. How are we to understand the notion of need or dependence used in both definitions? In what way do a particular rock and the union of Descartes's mind and body 'need' only the concurrence of God to exist? Does not the rock also 'need' and 'depend on' its material parts? Does not the union of Descartes's mind and body 'need' and 'depend on' Descartes's mind and Descartes's body? Do not God, a rock, Descartes's mind, and Descartes's body all 'depend' on their essential attributes since they could not exist without them, and on qualities in general since they could not exist without at least some?

Two assumptions enable us to move forward. First, let us assume that Descartes takes the concept of a thing as an undefined primitive and understands it so that the set of things is the set of all there is, from attributes such as thought and extension, to modes such as doubt and roundness, to minds, bodies, and their unions. Descartes understands the concept of a thing in this way in the extra remark in the French version of his definition of substance$_1$ at *Principles*, pt. I, art. 51, quoted earlier, and this assumption will let us state his definition in a noncircular way.[3] Secondly, let us assume that Descartes is concerned, at least partially, with a form of causal independence. We may now try the following.

[3] The relevant part of the French text is: '*mais parce qu'entre les choses créées quelques-unes sont de telle nature qu'elles ne peuvent exister sans quelques autres, nous les distinguons d'avec celles qui n'ont besoin que du concours ordinaire de Dieu, en nommant celles-ce des substances, et celles-là des qualités ou des attributs de ces substances*' (AT IXB 47). There are, of course, texts in which Descartes may use 'thing' (*res/chose*) and 'substance' (*substantiam/substance*) interchangeably to refer to what has independent existence. Consider: 'On the contrary, it is clear that since I am a thinking thing [*rem/chose*] or substance [*substantiam/substance*], it would have been far more difficult for me to emerge out of nothing than merely to acquire knowledge of the many things of which I am ignorant—such knowledge being merely an accident of that substance' (*Meditations*: AT VII 48; AT IXB 38; CSM II 33).

D3 *x* is a primary substance$_1$ =df. *x* does not depend on the causal power of any other thing to remain in existence.

D4 *x* is a secondary substance$_1$ =df. *x* does not depend on the causal power of any thing except God to remain in existence.

The definitions still contain at least one problem. Lots of bodies do not satisfy D4. Suppose you are holding a cup that will break if you drop it. Descartes is committed to the view that the cup depends on your causal power to remain in existence, for he thinks it will cease to exist if a part breaks off. Consider his remark to Mesland.

When we speak in general of a body, we mean a determinate part of matter, a part of the quantity of which the universe is composed. In this sense, if the smallest amount of that quantity were removed we would *eo ipso* judge that the body was smaller and no longer complete; and if any particle of the matter were changed we would at once think that the body was no longer quite the same, no longer numerically the same (AT IV 166; CSMK 242–3)[4]

Perhaps because of considerations like these, Louis Loeb offers the following interpretation of Descartes's definitions.

D5 *x* is a primary substance$_1$ =df. it is possible that *x*'s existence does not depend causally upon the existence of any other entity.

D6 *x* is a secondary substance$_1$ =df. it is possible that *x*'s existence

---

[4] Descartes modifies his position with regard to bodies that are substantially united with minds. Such a body may be said to be numerically the same despite changes in its material composition, so long as it remains united with the same mind: 'And so, even though that matter changes, and its quantity increases or decreases, we still believe that it is the same body, numerically the same body, provided that it remains joined in substantial union with the same soul; and we think that this body is whole and entire provided that it has all the dispositions required to preserve that union' (AT IV 166; CSMK 243).

Descartes's position here on the numerical diversity of bodies through changes in their parts is at odds with some of his other claims. In his account of refraction, he implies that, when a body changes shape, it takes on new particles of matter or loses old ones (*Principles*, pt. II, art. 6: AT VIIIA 43; CSM I 225); in the Second Meditation wax example, he says that the piece of wax changes shape but remains the same body (AT VII 30; CSM II 20). Descartes's best option is to give up the claim that the wax remains numerically the same; he might well say that it remains the same in the ordinary common sense of 'the same body', but not in a strict, philosophical sense of the phrase. This would accord with the fact that the wax example is presented as an appeal to our common-sense opinions. Consider Edwin Curley's fine account of the problem in *Descartes against the Skeptics*, pp. 213–14.

does not depend causally upon the existence of any other entity except God.[5]

Loeb's interpretation captures Descartes's view that only God is a primary substance$_I$, and that created minds, bodies, and combinations of minds and bodies are secondary substances$_I$. Yet, it contradicts Descartes's claim that qualities are not secondary substances$_I$. The quality of thought can exist with God as the sole cause of its continuing existence; consider a possible world in which God is the only thinking thing. Indeed, most, if not all, of God's qualities can exist in such a way that God is the sole cause of their continuing existence.

Let us take a closer look at some of Descartes's remarks to see where Loeb's definition of secondary substance$_I$ goes wrong. Why is it that particular minds and bodies are secondary substances$_I$ but qualities are not? At the start of *Principles*, pt. I, art. 52, Descartes writes:

But as for corporeal substance and mind (or created thinking substance) these can be understood to fall under this common concept: things that need only the concurrence of God in order to exist. (AT VIIIB 24; CSM I 210)

In the French version of *Principles*, pt. I, art. 51, we are told the following:

In the case of created things, some are of such a nature that they cannot exist without other things, while some need only the concurrence of God in order to exist. We make this distinction by calling the latter 'substances' and the former 'qualities' or 'attributes' of those substances. (AT IXB 47)

Consider, too, Descartes's remark to Hyperaspistes:

There is no doubt that if God withdrew his concurrence, everything which he has created would go to nothing; because all things were nothing until God created them and provided his concurrence. This does not mean that they

---

[5] L. E. Loeb, *From Descartes to Hume*, 96–7. Loeb does not explain the concepts of an entity and possibility used in these definitions. I assume that he takes the concept of an entity to be that of a thing and relies upon logical possibility. I also assume that the definitions are to be read as quantified formulas in which the variable x ranges over actual things and the phrase 'any other entity' is interpreted within the scope of the possibility operator. Thus interpreted, D5 implies that an actual thing is a primary substance$_I$ if and only if there is some possible world at which it exists and does not depend causally upon the existence of any of the other entities at that world. D6 implies that an actual thing is a secondary substance$_I$ if and only if there is some possible world at which it exists and does not depend causally upon the existence of any of the other entities at that world, except God.

should not be called substances, because when we call a created substance self-subsistent we do not rule out divine concurrence which it needs in order to subsist. We mean only that it is a thing of a kind to exist without any other creature; and this is something that cannot be said about the modes of things, like shape and number. (AT III 429; CSMK 193)

Secondary substances$_I$ are things that need only the concurrence of God to exist; they are things of a kind to exist without any other creature. Qualities are not secondary substances$_I$. They need more than the concurrence of God to exist. Yet, to say this is not to say or even imply, as Loeb's definition of secondary substance$_I$ assumes, that qualities are necessarily *causally dependent* on some created thing for their continued existence. We have just seen that the quality of thought is not so dependent. What more, then, do qualities need? Descartes does not say, but that may be because he gives the answer earlier in the *Principles*. At *Principles*, pt. I, art. 11, he says that 'whenever we find some attributes or qualities, there is necessarily some thing or substance to be found for them to belong to'. Each quality needs some entity to serve as the subject of its existence. This, I suggest, is why none is a secondary substance$_I$.

Consider, then, the following definitions:

D7 x is a primary substance$_I$ =df. (1) x is not dependent upon the causal power of any other thing to remain in existence, and (2) x is not a quality of some other thing.

D8 x is a secondary substance$_I$ =df. (1) x is necessarily dependent upon the power of God to remain in existence; (2) x can exist and not be dependent upon the causal power of any other created thing to remain in existence; and (3) x can exist without being a quality of some other thing.

So understood, the concept of a substance$_I$ involves two kinds of independence. One is causal independence: the ability to remain in existence independently of another thing's causal power. The other is subject independence: the ability to exist without being a quality of another thing, without depending on another thing to provide the subject in which existence occurs. God has subject independence and causal independence relative to everything. Created minds and bodies have subject independence, and they have causal independence relative to everything but God. Qualities lack subject independence, although they may have causal independence relative to things other than God.

The definitions capture Descartes's examples. God is the only primary substance$_I$; for only God exists both without depending on the causal power of something else and without being a quality of something else. Created minds, bodies, and their substantial unions are secondary substances$_I$. All are necessarily dependent upon God's causal power, can remain in existence without the aid of any causal power other than God's, and can exist without being a quality of any other thing. Attributes and their modes are not substances$_I$, since they can exist only as qualities of things.[6]

Two likely objections to my interpretation merit consideration. One is that my view conflicts with Descartes's metaphysical principle that every substance$_I$ has one essential attribute of which all its other qualities are modes.

A substance may indeed be known through any attribute at all; but each substance has one principal property which constitutes its nature and essence, and to which all its other properties are referred. Thus extension in length, breadth and depth constitutes the nature of corporeal substance; and thought constitutes the nature of thinking substance. Everything else which can be attributed to body presupposes extension, and is merely a mode of an extended

---

[6] Note that in one way the second condition of D8 is redundant: everything that satisfies the third condition satisfies the second as well, given Descartes's metaphysical commitments. We should not drop the second condition, however. If we do, we shall have a definition of substance$_I$ that, *in conjunction with Descartes's basic metaphysical commitments*, implies that every substance$_I$ can exist without being dependent on the power of any other created thing, but we want a definition that has that implication all by itself, independently of any other metaphysical commitments Descartes might have. The ability to exist independently of the causal power of any other created thing is part of Descartes's concept of a substance$_I$.

I have not bothered to examine an inadequate interpretation of Descartes's position, which I propose in *Descartes's Gambit*:

x is a substance$_I$ =df. (1) x has a real attribute, and (2) there is no y such that y has a real attribute, y is numerically distinct from x, y exists contingently, but it is logically impossible that x exists and y does not.

The set of substances$_I$ is defined as the set of entities that have real attributes and are capable of existing apart from every other contingent entity with real attributes. Real attributes are thought, extension, and their modes. This definition has at least three flaws. First, it says that qualities are not substances$_I$ because they lack real attributes, but Descartes clearly thinks they are not substances because they lack the proper sort of independent existence. Secondly, the union of Descartes's mind and body does not satisfy the definition, since that union cannot exist without Descartes's mind. Thirdly, a particular body, such as a coffee cup, does not satisfy the definition, given Descartes's position that no particular body can exist without all of its parts. The handle of the cup has a real attribute, is numerically distinct from the cup, exists contingently, and yet, according to Descartes, the cup cannot exist unless the handle exists.

thing; and similarly, whatever we find in the mind is simply one of the various modes of thinking. (*Principles*, pt. I, art. 53: AT VIIIA 25; CSM I 210)

My interpretation counts the substantial union of a mind and body as a substance₁ but such unions have no one attribute of which all their other qualities are modes.

I think Descartes's concentration on the categories of minds and bodies here simply makes him forget to build an exception for mind–body unions into his metaphysical principle. Recall that in the Fourth Replies he introduces the concept of substance as an independent existent and explicitly treats mind–body unions as substances₁. Note, too, that his formulation of his metaphysical principle in the *Principles* is loose in other ways: it is not the case that *everything* we find in a body is a mode of extension; being a substance₁ and having existence are not modes of extension. In the *Comments on a Certain Broadsheet* Descartes restates his metaphysical principle so that it contains an exception for mind–body unions.

As for the attributes which constitute the natures of things, it cannot be said that those which are different, and such that the concept of one is not contained in the concept of the other, are present together in one and the same subject; for this would be equivalent to saying that one and the same subject has two different natures—a statement that implies a contradiction, *at least when it is a question of a simple subject (as in the present case) rather than a composite one.* (AT VIIIB 350; CSM I 298; emphasis added)

Finally, we have a good philosophical justification to interpret Descartes's principle so it excepts mind–body unions rather than interpreting his definition of substances₁ so it excludes them. Any reason to exclude mind–body unions from the category of substances₁ is an equally good reason to exclude particular bodies from the category. Mind–body unions have just as much subject independence as particular bodies; they are just as causally independent of other things as particular bodies are. Mind–body unions contain other substances₁ as necessary parts, but so too do particular bodies.

Another objection concerns Descartes's account of how we can know that a particular object is a substance₁. He combines his definition of a substance₁ with the statement:

We can, however, easily come to know a substance by one of its attributes, in virtue of the common notion that nothingness possesses no attributes, that is to say, no properties or qualities. Thus, if we perceive the presence of some attribute, we can infer that there must also be present an existing thing or substance to which it may be attributed. (*Principles*, pt. I, art. 52: AT VIIIA 25; CSM I 210)

Descartes seems to endorse inferences of the form: I perceive that this has property P; whatever has a perceived property is a substance$_I$; therefore, this is a substance$_I$.[7] He seems to regard the second, general premiss as self-evident; indeed, he presents it as the common notion that 'nothingness possesses no attributes, that is to say, no properties or qualities'.[8] Yet, my interpretation implies that the general premiss is not self-evident. The premiss asserts that whatever has a perceived property also has subject independence and causal independence from everything, except perhaps God, which may be true but surely is not self-evident.

We have not found a problem in my interpretation, though we have found a problem in Descartes's philosophy which no plausible account of the concept of a substance$_I$ can avoid. Every plausible interpretation must take seriously Descartes's explicit requirement that to be a substance$_I$ is, at least in part, to be causally independent of other created things. Yet, to make this requirement part of the concept of a substance$_I$ is to deny self-evident status to the general premiss that whatever has perceived qualities is a substance$_I$. Descartes cannot both define the concept of substance$_I$ so it involves significantly more than the possession of perceived qualities and have it be self-evident that whatever has perceived qualities is a substance$_I$.[9]

---

[7] I have restricted Descartes's second premiss to perceived properties, since it clearly does not cover any property, including being an essential property, for example, and he is explicitly concerned with qualities we perceive. He indicates at *Principles*, pt. I, art. 48 (AT VIIIA 22–3; CSM I 208–9) that the qualities we perceive things to have include thought and its modes, extension and its modes, appetites such as hunger, emotions such as anger, and sensations such as pleasure and pain.

Some commentators take Descartes to be endorsing inferences of a slightly different form: 'This is a (perceived) property, every (perceived) property exists in a substance$_I$, therefore, there is a substance$_I$ in which this exists.' I believe this is a mistaken reading of Descartes's remarks. I shall not go into the reason here; those interested might examine my treatment of this point in *Descartes's Gambit*. Nothing I say here hinges on whether we accept or reject this reading of Descartes's remarks.

[8] Descartes's maxim, 'Nothing has no properties', contains an interesting ambiguity. We can read it as the claim that whatever has (perceived) properties is something (a substance$_I$), or we can read it as the claim that whatever is something (a substance$_I$)— and so not nothing—has some properties. I take it that he intends us to read it in the former fashion. This is the way in which it at least comes close to the general premiss used in his inference here. See *Descartes's Gambit* for an interpretation that reads Descartes's maxim in the latter way; I now think that interpretation is mistaken, for reasons I shall not consider here.

[9] I shall later suggest an explanation of why he misses this point.

Now that we understand Descartes's concept of substance₁, we can examine some related points. Consider a familiar point made by Leibniz:

I do [not] know whether the definition of substance as that which needs for its existence only the concurrence of God fits any created substance known to us, unless we interpret it in some unusual sense. For not only do we need other substances; we need our own accidents even much more. Therefore, since substance and accident depend upon each other, other marks are necessary for distinguishing a substance from an accident.[10]

The definitions of substance₁ do indeed use some particular notions of independence (causal independence and subject independence), while ignoring others, such as quality independence (the ability to exist without any qualities) and mereological independence (having no necessary parts). Perhaps, this amounts to using an 'unusual sense' of independence. None the less, the definitions distinguish between substances₁ and qualities.

Descartes's concept of a substance₁ does not contain much metaphysical content. His claim to be such a substance is consistent with his being material and with his being immaterial. It is consistent with his being a bare substratum–qualities combination, with his being a bundle of qualities, and with his being neither. It is consistent with his being divisible into other substances₁ and with his not being so divisible. It is consistent with his being immortal and with his being mortal, as well as with his remaining the same person through changes in his mental state and with his not remaining the same.

Descartes's claim to be a substance₁ gains metaphysical weight from being combined with additional synthetic principles about the metaphysical status of substances₁. He follows his definition of substance₁ in the *Principles* with the claim that substances₁ have one essential attribute of which all their other qualities are modes (pt. I, art. 53: AT VIIIA 25; CSM I 210). In the Third Meditation he combines his claim to be a substance₁ with the principle that it is a greater act to create a substance₁ than to create its particular qualities and uses the combination to argue that he could be the source of his own creation only if he could have given himself all the knowledge he lacks (*Meditations*: AT VII 48; CSM II 33).

Is the metaphysical content of Descartes's concept of a substance₁ so minimal that he thinks he can know beyond the slightest doubt that

---

[10] Leibniz, *Philosophical Papers and Letters*, ed. L. E. Loemker, 389.

he is a substance₁ prior to proving God's existence? If he does, is he right? Descartes says in the Fifth Replies (AT VII 355; CSM II 245) that his Second Meditation certainties include his claim to be a substance, though he does not explain what conception of substance he has in mind. As already noted, he claims to be a substance₁ in the Third Meditation, prior to arguing for God's existence, and uses that claim in his argument. So, we have some reason to think he counts his claim to be a substance₁ among his initial certainties. Yet, the evidence is inconclusive. Descartes may have a different conception of substance in mind when he describes his Second Meditation certainty in the Fifth Replies. The Second Meditation passage itself (AT VII 27; CSM II 18) contains only the claim to be a thinking thing (*res cogitans*). Moreover, according to some plausible interpretations of Descartes's method, he does not think the premisses of his argument for God's existence are beyond the slightest doubt, when he initially presents them.[11]

We cannot settle the issue by appeal to the *Principles*. Descartes does not define the concept of a substance₁ until after he argues for God's existence, but he might still use it beforehand. *Principles*, pt. I, arts. 8 and 20, which correspond to his Second Meditation account of his nature and his Third Meditation argument for God's existence, contain unclear references to things, which might or might not be intended as references to substances₁ (AT VIIIA 7, 12; CSM I 195, 200).

It is hard to see how Descartes's claim to be a substance₁ could be one of his Second Meditation certainties. It lacks the characteristics that make his beliefs in his existence and mental state plausibly immune to the Deceiver Hypothesis. Unlike the fact that he exists and thinks, it is not entailed by the Deceiver Hypothesis. Unlike the fact that he seems to see light, it is not something of which he is immediately aware. The Deceiver Hypothesis seems to cast doubt on his belief that he is a substance₁ just as effectively as it casts doubt on his senses. For all he knows, a deceptive god may cause him to think his ideas are caused by and correctly represent reality, when they are actually caused by the deceptive god and misrepresent reality; so too, for all he knows, a deceptive god may cause him to think he can exist independently of everything but God, when he actually necessarily depends on that deceptive god for his continued existence.

---

[11] Consider e.g. A. Gewirth, 'The Cartesian Circle' and F. Feldman, 'Epistemic Appraisal and the Cartesian Circle'.

So much for Descartes's definition of a substance₁ at *Principles*, pt. I, arts. 51–2; it is time to consider his definition of substance in the Second Replies.

II. The Second Replies

Descartes defines the concept of substance as a subject, what I shall call substance$_S$, in the Second Replies.

Substance. This term applies to every thing in which whatever we perceive immediately resides, as in a subject, or to every thing by means of which whatever we perceive exists. By 'whatever we perceive' is meant any property, quality or attribute of which we have a real idea. The only idea we have of a substance itself, in the strict sense, is that it is the thing in which whatever we perceive (or whatever has objective being in one of our ideas) exists, either formally or eminently. For we know by the natural light that a real attribute cannot belong to nothing. (AT VII 161; CSM II 114)

Descartes gives us:

D9 S is a substance$_S$ =df. some perceivable qualities exist in S.

This is almost the flip-side of the concept of substance₁. Being a substance$_S$ consists, not in being independent of other things, but in being something of which other things are not independent, something on which they depend as a subject for their existence.

Descartes's definition is ambiguous. The phrase 'exist in' in the definiens has two readings. It may be read so that the exist-in relation holds only between bare substrata, in the sense of bare particulars, and qualities, in which case the definition is satisfied only by bare substrata and not by such concrete objects as Descartes's mind and a piece of wax. This is the bare substratum reading. The phrase 'exist in' may also be read so that the exist-in relation holds between concrete objects, such as Descartes's mind or a piece of wax, on the one hand, and qualities, on the other, in which case the definition is satisfied by those concrete objects and does not presuppose their analysis into bare substrata and qualities. This is the subject reading. The readings have different implications for the relation between the concepts of a substance$_S$ and a substance₁. The concepts are not co-extensive on the bare substratum reading, since the set of substances₁ includes particular minds, bodies, and unions of minds and bodies, none of which is a bare substratum. They are co-extensive on the subject reading. Within the context of Descartes's metaphysical assumptions, every substance$_1$ is the subject of a perceivable quality, and every subject of a perceivable quality is a substance$_1$.[12]

At least one commentator, Louis Loeb, attributes the concept of a bare substratum to Descartes, but several considerations justify the subject reading of the definition.[13] Burman reports that Descartes gave him the following explanation of the definition: 'In addition to the attribute which specified the substance, one must think of the substance itself which is the substrate of that attribute. For example, since the mind is a thinking thing, there is in addition to the thinking a substance which does the thinking, and so on' (AT V 156).[14] He also reports that, when he observed to Descartes that, since the attributes are the same as the substance$_S$, it cannot be a greater thing to create a substance$_S$ than to create its attributes, Descartes replied as follows: 'It is true that the attributes are the same as the substance, but this is when they are all taken together, not when they are taken individually, one by one. So it is a greater thing to produce a substance than its attributes, if by producing all the attributes you mean producing one individually, one after the other' (AT V 154–5).[15] The first report does not help us on its own, since it retains the definition's ambiguity in its talk of a substrate: is the substrate of an attribute a bare particular or a concrete object? Yet, the second report quite clearly has Descartes adopting the view that each substance$_S$ is a collection of qualities, which is directly at odds with the view that each is a bare substratum though consistent with the view that each is a subject of qualities.[16]

Descartes's use of the concept of substance$_S$ strongly supports the

---

[12] The concepts of a substance$_1$ and a substance$_S$ are, of course, nonidentical on either reading of Descartes's definition of the latter, for on either reading it is possible to doubt that one is a substance$_1$ without doubting that one is a substance$_S$.

[13] Loeb, *From Descartes to Hume*, 78–83.

[14] J. Cottingham (ed.), *Descartes' Conversation with Burman*, 17.   [15] Ibid. 15.

[16] There is also evidence that Descartes adopts a bundle theory of substances$_1$, which would fit well with the subject of qualities interpretation of substance$_S$ since that interpretation makes the two conceptions of substance co-extensive. At *Principles*, pt. I, art. 63, after he has introduced the concept of substance$_1$, Descartes claims that: 'Thought and extension can be regarded as constituting the natures of intelligent substance and corporeal substance; they must then be considered as nothing else but thinking substance itself and extended substance itself—that is, as mind and body' (AT VIIIA 30–1; CSM I 215). If Descartes is endorsing a bundle theory of substances$_1$, he is careless in his statement of it, for it ignores the fact that each substance$_1$ has other qualities besides thought, extension, and their modes. All have duration and existence, for example. We have already seen him make a similar slip in his assertion of the 'principal attribute' claim at *Principles*, pt. I, art. 53.

subject reading. The Second Replies seems to be the only place where Descartes introduces the concept of a substance$_S$, and he uses it to present in 'geometrical fashion' arguments concerning God's existence and the real distinctness of mind and body that he presents in the *Meditations* and *Principles* using the concept of a substance$_I$. In the Third Meditation, Descartes claims that he, like a rock, is a substance$_I$ (AT VII 44; CSM II 30), as already noted; he then argues that, since it is a greater act to create a substance$_I$ than to create its qualities, he could have created himself only if he could and would have given himself all the knowledge he lacks (AT VII 48: CSM II 33).

Yet if I derived my existence from myself {and were independent of every other being}, then I should neither doubt nor want, nor lack anything at all; for I should have given myself all the perfections of which I have any idea, and thus I should myself be God. I must not suppose that the items I lack would be more difficult to acquire than those I now have. On the contrary, it is clear that, since I am a thinking thing or substance, it would have been far more difficult for me to emerge out of nothing than merely to acquire knowledge of the many things of which I am ignorant—such knowledge being merely an accident of that substance (AT VII 48; CMS II 33; the section in curved brackets is added in the French version (AT IXA 38)).

He repeats the argument in the Second Replies, using the concept of a substance$_S$.

If I had the power of preserving myself, how much more would I have the power of giving myself the perfections which I lack (Axioms VIII and IX); for these perfections are merely attributes of a substance, whereas I am a substance. But I do not have the power of giving myself these perfections; if I did, I should already have them (Axiom VII). Therefore I do not have the power of preserving myself. (AT VII 168; CSM II 118)[17]

---

[17] Descartes presents the Third Meditation argument in terms of his ability to create himself; he presents the Second Replies argument in terms of his ability to preserve himself. The difference is unimportant for our purposes, since Descartes explicitly adopts the axiom that 'no less a cause is required to preserve something than is required to create it in the first place' prior to presenting his Second Replies version of the argument (AT VII 165; CSM II 116).

Descartes's version of this argument in the *Principles* does not clearly use the concept of a substance$_I$. He presents the argument before he defines the concept of a substance$_I$, he writes of things rather than substances, and he states the argument without explicitly using the premiss that it is a greater act to create (maintain) a substance than to create its qualities: 'Now it is certainly very evident by the natural light that a thing which recognizes something more perfect than itself is not the source of its own being; for if so, it would have given itself all the perfections of which it has an idea. Hence, the source of its being can only be something which possesses within itself all these perfections—that is, God' (*Principles*, pt. I, art. 20: AT VIIIA 12; CSM I 200). Perhaps Descartes would have us interpret the argument so it uses the concept of a thing that recognizes something more perfect than itself instead of the concept of a substance$_I$.

In the *Principles*, as we have already seen, Descartes presents the concept of a substance$_I$, introduces real distinctness as a relation between substances$_I$, and appeals to his clear perceptions and the power of God to argue that his mind is really distinct from every other substance$_I$, especially the body to which God has united him (*Principles*, pt. I, art. 60: AT VIIIA 28–9; CSM I 213).[18] He gives the same argument in the Second Replies, using the concept of a substance$_S$.

God can bring about whatever we clearly perceive in a way exactly corresponding to our perception of it (preceding Corollary). But we clearly perceive the mind, that is, a thinking substance, apart from the body, that is, apart from an extended substance (Second Postulate). And conversely we can clearly perceive the body apart from the mind (as everyone readily admits). Therefore the mind can, at least through the power of God, exist without the body; and similarly the body can exist apart from the mind. (AT VII 169–70; CSM II 119)

Given the similarity between the arguments in the *Meditations* and the *Principles*, which use the concept of a substance$_I$, on the one hand, and those in the Second Replies, which use the concept of a substance$_S$, on the other, it is reasonable to expect that those concepts of substance are at least co-extensive. They are co-extensive only on the subject reading of the definition of substance$_S$.

Finally, Descartes's remark at *Principles*, pt. II, art. 9, counts heavily against the view that he gives the concept of a bare substratum an important place in his philosophy:

Others may disagree [with my view that if corporeal substance is distinguished from its quantity, it is conceived in a confused manner as something incorporeal], but I do not think they have any alternative perception of the matter. When they make a distinction between substance and extension or quantity, either they do not understand anything by the term 'substance', or

---

[18] A similar argument is, of course, given in the Sixth Meditation (AT VII 78; CSM II 54). I emphasize the *Principles* argument here simply because Descartes explicitly writes of substances in his formulation of it; he writes less clearly of things in the Sixth Meditation argument. We are told, for example: 'Hence the fact that I can clearly and distinctly understand one thing apart from another is enough to make me certain that the two things are distinct, since they are capable of being separated, at least by God' (AT VII 78; CSM II 54). Commentators generally assume that this is one place where Descartes's references to things may simply be interpreted as references to substances, though little attention, if any, is given to the question of which concept of substance— the concept of a substance$_I$ or the concept of a substance$_S$—we should use in interpreting and evaluating Descartes's claim to know the argument's premises with certainty.

else they simply have a confused idea of incorporeal substance, which they falsely attach to corporeal substance; and they relegate the true idea of corporeal substance to the category of extension, which, however, they term an accident. (AT VIIIA 45; CSM I 226–7)

Suppose we take a material object, say a piece of wax, and attempt to conceive of a bare substratum underlying its modes of extension. We do not succeed. Either we end up with no conception of substance at all—we 'do not understand anything by the term "substance" '—or we have a confused idea of incorporeal substance. It is most unlikely that Descartes would adopt a conception of substance he thinks we cannot grasp.[19]

Now that we understand Descartes's concept of a substance$_S$, we can appreciate some further points. Note that his claim to be a substance$_S$ contains even less metaphysical content than his claim to be a substance$_I$. It simply says he has perceivable qualities. It is consistent with his being material and with his being immaterial. It is consistent with his being a bare substratum–qualities combination, with his being a bundle of qualities, and with his being neither. It is consistent with his being divisible into other substances$_S$ and with his not being so divisible. It is consistent with his being immortal and with his being mortal, as well as with his remaining the same person through changes in his mental state and with his not remaining the same. It does not even entail that he has subject independence or causal independence.

Even more than his claim to be a substance$_I$, Descartes's claim to be a substance$_S$ must gain its metaphysical weight from being

---

[19] Dan Garber brought this passage to my attention. Consider a similar point by Leibniz in the *New Essays Concerning Human Understanding*: 'If you distinguish two things in a substance—the attributes or predicates, and their common subject—it is no wonder that you cannot conceive anything special in this subject. That is inevitable, because you have already set aside all the attributes through which details could be conceived' (2.23.2).

Louis Loeb (*From Descartes to Hume*, 91) thinks Descartes relies on the concept of a bare substratum in the Second Meditation wax example; he takes Descartes's position to be that a bare substratum lies hidden beneath the wax's qualities just as the men in the street lie hidden beneath their clothes. Yet, when Gassendi interprets the wax example in just this way in the Fifth Objections (AT VII 271–2; CSM II 189–90), Descartes objects that he has been misunderstood: 'I did not abstract the concept of the wax from the concept of its accidents' (AT VII 359; CSM II 248). Several commentators interpret the wax example without attributing the concept of a bare substratum to Descartes. See G. E. M. Anscombe, 'Substance'; Curley, *Descartes against the Skeptics*, 211–16; Williams, *The Project of Pure Enquiry*, 213–27; and M. Wilson, *Descartes*, 76–92.

combined with additional principles about the status of substances$_S$. Descartes seems to adopt the same metaphysical principles for both concepts of substance. We have already seen how he gives one set of arguments in the *Meditations* and *Principles*, using some metaphysical principles about substances$_I$, and then repeats the arguments in the Second Replies, substituting the concept of a substance$_S$ but otherwise keeping the metaphysical principles the same.

It is quite appropriate for Descartes to adopt the same metaphysical principles about both kinds of substance; the categories are after all co-extensive. Yet, an exchange of even co-extensive concepts can change the logical and epistemic status of a metaphysical principle. Consider, for example, Descartes's principle that whatever has a perceived quality is a substance$_I$. We have already noted the implausibility of Descartes's suggestion that this principle is self-evident. His position gains plausibility when we restate the principle as the claim that whatever has a perceived attribute is a substance$_S$. This principle is true by the definition of a substance$_S$ and so a plausible candidate for self-evident knowledge by the natural light.[20] In the case of some principles, things appear to work the other way. That it is a greater act to create a substance than to create its qualities is more plausible when substances are understood to have a kind of independence that qualities lack rather than simply being thought of as the subjects of perceivable qualities.

The slim metaphysical content of Descartes's concept of a substance$_S$ makes it tempting to use it to interpret his claim in the Fifth Replies to be certain he is a substance as early as the Second Meditation. Descartes could plausibly explain how his claim to be a substance$_S$ resists the Deceiver Hypothesis: 'Suppose there is a deceptive god; let him deceive me as much as he will, so long as he does so, I have the perceivable property of thought and so am a substance$_S$. To hypothesize that I am deceived is not to cast doubt on my claim to be a substance$_S$; it is to reaffirm it by assuming that I have the perceivable property of thought. To have a perceivable property is, by definition,

---

[20] This may explain Descartes's mistake in the *Principles* of presenting the claim that whatever has a perceived property is a substance$_I$ as self-evident. Perhaps, he simply switches from the Second Replies, substance$_S$, version of the principle, which is plausibly self-evident, to the *Principles*, substance$_I$, version, which is not, without catching the difference between them. Descartes would not be the first or last great philosopher to make the mistake of treating co-extensive concepts as though they were identical and so missing the logical and epistemic differences between the principles that contain them.

to be a substance$_S$.' Descartes never gives such an explanation, of course, and there is no clear indication that he has the concept of a substance$_S$ in mind when he claims to be certain he is a thinking thing. My only point here is that his claim to certainty is weaker, and so more plausible, when understood in terms of the concept of a substance$_S$ rather than that of a substance$_I$.[21]

Now that we have examined Descartes's concept of a substance$_S$ and its close relation to his concept of a substance$_I$, it is time to consider a third conception of substance that applies to a different part of reality and contains more metaphysical content.

III. The *Meditations* Synopsis

Descartes writes of pure substances, substances$_P$, in the Synopsis of the *Meditations*.

[T]he premises which lead to the conclusion that the soul is immortal depend on an account of the whole of physics. This is required for two reasons. First, we need to know that absolutely all substances, or things which must be created by God in order to exist, are by their nature incorruptible and cannot ever cease to exist unless they are reduced to nothingness by God's denying his concurrence to them. Secondly, we need to recognize that body, taken in the general sense, is a substance, so that it too never perishes. But the human body, in so far as it differs from other bodies, is simply made up of a certain configuration of limbs and other accidents of this sort; whereas the human mind is not made up of any accidents in this way, but is a pure substance. For even if all the accidents of the mind change, so that it has different objects of the understanding and different desires and sensations, it does not on that account become a different mind; whereas a human body loses its identity merely as a result of a change in the shape of some of its parts. And it follows from this that while the body can very easily perish, the mind is immortal by its very nature. (AT VII 13–14; CSM II 10)

[21] We could, of course, weaken Descartes's position further. Perhaps, when he claims that his Second Meditation certainties include his claim to be a substance, he has in mind the concept of a thing, as used in the definition of substance$_I$ to cover all there is. Surely, the Deceiver Hypothesis only reaffirms, rather than casts doubt upon, his claim to be a thing. This makes Descartes's claim to certainty more plausible at the cost of removing almost all content from the object of his certainty. As Gassendi puts it: 'And so you refer us to your principal result, that you are a thing that thinks—i.e. a thing that doubts, affirms, etc. But to say first of all that you are a "thing" is not to give any information. This is a general, imprecise and vague word which applies no more to you than it does to anything in the entire world that is not simply a nothing' (Fifth Objections and Replies: AT VII 276; CSM II 192).

This conception of substance is neither identical nor co-extensive with either of the ones considered so far. The set of pure substances consists solely of particular minds and matter in general; it contains more than the set of primary substances$_I$, less than the set of secondary substances$_I$, and less than the set of substances$_S$.

How are we to understand the concept of a pure substance? Descartes's contrast of particular minds, which are substances$_P$, with particular bodies, which are not—'For even if all the accidents of the mind change, so that it has different objects of the understanding and different desires and sensations, it does not on that account become a different mind; whereas a human body loses its identity merely as a result of a change in the shape of some of its parts'—encourages us to accept the following definition:

> D10 *x* is a substance$_P$ =df. *x* is such that at least some of its
> properties are not necessary to it (i.e. it can exist without
> them).

Minds satisfy this definition, since they presumably continue to exist as their thoughts, desires, and the like change. Particular bodies do not satisfy it, since they presumably cease to exist whenever one property is replaced by another mode of extension. Yet, the definition is also satisfied by the union of Descartes's mind and body, since at least some of its properties, those associated with the mind, are not necessary to it. Moreover, the definition does little or nothing to help us appreciate some of Descartes's major claims about pure substances, such as that they can be destroyed only by annihilation and they must be created.

We can best understand the concept of pure substance by considering the context in which Descartes presents it. Just before he says minds are substances$_P$ but bodies are not, he tells us the following:

[W]e cannot understand a body except as being divisible, while by contrast we cannot understand a mind except as being indivisible. For we cannot conceive of half a mind, while we can always conceive of half a body, however small; and this leads us to recognize that the natures of mind and body are not only different, but in some way opposite. (AT VII 13; CSM II 9–10)

Bodies have parts, but minds do not. This is what is behind Descartes's contrast of the ability of minds and bodies to survive change. Recall his remark to Mesland: every body has parts, and whenever parts are removed, added, or exchanged in a change of shape, the body is no longer numerically the same. Minds do not have parts to lose when their thoughts change.

I suggest that the best way to understand the concept of substance$_P$ is the following:

D11 x is a substance$_P$ =df. x is a substance$_I$ and x has no substantial parts.

The set of pure substances is the set of those substances$_I$ that do not contain another substance$_I$ as a part. Two necessary conditions help explain the concept of a substantial part: every substantial part of a substance$_I$ is itself a substance$_I$, and no substance$_I$ can exist apart from any of its substantial parts (a substance$_I$ and its substantial parts are not really distinct).[22] So understood, Descartes's concept of substance$_P$ is a refinement of his concept of substance$_I$. A substance$_I$ has causal independence and subject independence. A substance$_P$ has causal and subject independence, by virtue of being a substance$_I$, and it also has mereological independence; it does not depend on any other substance$_I$ as a necessary part.

This interpretation captures Descartes's examples. Particular minds are substances$_P$, since they have no substantial parts, which Descartes says can be seen from our inability to conceive of half a mind. Particular bodies are not substances$_P$, since they have substantial parts, which Descartes says can be seen from our ability to conceive of half of any body. There are no atoms of matter.

We also know that it is impossible that there should exist atoms, that is, pieces of matter that are by their very nature indivisible. For if there were any atoms, then no matter how small we imagined them to be, they would necessarily have to be extended; and hence we could in our thought divide each of them into two or more smaller parts, and hence recognize their divisibility. (*Principles*, pt. II, art. 20; AT VIIIA 51; CSM I 231)

Matter in general is a substance$_P$. It is a substance$_I$, and it contains particular bodies, which are substances$_I$, but none of those bodies is a substantial part of it. Each can cease to exist without affecting the existence of matter in general. We can destroy any particular body by replacing some of the matter of which it is composed by other matter that is available, and if we do, the particular body ceases to exist but

[22] These conditions are not sufficient. God is a substance$_I$ and Descartes's mind cannot exist apart from God, but God is not a substantial part of Descartes's mind.

matter in general continues to exist.[23] The union of Descartes's mind and body is not a substance$_P$, since it has parts, and qualities are not substances$_P$, since they are not substances$_I$.

Descartes's concept of substance$_P$ clearly has more metaphysical content than the other two concepts of substance. His claim to be a substance$_P$ implies that he is a simple substance$_I$ in that he has no substantial parts. It implies, on the assumption that he is not matter in general, that he is immaterial, since every material substance$_I$, other than matter in general, has substantial parts. It explains what makes him the numerically same substance$_I$ despite changes in his mental state. He remains the same substance$_I$ so long as he does not gain or lose any substantial parts, and he has no such parts to gain or lose. Descartes's claim to be a substance$_P$ does not explain why he remains the same person, however. Personal identity requires a continuity in mental states, and nothing in Descartes's concept of a substance$_P$ guarantees that.[24]

Descartes implies in the Synopsis passage above that his claim to be a substance$_P$ entails that he can cease to exist only by annihilation, must be created by God, and is immortal. Let us consider each of these points to complete our examination.

Descartes does not say why each substance$_P$ can be destroyed only by annihilation, but it is easy to construct a plausible explanation. Since every substance$_P$ lacks substantial parts, none can be destroyed by decomposition (division into substantial parts); what cannot be destroyed by decomposition can be destroyed only by annihilation; so, every substance$_P$ can be destroyed only by annihilation. There is a minor catch here, however. Descartes seems to be committed to the view that matter in general can be destroyed without being decomposed and without being annihilated. Suppose God just annihilates one particular body. Descartes seems willing to countenance the possibility, when he argues for the impossibility of a vacuum at

[23] Note that for matter in general to be a pure substance, each particular body must have at least some way of ceasing to exist while matter in general continues to exist. As we shall soon see, Descartes seems to be committed to the view that there are also ways in which a particular body can cease to exist which require that matter in general also ceases to exist and is replaced by a new, numerically distinct, matter in general.

[24] Descartes appears to be insensitive to the distinction between a mind's continuing as the same substance$_I$ through changes in its mental states and its continuing as the same person through such changes. For an informative discussion of the extent to which Descartes, Spinoza, Locke, and, especially, Leibniz were sensitive to this difference, see M. Wilson, 'Leibniz: Self-Consciousness and Immortality in the Paris Notes and After'.

Principles, pt. II, art. 18.[25] Yet, even though God's annihilation of a particular body does not decompose or annihilate matter in general, Descartes should say that one matter in general is replaced by another, for, as we have seen, he maintains that, whenever one part of some matter is removed or replaced, we have a new, numerically distinct, piece of matter.

The situation is similar with regard to Descartes's claim that every substance_P must be created by God. He does not explain his position, but a plausible account is obvious. No substance_P can come into existence by a natural process in which already existing substances_I are united to form a new whole; what does not come into existence in this way must be created by God. Matter in general again poses a problem. Suppose that God decides to create more matter by making a new body and adding it to the matter already existing. Nothing in Descartes's philosophy seems to preclude this possibility, and he has to say that in this case new matter in general comes into existence, even though it is formed by the union of already existing substances_I.

Descartes asserts in the Synopsis passage above that the mind's status as a substance_P implies that 'the mind is immortal by its very nature'. He is right, if immortality is mere immunity to death, for death as a natural process of decay into substantial parts does not apply to substances_P. He is wrong, if immortality requires that the mind continue to exist after the body is destroyed. Mersenne indicates this much in the Second Objections: 'What if its [the created mind's] nature were limited by the duration of the life of the body, and God had endowed that it came to an end with the death of the body?' (AT VII 128; CSM II 91). In reply, Descartes admits that the mind's continued existence is not implied solely by its status as a substance_P; he appeals to God for extra support.

[I]t could still be claimed that God gave it [the mind] such a nature that its duration comes to an end simultaneously with the end of the body's life. Here I admit that I cannot refute what you say. . . . [N]atural knowledge tells us that the mind is distinct from the body and that it is a substance. But in the case of the body, the difference between it and other bodies consists merely in the arrangement of the limbs and other accidents of this sort; and the final death of the body depends solely on a division or change of shape. Now we have no

[25] He writes: 'Hence, if someone asks what would happen if God were to take away every single body contained in a vessel without allowing any other body to take the place of what has been removed, the answer must be that the sides of the vessel would, in that case, have to be in contact' (*Principles*, pt. II, art. 18: AT VIIIA 50; CSM I 231).

convincing evidence or precedent to suggest that the death or annihilation of a substance like the mind must result from such a trivial cause as a change in shape, for this is simply a mode, and what is more not a mode of the mind, but of the body which is really distinct from the mind. Indeed, we do not even have any convincing evidence or precedent to suggest that any substance can perish. And this entitles us to conclude that the mind, in so far as it can be known by natural philosophy, is immortal.

But if your question concerns the absolute power of God, and you are asking whether he may have decreed that human souls cease to exist precisely when the bodies which he joined to them are destroyed, then it is for God alone to give the answer. And since God himself has revealed to us that this will not occur, there remains not even the slightest room for doubt on this point. (Second Replies: AT VII 153–4; CSM II 108–9)

Descartes's comment that we lack convincing evidence that any substance can perish indicates his use of the concept of a substance$_P$. Note that his appeal is not to God's nondeceptive nature as the designer of our intellectual faculties, but to what God has revealed. In the end, the mind's continued existence after the death of the body is not known by our reason under the guarantee provided by God's nondeceptive nature as the designer of our reason; it is known by being revealed to us by God.

IV. Conclusion

Let me sum up my main results by way of conclusion. *Principles*, pt. I, arts. 51–2, defines substance$_I$, substance as an independent existent, by two types of independence: causal independence, existing without depending on some other thing's causal power to remain in existence, and subject independence, existing without being a modification of some other thing. The Second Replies defines substance$_S$, substance as a subject, by a form of dependence: being something on which other things depend as a subject for their existence. The Synopsis of the *Meditations* contains the concept of substance$_P$, pure substance, in which mereological independence, existing without any necessary parts, supplements the two that define substance$_I$.

The concepts of substance$_I$ and substance$_S$ are exclusively satisfied by individual minds, bodies, and substantial unions of minds and bodies, and they are limited in their metaphysical implications. The concept of substance$_P$ is satisfied just by individual minds and matter in general and is more significant in its metaphysical content.

Several questions remain. I have not considered what arguments Descartes offers or might offer to show that he is a substance of each type. I have not considered the question of which conception of substance, if any, provides the more accurate or true description of the world. Is it in any way more accurate or true to say that the world contains individual minds and matter in general than to say that it contains minds and particular bodies? These questions and others are best left for another time.[26]

[26] An earlier version of this chapter was presented to the Central Division of the American Philosophical Association; participants in the discussion made many helpful comments, especially James Van Cleve, the commentator. Several of the ideas presented here were first aired at a symposium on Descartes at Vanderbilt University; participants there, especially Margaret Wilson, Dan Garber, and Calvin Normore, made helpful comments. I am also indebted to Jeffrey Tlumak for his comments on even earlier work on the topic.

5

God without Cause

CAROL ROVANE

Descartes's heavy reliance on a version of the principle of sufficient causation (henceforth 'the Principle') in his first proof of the existence of God is bound to frustrate—if not alienate—readers of the *Meditations*. However intuitive the Principle might be, its truth is not so evident (at the point of its introduction) as to meet the stringent requirements Descartes himself sets for rational credence. Granted, Descartes begins with what must have seemed in his time an absolutely straightforward point about sufficient causation:

> Now it is manifest by the natural light that there must be at least as much [reality] in the efficient and total cause as in the effect of that cause. For where, I ask, could the effect get its reality from, if not from the cause? And how could the cause give it to the effect unless it possessed it? It follows from this both that something cannot arise from nothing, and also that what is more perfect—that is, contains in itself more reality—cannot arise from what is less perfect. (AT VII 40–1; CSM II 28)

But even if scholastic training rendered this conception of causality (with its implication that reality comes in degrees) more 'evident' to Descartes and his contemporaries than it is to us, that would not absolve him of the charge of helping himself to rather too much. His application of the Principle to the case of ideas represents a highly controversial contribution to a prior debate within the scholastic tradition about the nature of ideas:

> The nature of an idea is such that of itself it requires no formal reality except what it derives from my thought, of which it is a mode. But in order for a given idea to contain such and such objective reality, it must surely derive it from some cause which contains at least as much formal reality as there is objective reality in the idea. For if we suppose that an idea contains something

which was not in its cause, it must have got this from nothing; yet the mode
of being by which a thing exists objectively [or representatively] in the intellect
by way of an idea, imperfect though it may be, is certainly not nothing, and
so it cannot come from nothing.

   ... And although one idea may perhaps originate from another, there
cannot be an infinite regress here; eventually one must reach a primary idea,
the cause of which will be like an archetype which contains formally [and in
fact] all the reality [or perfection] which is present only objectively [or
representatively] in the idea. (AT VII 41–2; CSM II 28–9)[1]

This application of the Principle to the case of ideas, taking their
objective reality (or content) to be what requires a sufficient cause
rather than their formal reality, is a departure from the dominant
scholastic view, and hence it calls for more justification than Descartes
provides. (This is especially so since Descartes goes to such lengths
in the First Meditation to unseat our conviction that the contents of
our ideas correspond to or resemble their causes, a point to which I
shall return shortly.)

When Descartes introduces the Principle in the Third Meditation,
the reader is supposed to believe that her experiences could be like a
dream, corresponding to nothing at all, perhaps caused by an evil
demon. The Principle implies that such an evil demon could not
produce in her an idea whose objective reality is greater than its (the
demon's) formal reality. But if the reader can think away the entire
material world and abandon all but the most obvious truths of reason
(having until recently abandoned even them), why should she be
unable to imagine herself tricked by the evil demon when it comes to
her complex, and therefore possibly indistinct, idea of sufficient
causation? Although she has by now been allowed to know some
truths—that she exists, that she doubts, that she knows what it is to
know, and the very simplest truths of reason (those which can be
intuited in an instant)—her confidence in her ratiocinative capacities
is still severely shaken by the thought of the evil demon. Surely, then,
the truth and implications of the Principle are among the things still
beyond her grasp. My complaint is not that Descartes argues in a
circle, assuming the legitimacy of reason while trying to secure it, for

---

  [1] See C. Normore, 'Meaning and Objective Being', for an account of the scholastic
background of Descartes's discussion of sufficient causation in the Third Meditation.
According to Normore, Descartes was not the first to propose that, when we enquire
into the possible causes of ideas, we must take into account not only their formal, but
also their objective, reality.

I think that Descartes is interested in *rational* doubt. I therefore want to allow him—at the start of the Third Meditation, before the existence of God is secured as antidote to the evil demon hypothesis—as much reason as he needs in order to entertain and understand the force of the hypothesis.

However, it is dubious at best that such a minimal framework for rational doubt would include the Principle, and this paper will explore what Descartes could accomplish (given the aims of the Third Meditation) if we rejected it. This may seem a strange exercise, since the Principle is the cornerstone of Descartes's first proof of God's existence. It should seem less strange if viewed as an attempt to be even more faithful than Descartes himself to his own method. By this I mean a step-by-step procedure that works from the presuppositions of rational doubt to the existence of God.

However, I have a second and subsidiary motive which is not so faithful to the real Descartes. We claim Descartes as the father of modern philosophy, and it is tempting to press him into that mould even though he does not quite fit. The modern aspect of his philosophy that I wish to stress, and perhaps exaggerate, is his tendency to a rationalistic conception of the relation between thought (or ideas) and objects. As I said earlier, the First Meditation attempts to break the tie between an idea's content and its cause. We might see this as just a temporary rupture brought on by a sceptical manœuvre, a rupture whose repair would then be regarded as the main event in the later refutation of scepticism. But we might also see the matter quite differently; we might well wonder whether Descartes broke the tie between content and cause merely to put it back again. As the wax example of the Second Meditation—in which scepticism is suspended—shows, the ideas we have of objects through our senses may provide what is from the causal point of view our most direct relations to objects, and yet fail to show us their true natures, or worse yet mislead us about them (AT VII 30–2; CSM II 20–2).[2] Proper understanding (or knowledge) of objects rests not on causal contact but on judgement according to principles. This rationalistic point is reiterated in the Third Meditation with respect to our idea of the sun (AT VII 39;

---

[2] See R. Adams, 'Where do Our Ideas Come from?', for an account of some of Descartes's detailed reasons for abandoning the scholastic view according to which ideas resemble their causes.

CSM II 27).[3] Since Descartes was so careful to distinguish between the grounds of belief and the causes of ideas, his urge to ground his idea of perfection in a causal relation to God appears out of place. Thus my secondary motive for providing an alternative to his causal proof of God's existence is to provide a proof that would be in conformity with a rationalistic conception of knowledge as deriving from principles rather than from causal contact with objects.[4]

Sympathizers with Descartes will of course maintain that there is good reason to see the idea of God as the one interesting exception in which the content of an idea and its causal ground must coincide. I want, therefore, to stress that my *main* dissatisfaction with this stems from the problem I stated at the outset: the Principle that provides our understanding of the causal link must be subject to the doubt of the First Meditation. But I also think Descartes's manifest inclination to move away from a causal theory of content, and towards a more rationalistic theory, provides an additional reason for dissatisfaction.

The question is, can Descartes get from his idea of God to God's existence without invoking the cosmological argument that employs the Principle and, along with it, a causal or exemplar model of content? He can get closer than one would expect. His treatment (in the text of the Third Meditation) of three objections which he poses for himself immediately after presenting the causal proof is, in this regard, more interesting than the proof itself. It is more interesting because it suggests a strategy for a more modern and rationalistic proof that respects the difference between the grounds of belief and the causes of ideas.

The three main points, for my purposes, that emerge in Descartes's discussion of the three objections he raises are the following: (1) that the ideas of perfection and infinity are not constructible out of the ideas of imperfection and finitude, (2) that the idea of God is not

---

[3] Although the specific view that ideas represent in virtue of their resemblance to their causes has been largely discredited (with the possible exception of 'information' theory), causal theories of content are, of course, still very much alive. I do not mean to suggest that Descartes's criticisms were so thoroughgoing that they would apply to all contemporary causal theories, as well as to the scholastic view that underlies the Principle. That the Principle does involve the resemblance doctrine (at least in the case of God) is persuasively argued by Normore ('Meaning and Objective Being', 236–7).

[4] There will necessarily be some resemblance between any rationalistic proof of God's existence and the ontological proof, for such a proof must derive God's existence from the very idea or concept of God. The primary difference between my rationalistic proof and the ontological proof is that it does not begin with the canonical description of God as 'that than which no greater can be conceived'.

materially false, and (3) that the various divine attributes are inter-dependent. My aim is to employ all these points in an alternative proof of God's existence, one that not only avoids appeal to the Principle, but also accords better with what has been established in the First and Second Meditations. The strategy of my proof is to show first that the method of doubt requires essential reference to a notion of perfection (perfect knowledge), and, secondly, that reflection on this notion brings in its train an irreducible notion of absolute perfection, or God. Its general thrust is that Descartes can only call God's existence into question on pain of giving up the line of reasoning that made his doubt intelligible to begin with.

I will take Descartes's discussion of the irreducibility of the idea of God as the point of departure for my alternative proof of God's existence. Only the first objection that Descartes considers explicitly raises the possibility of constructing or deriving the idea of God from another idea—his idea of himself (or of a thinking thing). Nevertheless Descartes is quite preoccupied in the Third Meditation with the general question of how some ideas may be constructed from others. After declaring that the Principle passes the test for truth (having somehow been made clear and distinct by the natural light), and after explaining how the Principle is to apply to ideas according to their objective reality, Descartes enquires which of his ideas have objective reality such that they could have been caused by himself rather than by something distinct from himself. What follows is an argument which purports to show that Descartes (or the reader) could construct his ideas of corporeal things out of elements in his idea of himself (AT VII 43–5; CSM II 29–31). It is initially hard to see why Descartes does not simply *assert* that, in the order of things according to their degrees of reality, a thinking substance has greater reality than a corporeal substance, and hence is clearly sufficient to cause the idea of a corporeal substance. For some reason, Descartes becomes interested in details at this point, and offers an actual account of how the notions of substance, mode, and number (which belong to his idea of himself) can be combined so as to constitute the idea of a corporeal thing.

It makes sense to suppose that Descartes is preoccupied by this issue because he recognizes that, if his idea of God were similarly constructible from the ideas belonging to his self-conception, he would not be in a position to infer God's existence from his having an idea of God. Thus, although the argument that the idea of God is not so constructible does not strictly belong to Descartes's proof of God's existence, but rather accompanies the proof as extra support, that argument is nevertheless essential to the proof's ultimate success. The proof itself turns on a flat assertion that a finite thinking thing is not sufficient to cause the idea of any infinite substance, and that only an infinite substance is sufficient. It is a short step from there to the existence of God (AT VII 45; CSM II 31). The three objections follow, and it is in the treatment of the first, as I have said, that we find an argument that the idea of God is not constructible from or reducible to other ideas. In the light of the importance of this argument for Descartes's actual proof employing the Principle, and given the dubitability of the Principle, it is natural to take the argument as the point of departure for my alternative proof of God's existence.

I. The Idea of Perfect Knowledge in the Method of Doubt

When Descartes poses the question whether his ideas of infinitude and perfection are derivable from his ideas of his own finitude and imperfection, he answers as follows:

And I must not think that, just as my conceptions of rest and darkness are arrived at by negating movement and light, so my perception of the infinite is arrived at not by means of a true idea but merely by negating the finite. On the contrary, I clearly understand that there is more reality in an infinite substance than in a finite one, and hence that my perception of the infinite, that is God, is in some way prior to my perception of the finite, that is myself. *For how could I understand that I doubted or desired—that is, lacked something— and that I was not wholly perfect, unless there were in me some idea of a more perfect being which enabled me to recognize my own defects by comparison?* (AT VII 45–6; CSM II 31; emphasis in original)

Although Descartes has already presented his causal proof for the existence of God at this point, we can see in the last words of this passage the basis for another sort of proof. The method of doubt rests on the recognition of epistemic limitations and imperfections, and Descartes here claims that this recognition presupposes a standard of perfection against which these imperfections can be seen as such. This claim is a better starting-point for a Cartesian enquirer than is the Principle, simply because it posits a direct link between the doubts that surround reason and the idea of perfection, thereby escaping the sort of criticism that applies to the Principle (namely, that the latter is so complex that it cannot be known until reason has already been validated).

This starting-point has the further advantage that it makes the entrance of the idea of God in the Third Meditation less fortuitous. One might complain that Descartes's idea of God is too handy; it just happens to be floating around among his other ideas standing in need of explanation in accordance with the Principle. It will not do to say in response that the idea of the evil demon occasions reflection on the idea of perfection in so far as the demon is conceived as all-powerful. While it is true that Descartes conceives it as all-powerful, it is not the case that it must be all-powerful in order to deceive us in the way described in the First Meditation. All that is required is that the demon be powerful *enough* to fool us, and we have been given no reason to think that omnipotence alone would enable it to do so. Thus Descartes's claim that the project of rational doubt requires an implicit reference to a notion of perfection constitutes the only available ground for thinking that his introduction of the notion of God is not gratuitous.

If we were to proceed by drawing a connection between the possession of Cartesian self-consciousness and the possession of a notion of perfection, however, it is not clear whether the latter must be a notion of perfection *simpliciter* or the more restricted notion of perfect *knowledge*. There seem to be at least four ways in which Descartes conceives of perfection, and it is not obvious that they are all equivalent.[5] First, there is the 'degrees of reality' conception associated with the Principle: what is more perfect is literally more real. Secondly, Descartes introduces the notion of perfections in the plural: one thing can possess various perfections. Thirdly, there is the more familiar notion of attributive perfection: with respect to a given property, one thing may be perfect or imperfect. And, finally, there is the notion of absolute perfection associated with the idea of God. In the course of the Third Meditation Descartes speaks freely of perfection in all four senses, and he never displays any doubt about whether the notion of perfection is univocal. I shall explore later whether Descartes might think that judging about perfection in the first three senses must always involve an implicit reference to absolute perfection. For the moment, however, I shall not assume that this is

---

[5] See A. Kenny, *Descartes: A Study of his Philosophy*, 134–5, for clarification of these different senses of perfection.

so. In proceeding without the assumption, I can only invoke perfection in the attributive sense: the enquirer who doubts must recognize her *epistemic* imperfection, and the passage I have quoted provides her with a reason to think that this recognition presupposes a standard of perfect knowledge which she lacks and to which she aspires.

The possibility that the quoted passage raises is that we could construct the idea of perfect knowledge simply by negating the idea of our own limited and imperfect knowledge. The answer suggested by the passage is that it goes the other way round, that one's idea of one's own epistemic limitation is actually the negation of the idea of what one *lacks*, namely perfect knowledge. Unfortunately, Descartes's commitment to such a view cannot be established on the basis of what he says in the passage, for there he is speaking of God's absolute perfection and actual infinitude, and it would take further argument to show that the same reasoning must apply to the sort of attributive perfection contained in the idea of perfect knowledge.

In fact, there is a serious question whether the same reasoning should apply to attributive perfections, and this can be brought out by refining the objection Descartes has raised for himself. As it stands, the objection confines itself to the issue whether the notions of perfection and infinitude are mere negations of the notions of imperfection and finitude. In the light of the wording of the quoted passage, however, I think it would be unsympathetic to interpret Descartes as defending the restricted claim that the notions of infinitude and perfection are positive ideas of which the notions of finitude and imperfection are negations. The notions of perfection and infinitude that he employs are not simply standards against which we can make sense of their complete absence or negation—they are standards against which we can make *comparative* judgements concerning one thing being more perfect or greater than another. Thus a more sophisticated version of the objection Descartes has raised would maintain that these comparative judgements involve ideas of one thing's being better or greater than another, ideas out of which we can construct the relevant ideal notion by a process of extension of amplification.

This would imply the following account of the idea of perfect knowledge. In the course of the first two Meditations Descartes has observed the improvement of his epistemic situation, first by jettisoning all beliefs for which he has insufficient warrant, and secondly by arriving at true and certain knowledge of his own existence and of his mental states. Suppose, then, that the idea of perfect knowledge is nothing but an extension or amplification of this process by which Descartes has improved and expanded his own imperfect and finite knowledge. The contention of the refined objection would be that one's capacity to produce this conception of the ideal state towards which imperfect knowledge can be seen as progressing is quite independent of there being any such thing as actually perfect knowledge.

This more sophisticated account of how the notion of perfect knowledge could be constructed cannot be dismissed as something that Descartes would reject outright, because he often distinguishes between an indefinite progression whose end cannot be reached and actual infinity.

Our reason for using the term 'indefinite' in these cases is, in the first place, so as to reserve the term 'infinite' for God alone. For in the case of God alone, not only do we fail to recognize any limits in any respect, but our understanding positively tells us that there are none. Secondly, in the case of other things, our understanding does not in the same way positively tell us that they lack limits in some respect; we merely acknowledge in a negative way that any limits which they may have cannot be discovered by us. (AT VIIIA 15; CSM I 202)[6]

When he speaks of indefiniteness, Descartes usually has space and number in mind. In each case, we recognize that for us the ultimate limit—of, respectively, the material world and the positive integers—is not something that we can reach even in thought. Every spatial bound that we can imagine must have something beyond it, and for every integer we can count there is a greater one. This negative idea of indefiniteness could, it seems, be grasped by attending to the process by which the understanding amplifies or extends the relations in question just as the objection we have been considering maintains.

And so we must ask: should the idea of perfect knowledge, in contrast with which Descartes's idea of his own epistemic imperfection can be made intelligible, be construed as the (negative) idea of

---

[6] See M. Wilson, 'Can I be the Cause of my Idea of the World?', for a revealing account of Descartes's views concerning the distinction. Wilson calls attention to scattered remarks Descartes makes about the two notions which seem—at least superficially—to be incompatible. She manages to bring them into line by identifying two ways in which Descartes draws the distinction: epistemically and metaphysically. At this point I am interested only in the epistemic version, though later I shall appeal to the metaphysical version as well. (Much of the textual material on indefiniteness which I discuss below I discovered through Wilson's article.)

indefinitely perfected knowledge, and could this idea be derived from
Descartes's ideas of his actual states of knowledge and their relative
perfection? It is tempting to answer 'no'; Descartes ought to hold that
the idea of perfect knowledge is presupposed as a standard in judging
the relative perfection of his various states of knowledge and therefore
cannot be constructed out of the ideas involved in those judgements.
If we did not credit Descartes with such a view, how could we make
sense of his declaration that the ideas of the infinite and the perfect
are *prior* to his ideas of his own finite and imperfect nature? But we
have already seen what stands in the way of this all-too-quick
transition from the recognition of one's epistemic imperfection to an
irreducible idea of perfect knowledge. The only standard of perfection
of which Descartes thinks we have a positive and irreducible idea is
God's absolute perfection. Until we have shown that perfect knowledge is unintelligible apart from God's absolute perfection, we have
no reason to attribute to Descartes the view that the idea of perfect
knowledge is itself a positive and irreducible idea (or at least presupposes one), rather than a negative and indefinite idea constructible
from ideas of oneself in the manner we have been considering.

What we seek, then, is some sort of *conceptual* dependence of the
notion of indefiniteness on a positive notion of perfection. In other
words, we need a reason for accepting the following sort of argument:
(1) a Cartesian enquirer who doubts recognizes her epistemic imperfection; (2) this presupposes a standard of epistemic perfection against
which she can recognize both that she falls short of it and that in the
course of the first two Meditations she has come closer to it; (3)
perhaps her idea of this standard of perfect knowledge is a negative
or indefinite idea that can be arrived at by amplifying and extending
her ideas of her actual states of knowledge; (4) but she could not
generate this negative idea unless she also had a positive idea of
perfection which is not similarly constructible and which is therefore
irreducible to any other ideas.

There is some evidence that Descartes thinks our capacity to
generate indefinite progressions does depend in some way on having
a positive conception of actual infinity or perfection: 'And how could
we have a faculty for amplifying all created perfections (i.e. conceiving
of something greater or more ample than they are) were it not for the
fact that there is in us an idea of something greater, namely God?'
(AT VII 365; CSM II 252). This is not a claim to the effect that every
indefinite progression (e.g. the number series, spatial extension,

progressively greater knowledge) presupposes its own completion (e.g. the cardinally infinite set of integers, infinite space, complete and perfect knowledge). If it were, then it would rest on a pseudo-Platonic vision of a host of attributive perfections—one for each of our concepts—each of which was presupposed in applying the relevant concept. What Descartes affirms instead is that all of these attributive perfections presuppose *one* idea of absolute perfection, i.e. the idea of God.

While the above passage suggests that there is a *conceptual* dependence of the indefinite notions on the idea of God, Descartes more often affirms a sort of cosmological or causal dependence of indefinite things on infinite substance. In a letter to Regius he puts it as follows:

> Now for your objections. In your first you say: 'it is because we have in ourselves some wisdom, power and goodness that we form the idea of an infinite, or at least indefinite, wisdom, power, goodness and the other perfections which we attribute to God; just as it is because we have in ourselves some degree of quantity that we form the idea of an infinite quantity.' I entirely agree, and am quite convinced that we have no idea of God except the one formed in this manner. But the whole point of my argument is this. These perfections are so slight that unless we derived our origin from a being in which they are actually infinite, my nature could not enable me to extend them in thought to an infinite degree. Similarly, I could not conceive of an indefinite quantity by looking at a very small quantity or a finite body unless the size of the world was actually or at least possibly indefinite. (letter to Regius of 24 May 1640: AT III 64; CSMK 147)

It is somewhat obscure why our capacity to generate indefinite progressions should depend on our having our *origin* in something actually infinite and perfect. Descartes elaborates the thesis near the end of the Third Meditation:

> But the mere fact that God created me is a very strong basis for believing that I am somehow made in his image and likeness, and that I perceive that likeness, which includes the idea of God, by the same faculty which enables me to perceive myself. That is, when I turn my mind's eye upon myself, I understand that I am a thing which is incomplete and dependent on another and which aspires without limit to ever greater things; but I also understand at the same time that he on whom I depend has within him all those greater things, not just indefinitely and potentially, but actually and infinitely, and hence that he is God. (AT VII 51; CSM II 35)

Descartes displays here the very tendency to causal reasoning that I aim to avoid in my alternative proof—namely, the tendency to

assimilate ideas to images whose power of representing derives from
their resemblance to their causes. I take it that the reasoning goes
something like this. When creatures doubt and reflect upon their own
nature, they perceive themselves as standing in a relation to God which
is a metaphysical version of the conceptual relation that might be
thought to hold between our idea of an element in an indefinite
progression and our idea of the completion of that progression. In
other words, we cannot perceive ourselves except as indefinitely
progressing towards some kind of perfection. What we want is an
explanation or account of our capacity to perceive ourselves in these
terms. Descartes's view seems to be that we have the account as soon
as we suppose that we are ourselves images of God's perfection.[7] This
requires the assumption that we cannot perceive an image without
understanding what it is an image of, and that we therefore cannot
perceive ourselves without perceiving God. A goal of my alternative
proof is to supply a different sort of explanation, by drawing conceptual—
rather than causal—connections between rational doubt and a notion
of perfect knowledge, and between the notion of perfect knowledge
and the idea of God's absolute perfection.

Rather than launch directly into an argument that would establish
the second connection, I want to return to the issue whether the idea
of perfect knowledge could be an indefinite idea that is constructible
by Descartes from his ideas of his actual epistemic states. Let us
suppose for the sake of argument that it might be, and re-examine
Descartes's response to Regius. I have already complained that it is
obscure why the capacity to amplify or extend our ideas depends on
our having our origin in something actually perfect and infinite (though
we have seen that a causal, or 'exemplar', model of representation goes
some distance towards supplying the reason). It is perhaps less obscure
why forming an idea of the size of the world as indefinite should
depend on the world being 'actually or at least possibly indefinite'.
There, I take it, Descartes means that it is part of our concept of spatial
extension that no spatial boundary can be perceived by us as absolute,
and that it follows that a spatially extended world could in fact be
*un*bounded, that is to say, indefinite. How does this bear on the status
of perfect knowledge? If we think of our actual knowledge as being

---

[7] See A. Baier, 'The Idea of the True God in Descartes', for an extraordinary reading
of the entire Third Meditation that is based on the passage just quoted. Baier argues
that Descartes himself must be his idea of God (qua image of God).

indefinitely perfectible or extendable, it ought to follow that there could in fact be such a thing as unlimited knowledge.

This reasoning does not, of course, establish that there must *be* such a thing as unlimited knowledge. But what of the weaker claim that doubt and enquiry presuppose at least the *idea* of unlimited knowledge? In attempting to answer this question, it will help to pause over the process by which the refined version of Descartes's first objection maintains that the idea of perfect knowledge might be reached. The process begins with the recognition, on the part of a Cartesian enquirer, that her knowledge has grown and improved over the course of the first two Meditations. At each stage, what she knows is established as certain and indubitable, which ensures that, when she knows, she knows that she knows. Thus, when she imagines an extension of her actual knowledge, she must suppose that none of her actual knowledge is subject to revision. So, in so far as she can imagine knowledge more perfect than her actual knowledge, she must suppose that at some later stage she could know *more*.

One question which naturally arises is this: could there ever be an end to this extension or amplification of her knowledge? Fortunately, the analogy I want to explore between Descartes's conceptions of space and knowledge does not require that this question have a definitive answer. The point about space is that no spatial boundary discoverable by us could be regarded as absolute, and Descartes is quite clear that this negative point does not by itself entail that space is actually without any limits. The parallel point about knowledge follows from the fact that the Cartesian enquirer knows herself to be temporally bounded—not in the sense that her life must come to an end, but in the sense that her acquisition of knowledge takes place in time. In consequence, no state of knowledge attainable by such an enquirer could be regarded by her as complete. This is compatible with the supposition that complete knowledge might be finite. Even if all there was to know were finite, a temporally bounded subject who possessed that knowledge would not be in a position to know that her knowledge was complete. From her temporal point of view, it would remain a possibility that at some future time new ideas could present themselves and occasion additions to her body of knowledge. Thus, so far as she is concerned, the growth or extension of her knowledge may be without limit in precisely the sense in which space may be unlimited. In other words, doubt and enquiry do presuppose at least the possibility—if not the actuality—of unlimited knowledge. What remains to be seen is whether the idea of unlimited knowledge is constructible from our ideas of ourselves and our actual states of knowledge.

At this stage of reflection, a Cartesian enquirer must acknowledge that she is, from an epistemic point of view, intrinsically limited. Even if her epistemic life continued indefinitely into the future, she could never regard herself as possessing complete knowledge, and this is a respect in which her knowledge is destined to be imperfect. Now for Descartes the recognition of imperfection is always a recognition of a lack or deficiency, and this always involves a reference to something positive against which the lack can be seen as such. In this case, the negative idea of indefinitely extendable knowledge (possibly constructible from ideas of oneself) does not seem to provide what is needed. What is needed is the idea of a kind of epistemic access which is not subject to the limitation we recognize on our own. We need the idea of a being that could actually survey all of time from a point outside it, thereby gaining a direct grasp of what we can only approach but never reach. Whether complete knowledge be finite or not, only this sort of knower would be in a position to regard her knowledge as complete. And, although we come to reflect on the idea of such a being by exploring what is presupposed by our own progress of doubt and enquiry, and by imagining extensions of our actual knowledge, we must acknowledge that the idea of such a being is not just an indefinite extension of our ideas of ourselves: it is the positive idea of a being that is essentially unlike us. For this reason, we cannot suppose that our idea of actually perfect knowledge is constructible by amplifying or extending our ideas of ourselves and our actual states of knowledge.

Given Descartes's understanding of the relations between the concepts of time and number, and space as well, the idea of a being which could survey all of time would be, for him, the idea of a being that could in principle survey other unlimited domains. Thus, by framing for ourselves the idea of a being that does not share our peculiar epistemic limitation, we arrive at the idea of a being that could positively grasp whatever we conceive negatively through indefinite progressions. This accords well with Descartes's vision of how his ideas of indefinitely extended (created) perfections relate to the idea of the one being—God—of which he understands positively that it is not limited. However, it has not been established that the idea of a being with complete and perfect knowledge is the idea of God, since

Descartes understands God to be unlimited in *all* respects,[8] while this being is (at this stage) to be thought of as unlimited with respect to knowledge alone. Nor has it been established that this being exists. If we subscribed to the Principle, the fact that we conceive it as having greater epistemic powers than our own would be enough to establish its existence. But the alternative proof must find another ground for that conclusion, as well as for the lemma that the positive idea of perfect knowledge presupposes, or coincides with, or in some other way involves, the idea of a supremely perfect being, i.e. God.

II. The Idea of Perfect Knowledge is not Materially False

The exercise of trying to supply links between the idea of perfect knowledge, the idea of God, and God's existence would, of course, be futile, and in fact unfeasible, if it turned out that the positive idea of perfect knowledge was either empty or incoherent. In Descartes's terms that would amount to material falsity, and the second objection he considers to his own proof of God's existence is whether the idea of God could be materially false. It will emerge that by Cartesian reasoning the idea of complete and perfect knowledge (and/or the sort of being who could have it), like the idea of God, is a true one, and that our grasp of it does not depend on our being able actually to attain perfect knowledge ourselves. I will quote Descartes's discussion of the possible material falsity of the idea of God at length and then proceed to show how the same reasoning applies to the idea of perfect knowledge.

Nor can it be said that this idea of God is perhaps materially false and so could have come from nothing . . . On the contrary, it is utterly clear and distinct, and contains in itself more objective reality than any other idea; hence there is no idea which is in itself truer or less liable to be suspected of falsehood. This idea of a supremely perfect and infinite being is, I say, true in the highest degree; for although perhaps one may imagine that such a being does not exist, it cannot be supposed that the idea of such a being represents something unreal, as I said with regard to the idea of cold. The idea is,

---

[8] Wilson ('Can I be the Cause of my Idea of the World', 342–3) identifies this as the metaphysical criterion of actual infinitude as distinguished from indefiniteness. We can view the problem for my alternative proof as one of finding a way to derive the metaphysical distinction from the epistemic distinction. (See above, n. 6, for more on the epistemic and metaphysical versions of the distinction.)

moreover, utterly clear and distinct; for whatever I clearly and distinctly perceive as being real and true, and as implying any perfection, is wholly contained in it. It does not matter that I do not grasp the infinite, or that there are countless additional attributes of God which I cannot in any way grasp, and perhaps cannot even reach in my thought; for it is in the nature of the infinite not to be grasped by a finite being like myself. It is enough that I understand the infinite, and that I judge all the attributes which I clearly perceive and know to imply some perfection—and perhaps countless others of which I am ignorant—are present in God either formally or eminently. This is enough to make the idea that I have of God the truest and most clear and distinct of all my ideas. (AT VII 46; CSM II 31–2)

With this objection, as with the first, we are faced with the problem of deciding how to apply what Descartes says about absolute perfection or God to (merely attributive) epistemic perfection. In Section I we saw that Descartes's arguments about the irreducibility of the idea of God do not automatically transfer to the idea of perfect knowledge, in part because they rest on causal claims of the sort I aim to avoid in my alternative proof, and in part because Descartes distinguishes indefiniteness from actual infinity. By the end of the section, however, we managed to effect a transition from a negative conception of indefinitely extendable knowledge to the irreducible idea of a being with a positive grasp of the extent and completeness of its knowledge. Because this idea is the idea of a being that transcends human limitations, it has something in common with Descartes's idea of God. As a result, his claims against the material falsity of the idea of God transfer quite smoothly to the idea of perfect knowledge. I shall paraphrase the key passages, replacing references to God, perfection, and infinity with references to perfect knowledge. It will emerge that for the most part the results are plausible, and I will pause along the way to say why.

First: *Nor can it be said that this idea of perfect knowledge is perhaps materially false and so could have come from nothing . . . On the contrary, it is utterly clear and distinct, and contains in itself more objective reality than any other epistemic idea; hence there is no epistemic idea which is in itself truer or less liable to be suspected of falsehood. This idea of perfect knowledge is, I say, true in the highest degree; for although perhaps one may imagine that such a state does not exist, it cannot be supposed that the idea of such a state represents something unreal, as I said with regard to the idea of cold.* The idea of perfect knowledge cannot be derived from nothing, but can be derived only from positive ideas of one's actual states of knowledge and their relative perfections. Since the idea involves the greatest conceivable extension of the positive ideas we have of our actual knowledge, the former represents something greater and better than any other epistemic idea. And although there may in fact be no such thing as an actual state of perfect knowledge, we cannot suppose that the idea of such a state is empty. Given the procedure by which we arrive at the idea (by extending our positive ideas of actual states of knowledge), we cannot think of perfect knowledge as a mere absence of something else, as cold is an absence of heat.

Secondly: *The idea is, moreover, utterly clear and distinct: for whatever I clearly and distinctly perceive as a real or true state of knowledge, and as implying any degree of epistemic perfection, is wholly contained in it.* This claim is quite straightforward: everything I (or anyone else, for that matter) might know would have to belong to complete and perfect knowledge.

Thirdly: *It does not matter that I do not grasp the completeness of perfect knowledge, or that there are countless additional aspects of perfect knowledge which I cannot in any way grasp, and perhaps cannot even reach in my thought; for it is in the nature of complete knowledge not to be grasped by a finite being like myself.* We saw at the end of the last section that in contemplating perfect knowledge we come to see that we are essentially limited in so far as we can never be in a position to know that our knowledge is complete, and that this is so regardless of whether complete knowledge is infinite or finite. The point Descartes wishes to make here is that this concession does not require us to conclude that the idea of perfect knowledge is not a genuine idea: we need not fully comprehend all that would belong to perfect knowledge in order to have an idea of it. Indeed the very activities of doubt and enquiry that presuppose the idea also presuppose that it is a genuine idea of something that we have not got.

Fourthly: *It is enough that I understand complete knowledge, and that I judge that all the states which I clearly perceive and know to imply some epistemic perfection—and perhaps countless others of which I am ignorant— are present in perfect knowledge either formally or eminently. This is enough to make the idea that I have of perfect knowledge the truest and most clear and distinct of all my epistemic ideas.* This paraphrase works quite naturally. All that belongs to Descartes's actual knowledge would either be contained in perfect knowledge just as it is (formally) or would belong to perfect knowledge in some enhanced or perfected way (eminently).

I see no obstacle to the conclusion that Descartes would accept all the foregoing. Which is to say, the irreducible idea of perfect knowledge which is presupposed in the course of rational doubt represents something that is really possible even though it is not achievable by us.

III. The Interdependence of God's Attributes

We are now in a position to ask what would follow if perfect knowledge were actual, i.e. if there were a being that was not subject to our epistemic limitations. In the third objection Descartes raises in the Third Meditation he suggests that a being with perfect knowledge could by its means acquire the rest of the divine attributes:

But perhaps I am something greater than I myself understand, and all the perfections which I attribute to God are somehow in me potentially, though not yet emerging or actualized. For I am now experiencing a gradual increase in my knowledge, and I see nothing to prevent its increasing more and more to infinity. Further, I see no reason why I should not be able to use this increased knowledge to acquire all the other perfections of God. (AT VII 46–67; CSM II 32)

Descartes goes on to argue that his idea of God is an idea of something in which nothing is merely potential, and furthermore, that he has no reason to believe that his own knowledge could ever actually be infinite. Since we produced an argument in Section I to the effect that we could never attain perfect knowledge, once again it is clear that what Descartes argues with respect to the idea of God also applies to the idea of perfect knowledge.

The issue at hand is how seriously to take Descartes's commitment to the supposition of the objection—namely, that perfect knowledge would go hand in hand with the rest of the divine attributes. It may be a mistake to take it too seriously. After all, Descartes may be granting for the sake of argument a strong claim to which he is not entirely committed. On the other hand, the doctrine that the divine attributes are thoroughgoingly interdependent is both familiar and widely subscribed to, and it is manifest in much of what Descartes says about the divine nature. Here is how he conceives the divine attributes: 'By the word "God" I understand a substance that is infinite [eternal, immutable], independent, supremely intelligent, supremely powerful, and which created both myself and everything else (if anything else there be) that exists' (AT VII 45; CSM II 31). I do not claim to be able to produce a compelling argument for the thesis that all these attributes are logically or metaphysically interdependent. But we have good reason to suppose that infinitude, eternity, and immutability would follow from perfect knowledge, in so far as the latter involved both its completeness and a recognition that it was complete. We argued in Section I that a being that could recognize the completeness of its knowledge could not be temporally bounded, and if it could survey all of time it could presumably survey other infinite domains as well. Thus a being that possessed perfect knowledge would in some sense be both eternal and infinite. It would also be immutable, at least with respect to knowledge, for that could not change except by becoming less complete and perfect.

Although the other divine attributes do not follow so straightforwardly from the idea of perfect knowledge, there is some reason to suppose that they are interconnected. In the objection under consideration Descartes suggests that omniscience would lead to omnipotence, though we might reason the other way round and ask whether a being with limited power could ever achieve omniscience. Of course, if we somehow worked omnipotence into the picture, independence would not be far behind. A dependent being is by definition a being whose power is circumscribed by its dependence on another thing. If omnipotence implies independence, then we are close to the conclusion that any being with the divine attributes of omniscience, infinitude, eternity, immutability, and omnipotence could not fail to exist. An independent being could not depend on anything besides itself for its existence. If it existed at all, it would be in virtue of its intrinsic nature—its possibility would imply its necessity. Thus, once we accept that omnipotence and independence follow from omniscience, we seem to be committed to the conclusion that a being with these attributes must exist. It would not take much more argument to show that there could be only one such being, and that all dependent things are ultimately dependent upon—and in that sense created by—it. In short, not only are all the divine attributes which Descartes associates with the idea of God arguably interdependent, but they also arguably entail God's existence.[9]

[9] Descartes takes up many of these issues further on in the Third Meditation (AT VII 50; CSM II 34), in the course of pursuing the ultimate cause of his own existence. He states that this ultimate cause must be self-causing, and that, if it is, then it has the power to give itself all the divine perfections. Although this is not the order in which my alternative proof provides for relations of interdependence among the divine attributes, it at least constitutes clear evidence that Descartes affirms these relations. I am indebted to Michael Della Roca for bringing this passage to my attention in this connection.

If all this reasoning were sound, we would have shown that the existence of Descartes's God can be derived from the idea of perfect knowledge which is presupposed by the Cartesian project of doubt and enquiry. The only (and to my mind plausible) ways to avoid the conclusion that this God exists are (1) to deny that the other divine attributes really do follow from perfect knowledge, or (2) to argue that the idea of an absolutely perfect being is incoherent (in Descartes's terms 'materially false'), and hence not the idea of something possible after all.

It has not been my aim to provide a sound or even valid proof for the existence of God, but only to provide one that Descartes would accept. The aspect of my 'proof' for which I have given the least textual support is the thesis that the divine attributes are interdependent. Nevertheless it seems reasonable that Descartes's view would include a commitment to the thesis. Apart from the evidence provided by the passage I quoted at the beginning of this section, I would like to speculate on another, possibly deeper, reason for ascribing the thesis to Descartes. We have seen that there are four senses of perfection at work in the Third Meditation, and yet Descartes never displays any doubt that he employs a univocal notion of perfection throughout. He cannot speak of God's attributes except attributively, and when he does, he refers to God's perfections in the plural. He also claims that God's perfections are greater or more real than created perfections. If we credit Descartes with the interdependence thesis, then these three ways of characterizing God's perfection may not really be in tension with the fourth—the absolute and unqualified perfection of the divine being. In that case omniscience and the rest need not be construed as properties that God *has*, exactly, but rather as what God *is*. In other words, infinitude, eternity, immutability, omniscience, omnipotence, independence, and creator might all be one and the same *thing* which is called 'God'. Given our ways of talking they seem separable (i.e. they seem like different kinds of attributive perfections in the plural that may come in degrees), but they might just be different ways in which we apprehend the same identical nature. I am tempted to make the further claim that this idea of absolute perfection could serve as the ultimate reference point to which Descartes thinks all indefinite progressions and comparative reasoning in the end relate. The number series would not have its own (purely numerical) ideal limit, nor would time and space have theirs, and our judgements concerning degrees of different attributive perfections would not be associated with different ideal or wholly realized attributes. These orderings would involve just *one* capacity, which is associated with the idea of just *one* ideal standard (i.e. God's absolute perfection), against which degrees of perfection in quantity, knowledge, power, goodness, etc., can all be judged. I think this view is Cartesian in spirit, and serves to unify Descartes's various remarks about perfection.

There are a great many weak links in the proof I have offered as an alternative to Descartes's causal proof of God's existence. But it is in many respects an attractive alternative. It avoids the charges of gross circularity and of begging the question that are often levied against Descartes's proof. I admitted at the beginning that there is no hope of avoiding circularity altogether: some bit of reason must be assumed as part of the framework of rational doubt. Nevertheless, unlike Descartes's proof employing the Principle, this proof does not begin with any more than the minimum assumptions needed for rational doubt and enquiry. There are no unmotivated assumptions—not even the idea of God is assumed. Each stage of the proof attempts to uncover something that is presupposed by the stage before, beginning with nothing more than reflection on one's actual epistemic situation, and always employing concepts and principles that Descartes would clearly accept.[10] The proof shows how we can build a bridge between Cartesian reflection on the doubting, enquiring self and the idea of a being that transcends the limits that such enquirers perceive in themselves, and a further bridge between this idea and the conclusion that God exists. At no point does it posit the sort of relation between the content of an idea and its cause that other vital sections of the *Meditations* speak against.

---

[10] Some readers of the *Meditations* are sceptical of Descartes's professed theological commitments, arguing that they amount to dissimulation. Of course, if that interpretation is correct, then my claim that Descartes would accept the concepts and principles employed in my alternative proof is false. Although I myself am not persuaded of the dissimulation interpretation, my arguments in this chapter may provide fodder for it. If I am right, my alternative proof of God's existence rests on premises that Descartes professes to accept, and at the same time avoids some of the manifest difficulties of his own causal proof employing the Principle. Since Descartes could presumably think of any proof I can think of, he must have been aware of the availability and advantages of the proof I have presented here. So there is a question why he chose to offer the one he did instead. The dissimulation interpretation provides a perverse, but not entirely discreditable, answer: he offered the causal proof *because* of its manifest difficulties, as a sort of tip-off about his 'true' commitments.

6

Descartes's Denial of the Autonomy of Reason

HOWARD WICKES

There is always a temptation to treat the texts of the philosophical canon as complete historical entities in their own right. Celebrating the anniversary of the publication of the *Meditationes* invites a reading of this work as representing a definitive, self-contained, and fixed position. Yet we know that Descartes had engaged in metaphysical speculations long before 1641 and even before the familiar discussions in the fourth part of the *Discours de la méthode* (1637). The correspondence refers more than once (letters to Mersenne of 25 November 1630: AT I 182; 15 April 1630: AT I 144, etc) to a 'Traitté de Metaphysique' composed during the first months of Descartes's residence in the United Provinces in 1629.[1] Although the 'Traitté' is lost, the 1630 letters on the 'eternal truths of mathematics' and the natural philosophy of *Le Monde* (1629–33?) clearly reveal something of Descartes's metaphysical concerns. Scholarly discussions of these early writings have generally assimilated them into the 'mature' metaphysics of the *Meditationes*, as 'rough drafts' or telling 'anticipations'.[2] But such dismissive, proleptic readings look questionable in their deference to the authority of the canonical text. Surely we need not be so overawed by the reputation we have given to the *Meditationes* as to presume that all other writings offer no more than either an inadequate or an equivalent rendering of its uniquely valid statements. We can at least entertain the possibility that the *Meditationes* itself is to be read more profitably as part of the dynamic process of a

---

[1] Descartes claims that he began the 'Traitté' whilst in Friesland (letter to Mersenne of 25 November 1630: AT I 182). Baillet, however (*La Vie de M. Des-Cartes*, i. 170–1), remarks that work on this project began in France.

[2] This tradition goes back to Baillet (ibid. i. 190). It is followed in most modern accounts. Adam and Tannery endorse it (AT I 30).

developing metaphysics, rather than as a single, static, historical event, whose interpretation is to be limited to the range of its own direct textual assertions.

This chapter considers an instance where attending to the 'process' of Descartes's metaphysics arguably makes a difference to the interpretation of a well-known problem area in the *Meditationes*: the question of the autonomy of reason. The easiest way to describe this question is to rehearse the situation in which it arises. Having subjected himself to the rigours of systematic doubt, Descartes's mediator finds himself left with a stock of ideas, whose provenance is unknown to him. He wishes to proceed from this position to conclusions about things as they are outside the mind. The only possible means he has to this end is a heterogeneous variety of mental capacities and faculties, which can be applied to his ideas and can perform various operations on them and make various judgements about them. And this is where the slippery term 'reason' comes in. In so far as the question of the autonomy of reason is at issue, we can most generously take 'reason' in a large sense to cover all of this varied human mental apparatus, seen as a means of trying to get at knowledge of things. If it is Descartes's contention that it is possible for us to get from our ideas to absolutely valid knowledge of things as they actually are in the world, uniquely by our own intellectual, intuitive, logical, or other mental endeavours of whatever kind, then we can say that he is affirming the autonomy of reason.

When he discusses the available means of proceeding from ideas to conclusions about the world, Descartes distinguishes different categories of ideas according to the ways in which we apprehend them. He gives pride of place to those ideas which we can perceive 'clearly and distinctly' and to what is 'manifest by natural light'. The ideas which we apprehend in these ways constitute a privileged class. They are installed as the foundations and first premises of a vast philosophical reconstruction of the world, and, for the time being at least, other ideas perceived in different ways are dismissed from consideration. Given the way in which the question of the autonomy of reason arises in the *Meditationes*, the epistemic status of these foundational principles is evidently the crucial issue.

Most commentators have read the *Meditationes* as involving the view that perceiving something clearly and distinctly, or finding it manifest by natural light, is indeed to embark upon the royal road to absolute knowledge. However, they have failed to agree on the precise route that the road takes. Some say Descartes regards these foundational principles as somehow self-validating, so that when we perceive an idea in the requisite ways we know immediately and absolutely that it corresponds to reality as it actually is.[3] And in this case the road to knowledge is short indeed. All we have to do is satisfy ourselves about one or two potentially awkward eventualities[4] before getting on to explore the expanses of absolute knowledge which open up before us. Others have understood Descartes to say that, although clear and distinct perceptions and things manifest by natural light are indeed of extreme importance, we have to follow a more arduous (perhaps more picturesque) detour before they lead us to absolute knowledge as such. For all that our foundational principles *seem* to give us knowledge, we need to verify this by proving that there is a truthful God who is the author of our nature and of our ideas.[5] It is only after the performance of this proof that we can say that our clear and distinct perceptions and things manifest by natural light must in fact correspond to reality. But, since the proof of God is itself a purely human construct, involving no more than the work of reason on ideas present to the mind, it remains the case that, however indirectly, unaided reason is a means to absolute knowledge. On either of these two well-known accounts then, the meditator has the power to break out from his closed world of ideas into full knowledge of reality as it actually is and his own rational capacities are the only tools he needs. Reason is emphatically autonomous.

This chapter takes the view that both of these standard readings are ultimately on the wrong track. The textual and logical objections to each of them are already familiar enough and I do not propose even

---

[3] Of the many papers which have argued for a version of this thesis, two of the most frequently discussed have been W. Doney, 'The Cartesian Circle', and P. A. Schouls, 'Descartes and the Autonomy of Reason'. The present chapter certainly takes a different line from that of Schouls's article. However, the similarity of titles should not be taken as implying that Schouls is in any sense the main target of my arguments.

[4] These sorts of account have great difficulty in making sense of the passage in the Third Meditation where Descartes claims 'I must examine whether there is a God, and, if there is, whether he can be a deceiver; for, so long as I am ignorant of this, I do not seem ever to be able to be fully certain of anything else [*non videor de ulla alia plane certus esse unquam posse*]' (AT VII 36). A cluster of papers has followed Doney's lead in suggesting that the proofs of God are required only to establish the reliability of memory and the trustworthiness of remembered clear and distinct perceptions.

[5] This would presumably be the most orthodox reading of the *Meditationes*. The problem it poses is that it appears to involve a circular argument. A legion of scholarly essays has attempted to uphold this general line of argument, whilst exonerating Descartes from the charge of circularity.

to attempt a further systematic critique of them. Rather, I wish to offer what is, I think on its own merits, a preferable reading of the texts. It seems to me that, when we enlarge the horizons of our discussion of the *Meditationes* to include the longer 'processes' of Descartes's metaphysics, we shall best come to the conclusion that he does not believe either that the meditator has it within his own power to attain absolute knowledge, or therefore that reason is autonomous at all.

There is another well-known reading of the *Meditationes*, associated chiefly with Harry Frankfurt, which also denies that the meditator achieves absolute knowledge. But on this account reason nevertheless remains autonomous in a somewhat diminished sense. On Frankfurt's interpretation, what the world is actually like is not a matter of human concern.[6] He has Descartes think that philosophy is limited to exploring whatever it is that our reason endorses. The findings of human reason constitute a closed system of mutually consistent, incorrigible propositions which are entirely accessible to us—even if they do not correspond to external reality. And (put crudely), because this system of rational propositions constitutes the only sort of certainty available to human beings, unaided reason is plainly an autonomous means to certainty. I think Frankfurt is right to insist that Descartes is interested in the constraints which our human cognitive apparatus places upon the scope and validity of our beliefs. But in the end we shall have to discard his interpretation too. I shall argue that Descartes denies the autonomy of reason not just in the strong sense of promising a more or less direct means to absolute knowledge, but even in the weaker sense of providing a detached, closed realm of speculation cosily insulated from all contact with external reality.

I

1. From the outset, Descartes's early metaphysical texts focus attention upon the central issue for the question of autonomy: the problematic relationship between the ideas which are perspicuous to the mind and the 'truth' (which generally means for Descartes 'ontological truth', 'the nature of the world as it actually is'). Although there is no systematic reference to clear and distinct perceptions or things manifest by natural light in these early writings, the *Regulae*

---

[6] See H. Frankfurt, *Demons, Dreamers and Madmen*, 184–5.

(1628?) provides us with the concept of 'intuition' and its definition: 'such an easy and distinct conception of pure and attentive mind, that no doubt may henceforth remain concerning what it is that we understand . . . a non-doubtful conception of pure and attentive mind, which is born of the sole light of reason' (AT X 368).[7] Even if the early *intuitus* is strictly speaking different from the successor notions of the clear and distinct and *lumen naturale*, a close functional similarity is undeniable.[8] Descartes himself helps us with a reference to 'la lumiere naturelle, ou *intuitus mentis*' (letter to Mersenne of 16 October 1639: AT II 599) and with instances of the language of 'intuition' surviving into the *Meditationes*.[9] An 'intuition' may give us an indubitable awareness that we understand an idea fully, but the question remains: does this necessarily imply that whatever we intuit is true, in that it corresponds to external reality?

2. That this issue profoundly worried Descartes is best shown in a place which we might find surprising. His early natural philosophy, *Le Monde*, constructs a cosmogony, starting from a set of principles, each of which is described in the language of 'intuition'. But the perspicuity of the ideas in question is never taken as a guarantee of their correspondence to reality. Nor indeed does *Le Monde* furnish any single blanket proof of this correspondence, of the sort usually said to be constituted by the later appeals to divine veracity in the *Meditationes* and elsewhere. In terms of their epistemic status, these principles fall into three distinct categories.

In the case of two of these categories, Descartes is somewhat vague and equivocal. His cosmogony depends firstly upon laws of nature summarizing God's general and particular conservation of what he has once created. The truth of these laws for any possible world is said to be a deductive consequence of God's immutability (AT XI 43, 44). However, we are not told how it is that we are supposed to know that there is a God or that he is immutable in the first place. All we have is an uninformative reference to 'God, who, as everyone must know, is immutable' (AT XI 38) and a refusal to delve further into 'metaphysical considerations' (ibid.). Whether this is an appeal to unstated proofs of God, to universal consent, or to presumed religious faith can only be a matter of speculation.

In a separate category are the rules governing the impact of bodies.

---

[7] This and all other translations are my own.
[8] For the purposes of this chapter I shall take these terms (somewhat loosely perhaps) as equivalents. [9] See e.g. AT VII 36.

They are said to follow from 'eternal truths', the knowledge of which 'is so natural to our souls that we could not fail to judge them infallible, when we conceive them distinctly' (AT XI 47). But whether the perspicuity of these 'truths' is itself sufficient for us to be able to know that they correspond to reality remains in doubt. Descartes also feels the need to refer to them as those truths 'according to which God himself has taught us that he had disposed all things in number, in weight and in measure' (AT XI 47). We are left to wonder if the truth of these propositions is something which is self-evidently attached to them, which is involved in their being innate in our minds as a sort of natural revelation, or whether, as the tacit scriptural reference suggests, it is a privileged supernatural revelation. Perhaps these references are not particularly helpful in themselves. But, if Descartes is indeed the champion of the autonomy of reason, it seems at least odd that he should leave the relationship between our intuited ideas and reality quite so indefinite.

Fortunately Descartes's discussion of his remaining principles is more fully developed. The substantive constituent of his world, matter, and the motion which informs it, are both described in intuitive terms. Of the primitive material chaos, we are asked to 'note that it contains nothing but what is so perfectly known to you that you could not even pretend to be ignorant of it' (AT XI 35; also XI 33). The definition of motion is characterized as being 'easy to know', 'simple', 'intelligible', and 'easy to conceive' (AT XI 39–40). But what is remarkable here is the absence of any claim that our ideas of matter and motion, however clearly understood, can be shown necessarily to correspond to anything existing in the real world. Indeed, the latter stages of *Le Monde* serve as a purely hypothetical proof that, *if* matter and motion were created so as to correspond to our ideas of them, then, with the ordinary operation of the laws of nature and rules of impact, they would come to form a cosmos resembling in all particulars the world of actual experience which we inhabit.[10] Implicit in this argument is the very high probability that the real world is in fact constituted of the principles which Descartes supposes and in the way that he describes it. But even if he had successfully completed his hypothetical cosmogony, we could not be said to know *absolutely* that our ideas of matter and motion must correspond to reality as it actually is. He acknowledges (letter to Morin of 13 July 1638: AT II 199–200) that

[10] See AT XI 34–5.

the most thorough confirmation of the largest possible hypothesis may 'persuade' us of its truth, but this persuasion plainly amounts to something less than absolute knowledge.

We should not read too much into *Le Monde*, which, after all, is not concerned primarily with metaphysical issues. But at a number of points it has a bearing on the question of the autonomy of reason: (i) Descartes is plainly aware of the problems of proceeding from intuited ideas to reality; (ii) he does not claim that the correspondence between intuited ideas and reality is always or simply self-evident, nor does he furnish a consistent a priori proof of this correspondence; (iii) in one instance at least he finds hypothetical, as opposed to absolute, knowledge of external reality a sufficient basis for his philosophy. And this is worth underlining, not merely because it involves a recourse to non-absolute forms of knowledge, but because it constitutes a precedent to which we may need to return in due course.

3. If the metaphysical passages of *Le Monde* have received relatively little attention from commentators, the same cannot be said of the 1630 letters to Mersenne on the 'eternal truths of mathematics'.[11] They have spawned a minor interpretative industry of their own. But even here our understanding of the early texts may have been unduly overshadowed by the more familiar frames of reference of the *Meditationes*.[12]

The main point at issue is presented in the letter of 15 April and can be summarized quickly. The truths of mathematics are described in the language of intuition, so that 'there is none in particular that we cannot understand if our mind turns to consider it, and they are all innate in our minds' (AT I 145). But, on the surface at least, Descartes has something slightly more recondite to worry about than whether or how we can know that intuited mathematical propositions correspond to the way things actually are in the world. His problem is that, even if a mathematical proposition is true at the present moment, this carries no logical implication that it will also be true at any subsequent moment. (The discussion relates to Descartes's peculiar theory of the discontinuity of time.) He suggests that mathematics is not a reliable

---

[11] Letters of 15 April 1630, 6 May 1630, and 27 May 1630? (AT I 135–54). The last of the three is a fragment for which date and name of recipient have been supplied by Adam and Tannery.

[12] However, J. G. Cottingham ('The Cartesian Legacy') and S. Gaukroger (*Cartesian Logic*, 60–71) suggest interpretations of Descartes's theory which are in important respects consistent with my own.

or valid discipline, unless we have some guarantee of the permanency of the truth of its propositions. In Descartes's view the guarantee is provided only by a prior acknowledgement of the existence of an immutable God. Because such a God must continuously conserve the being of all created things, including the world and the mathematical propositions innate in our mind, if such propositions are once true, they must always remain true.

Put in this way, the argument of the 1630 letters does not tell us appreciably more about the ultimate status of reason than does *Le Monde*. Descartes is still worried about the relationship of intuited ideas to reality and there is still an annoying reticence about our entitlement to say that we have absolute knowledge of the truth of mathematical propositions, or of the existence of an immutable God in the first place. Even though he apparently wishes to establish the dependence of the reliability of mathematics upon our idea of God, this only implies the non-autonomy of mathematics as a discipline. It does not necessarily carry the wider implication that human reason itself must be non-autonomous.

The importance of the 1630 letters is, however, less in their explicit arguments than in their more general discussion of the status of the human mind and of human rationality in the universe. The arguments for the non-autonomy of mathematics are presented within a larger metaphysical framework which seeks to establish the total dependence of *all* things (and not just the permanency of truths) upon God. The constant theme of these letters is the transcendence and dignity of God, as opposed to the relatively humble and insignificant position of human beings in the universe. Without exaggeration this can be termed an anti-humanist metaphysic, revealing a profound antipathy towards claims for the power of human reason and those who make them.

The 1630 letters insist upon those attributes of God which elevate him furthest from human understanding. Above all, God is 'an infinite and incomprehensible being' (AT I 150). And again, 'I say that we can know that God is infinite and all-powerful, even though our soul being finite cannot comprehend him or conceive of him' (AT I 152). The huge distance which separates God from mankind is forced home by affirming that, although human thought may bring us into contact with God, it can never truly embrace his nature. The fact that 'we cannot comprehend the grandeur of God even though we can know it' (AT I 145) is said to be a reason for esteeming his grandeur all the more.

His 'power surpasses the bounds of human understanding' (AT I 150) and 'generally we can be sure that God can do everything that we can comprehend, but not that he cannot do what we cannot comprehend' (AT I 146).

This bleak picture of a remote omnipotent God, without a hint of benevolence, is enough to suggest that there need be no direct analogy between our minds and the divine nature. Finite human beings are different from the infinite God not only in degree but in kind. The absence of analogy seems confirmed by Descartes's denial of the division of the divine 'mind' into faculties: 'it is in God one same thing to will, to understand and to create, without even a logical priority of the one over the other' (AT I 153). Again, God is the 'efficient and total cause' of all things (AT I 152) and he is 'the Author from whom all things depend' (AT I 150). In that great divide which separates all being into the two categories of the creator and the freely created, human nature is plainly in the second camp. Our minds are not a participation in the divinity, privy to the workings of creation itself, but contingent entities, dependent creatures amongst all other dependent creatures. The general tenor of this account already looks worrying if we wish to maintain that human beings have some inherent natural ability to know the world. But the further consequences of Descartes's view seem virtually fatal to such claims.

The most remarkable feature of the metaphysics of dependence is not the contingent status of the mind itself, so much as the strictly non-necessary character of those mathematical (and, by implication, logical) propositions which appear to us necessarily true. Descartes is adamant that what seems necessary to us is not necessary for God. God's action is not constrained by the laws of logical possibility as we perceive them, nor are these laws part of his essence and, as it were, expressions of the divine nature itself. Rather, the truths of logic and mathematics are freely created by God: 'he was as free to make it the case that it should not be true that all the lines drawn from the centre to the circumference [of a circle] were equal, as he was not to create the world' (AT I 152). Since he knows no necessity, God himself is not a logical agent. Logic itself is an accident of created human minds, rather than the absolute universal arbiter.

When followed through, the strict contingency of the 'truths' of logic and mathematics strikes at the very heart of claims for the autonomy of human reason. The obvious way in which we might think that we can attain absolute knowledge of the world is if ontological

conclusions can be shown to follow *necessarily* from ideas present to
the mind. But this procedure is useless as a means to knowledge once
we deny that what *seems* necessarily true to us must also in fact *be*
necessarily true. No matter how valid and conclusive any ontological
argument may seem, it cannot be said to tell us anything definite or
true about the world, so long as we regard logic as a contingent part
or accident of our human nature. All that any ontological argument
could establish is that we are of such a nature that we must think that
certain things exist, regardless of whether or not they do in fact exist.
Since Descartes's later metaphysics, from the Cogito onwards, may be
taken as a tissue of ontological arguments, we might conclude that he
ought to be interested in what we must rationally think about the
world, not in the world as it actually is.[13]

It is hard to read the 1630 letters as anything other than a
theologically motivated[14] attack on human logic and mathematics seen
as means of knowing the world. Descartes, of course, never denies
that our logical and mathematical conclusions *may* correspond to the
way the world is. But the crucial point is that there seems to be nothing
about such conclusions in themselves which would entitle us to say
that they must provide absolute knowledge. The letters of 1630, along
with the more equivocal assertions of *Le Monde*, provide a suggestive
context in which we can reconsider the status of reason in the later works.

II

4. Descartes's early views on human frailty and dependence need
not, of course, mean that he maintains the same position in the
Meditationes. If so many modern critics have understood Descartes as
celebrating the power and adequacy of human reason, and if Descartes
himself can describe the *Meditationes* as providing the foundations for
a wide-ranging natural philosophy,[15] then may it not be that he has
simply changed his mind about the status of human beings and their
rational capacities?

---

[13] This is not the situation envisaged in Frankfurt's account of Descartes's epistemology. The sorts of belief involved here are ones which we would be *obliged* to think
truly correspond to the way the world actually is: even if such beliefs could conceivably
be mistaken.
[14] See E. H. Gilson, *La Liberté chez Descartes et la théologie*, esp. pt. 1, ch. 5, and pt.
2, ch. 3.   [15] See letter to Mersenne of 28 January 1641 (AT III 298).

There are indeed signs of a reorientation of Descartes's meta-physics, of a sort consistent with more optimistic views about human potentials. The God of the *Meditationes* is a less remote figure than that of the 1630 letters. Descartes discusses the 'perfections' of God rather than insisting only upon his 'infinity', admitting the possibility of a more positive understanding of him. The appeal to the 'veracity' of God involves an a priori conception of his moral goodness or benevolence, absent from the earlier texts. There are also hints of analogy between human and divine natures, according to which human beings are created in the image of God (AT VII 51).[16] All of these modifications would seem to commend and elevate the status of humanity in the universe, integrating the mind more fully into the planned order of things. And they might be expected to have some bearing on the problems of knowledge. Indeed the *Meditationes* tends to discuss these problems in terms of possible weaknesses of the human mind (defects of perception and understanding), rather than in terms of our unrelatedness, contingency, and isolation in an alien world. Attention shifts from our ontological status to our psychological fallibility.

The difficulty with this account is that it neglects the extent to which the central concerns of the earlier texts continue to be of importance in the *Meditationes*. This is not so much a new metaphysics as one which exhibits a series of tensions between older and newer views. So, for example, the 'perfection' of God in the Third Meditation is a highly equivocal concept. For the most part, it is a morally neutral ontological principle, a plenitude of being, where the attributes of the 'perfect' God are very much the same as those of the omnipotent creator in the 1630 letters.[17] It is only at the very end of the Third Meditation that there is a sudden switch to the use of 'perfection' as a moral term, involving benevolence and veracity (AT VII 52). Similarly, whilst the main text of the *Meditationes* does tentatively endorse the analogy of God and humanity,[18] there are also passages in the Sixth Replies which seem to deny it.[19] It is even arguable

---

[16] See also *Conversation with Burman* (AT V 156).

[17] See the list of divine attributes (AT VII 40) and the account of the idea of God (AT VII 45).

[18] See AT VII 57: the meditator feels able to compare his own faculties with those of God.

[19] See AT VII 433 ('no essence can be applied univocally to God and his creatures') and AT VII 435–6, where Descartes gives a revised rendering of his theory of God's creation of the eternal truths. The account of the differences between human and divine liberty (AT VII 431–3) could also be used as an argument against analogy.

that, like the *Regulae* and the *Discours*, the *Meditationes* is a composite text, including passages originally drafted for Descartes's earlier projects. There are enough discontinuities of style and vocabulary in the Third Meditation in particular to make us wonder about the process of its composition.

Be that as it may, it is part of the intriguing, puzzling character of the *Meditationes* that its arguments pull in two directions at once. On the one hand, it seems to favour human rational enterprises and to establish the credentials of a dogmatic philosophy. Yet, on the other, the assertions of severely circumscribed human potential remain strong. And this plainly poses problems of interpretation.

5. Nevertheless, the crucial issue for the question of autonomy has to be the epistemic status of the foundational clear and distinct perceptions and things manifest by natural light. And the discussion of these principles is much more fully developed in the *Meditationes* than in the earlier texts. There is, of course, already a vast literature on clear and distinct perceptions, but much less has been written about things manifest by natural light (*lumen naturale*).[20] The two are plainly related, but, even if we attend only to the terms which Descartes uses, there seems to be a formal distinction between them. The different phrases used point to different aspects of Descartes's understanding of the status of the foundational principles available to the meditator and invite us to see how far this distinction goes.

6. 'Clear and distinct perception' is, I think, best seen in logical terms. To have perceived something clearly and distinctly is to have subjected an idea to a full and successful logical analysis, so that it is reduced to simple notions, which are fully perspicuous to our intellect (or, in the case of propositions, to terms signifying simple notions which are intellectually perspicuous). This is very much the account of the proper procedures of human intellect given in the *Regulae*,[21] with its theory of 'simple natures' as the ultimate units of cognition. And it is echoed in a letter to Mersenne, where Descartes elaborates upon the 'clarity' of simple ideas in terms of their logical irreducibility: 'One cannot give any definition of Logic which helps us to understand its nature. And I think the same of several other things which are very simple and are naturally known, such as shape, size, movement, place, time, etc., so that when one wishes to define these things one only

---

[20] Perhaps the most thorough account is J. Morris, 'Descartes' Natural Light'.
[21] Esp. rule XII (AT X410 ff.).

obscures them and gets into a muddle' (16 October 1639: AT II 597). Since the intellectual perspicuity of 'simple natures' is presumably the same for all human beings, this insistence upon logical analysis or reduction ought to counter the common charge that the criterion of clarity and distinctness is purely subjective. Perhaps the resolutive–compositive method of rule XII and what one might call the 'logical atomism' of the 1639 letter are not as prominent in the later comments on the clear and distinct.[22] However, it is difficult to see just what is meant by these comments, unless Descartes takes the view that clear and distinct perceptions are such as are seen to be composed solely of logical simples.

Even so, this account prompts two objections already foreshadowed in Descartes's earlier writings. (i) It looks difficult to justify any claim to know that our analysis has indeed successfully reduced a complex idea or proposition to logical notions which are in fact absolutely simple. More bluntly, how can we be sure that something really is 'simple', even when it looks perfectly simple to us? (ii) There is the special problem with claims that clear and distinct perceptions are 'true', in the sense of corresponding to the way things are in the world. Even if our analysis of an idea or proposition into logical simples were known to be adequate, all that this would entitle us to say would be that we had fully grasped and understood this idea or proposition. The perspicuity of something to the human intellect hardly looks like a ground for affirming its ontological truth.

7. If this is all fairly familiar, Descartes's concept of *lumen naturale* is much less well known. To see that something is 'manifest by natural light' is not to say anything at all about its *logical* status. It appears on the contrary to be a statement of a purely *psychological* response to whatever we have perceived clearly and distinctly.[23] Descartes seems to say that it is an observable fact of human psychology that, whenever we are confronted with ideas or propositions which the intellect has

---

[22] The fullest definition of clear and distinct perceptions is the one found in *Principia*, pt. I, art. 45 (AT VIIIA 21–2). Most commentators would agree that it leaves much to be desired.

[23] Descartes's concern with the psychology of assent has only recently begun to receive the critical attention that it deserves. General accounts are provided by R. Rubin, 'Descartes' Validation of Clear and Distinct Apprehension', and C. L. Larmore, 'Descartes' Psychologistic Theory of Assent'. L. E. Loeb's essay 'The Cartesian Circle' was published when the present chapter was already into its final draft. Loeb offers a much fuller development of the 'psychological interpretation' of Descartes than is given in the earlier discussions. In important respects, he anticipates my own conclusions in Section III of this chapter. See also S. Gaukroger, *Cartesian Logic*, 48–60.

analysed thoroughly, we find ourselves obliged unconditionally, totally, and spontaneously to assent to their complete simplicity and to their ontological truth. Indeed, the adequacy of our logical analysis and the ontological truth of our apparently clear and distinct perceptions are such closely linked issues that we seem to be convinced of both in a single, instantaneous act of assent. The meditator finds, 'whenever I turn my attention to those things which I think I perceive very clearly, I am so fully persuaded by them, that I spontaneously break out into these affirmations: let whoever can deceive me, but he shall never bring it about that I should be nothing whenever I shall think that I exist . . . ' (AT VII 36). Repeatedly Descartes observes that we cannot help ourselves from saying that some things are true whenever we perceive them. We hear, 'for I am of such a nature that so long as I perceive something very clearly and distinctly, I cannot not believe it to be true' (AT VII 69). There are further propositions which are such that 'we can never think of them without believing them to be true' (AT VII 145–6).

Descartes frequently telescopes this act of unconditional assent into his account of what it is to perceive something clearly and distinctly in the first place. But it must be apparent that assenting to something is not at all the same thing as perceiving its logical structure. Descartes refers to the need 'to distinguish between the matter or thing to which we assent and the formal cause [*ratio*] which moves the will to assent' (AT VII 147). And when he describes the psychological status of natural light, Descartes suggests that it is specifically the *ratio* determining our assent. Where the function of the intellect is to perceive clearly and distinctly, it is the immediate illumination of the will by natural light which transforms our perceptions into certain beliefs or 'knowledge'. In the *Principia*, we hear of 'natural light, or the faculty for knowing [*cognoscendi facultatem*], given to us by God' (AT VIIIA 16). Again, in the *Meditationes*, natural light is presented as the ultimate arbiter of certainty, 'showing' and 'teaching' us that our perceptions are true: 'whatever things are shown to me by natural light . . . can in no way be dubious, because there can be no other faculty which I can trust to the same extent as that light, and which could ever teach me that they were not true' (AT VII 38–9).

What is remarkable about Descartes's account of assent (as opposed to perception) is the strength of the language used. If we take his texts literally, the psychological force of natural light is utterly irresistible and incorrigible. It is *impossible* for us to dissent from those things which we perceive very clearly. Descartes commonly appeals to natural light in contexts suggesting that it is the origin of what we experience when something appears logically or mathematically 'necessary'. So, he remarks, 'it is manifest by natural light that there must be at least as much in the efficient and total cause, as in the effect of that same cause' (AT VII 40). Again, he refers to 'whatever things have been shown to me by natural light, such as that from my doubting, it follows that I exist, and similar things' (AT VII 38). Here it is not the logical structure of propositions that commands our assent so much as the natural light which 'shows' us their truth. If my account is correct, we need to dispense with any expectation that Descartes's foundational principles should conform to purely logical criteria of certainty, or that our grounds for certainty must be open to intellectual scrutiny. These principles are derived not from the intellect alone, but from the intellect and natural light, as separate faculties of the mind, functioning in tandem. And it is the God-given natural light that Descartes refers to as his unique 'rule of truth' (letter to Mersenne of 16 October 1639: AT II 597). It is this natural light, rather than the intellectual perspicuity of the propositions themselves, which is the ultimate psychological ground of all our logical and mathematical judgements.

This implicit repudiation of claims for the self-sufficiency of logic and mathematics involves a mystification of the concept of 'necessity'. For all its coercive force, natural light is a hidden faculty of mind (it seems odd to call it a faculty at all[24]). As compared with the intellect, it is unfathomable in its spontaneous intuitive workings. The invincible psychological certainty it produces in us in the presence of clear and distinct perceptions is a persuasion of their truth which we can experience in its effects, but not justify in its reasons. One is tempted to speak of an epistemic 'enthusiasm', in which the mind is spontaneously filled with the dazzling light of evidence.

8. But how secure is any clear and distinct perception against doubt? In principle, we might think the sceptic could refuse to give his assent to such perceptions, because he has no logical grounds for accepting them. But this would be to miss the point of Descartes's theory. He maintains that all human beings share 'one same natural light' (letter to Mersenne of 16 October 1639: AT II 598), and, as such, its coercive power would seem to mean that the same propositions must

---

[24] Descartes's equivocations about the status of natural light as variously 'God-given' and 'facultative' perhaps suggest links with debates about illuminative theories of epistemology in the Augustinian and Thomist traditions.

be totally convincing for everyone. Even the sceptics have the same psychological make-up as other human beings. If they are honest with themselves (and with us[25]) they must admit that they are fully persuaded, and therefore certain, of things made evident by natural light—even without logical grounds for this certainty. They *cannot* simply suspend judgement in the face of such an overwhelming and instantaneous determination of the will. The power of natural light is such that it abolishes our liberty of indifference[26] and commands us to accept those things which it makes manifest.

If this line of attack fails, we might imagine that a stronger one remains available. The sceptic could argue that we have positive grounds for withholding our assent from clear and distinct perceptions. Any feeling of certainty we may have when we encounter a proposition is, from a purely logical point of view, quite compatible with the falsity of that proposition. To say that we find ourselves fully persuaded that something is the case in the world is an observation about our own state of mind, not about the order of external reality. The possibility that our beliefs do not correspond to the absolute truth about the nature of things looks like a perfectly good reason for doubting them, which ought to be taken into account when we grant or refuse our assent.

But this too misrepresents the psychology of certainty. Descartes's account of natural light involves the view that, when something becomes manifest, the force of our conviction is such that we are spontaneously persuaded of its truth, *even if* there could be logical reasons for doubting it.[27] The immediacy of natural light gives us no opportunity to attempt a balanced judicial appraisal of reasons for assent or doubt. If we assent to something, it is not merely that our intellectual grounds for affirming it 'outweigh' or 'refute' our reasons for doubting. Rather the instantaneous evidence of natural light suppresses the possibility of doubt. It pre-empts any logical qualms and makes us deaf to them. This is surely the sort of thing Descartes has in mind in the Second Replies, when he notes: 'it is no objection

---

[25] For an example of 'dishonesty', see letter to Father Mesland (?) of 9 February 1645 AT IV 173. Even if we see that something is perspicuously true, we can still *say* that we deny it.

[26] The question of liberty is as much an epistemic as a moral one. One suspects that Descartes's denial of liberty of indifference in the Sixth Replies is largely to do with the requirements of his epistemology.

[27] In general terms, this part of my account takes issue with E. M. Curley, *Descartes against the Skeptics*, 84–6, 116–23.

if someone pretends that those things [of which we are so firmly persuaded] appear false to God or an Angel, because the evidence of our perception does not permit the case that we should hear [*audiamus*] a person who pretends such things' (AT VII 146). Appeal is made to an empirical observation about human responses to clear and distinct perceptions. Under no circumstances can we honestly claim to believe that something which is at present manifest by natural light could be false. Indeed, the certainty experienced when we intuit a truth appears to involve the persuasion that it could *never* be false. An intuited truth is for all time. In 1630 Descartes had discussed the truths of mathematics as things which we perceive as 'eternal'. And the same sense of the perpetual truth of intuitions is conveyed in the Third Meditation. Present intuitions cover beliefs about what can possibly be true in the future: 'I spontaneously break out into these affirmations: let whoever can deceive me, he shall never bring it about [*nunquam efficiet*] that I should be nothing, for so long as I shall think [*cogitabo*] that I am something; or that it should at some time [*aliquando*] be true that I never existed when it is true that I exist now . . .' (AT VII 36).

9. On this interpretation, then, clear and distinct perceptions are certified by a total psychological persuasion of their truth. Although this persuasion guarantees our perceptions against scepticism, it leaves open the (strictly incredible) logical possibility that they could be false from an absolute point of view. That is to say, our obligatory assent to the truth of present clear and distinct perceptions may secure our unconditional belief in them. But this belief could never amount to an absolute knowledge. If, as seems to be the case, the scheme of clear and distinct perceptions constitutes the sum total of the foundational principles available to human reason, then reason itself cannot be fully autonomous. It appears to have no means of access to absolute knowledge of the world as it actually is. And it is not so much that Descartes has *failed* to provide a proof of the autonomy of reason. Rather, if we understand the psychology of human cognition correctly, the autonomy of reason and the pursuit of absolute knowledge are illusory quests. Such goals are simply beyond the capacity of our common human nature.

Nevertheless, the strength and value of our certainties should not lightly be dismissed. For all that we cannot have absolute knowledge of the truth of any clear and distinct perceptions, they remain so convincing and appear so *necessary* that we feel ourselves obliged to believe in them unconditionally. 'Our mind', as Descartes tells us, 'is of such a nature that it cannot fail to assent to things which are clearly understood' (letter to Regius of 24 May 1640: AT III 64). And this is surely an adequate basis for some sort of rational philosophy. Nor need this philosophy be confined to a coherence theory of knowledge, detached from actual reality (of the sort suggested by Frankfurt[28]). Our belief that we know reality as it is will be insurmountable, even if logically unjustifiable. Our obligatory beliefs about the world will be psychologically indistinguishable from absolute knowledge. We might indeed describe Descartes's theory of clear and distinct perceptions— including the Cogito and the proofs of God—as a system of 'absolute persuasions' about reality.

III

10. But this interpretation of Descartes's epistemology could hardly be thought complete. It conspicuously omits any account of the proofs of God in the Third Meditation. Descartes plainly sets great store by his demonstration that we can have a clear and distinct perception of the existence of a truthful God. And many commentators have argued that it is only when epistemology takes the metaphysical turn and divine veracity is invoked that absolute knowledge (somehow) becomes a viable possibility. The case for Descartes's denial of the autonomy of reason must stand or fall on our reading of these much discussed texts.

11. Glancing back to the letters of 1630, one of Descartes's main concerns was to do with the problem of time, or, more specifically, of the temporal character of human thought and consciousness. What was at issue was the permanency of the 'eternal truths' of mathematics. This early preoccupation points to a central, but not identical, issue in the *Meditationes*, where time is again brought into play. Descartes here enquires whether a subsequent reflection upon an antecedent certainty might allow us to cast doubt upon it after the fact. Essentially the problem is the *permanency* of our certainties. To see what the problem is involves rehearsing Descartes's account of the psychology of knowledge.

[28] See *Demons, Dreamers and Madmen*, 184–5. Frankfurt's account considers only the *logic* of the *Meditationes*. He fails to acknowledge the strictly psychological force of natural light as a principle of belief.

The way our mental faculties work is that when we encounter intellectually perspicuous propositions they become manifest by natural light. This involves an experience of total persuasion, overwhelming us with a sense of the truth of what we perceive and of the impossibility that it could ever be false. Whilst we continue to attend to such propositions, we are constitutionally incapable of regarding them as dubious. However, we cannot pass our entire life intuiting clear and distinct propositions. The moment of epistemic enthusiasm must pass and we must cease to be helplessly dazzled by the glow of natural light. It is in this new state of mind that potential doubts can arise. We pass from a subjective experience of intuitive certainty to a position of detachment, in which we can cognize that experience and the functioning of our mental faculties objectively. Descartes appears to ask just what we should make of our certainties when we look at them retrospectively in this cold spirit of disenchantment.

The mere fact that we are no longer currently experiencing the coercive force of natural light is of itself insufficient to throw the propositions it certified back into the epistemic melting-pot of things uncertain. Without some new reason for doubting them, the contents of our remembered certainties remain certain, even when the original cause inducing persuasion is no longer present. And Descartes is confident that genuinely intuitive judgements are irrevisable. Intuiting a proposition involves such a total certainty of its perpetual truth as to make us sure that, if we were ever to reconsider the proposition, we should again be infallibly obliged to regard it as true. The recollection of this sense of certainty ought to be enough to persuade us that all intuitions are indefinitely reproducible. Once we have intuited a proposition, even in our mood of retrospective detachment, we can say that it is in our nature that we must always think that it is true whenever we consider it.

But this does not mean that we cannot subsequently doubt intuitions in a more roundabout way. The meditator can turn his attention from the *contents* of these propositions to a consideration of the mental procedures by which he first arrived at them. In his position of retrospective detachment, he can think about the reliability of his own mental faculties in a way that was impossible whilst he was in the process of intuiting particular truths. The doubt which occurs to him—he indicates that there is no other reason for doubt (AT VII 36)—is that perhaps those parts of his mental apparatus which induce him to assent are delusive. And, since it is the faculty of natural light that is chiefly concerned with assent, this inevitably becomes the focus of critical reappraisal.

When we reflect upon the faculty of natural light as a psychological phenomenon, rather than experiencing it at work, it is by no means obvious that it must be reliable. It could make us certain of things which are simply false (even though they look absolutely true whenever we intuit them). Moreover, because natural light is the sole 'rule of truth' (letter to Mersenne of 16 October 1639: AT II 597) and because it is the ultimate ground of all our logical and mathematical judgements, the retrospective doubts about its reliability would seem—at one remove, as it were—to make all of our clear and distinct perceptions dubious.[29] The meditator observes,

Thus, for example, when I consider the nature of the triangle, it seems very evident to me, in as much as that I am versed in the principles of Geometry, that its three angles are equal to two right angles, nor can I not believe that it is true, so long as I attend to its demonstration; but as soon as I turn aside the full intensity of my mental attention, even though I still remember that I perceived it very clearly, it can easily happen that I doubt whether it was true . . . (AT VII 69–70)

Although the meditator had experienced a total certainty of the content of the proposition about triangles, when he reconsidered this experience he could not rule out the possibility that the natural light, which had first made him certain, was unreliable.

But this retrospective doubt leaves us in a thoroughly bizarre situation. Our suspicions about the reliability of natural light when cognized objectively as a faculty of mind might well cast a 'procedural doubt', so to speak, upon all past clear and distinct perceptions (in so far as we could think about them without once more intuiting their truth). But such suspicions could never affect our spontaneous experience of an overwhelming psychological certainty when in the presence of anything that was clearly and distinctly perceived. That is, we cannot simply *decide* that because natural light now seems a dubious faculty we shall never again accept it in future. The power of natural light is such that when we actually experience it we can never acknowledge any merely logical quibbles about its validity. Perhaps, in our present mood of detachment, we can doubt the proposition that

---

[29] The only propositions which would escape this doubt would be such simple ones that they could not be thought of without being re-intuited and so having their certainty reaffirmed by the actual operation of natural light. The Cogito is the obvious example.

the angles of a triangle are equal to two right angles, because we have grounds for mistrusting the faculty which originally persuaded us of its truth. But the fact remains that the next time we consider a triangle, run through the demonstration, and once more intuit the conclusion about the sum of the angles, we shall again feel ourselves to be totally certain of the truth of this conclusion.

Retrospective suspicions about the reliability of natural light do not then open the door to any stable scepticism. Instead of comfortable suspension of judgement, the aspiring sceptic would face a bewildering confusion. He would alternate between bouts of doubt and of total certainty. There could be no happy *ataraxia* in this, only an intolerable, morally debilitating fluctuation in his rational dispositions. Having come this far with Descartes, the honest sceptic would be reduced to a position where he must positively hope that the doubts about the reliability of natural light should be removed.

12. Before Descartes proceeds to the solution of these doubts, the problem is redefined in more manageable terms. At the start of the Third Meditation, the meditator is certain that he is '*res cogitans*'. What makes him sure of this is 'a clear and distinct perception of what I affirm'. This leads him to propose as a 'general rule [*regula generali*]' that 'everything is true which I perceive very clearly and distinctly' (AT VII 34–5). This does not, of course, mean that the meditator is certain of the truth of this proposition. A 'rule' is a procedural hypothesis or directive rather than a truth as such. However, the epistemic status of the 'rule' can be seen as the key issue in Descartes's subsequent argument. He attempts to ascertain whether the proposition laid down by the 'rule' can itself be intuited. And the reason for making the status of the 'rule' so central is not hard to find. It encapsulates very neatly the question of the reliability of natural light in particular and of our mental faculties in general. The way our minds work is that they compel us to assent to clear and distinct perceptions; if what the 'rule' says is true, then, by implication, our mental faculties are reliable; if it is false, they are delusive.

Let us suppose that the meditator were to discover some argument in the context of which he could perceive the proposition laid down by the 'rule' clearly and distinctly, so that its truth were certified by natural light. We might gloss this even as follows:

(i) Even if the meditator had previously entertained doubts about the reliability of his own mental faculties as a means to truth, this could not prevent him giving his total assent to anything which was actually manifest by natural light.

(ii) His experience of an actual natural light convincing him totally that 'everything is true which [he] perceives very clearly and distinctly' would amount to an actual persuasion that his mental faculties (including natural light) were reliable.

(iii) This could not mean that his natural light was not in fact delusive from an absolute point of view. All that the meditator could say at the conclusion of his argument would be that he presently found himself psychologically incapable of believing that his natural light was, or could ever be, unreliable.

Regardless of whether the meditator's natural light and other mental faculties were in fact delusive, when he examined the matter for himself, making best use of his faculties such as they were, an intuition of the truth of the 'rule' would oblige him to *believe* in the reliability of his own faculties.[30]

But the question remains, if the meditator were to intuit the truth of the 'rule', could he still doubt this truth retrospectively?

As we have noted, even in our mood of detached reflection we cannot doubt the contents of a past intuition as such. If we have once intuited the proposition (say) 'the angles of a triangle equal 180 degrees', then, even when we are no longer intuiting it, we remain sure that whenever we think about triangles we shall find that the proposition is true. It is part of our mental nature that, in itself, the proposition must always appear true to us. Similarly, if the meditator were to succeed in intuiting the truth of the 'general rule', he could be sure that he would never have grounds to revise this intuition as such. He could say that it was part of our nature that we must think our mental faculties reliable. The problem is that, where the proposition about triangles contains nothing which precludes the subsequent worry that our mental faculties may be delusive, an intuition of the 'general rule' would in some sense appear to pre-empt that doubt.

And this starts to look decidedly difficult. We can perhaps restate the problem schematically:

(i) Human psychology is such that, for any particular intuition, we can never (i.e. not even retrospectively) doubt its contents as such.

(ii) But we have a reason for doubting the procedural validity of intuitions in general.

(iii) This reason permits us retrospectively to doubt the contents of

[30] It is perhaps worth observing that there is nothing circular in this procedure.

intuitions in general (and therefore of any particular intuition) not as such, but as dependent upon an invalid procedure.

(iv) Problem: what would happen when we considered retrospectively a particular intuition whose contents as such confirmed the procedural validity of intuitions in general?

An intuition of the 'general rule' would place the meditator in a situation where his psychological dispositions and his purely logical judgements were in direct opposition. On the one hand, he would have an enduring psychological certainty that his mental faculties were reliable. On the other, we might think that he ought to acknowledge the logically conceivable possibility that all our certainties (including this one about the reliability of our faculties) might be mistaken—because our faculties could be delusive. Whilst the meditator might say 'I find that I am of such a nature that I must always believe in the reliability of my mental faculties', he could imagine the would-be sceptic replying 'that may be true, but perhaps your nature is so flawed that it makes you think your faculties are reliable when they are not'. Even in this case, however, the meditator might conclude the dialogue with the rejoinder, 'my nature may indeed be flawed as you suggest, but as a matter of fact, I can by no means believe that it is—and neither you nor anyone else can honestly believe this of their own nature'.

When Descartes comments on this question for himself, he plainly takes the view that our *inability to believe* that our faculties are delusive would be the clinching point. He discusses a closely related case in a much quoted passage of the Second Replies:

> Firstly, as soon as we think something has been correctly perceived by us, we spontaneously persuade ourselves that it is true. But if this persuasion is so firm that we can never have any cause for doubting that of which we persuade ourselves, there is nothing at all about which we can enquire further; we have everything that we are reasonably entitled to wish for. For what is it to us, if by chance anyone pretends [*fingat*] that the very thing of whose truth we are so firmly persuaded, should appear false to God or an Angel, and so, absolutely speaking, be false? What do we care for that absolute falsity, since we in no way believe it [*nullo modo credamus*], nor in the least suspect it? For we suppose such a firm persuasion that it can in no way be overthrown; and that persuasion henceforth is just the same as perfect certainty. (AT VII 144–5)

The 'general rule' seems to be the unique instance where the psychological force of an intuited certainty would be sufficient to silence even *subsequent* logical quibbles about its truth.

Furthermore, if we were once to intuit the 'general rule', all doubts about the reliability of our faculties would be permanently removed. The recollection of our certainty of the truth of the 'rule' would be sufficient to guarantee the reliability of our faculties in respect of all other particular clear and distinct perceptions, when we subjected them to detached scrutiny. Even when we reflected upon the clear and distinct perception, 'the angles of a triangle equal 180 degrees', the recollection that we are of such a nature as to be totally certain that 'everything is true which I perceive very clearly and distinctly' would render this proposition indubitable. Once we had intuited the truth of the 'rule', we could be as sure of the reliability of other particular past (and future) clear and distinct perceptions as we had always been of those actually present to the mind.

Just as much as the Cogito, an intuition of the 'general rule' would be a very special case. Indeed, it would exhibit many of the same features of self-referentiality that make the interpretation of the Cogito so perplexing. But, whereas the Cogito is so strikingly and immediately evident that we cannot think of it without intuiting it, the 'general rule' is plainly much harder to pin down. Descartes might be confident that, *if* he could intuit the truth of the 'rule', this would permanently validate the reliability of the faculty of natural light. But the difficulty is to know how it could possibly be perceived clearly and distinctly in the first place. And the question is urgent, because, until the truth of the 'rule' can be intuited, we must remain in that intolerable confusion, fluctuating between certainty and doubt, as moments of illumination by natural light and of detached reflection succeed each other.

13. The context for providing a clear and distinct demonstration of the truth of the 'general rule' is, of course, one that Descartes has ready to hand: enter the proofs of God. The Third Meditation initially takes up questions to do with the existence of a God as means of heightening our doubts about the reliability of past certainties (and indeed of making these doubts more vivid and alarming). So, the meditator comments, 'I later judged that there was no other ground for doubting those things [which I see with intuitive clarity] than that it occurred to me that perhaps some God could have endowed me with such a nature that I should even be deceived about those things which seem most manifest'; and, if there were an omnipotent God, 'it would be easy for him to bring it to pass that I should be mistaken even about those things which I think I intuit as evidently as possible in my mind's eyes' (AT VII 36). However, the main purpose of these speculations

is soon made clear. The meditator does not propose to examine these doubts in a neutral way. His concern is to remove them as a matter of the highest priority: 'But so that this [reason for doubting which supposes a deceiving God] may also be removed [*tollatur*], as soon as occasion arises, I must examine whether there is a God, and, if there is, whether he can be a deceiver, for whilst I am ignorant of this thing, I do not seem ever to be able to be fully certain of any other' (AT VII 36).

So the meditator sets out on to the familiar line of argument in order to establish that we can have actual clear and distinct perceptions, certified by natural light: (i) that there is an infinitely perfect God;[31] (ii) that he is the author of our nature (i.e. of our mental faculties); and (iii) that he is truthful. And from these premisses, the meditator, in continuous deduction, can find the further actual clear and distinct conclusions, certified by natural light: (iv) that, when, in so far as we can possibly tell, we use our faculties rightly, they cannot be a source of error;[32] and (v) that, because we use our faculties rightly when we give our unconditional assent to clear and distinct perceptions, the proposition 'everything is true which I perceive very clearly and distinctly' is not merely a 'rule', but is certainly true. Even though the meditator had his doubts about the reliability of clear and distinct perceptions before embarking upon this proof, and even though he had been worried about the possibility of a deceiving God, these doubts could not be entertained whilst he was actually intuiting the proof itself and whilst he was under the indomitable influence of natural light. And by the time he had finished his proof he had at his disposal an invincible certainty of the reliability of clear and distinct perceptions, which would make further doubts about them psychologically impossible.[33]

[31] In 1630 Descartes was worried that we might be deceived in our rational judgements because the truth itself could be changeable. In so far as I can tell, this specific worry is not present in the *Meditationes*. But, in any case, because God must be the author of all truth and because an infinitely perfect God must be immutable, the proof of the existence of such a God is enough to dispel doubts of this kind.

[32] Following Doney, some commentators have suggested that Descartes's comments on the possibility that our natural faculties may be delusive refer to the fallibility of memory. As I read the *Meditationes*, this is never in fact an issue for Descartes. Nevertheless, the proof of the necessary reliability of all our faculties would clearly cover possible doubts of this kind.

[33] The nature of this psychological certainty would mean that the meditator could not even entertain (*pace* Frankfurt, 'Descartes on the Consistency of Reason', 38) the possibility of an alternative proof demonstrating the existence of a demon, even though this may be a *logically* conceivable possibility.

On this view, then, the primary function of the proofs of God is nothing more than to allow us to remove retrospective doubts about the reliability of the natural light. They serve only to make our certainties permanent. That Descartes conceives of the proofs of God as a device of this kind is perhaps best shown by a letter to Regius of May 1640. Since the letter also draws out the epistemological consequences of Descartes's position, it is worth citing at some length:

you say 'the truth of clearly and distinctly understood axioms is manifest in itself'; indeed I concede that this is so, for as long as these axioms are being clearly and distinctly understood, because our mind is of such a nature that it cannot fail to assent to things which have been clearly understood; but because we often remember conclusions derived from premises of this kind even when we do not attend to the premises themselves, I say that in these cases, if we are ignorant of God, we can imagine [*fingere*] them being uncertain, even though we remember that they were deduced from clear premises; because we are, to be sure, perhaps of such a nature that we may be mistaken about the most evident things; and from that time forward, indeed immediately after we have deduced these things from those principles, we should have not so much a knowledge [*scientiam*] of them, as merely a persuasion [*persuasionem*]. These two terms I distinguish thus: that there is *persuasio* when there remains some reason that could force us to doubt; but *scientia* is a *persuasio* by means of such a strong reason, that it could never be shaken. But for anyone who has once understood the reasons which persuade him [*persuadent*] that God exists and that he is not a deceiver, even when he no longer attends to those reasons, but only remembers this conclusion: *Deus non est fallax*, there will remain in him not merely a *persuasio*, but a true *scientia* both of this conclusion, and also of all other conclusions for which he will have once clearly perceived the reasons. (AT III 64–5)

Our 'persuasion' that God exists and is not a deceiver is important because (implying the truth of the 'general rule') it serves to transform this and other 'persuasions' into 'scientific knowledge'. The pedigree of the term *scientia* might suggest that it is meant to denote absolute knowledge.[34] Yet from the context in which Descartes uses the term, it is apparent that his *scientia* is no more than a permanently indubitable human belief. And an obligation to believe something, even an unshakeable obligation, is no guarantee of its absolute truth. Descartes appears to have redefined 'scientific knowledge' to mean that set of

---

[34] The philosophical use of the term *scientia* derives primarily from Latin editions of the works of Aristotle. 'Scientific knowledge' is defined in the *Posterior Analytics* I. 2, 71^b.

certainties, of whose reliability we are naturally obliged to be totally persuaded.[35]

Even though the persuasive proofs of God make a major contribution to Descartes's epistemology by offering us permanent certainty, they cannot change these certainties into absolute knowledge as such. They cannot make human reason autonomous. But because permanent certainties are all that is available to human beings, endowed with ordinary human faculties, and because we must always *believe* that these certainties correspond to reality as it actually is, we can describe the world in total confidence and without fear of error. For all practical purposes our certainties will perform as if they were true knowledge. Even so, in the end our *scientia* can only ever amount to what one might call 'virtual knowledge', rather than the full-blown 'absolute' variety.

14. But perhaps we can take Descartes's argument one stage further. So far we have considered the Third Meditation essentially as an exercise in phenomenology, describing and investigating what it is like to experience natural light and what it is like subsequently to reflect upon this experience. On this account, the proofs of God are reduced to the status of a heuristic device. They are particular patterns of human thought, mere useful arguments, allowing us to establish our capacity for achieving 'virtual knowledge' of reality. However, the *Meditationes* is a densely written text in which a variety of themes unfold simultaneously. It admits of a range of different interpretations according to which of these themes we emphasize.

One of the more conspicuous features of the *Meditationes* is its interweaving of epistemological and properly *ontological* concerns. A fairly straightforward interpretation of the Third Meditation sees in it the meditator's project of discovering what other certainties about reality he can achieve besides that of his own existence as *res cogitans*. A total persuasion of the existence of God is, in this context, not just the premiss from which we happen to be able to deduce the reliability of our mental faculties. It is also an important ontological conclusion in its own right: a significant discovery about how we must see the world.

---

[35] At the start of the Third Meditation, Descartes lists the things which he 'knows', using the verb *scire*. This list includes the proposition *ego sum res cogitans* (AT VII 34–5). Presumably the point is that, because we cannot even think of such propositions without re-intuiting them, they are invulnerable to retrospective doubt and therefore count as *scientia* under Descartes's definition, even before the proofs of God. The letter to Regius makes it clear that, despite the use of the language of *scientia*, we should not suppose that the Cogito is an item of absolute knowledge.

If we adopt an 'ontological' reading of the Third Meditation, something more than (or at least different from) 'virtual knowledge' becomes possible. By performing the proofs of God for ourselves, we find that we are of such a nature that we must think that as a matter of fact there exists independently of us a truthful God who is author of our being. This is, of course, only a permanent persuasion, an item of 'virtual knowledge', which could in principle be absolutely false. However, we can surely convert this human certainty into a meta-physical hypothesis. We can say, 'let us suppose that a truthful God of this sort really does exist from an absolute point of view'. On this hypothesis, the reliability of our mental faculties and the truthfulness of clear and distinct perceptions would no longer be mere permanent psychological certainties. They would be transformed into necessary deductive conclusions, valid even from an absolute perspective.

As a supplement to 'virtual knowledge', we can tentatively ascribe to Descartes the ontologist a theory of 'hypothetical knowledge'. However, this constitutes a much firmer epistemological base than that provided by *Le Monde*'s earlier forays into hypothetical constructions of reality. The hypothesis that a truthful God exists is not randomly selected, nor is it arrived at a posteriori, justified only by its explanatory power. Rather the hypothesis in question is one to which all human beings are, by their very nature, obliged to assent. Because we see clearly and distinctly that a truthful God exists and because we are certain of the reliability of such perceptions, Descartes's hypothesis would be an example of the strongest sort of belief of which human beings are naturally capable. We could interpret the *Meditationes* as involving the argument that, *if* a truthful God exists, as everyone in fact is psychologically obliged to believe, then, whenever we use our mental apparatus aright, our beliefs must correspond to reality as it actually is from an absolute perspective.

15. The textual evidence suggests that Descartes himself favours the scheme of 'virtual knowledge' rather than a 'hypothetical' variation upon it. But the choice between the two makes no more than a tactical difference to the way in which we interpret the overall epistemological claims of the *Meditationes*. In either case, human beings are incapable of an independent rational mastery of the universe. All that is available to us are unshakeable psychological certainties and hypothetical truths. And, even in the pursuit of such qualified forms of knowledge as these, Descartes insists that we remain tied to the condition of dependent creatures. He finds that our firmest persuasions are not born of human

intellect alone, but stem from a fruitful co-operation between our understanding and a 'God-given' natural light which can be described on analogy with divine grace (AT VII 147–8);[36] and he shows that our ability to translate these persuasions into 'virtual' or 'hypothetical' knowledge comes only through a further persuasion that God exists and is infinitely perfect.

In 1630 Descartes had engaged in his critique of logical and mathematical necessity as an expression of disquiet about the implicit atheism of contemporary intellectual fashions. He hoped that 'the world might become accustomed to hear God spoken of more worthily' (AT I 146). These letters remind us that seventeenth-century epistemology was as much part of theology as of humane philosophy. And perhaps it is Descartes's continuing sensitivity to theological issues that best accounts for his subsequent theories of knowledge, as I have sketched them. He seems to ask whether it is possible to be both a good Christian and a good philosopher. At its most positive, the *Meditationes* suggests that, if we once abandon our claims to rational autonomy and acquiesce in our submission to God, we can still construct an account of reality whose truthfulness will be as certain as anyone could possibly desire. But still this promises no more than maximal psychological certainty. Perhaps with divine assistance the good philosopher can reach the very brink of absolute knowledge, but the final transition must remain forever beyond human powers.

---

[36] See also the letter to 'Hyperaspistes' of August 1640 (AT III 425–6). These references pose tantalizing questions about the precise relationship between philosophical beliefs and revealed articles of faith. Descartes's theory ought to establish a direct analogy, in terms of their epistemological status, between revealed and rational knowledge. Such a theory might suitably safeguard the faith against atheistic rationalism and (just as important) protect natural philosophy against the theologians.

7

Truth, Error, and the Order of Reasons: Descartes's Puzzling Synopsis of the Fourth Meditation

DONALD A. CRESS

After he had decided to publish his *Meditations on First Philosophy*, Descartes sent pre-publication copies of the work to several philosophers and theologians who were asked to study it and to forward to him their queries and objections (letter to Mersenne of 13 November 1639: AT II 622, CSMK 141; letter to Mersenne of 30 July 1640: AT III 126–7, CSMK 149–50; letter to Mersenne of 30 September 1640: AT III 183–4, CSMK 153). Eventually Descartes decided to append these queries and objections to the printed edition of the *Meditations*, along with his own replies to each set of queries and objections (letter to Mersenne of 24 December 1640: AT III 265–7, CSMK 163–4). Descartes had hoped that, by raising and answering in advance problems voiced by learned critics in their own words, he could pave the way for greater acceptance of the method and the doctrines espoused in his *Meditations*. Moreover, to assist them in locating various doctrines and arguments and in better grasping the work's order of reasons, Descartes forwarded to his readers an abstract which would eventually become the Synopsis that has accompanied the printed editions of the *Meditations* (letter to Mersenne of 24 December 1640: AT III 268, CSMK 164; letter to Mersenne of 31 December 1640: AT III 271–2, CSMK 165).

Such a finding-aid is particularly welcome, given the fact that Descartes's order of reasons is somewhat complicated by recapitulations that seem to contain more or to advance a line of reasoning further than the original discussions themselves. Thus the question of where Descartes first formulated or established this or that claim at times becomes a bit clouded. A case in point is whether clear and distinct ideas actually came to be doubted in the First Meditation.[1] We do not find it explicitly enunciated in the First Meditation, yet a subsequent recapitulation seems to presume that clear and distinct perceptions were in fact subjected to doubt in the First Meditation (AT VII 35–6; CSM II 24–5). Given this interpretive challenge, it is well to pay closer attention to the argumentative finding-aid which Descartes has left us.

The portion of the Synopsis upon which I will focus in this chapter is Descartes's brief sketch of the Fourth Meditation. This portion of the Synopsis is particularly challenging in that Descartes presented in it some rather remarkable claims regarding both the content and the role of the Fourth Meditation in the analytic order of reasons of the *Meditations*. Such a study is overdue, especially given the fact that Cartesian scholarship has not generally paid a great deal of attention to the Fourth Meditation or to Descartes's own appraisal of its role in the overall order of reasons.[2] In this chapter I will indicate several of the questions that need to be asked about the Fourth Meditation, the Synopsis, and Descartes's own understanding of the role of the Fourth Meditation in the overall order of reasons in the *Meditations*.

By the end of the Third Meditation we are provided with what Descartes considered to be solid grounds for holding that a supremely good God exists and that, as a consequence, there is no all-powerful deceiver (AT VII 51–2; CSM II 35). Nevertheless, Descartes remained acutely aware of the fact that these conclusions were at apparent odds with the very difficulties that had initially delivered him to the depths of scepticism and which eventually brought him to acknowledge the existence of a supremely good God (AT VII 53–4; CSM II 37–8). So it remained to answer the question: if in fact God is all good and if we have not been given a dedicated faculty of erring, then how could we, as creatures endowed by this God with intellect, fall *even once* into the sorts of errors in judgement chronicled in the First Meditation (AT VII 53–4; CSM II 37–8)?[3]

[1] On the basis of a close reading of the First Meditation, Harry G. Frankfurt has argued that clear and distinct perceptions do not become the target of the methodic doubt in the First Meditation, owing to the fact that clear and distinct perceptions are not discussed there. See his *Demons, Dreamers and Madmen*.

[2] Martial Gueroult's treatment of the Fourth Meditation in vol. i of his *Descartes selon l'ordre des raisons* is virtually the sole exception to this generalization.

[3] In addition to displaying these errors, the First Meditation also anticipates the theodical problem they entail (AT VII 21; CSM II 14).

Some readers might view the Fourth Meditation as a moment of consolidation in the analytic order of reasons wherein an attempt is made to reconcile the results of the Third Meditation with the sorts of errors which mark the starting-point of the First Meditation. In other words, the Fourth Meditation's primary objective is to show how a God who is all good could have made a finite intellectual creature that errs. Thus the Fourth Meditation might be seen as a special-case theodicy, a justification of the epistemic ways of God to man. And because the Fourth Meditation is taken to be a moment of consolidation, it might even be said to constitute a break or a respite, rather than a fresh advance in the analytic order of reasons. But what does the Synopsis tell us?

In the Fourth Meditation it is proved that everything that we clearly and distinctly perceive is true, and I also explain what the nature of falsity consists in. These results need to be known both in order to confirm what has gone before [*ad praecedentia firmanda*] and also to make intelligible what is to come later [*ad reliqua intelligenda*]. (But here it should be noted in passing that I do not deal at all with sin, i.e., the error which is committed in pursuing good and evil, but only with the error that occurs in distinguishing truth from falsehood. And there is no discussion of matters pertaining to faith or the conduct of life, but simply of speculative truths which are known solely by means of the natural light.) (AT VII 15; CSM II 11)

Contrary to what one might expect, there is no mention of any special-case theodicy of error; we are told nothing about any reconciliation of the primordial fact of error with the conclusion that an infinitely perfect God exists. Nor are we led to believe that the Fourth Meditation represents a respite or a consolidation of gains made in the analytic order of reasons prior to the Fourth Meditation. Instead we are told that two things will take place in the Fourth Meditation: first, it will be proved that everything that we clearly and distinctly perceive is true; secondly, the nature of falsity will be explained. Moreover, we are told that these two doctrines need to be known both to confirm what had gone before (presumably the first three Meditations) as well as to render intelligible what is to come later (presumably the last two Meditations). At the specific urging of Antoine Arnauld, author of the Fourth Set of Objections, Descartes added parenthetically that he would consider only those errors that are committed in distinguishing truth from falsehood, when the matter at hand is purely speculative and is knowable by means of the natural light of reason alone (letter to Mersenne of 18 March 1641, AT III 334–5:

CSMK 175). Moreover, Descartes specifically put the reader on notice that he was not about to deal with certain issues—namely sin, matters pertaining to faith, and matters pertaining to the practical conduct of life.[4] Let us review the elements of this synopsis more carefully.

I. Topics Treated in the Fourth Meditation

We are informed that it is in the Fourth Meditation that Descartes will prove that 'everything that we clearly and distinctly perceive is true'. This, of course, is what we find in the Latin text; the French translation reads somewhat differently: 'everything that we *very* clearly and *very* distinctly perceive is true' (AT IXA 11; emphasis added). I am not prepared to argue that the Latin text and the French translation are making two distinct claims. It would be stretching the point to claim that Descartes himself took clarity and distinctness to be all or nothing, whereas the French translation has clarity and distinctness admitting of degrees. Descartes's many enunciations of the criterion of clarity and distinctness are much too fluid for so strong a reading. As a matter of fact, there are passages in Descartes's own words, both in the *Discourse* as well as in the Latin text of the *Meditations*, which do express the criterion of clarity and distinctness in terms of degrees.[5]

But I am most concerned here with Descartes's claim that it is in the Fourth Meditation that the criterion of clarity and distinctness, however it is worded, is first established. Recall, too, that the synopsis of the Second Meditation had gone so far as to claim that, prior to the Fourth Meditation, it was not *possible* to prove that what I clearly and distinctly perceive is true (AT VII 13; CSM II 9). Thus we are clearly put on notice by Descartes that the criterion of clarity and distinctness was not and could not have been proved until the Fourth Meditation, that some necessary condition would be fulfilled in the Fourth Meditation that had not and could not have been fulfilled previously in the *Meditations*, such that the criterion of clarity and

---

[4] See also the Second Replies, (AT VII 148–9; CSM II 106).
[5] See e.g. the Fifth Meditation (AT VII 69; CSM II 48): 'Admittedly my nature is such that so long as I perceive something very [*valde*] clearly and distinctly I cannot but believe it to be true.'

distinctness could at last be established.[6] Thus a proper discernment of Descartes's own understanding of the analytic order of reasons in the *Meditations* requires a closer reading of the Synopsis.

The Synopsis further states that a second result will have been achieved in the Fourth Meditation—namely, the nature of falsity will have been explained. Now anyone expecting a sustained and systematic treatment of falsity comparable, say, either to Q. 17 of Part One of Aquinas's *Summa theologiae* or to Suárez's Ninth *Metaphysical Disputation* will be rather disappointed. Despite the importance given to the definition of falsity in the Synopsis and despite the prominence of falsity in the title of the Fourth Meditation, Descartes's analysis of falsity is anything but systematic and sustained. Scattered throughout the Fourth Meditation are sketchy remarks to the effect that falsity is an instance of non-being, that it is a 'privation', a lack of something that by rights ought to have been present (AT VII 60–1; CSM II 42).[7] Nowhere in the Fourth Meditation do all of these pieces come together in anything like a sustained and systematic analysis; moreover, these scattered, almost off-handed remarks raise a number of questions in their own right. But even if we focus instead on the role played by this account of falsity in the order of reasons, we have to admit that Descartes's explanation of falsity, such as it is, is not actually argued for; it is merely taken for granted. Alternative explanations are not so much as mentioned, let alone demonstrated to be false.

It also remains for Descartes to establish the relationship of this explanation of error to his proof of the criterion of clarity and distinctness.[8] Moreover, even though the Synopsis makes no mention of a theodical role for the Fourth Meditation, we do find in the Sixth Meditation (AT VII 83; CSM II 58) that Descartes believed such a theodical analysis to have previously taken place. But most important, how does this all too brief, incomplete, and unsubstantiated discussion of falsity 'confirm' the First, Second, and Third Meditations or render the Fifth and Sixth Meditations 'intelligible'?

Finally, Descartes's discussion of falsity in the Fourth Meditation

---

[6] In his *Descartes: An Analytical and Historical Introduction*, Georges Dicker claims, without taking the Synopsis into account, that the criterion of clarity and distinctness is established in the Third Meditation.

[7] This equating of truth with being and falsity with non-being is discussed by Étienne Gilson in his edition of *Discours de la méthode*, 317, 363–5.

[8] In the Second Replies (AT VII 148–9; CSM II 106) Descartes refers to the Fourth Meditation as the place 'where I was looking into the cause of falsity'. No mention is made there of the criterion of clarity and distinctness.

is intended not only to instruct one about the nature of error but also to provide concrete guidance in avoiding error (AT VII 59–60; CSM II 41). It might appear at first blush that it is Descartes's explanation of falsity rather than any practical advice about error-avoidance that is called upon to confirm what had come before and to render intelligible what is to follow. Nevertheless, earlier remarks in the Fourth Meditation (AT VII 53–4; CSM II 37–8) make it quite clear that the proper use of one's cognitive faculties is a critical component of his theodicy.

II. The Role of the Fourth Meditation in the Order of Reasons

The proof of the criterion of clarity and distinctness and the explanation of the nature of falsity are said to confirm what had gone before. If 'confirm' means to provide essential evidentiary support, we might first ask whether these two points are needed to 'confirm' *all* that had gone before or just certain particular teachings contained in the First, Second, and Third Meditations. And if just some, then *which* ones? This is critical, for, if we are speaking not about ancillary discussions but about critical components of the analytic order of reasons, then the allegedly firm and certain foundations upon which the positive conclusions of the early Meditations rest are clearly compromised. If the Fourth Meditation arises of necessity through the order of reasons established in the First, Second, and Third Meditations, then the Fourth Meditation cannot possibly be called upon to provide confirmation for the First, Second, and Third Meditations without begging the question.

Indeed, if 'confirmation' means critically needed corroboration, then the relevant components of the Fourth Meditation would have to be known to be true independently of the First, Second, and Third Meditations—i.e. the Fourth Meditation would have to be knowable independently of the analytic order of reasons and hence must be known to be true independently of the natural light of reason. But, if the natural light of reason is not its source, then it is a matter either of faith or of wrongly formed preconceived notions (*praejudicia*), and thus constitutes a gross violation of Cartesian methodology.

On the other hand, if 'confirmation' means merely the provision of additional optional support of some unspecified nature, this strong language of 'confirmation' is unwarranted. Whatever 'confirmation' might mean, it clearly seems to be regarded by Descartes as something very critical to the order of reasons. If we take the Synopsis at face value, the Fourth Meditation has to be more than a mere interlude, a time-out in the analytic order of reasons. This 'confirmation' must mean more than merely a moment in which the reader takes stock of what has transpired and focuses particularly on the reconciliation of the fact of human error described in the First Meditation with the fact of divine goodness established in the Third Meditation. This latter hardly qualifies as a 'confirmation' in any usual sense of the term.

A third reading of *ad praecedentia firmanda* would seem to be called for. Let us suppose that a child is having difficulty with mathematics. The child is able to succeed in mathematics, but only with considerable encouragement and assistance from her parents and considerable investment of time on her own part. The child moves on to college, where she decides to major in physics, a subject in which she now excels. She reports to her parents that her success in college is a clear confirmation of the wisdom of her long hours of study and of their having taken the time to give her help and encouragement. Success in college could not have happened without those earlier sacrifices; it does show the *wisdom* of making those efforts of previous years.

The Fourth Meditation does not provide needed proof for the positive claims of the first three Meditations, for no additional proof is needed; nor, for that matter, could any independent proof be adduced. On the other hand, the Fourth Meditation is no mere interlude in the order of reasons wherein previous philosophical gains are merely consolidated. I would instead claim that the Fourth Meditation 'confirms' the first three Meditations in the sense that it shows the worthwhileness or the wisdom of entering into the sceptical doubts of the First Meditation and of the methodology observed in the First and Second Meditations. In short, it provides a certain 'pragmatic' justification for what had preceded it.

The second role assigned by the Synopsis to the Fourth Meditation is to 'render intelligible what is to follow'. Paralleling the degrees of clarity and distinctness indicated in the French translation, we also find in the French translation degrees of intelligibility: the Fourth Meditation is needed in order to make what follows *more* intelligible (AT IXA 11). I am not entirely certain what to make of this discrepancy between the Latin and French versions, but it should be noted. The more important question, however, is the sense in which these discussions of the criterion of clarity and distinctness and the nature of falsity are necessary in order to render the remaining two Meditations 'intelligible' or, if you will, 'more intelligible' (following de Luynes).

We can easily imagine the intelligibility of the Fifth and Sixth Meditations being impaired through one's failure to study either the First Meditation or the Second Meditation or the Third Meditation, but what about the Fourth Meditation? One is hard pressed to make the same case. Moreover, one could claim that Descartes's proof of the criterion of clarity and distinctness might just as well have been incorporated into the Third Meditation.[9] One might also make the somewhat hostile observation that, since no justification is given for his explanation of falsity, Descartes could have inserted that discussion virtually anywhere.

So in what sense do the remaining two Meditations really *require* these two teachings in order to be made intelligible? And what role does the remainder of the Fourth Meditation (e.g. the theodicy of error, the psychology of judgement, the infinity of the human will, the practical advice on error avoidance) have to play in rendering intelligible what is to follow? If it turns out that the Fourth Meditation is not an organized body of philosophically argued claims playing a pivotal role in the analytical order of reasons, but instead is found to be a loose collection of secularized religious claims and theologically inspired philosophical claims that are not rationally argued for, then what precise contribution could the Fourth Meditation be *expected* to make to the order of reasons? Just why did Descartes assign such importance to the Fourth Meditation? He wrote the Synopsis prior to any polemical exchanges; it was not written in the heat of battle. He was under no pressure to exaggerate the importance of the Fourth

---

[9] Throughout his *Descartes: An Analytical and Historical Introduction*, Georges Dicker operates on the assumption that it is in the Third Meditation that Descartes established the criterion of clarity and distinctness. Dicker's book lacks a formal treatment of the Fourth Meditation; it clearly remains for Dicker to explain away Descartes's own explicit statement of where the criterion is established.

It is fair to ask where in the Fourth Meditation Descartes actually provides a proof of the claim that all I clearly and distinctly perceive is true. One seems to search in vain until one finally reaches the final paragraph of the Fourth Meditation, wherein Descartes recapitulated what had just taken place in the Fourth Meditation. I believe the most explicit validation of the criterion of clarity and distinctness is to be found in that recapitulation. Admittedly this paragraph seems designed to recapitulate previous developments; nevertheless, it actually is much more tightly organized and far more explicit than the very discussions it was to summarize.

Meditation; in fact, but for Gassendi and Hobbes, the Fourth Meditation was largely ignored by Descartes's critics.

Finally there is the somewhat awkward empirical fact: many readers, indeed many teachers of the *Meditations*, routinely skip the Fourth Meditation and believe themselves (and their students) none the worse for wear.[10] Such readers certainly believe themselves to have survived this alleged intelligibility gap quite handily. Clearly the Fifth and Sixth Meditations are not so utterly bereft of intelligibility that they simply cannot be understood without the Fourth Meditation. One could conceivably skip over the Fourth Meditation and plausibly believe one is in a position to grasp both the content and the structure of the Fifth and Sixth Meditations. Just what then are we to make of Descartes's claim that the Fourth Meditation plays an essential role in rendering the Fifth and Sixth Meditations 'intelligible'?

III. Topics not Treated in the Fourth Meditation

There are plausible grounds for asserting that, apart from the explanation of the nature of falsity and the validation of the criterion of clarity and distinctness, the bulk of the Fourth Meditation constitutes a quasi-theological interlude in the analytic order of the *Meditations*. First, the principal components of the theodicy contained in the Fourth Meditation historically were once religious doctrines or, perhaps more accurately, religiously inspired philosophical doctrines for which philosophical arguments were later developed. But the important thing to note is that, whether philosophical or theological in nature, they are presented in the Fourth Meditation without proof. Descartes virtually takes it for granted that falsity is non-being or a privation; that he is a creature made *ex nihilo* through divine power; that what is a privation to him is merely a negation to God; that God is not subject to the same moral duties and obligations as we humans are; that he has no right to complain that God has not given to every creature the perfections enjoyed by the noblest; that he has no right to complain that he has not received every perfection that he could imagine for himself; that he, who lacks a full and complete understanding of the cosmos, has no right to complain about God's

---

[10] Georges Dicker, *Descartes: An Analytical and Historical Introduction*, is but the most recent example of this approach.

goodness in particular cases. In short, Descartes presents straightaway
and without proof an anti-Manichaean metaphysics.

Nevertheless, to this point Descartes knows only that God and he
exist; he knows nothing with certainty about whether human morality
is or is not binding upon God; moreover, he knows nothing about
whether there even is a larger cosmic context in which he unknowingly
does or does not play a part. (One may indeed wonder how Descartes
can doubt whether there is a world outside him and at the same time
speak about a complex cosmos in which he plays but a small part and
where privations are, from the correct perspective, only negations.)

In any event, these allegedly spontaneous outpourings of a historically disengaged natural light of reason were originally formulated only
slowly and with considerable difficulty over many centuries by numerous religious thinkers and largely brought to completion in Augustine.[11]
Recall the long and difficult road travelled even by Augustine, as he
slowly developed his own mature understanding of the nature and
origin of evil, an understanding strikingly similar to Descartes's
handling of the nature and origin of the problem of error. To claim
that these theodical components, supplied without proof, are the
spontaneous outpourings of the natural light of reason exhibits a
certain lack of historical awareness. At the very least, the Fourth
Meditation seems to indicate an inability on Descartes's part to
distinguish what had become second nature to him from what
supposedly is innate.[12] This betrays a curious ignorance of both the
intellectual struggles of his predecessors as well as the essentially
communal and theological nature of their enterprise, despite the fact
that many of the doctrines themselves are intrinsically philosophical
and ones for which philosophical arguments were eventually developed. Of course, looking at the matter from the point of view of the
analytical order of reasons, we are inclined to ask where, regardless of
their origins, we are to find the arguments for these theodical
components.

Now, if the theodical components of the Fourth Meditation—be
they intrinsically theological or theological merely in the sense of their
having originated in a theological context—are put forward without

---

[11] I say 'largely', because Augustine did not draw a sharp distinction between
negations and privations. In fact, there is but one passage in his writings in which
Augustine suggests that evil is the lack of an *owed* good.

[12] This, of course, is the observation made by Mersenne in the Second Objections
(AT VII 124; CSM II 88–9).

philosophical arguments to support them, then Descartes has contradicted his own remarks in the Dedicatory Letter, wherein he stated that the *Meditations* would proceed on the basis of reason alone, so as to avoid giving scandal to the infidel (AT VII 2; CSM II 3–4). Moreover, the Synopsis informed us that the Fourth Meditation would treat error only in matters which are speculative and are known solely by means of the natural light of reason. It would appear that, by Descartes's own words, the Fourth Meditation is pivotal in the analytic order of reasons of the *Meditations*. Nevertheless, Descartes seems to violate the prime directive of his own methodology when he makes unfounded theodical claims in the Fourth Meditation, even when they are intrinsically philosophical. Given all this, we have every reason to be troubled about Descartes's remark that the Fourth Meditation 'confirms' the First, Second, and Third Meditations or renders the Fifth and Sixth Meditations intelligible.

All that Descartes told us in the Synopsis was that he would provide a proof of the criterion of clarity and distinctness and an explanation of the nature of falsity. And these two points were what Descartes declared to be the basis for the confirmation of the First, Second, and Third Meditations and the illumination of the Fifth and Sixth Meditations. As we noted previously, he was silent in the Synopsis about his theodicy. Perhaps we should simply take Descartes at his word: what matters, what really counts, in the Fourth Meditation is precisely what Descartes told us in the Synopsis—and not the theodicy, whose components are presented in a somewhat unsystematic fashion and without proof. Of course, if we adopt this approach, we do need to explain the remark in the Sixth Meditation (AT VII 83; CSM II 58) to the effect that a theodical discussion had previously taken place. If we take him at his word, we may well wonder just what the point of the theodicy is, beyond filling the obvious need for a reconciliation of the First Meditation and the Third Meditation, but at least we would not be tempted to view the theodicy as undermining the order of reasons.

What matters to the order of reasons is the establishment of the criterion of clarity and distinctness and the explanation of the nature of falsity, not the theodicy. But it would be helpful if we could determine the relationship these two matters have to the Fourth Meditation's theodical components. Just how are the Fourth Meditation's more theologically inspired philosophical components related, if at all, to the philosophical project of establishing the criterion of clarity and distinctness and of explaining the nature of falsity? Somehow the Fourth Meditation is to confirm the First, Second, and Third Meditations; somehow the Fourth Meditation is to illuminate the Fifth and Sixth Meditations. Descartes tells us that it is the discussion of the criterion of clarity and distinctness and the nature of falsity which accomplish this.

Having defined sin as 'the error which is committed in pursuing good and evil', Descartes went on to state that he was not going to treat sin, matters of faith, or the practical conduct of life in the course of the Fourth Meditation. It was somewhat redundant for him to have specifically mentioned sin, since sin is at once a theological notion as well as a matter involving the practical conduct of life. Presumably Descartes believed his method to be neutral with respect to matters of faith. When Descartes asked the question 'why does a God who is all good permit him to commit errors?', he elected to answer this question by drawing heavily upon Augustinian teachings, while prescinding from the one doctrine that is the centrepiece of Augustinian theodicy and without which, at least to Augustine's way of thinking, one does not have a theodicy—namely, sin.

No contemporaneous Augustinian would have any difficulty recognizing that the theodicy contained in the Fourth Meditation possesses a distinctly Augustinian complexion. In fact, it is remarkable just how closely Descartes's explanation of falsity parallels major components of the Augustinian account of evil.[13] The Fourth Meditation made full use of virtually every major theme in Augustine's theodicy with the important exception of sin. What also would have caught our Augustinian's attention was the historically conditioned 'tilt' of the natural light of reason: throughout the Fourth Meditation (in fact throughout the *Meditations* generally) the utterances of the natural light almost invariably appear to be Augustinian in nature. But an Augustinian theodicy without sin is unthinkable. Augustine's doctrine of sin informs the whole of his theodicy. Without it there simply is no Augustinian theodicy.

Our Augustinian might well have wondered why, if he went this far with Augustine's theodicy, Descartes did not allow sin to enter his account of the origin and nature of error, for, our Augustinian might

---

[13] The one point of divergence, admittedly a significant one, is that Augustine uses the terms 'non-being', 'negation', and 'privation' interchangeably. A rigorous distinction between privation and negation, such as one finds in Thomas Aquinas, is simply not to be found in Augustine.

argue, error is adequately explained only in the larger context of the problem of evil, a context in which sin clearly plays a prominent role as a proximate cause. Remove sin from Augustine's account of the origin of evil and our Augustinian might well wonder whether one any longer had an orthodox, let alone Augustinian, account of the origin of evil or any clue as to how to reconcile divine goodness with the fact of evil. For Augustine, sin is an essential ingredient in explaining the twin facts of evil and error. To account for the origin and possibility of error in the absence of an appeal to sin is, in an Augustinian context, at least rather remarkable. Augustine would have agreed with Descartes that part of the explanation of the origin of error is to be found in the fact that we have been created from nothing. But Augustine made it abundantly clear in his anti-Manichaean writings that creation from nothing is an insufficient explanation of evil and error.[14] Failure to include sin as a necessary condition of evil would place the entire burden of explaining evil and error on the sheer fact of createdness, which, to Augustine at least, would not be orthodox teaching.

Descartes is, of course, perfectly free to be as much or as little an Augustinian as he wishes. In and of itself, there is nothing decisive about the observation of having assimilated all but one feature of Augustinian theodicy of evil into one's own theodicy of error. However, Descartes had made it clear that, although he would appeal to nothing but the natural light of reason, nothing in his philosophy would be contrary to true religion. Herein lies his problem; granted it is a theological problem, but it remains a problem none the less.

It is highly problematic how one is to attempt a complete and coherent theodicy by appropriating all of the *other* components of Augustine's theodicy while refraining for methodological reasons from any mention of the most important one: sin. Nevertheless, Descartes made it quite clear in the Synopsis that he was not going to treat sin in the course of the Fourth Meditation. The real question is, of course, not whether Descartes was a consistent and faithful Augustinian, but whether his partial Augustinianism is fully up to the task of providing a coherent and complete explanation of origin of falsity.

Again, when we note that so much of the theodicy of the Fourth Meditation is enunciated in the absence of proof, it seems too much

[14] See D. Cress, 'Creation *De Nihilo* and St. Augustine's Account of Evil in *Contra Secundum Juliani Responsionem Imperfectum Opus*, Book V'.

to accept the Cartesian claim that this theodicy is derived exclusively from the natural light of reason. This is especially so in view of the fact that the more general theodicy of evil from which the theodical components of the Fourth Meditation are based evolved slowly over time thanks to the contributions of many thinkers and, *pace* Plotinus, received its principal inspiration from theological rather than philosophical speculation. One marvels at the poignant account in his *Confessions* of Augustine's slow painstaking construction of this theory of the nature and origin of evil. Nevertheless, the chief components of Augustine's mature theodicy flow from Descartes's pen as truths of the natural light of reason, the sole source of knowledge. Mersenne was right: what his schooling had made second nature to Descartes was transformed into the deliverances of the natural light of reason (Second Set of Objections: AT VII 124; CSM II 88–9).

But for the fact that he occasionally committed errors, Descartes informs us he would have had no basis for judging himself to be finite. Perhaps our Augustinian might have observed that this admission is ironically the beginning of an answer as to why an infinitely perfect God would make a finite thinking thing that commits errors; however, such an observation would take us in a decidedly theological direction. Why would an infinitely perfect deity create a being endowed with a natural desire to know which occasionally commits errors? For that matter, why would an infinitely perfect deity create a being which has a natural desire to know, but which is not from the beginning in total possession of all truth? Why must one progress only slowly and fitfully from one truth to another? Why would such a God make one's cognitional life such a struggle, with or without the actual commission of errors? Descartes himself seems to take us in that same theological direction: 'I have no right to complain . . .'

I have drawn attention to certain rhetorical and philosophical problems inherent in discerning the order of reasons in the *Meditations*. I pointed out that, even though Descartes intended the Synopsis as an argumentative finding-aid to assist readers in locating arguments and in discerning more clearly the order of reasons in the *Meditations*, the Synopsis raises its own share of questions even as it reveals to us how Descartes in fact viewed the order of reasons.

The Synopsis raises major issues regarding the role of the Fourth Meditation in the overall argumentative structure of the *Meditations*. We are told that in the Fourth Meditation there would be (*a*) a proof of the maxim that all I clearly and distinctly perceive is true, and (*b*) an explanation of the nature of falsity. Descartes then informs us that 'these results need to be known both in order to confirm what has gone before and also to make intelligible what is to come later' (AT VII 15; CSM II 11). I take it that, when Descartes stated that the Fourth Meditation 'confirms' what preceded it, we should understand this confirmation to mean not a proof in any strict sense, but a further elaboration of the advantages inherent in the order of reasons developed in the First, Second, and Third Meditations. Thus the *retrospective* role of the Fourth Meditation is to provide a kind of 'pragmatic justification' for what preceded it.

Secondly, I take it that, when Descartes stated that the Fourth Meditation 'made intelligible' what was to come later, the dual achievements of establishing the criterion of clarity and distinctness and of explaining the nature and origin of falsity do not strictly speaking make intelligible an otherwise unintelligible Fifth or Sixth Meditation. After all, one does not need the Fourth Meditation in order to grasp the contents of the Fifth and Sixth Meditations. Rather, I take Descartes to be saying that, without these two achievements, the remainder of the *Meditations* would be in vain. Unless we were already warranted in our acceptance of the criterion of clarity and distinctness and unless we fully grasped the nature and origin, both proximate and remote, of falsity, the Fifth and Sixth Meditations would be utterly futile—i.e. without the Fourth Meditation we could make no sense of the argumentative strategy contained in them. Thus the *prospective* role of the Fourth Meditation is to provide an argumentative context for what follows after it.

No passage from the Synopsis is more problematic than the account of the content and role of the Fourth Meditation. In this chapter I have discussed several of the problems arising from this passage. It is my belief that an adequate treatment of the analytic order of reasons in the *Meditations* must take into account the Synopsis and particularly the Synopsis's account of the content and role of the Fourth Meditation in the overall order of reasons.

PART THREE

The Will

8

Human Nature, Reason, and Will in the Argument of Descartes's Meditations

PETER SCHOULS

Is human nature such that it allows human beings to know, that is, to be absolutely certain in matters both of everyday life and of science whether applied or pure? Since all human knowledge necessarily requires human activity, one way in which we may approach this question is through another one: are human beings capable of the requisite activity and are they capable of discerning when, or whether, they are so active? That is the question which I shall use as my Ariadne's thread in the reading of the *Meditations* which I am about to present.[1]

'I realized that it was necessary . . . to demolish everything completely and start again right from the foundations if I wanted to establish anything at all in the sciences that was stable and likely to last.'[2] Much has been written about these words from the opening paragraph of the *Meditations*, as commentators have paid attention to the grounds for the 'necessity' of the 'demolition', to the intended extent of the 'demolition' (how inclusive is 'everything' meant to be?) and to the 'foundations' and the 'sciences' to be (re-)constructed on them. These are matters I will explore from the vantage-point of what Descartes says about human nature: I will argue that the necessity and

---

[1] In P. Schouls, *The Imposition of Method*, chs. IV, V, and *Descartes and the Enlightenment*, chs. II, IV, I began a discussion of which this chapter is one possible conclusion. Whereas I then argued that in the first three of the *Meditations* Descartes meant to validate trust in the senses and in the deductive (i.e. compositive) function of reason, I now present grounds for a more extensive thesis. To make this chapter self-sufficient, it was necessary to introduce a minimal amount of the argument from the two earlier works.

[2] All translations from Descartes's works are from CSM or CSMK.

extent of the demolition, as well as the necessity and nature of the new starting-point for (re-)construction, are determined by his doctrine of human essence.

My chapter has two main sections: (i) human reason and the argument of the *Meditations,* and (ii) human freedom and that argument. Since a good deal of the first section follows well-trodden paths, I here present little more than the outline of the argument; I devote most of my time to the second section, in which I offer a new slant for our reading of the *Meditations.* Much of the second section will be parallel and complementary to the first, for in it I deal with the same argument as in the first but now considered from the vantage-point of freedom rather than reason. My main focus in this chapter is on the first three Meditations.

There are two preliminary points to be made, one about (*a*) activity and passivity and the other about (*b*) freedom and nature. Since both concern well-known Cartesian doctrines whose interpretation commentators have not made a matter of controversy, it will suffice to state them in brief.

(*a*) To Regius, Descartes writes, 'There is only one soul in human beings, the rational soul; for no actions can be reckoned human unless they depend on reason.' This 'rational soul' is thus 'the first principle' of human 'actions' (letter of May 1641: AT III 371; CSMK 182). In the same letter he states that 'willing and understanding' 'differ only as the activity and passivity of one and the same substance', with 'understanding . . . the passivity of the mind and willing . . . its activity'. At about the time of this letter, Descartes composed the part of his *Principles of Philosophy* where we read that

All the modes of thinking that we experience within ourselves can be brought under two general headings: perception, or the operation of the intellect, and volition, or the operation of the will. Sensory perception, imagination and pure understanding are simply various modes of perception; desire, aversion, assertion, denial and doubt are various modes of willing. (*Principles,* pt. I, art. 32)

The 'passivity' of the intellect is clear enough in 'sensory perception'. But it pertains also in 'pure understanding' when, once confronted with a truth which is clear and distinct to the intellect, there is no choice but to accept this truth as long as one pays attention to it.[3] Thus

---

[3] Descartes wrote to Regius that 'perception' is not, strictly speaking, an action; hence willing is the only activity of the soul. See AT III 454–5; CSMK 199.

one backdrop to this paper is Descartes's doctrine that, as *res cogitans*, we are passive and active, creatures of intellect and will, and that it is only when intellect and will are co-present and co-operate (in a manner which will demand attention later on) that action, as distinct from mechanistic behaviour, ensues.

(*b*) Another part of the setting for my chapter is Descartes's insistence, in the subtitle of the *Meditations* and beyond that in all of his works,[4] that this 'rational soul' is distinct from 'the body' or from 'nature' (where 'distinct' is meant to include the possibility of 'separate' existence). This doctrine is crucial once we relate it to Descartes's intent for humanity to achieve mastery over nature, for such mastery requires that we deal with nature (including the human body) mechanistically. We will not be able to relate to nature in the requisite ways unless we decide to do so. That decision, as well as its persistent application, requires acts of will, that is, presupposes that human beings are essentially free. Hence human essence must be taken as distinct from that of mechanistic nature so that, in crucial respects, there is no limitation of *res cogitans* by *res extensa*.

The immediate significance for my thesis of these two preliminary points is this. If 'no actions can be reckoned human unless they depend on reason', then there is no expression of human essence apart from reason. Similarly, there is no human essence apart from exertion of will, for there is no action (as distinct from mechanistically determined behaviour) unless it be willed. If we doubt whether there is reasoning or willing, we doubt the existence of the human being. Restating this and bringing out some of its implications will allow me to present my thesis clearly.

Once (in the part of the *Principles* where we find the counterpart to the *Meditations*) the existence of the *res cogitans* is established, Descartes says that we are still 'supposing that everything which is distinct from us is false' that is, unreal or non-existent (as the French version has it, we are 'now thinking that there is nothing outside of our thought which truly is or exists').[5] Thus that which can be doubted is counted as non-existent unless the doubt can be dispelled. If doubt can be directed to the *res cogitans*, then the question Descartes is asking becomes: is there in fact a *res cogitans*, a thinking willing being? This,

---

[4] For examples of relevant passages, see the *Regulae* (AT X 415, 421–2; CSM I 42, 46), the *Discourse* (AT VI 46, 58–9; CSM I 134, 140–1), the *Meditations* (AT VII 78; CSM II 54), and the *Principles* (AT IXB 4, 14–15; CSM I 180–1, 186; AT VIIIA 7; CSM I 195).   [5] *Principles*, pt. I, art. 8.

of course, is not the only question he is asking. An earlier question is: do we know anything about *res extensa?*, which, once answered negatively, is followed immediately by the question: is there a r̊es *extensa?* But these questions then lead to another set of questions, and that set is the more foundational in that the very possibility of answering the first depends on the possibility of answering the second set. And this second set is: do we know anything about the *res cogitans?*, which, once answered negatively, is then followed by: is there in fact a *res cogitans?* At a certain moment we do not know whether distant towers are round or square and this leads us to question whether both towers and senses exist. Similarly, at a certain moment we do not know whether two and three make more or less than five, and this makes us wonder whether both sciences and *res cogitans* exist. Thus my thesis about the *Meditations* is that it is an argument structured by the fundamental need to prove the existence of the *res cogitans* as an autonomous, reasoning, and willing being. I can now turn to the two main parts of my chapter, first to *human reason*, next to *human will* and the argument of the *Meditations*.

I. Human Reason

To be human is to be free to reason and to act on one's reason's precepts. Implied is the individual's radical epistemic autonomy, an autonomy grounded in the nature which God has given human beings.[6] Perhaps the best-known early statement of this epistemic autonomy is the striking passage in the *Discourse* where Descartes writes of his 'resolution to abandon all the opinions' which he 'has hitherto accepted', thus 'uprooting—*ie déracinois*—from my mind any errors that might previously have slipped into it' (AT VI 15, 28; CSM I 118, 125).[7] The doctrine requires that only such new opinions will

---

[6] See e.g. the *Discourse* (AT VI 27; CSM I 124). I shall deal with another passage (AT VII 60–2; CSM II 42–3), which has the same import, when, in the second section, I consider aspects of the Fourth Meditation.

[7] Other examples readily come to mind. The *Principles* are characterized as quite different from those of Aristotle (or, for that matter, from those of any other thinker) because of the way in which they are derived, a 'difference ... between these principles of mine and all those of other philosophers' (AT IXB 20; CSM I 190). In *The Search for Truth* he insists on beginning 'by overturning all the knowledge acquired up to the present' because it is like 'a badly constructed house, whose foundations are not firm' and for which there is 'no better way to repair it than to knock it all down, and build a new one in its place' (AT X 509; CSM I 406–7). And in *The Passions of the Soul* he feels 'obliged to write just as if I were considering a topic that no one had dealt with before me' (AT XI 328; CSM I 328).

be adopted (or only such old ones readopted) as can be 'squared . . . with the standards of reason' (AT VI 13; CSM I 117).[8]

This gives us the first vantage-point from which to approach the question why 'it was necessary, once in the course of my life, to demolish everything completely and start again right from the foundations . . .'. It is human nature itself which dictates as much through human reason. If anything is to be an item of knowledge for me, it must be clear and distinct to me.[9] Whatever experience initially gives is complex, hence not at first meeting clear and distinct and therefore cannot then be grasped by the intellect as true even if it is true. With respect to any complex item it will be *necessary*, at least once, to submit it to analysis until we reach the 'foundations', where we have items which are absolutely simple and therefore self-evident, entities known *per se* rather than *per aliud*.[10] Ultimately, it is only from such simplest items that we can commence our scientific construction. But such items are never given to begin with; they must always be established by whoever comes to know them.

In the First Meditation we go beyond this statement from the *Discourse*, radical though it is: now there are not just the questions whether what is given by the senses can be 'squared with reason' or whether what we take to be constructed by our understanding does indeed come from the understanding. There are the further questions whether we can know that sensation usually or ever gives us materials which allow us to construct accurate knowledge of our surroundings and, more broadly, whether the understanding provides

[8] Thus with respect to the doctrines of his own scientific works like the *Geometry*, the *Dioptrics*, and the *Meteors*, Descartes writes that 'I do not boast of being the first to discover any of them, but I do claim to have accepted them not because they have, or have not, been expressed by others, but solely because reason has convinced me of them' (AT VI 77; CSM I 150).

[9] Recall what Descartes says about clarity and distinctness: 'A perception which can serve as the basis for a certain and indubitable judgement needs to be not merely clear but also distinct. I call a perception "clear" when it is present and accessible to the attentive mind . . . [and] I call a perception "distinct" if, as well as being clear, it is so sharply separated from all other perceptions that it contains within itself only what is clear' (*Principles*, pt. I, art. 45).

[10] As we read in the *Regulae* with respect to items which are simple and hence 'self-evident' (*per se notas*): 'it is evident that we are mistaken if we ever judge that we lack complete knowledge of any one of these . . . For if we have even the slightest grasp of it in our mind . . . it must follow that we have complete knowledge of it. Otherwise it could not be said to be simple, but a composite made up of that which we perceive in it and that of which we judge we are ignorant' (AT X 420; CSM I 45).

correct accounts of whatever can be an object of thought.[11] In order to achieve the certainty which allows for the 'sciences' to be 'stable and likely to last', Descartes needs to authenticate these two 'sources' or 'principles' of knowledge. Here is one of the *Meditations*' grounds which made it 'necessary . . . to demolish everything completely and start again right from the foundations'. It is a necessity dictated by what Descartes has all along accepted as part of human nature.

This authentication is accomplished through a 'journey' on which he 'led the mind from knowledge of its own existence to knowledge of the existence of God and to the distinction between mind and body'—a distinction expressing the mind's essence (AT VII 550; CSM II 375). Most of the implications of this 'distinction' I must leave for the next section of my chapter; of importance now is the mind's 'knowledge of its own existence' and 'of the existence of God'. This knowledge will reveal several facts about the *rational* aspect of human nature and the argument of the *Meditations*.

The manner of achieving this knowledge introduces the sceptic's most 'excessive doubt' imaginable,[12] which is: not only do we not know that God exists, but for all we know there exists instead an omnipotent deceiver.[13] It is that supposition which demolishes 'everything' hitherto accepted as true or trustworthy; and, since no doubt about rational human nature can be legitimate after that supposition has itself been demolished, it was 'necessary . . . to demolish everything completely'— where 'everything' includes both all objects of, as well as the most far-fetched ground for, the sceptic's doubt.

[11] Some commentators argue that the doubt in the First Meditation is one limited to the senses. Recent statements of this position are J. Carriero, 'The First Meditation', and R. Smyth, 'A Metaphysical Reading of the First Meditation'. Of these two, Carriero tells the more plausible story. He reads the First Meditation as only an anti-Aristotelian attack on the senses as a foundation for science. Interpretations alternative to his own he dismisses in part because (so he claims without offering support for the claim) they result in a reading of the 'First Meditation' 'as a loosely connected string of sceptical challenges' (p. 243). My disagreement with a position like Carriero's concerns the extent of the doubt rather than the suggestion that, in doubting the senses, Descartes attacks Aristotelian philosophers.

[12] Hence Descartes can characterize the *Meditations* as 'arguments by means of which I became the first philosopher ever to overturn the doubt of the sceptics' (AT VII 550; CSM II 376).

[13] In Robert Stoothoff's terminology ('Descartes' Dilemma') I interpret the deceiver as allowing Descartes to entertain the possibility that he is subject to 'natural deception', that is, to 'deception or error resulting from Descartes' nature' (p. 296). Stoothoff's juxtaposition of 'natural deception' to 'ad hoc deception' (which corresponds to deception by an omnipotent God in the first and by a powerful but less-than-omnipotent

Demolishing this supposition itself is by way of proof of the existence of a veracious God. Once that proof is in place we are in the position to know that reason is the human being's self-authenticating capacity which establishes the stable foundations of science and authenticates sense. These revelations, given by reason to reason, in effect show the absolute validity of radical individual epistemic autonomy. Implicit is the doctrine that it is rational human nature which is necessary as the foundation of science.[14]

Since I have elsewhere[15] given close attention to the stages of this part of the journey, they need not be reconsidered here. However, in my earlier account I missed one important stage—a failure I shared with other commentators. I argued that Descartes submits both 'basic principles' of sense and reason to metaphysical doubt, but in the case of reason I believed he doubted only its compositive and not its intuitive function; that is, I believed Descartes exempted from doubt reason's capacity of grasping self-evident items. It was a mistake so to limit the extent of metaphysical doubt. Thus there remains an additional stage to the journey; it requires our attention for a moment.

With the introduction of the omnipotent deceiver, Descartes doubts the trustworthiness of reason even in its intuitive function. The central sentence of the First Meditation's ninth paragraph reads:

> What is more, since I sometimes believe that others go astray in cases where they think they have the most perfect knowledge, may I not similarly go wrong every time I add two and three or count the sides of a square, *or in some even simpler matter*, if that is imaginable? (AT VII 21; CSM II 14)

This 'even simpler matter' extends the doubt to reason's ability of cognizing the absolutely simple foundational items of knowledge, those

external agent in the second case) seems not fully plausible—both because of 'problem texts' he himself introduces and because of relevant texts which he fails to cite. For an example of the latter, see AT VII 195; CSM II 136–7. I hold that Descartes entertains the possibility of an omnipotent deceiver's existence in order to push methodological doubt beyond its normal boundaries to become metaphysical doubt. Hence I am among those who believe Descartes to make this move 'in order to counteract the force of habit . . .' (p. 300). My question in a moment will be 'Habit with respect to what?' And my suggestion will be that it is considerably more than 'habit, which threatens to impede the application of the method by preventing him from withholding assent to opinions that reason renders doubtful' (ibid.).

[14] As we shall see later, though necessary it is not sufficient as the foundation of science. Something additional is required, but for this addition we need introduce nothing beyond the other aspect of human nature, namely, the human will—a will whose existence is possible because of 'the distinction between the human soul and the body'.

[15] See Schouls, *The Imposition of Method*, chs. IV, V.

contextless items known *per se*. Descartes here imagines (*fingo*) that even self-evidence has lost its certainty.[16] As he puts this in *Principles*, pt. I, art. 5: 'Our doubt will also apply to other matters which we previously regarded as most certain—even the demonstrations of mathematics and even the principles [*principiis*] *which we hitherto considered self-evident* [*per se nota*].'

The intellect's nature is to sense, imagine, and understand. We have habitually believed these functions to be capable of giving us, or of leading us to, truth. Since these are *habitual* beliefs, they are prejudices. The first two can become rational beliefs if our reason can validate our trust in them—provided, of course, that our trust in reason is itself no longer habitual but is itself validated. Thus we have now placed ourselves in the position where we recognize that all our intellectual functions need validation—a recognition which frees us from all prejudice about intellectual human nature, and places us in the position to see whether we can in fact discover incontrovertible truth about this human nature—first about its existence and then about its essence.

On this path of discovery Descartes starts with establishing the mind's existence; this activity turns out to be the very same which validates trust in reason's ability to establish foundations; that is, it validates trust in reason's intuitive function. It· is the focus of the Second Meditation where (says Descartes in its Synopsis) 'the mind . . . supposes the non-existence of all the things about whose existence it can have even the slightest doubt'—the human intellect and its objects and therefore human nature and human existence itself—'and in so doing the mind notices that it is impossible that it should not itself exist during this time'. '*I am, I exist*, is necessarily true whenever it is . . . conceived [*concipitur*] in my mind'—as the first formulation in its third paragraph has it. It is an item *per se nota*, 'known without any affirmation or denial' (AT IXA 206; CSM II 271).[17] This first certainty is achieved with the omnipotent deceiver supposedly on the

[16] In 'Descartes' First Meditation' M. A. Olson excludes 'any "common notion" or inference rule "intuitively" or non-abstractively known' from being dubitable (p. 433). He is correct when he does so in the context of the Third Meditation (or, for that matter, in the Second after we have reached the Cogito. But if my interpretation is correct, then Olson is wrong in doing so in the context of the First Meditation—and that pulls the rug from under the central thesis of his interesting article.

[17] That we do not reach the Cogito through syllogistic argument is clear enough from Descartes's entire mode of procedure and, for those of his readers who missed this to Descartes elementary point, is spelled out also in the Second Replies (AT VII 140; CSM II 100).

scene. That is, reason in its awareness of absolutely simple items of knowledge has been shown to exist and to be unconditionally trustworthy, for it has withstood the test of metaphysical doubt greater than which cannot be conceived. Next he settles reason's absolute trustworthiness in its compositive function; this is the focus of the Third and, to an extent, the Fourth Meditations. Finally, in the Sixth Meditation, he confirms the trustworthiness of the senses.

Reason in its compositive function is shown to be absolutely trustworthy by reason functioning intuitively: it recognizes the contradictoriness[18] of the supposition, and hence the impossibility of the existence, of an omnipotent deceiver and so removes the ground for doubt of reason in its non-compositive function. This places us again where we were in the *Discourse* (at AT VI 15, 28; CSM I 118, 125): we may accept whatever the senses present provided we have determined that these givens can be 'squared . . . with the standards of reason'. But there is a difference, because there is an additional element: we now have metaphysical grounds for our acceptance of these givens.

II. Human Free Will

To be human is to be free to use one's freedom to reason and to act on one's reason's precepts.[19] The passive intellect's reception of truth, and the subsequent further actualization of one's humanity through action on that truth, become possible only through acts of will.

For Descartes, to the extent that one's freedom is limited by external constraints there is less of an expression (and hence less of a presence)

---

[18] See J. G. Cottingham (ed.), *Descartes' Conversation with Burman*, 4, 9, where it is explicitly stated that the idea of an omnipotent deceiver is incoherent. (The second of these passages is missing in the reproduction of this material in CSMK; the first appears on p. 333). The 'supposition' of the First Meditation which related utmost power and utmost cunning (*summe potentem et callidum*) is incoherent because perfection and imperfection cannot coexist in the same being: 'he cannot be a deceiver, since it is manifest by the natural light that all fraud and deception depend on some defect' and 'in every case of trickery or deception some imperfection is to be found . . .' (AT VII 52, 53; CSM II 35, 37).

[19] There is more to Descartes's position than this sentence states, for in an important setting Descartes holds that to be human is also to be free not to reason and not to act on one's reason's precepts. These statements point to what I believe to be an unresolved tension in Descartes's writings between his doctrines of autonomous will and authoritative reason. I have highlighted this tension in Schouls, *Descartes and the Enlightenment*, ch. V, pt. 1, and will say no more about it in this chapter.

of a *res cogitans*, just as there would be if one were deprived of part of one's reason. Our freedom is limited to the extent that we are passive rather than active. Which is to say that we give greater or lesser expression to our humanity depending on whether we are more or less active.

One way in which passivity dominates is through habit, when the habit in question is uncritically contracted through one's exposure to one's environment. The First Meditation states that we have domineering habits of precisely this kind in our trust of sense and of reason. It is (in the words of its eleventh paragraph) these 'habitual opinions' which 'keep coming back' and which 'despite my wishes . . . capture my belief, which is as it were bound over to them as a result of long occupation and the law of custom'. In this situation Descartes then adopts a strategy which promises escape from imprisonment in passivity:

I think it will be a good thing to turn my will in completely the opposite direction and deceive myself, by pretending for a time that these former opinions are utterly false and imaginary. I shall do this until the weight of preconceived opinion [*praejudiciorum*] is counter-balanced and the distorting influence of habit no longer prevents my judgement from perceiving things correctly. (AT VII 22; CSM II 15)

This undertaking to deceive oneself is an attempt at expressing the *res cogitans* as free being. In words from the Synopsis of the Second Meditation: 'the mind uses its own freedom [*propria libertate utens*] and supposes the non-existence of all . . . things . . .' The Synopsis of the First Meditation asserts the far-reaching consequences of persistence in this attempt: 'The eventual result of this doubt is to make it impossible for us to have any further doubts about what we subsequently discover to be true.' That (as we shall come to see in retrospect) is because this attempt at expressing human freedom inexorably will deliver us from the doubt we have imposed on ourselves through adoption of the belief that there may be an omnipotent deceiver.

If there is such a deceiver then we might be so malleable, so passive in his hands that we do not even know whether or not we are being imposed upon, whether or not what we take to be assertions of free will or experiences of passivity are so in fact. I may be active when I experience myself to be passive, and vice versa. Consider this example from the Third and Sixth Meditations. My experience tells me that 'there is in me a passive faculty of sensory perception, that is, a faculty for receiving and recognizing the ideas of sensible objects', and this implies that there is 'also an active faculty, either in me or in something else, which produced or brought about these ideas', and it is only my knowledge that 'God is not a deceiver' which allows me to conclude that these ideas are not 'transmitted from a source other than corporeal things' (AT VII 79–80; CSM II 55). As long as I entertain the possibility of an omnipotent deceiver, then, although my experience tells me that 'these ideas do not depend on my will', 'it does not follow that they must come from things located outside me' for 'there may be some . . . faculty not yet fully known to me, which produces these ideas without any assistance from external things' (AT VII 39; CSM II 27). Hence I may be active when I experience myself as passive and, conversely, I may be passive when I experience myself to be active.

Two paragraphs before he comes to his first articulation of the Cogito, strategically at the very opening of the Second Meditation, Descartes vividly pictures this situation of doubt about the efficacy, and even the existence, of free will:

So serious are the doubts into which I have been thrown as a result of yesterday's meditation that I can neither put them out of my mind nor see any way of resolving them. It feels as if I have fallen unexpectedly into a deep whirlpool which tumbles me around so that I can neither stand on the bottom nor swim up to the top. (AT VII 23–4; CSM II 16)

The experience described is one of passivity, of helplessly being 'tumbled around' by a force external to oneself, a force so powerful that both certainty ('standing on the bottom') and the pursuit of certainty ('swimming to the top' and so looking for a place to stand and making one's way to that) seem equally impossible. Whether there is any efficacy to either attempt we do not know: there may be, there may not. The only way to find out (if there is such a way) is to assume that this experience of passivity is not our ultimate state of being. Therefore: 'Nevertheless I will make an effort and once more attempt the . . . path . . .' And so: 'I have convinced [*persuasi*] myself that there is absolutely nothing in the world, no sky, no earth, no minds, no bodies. Does it now follow that I too do not exist? No: if I convinced [*persuasi*] myself of something then I certainly existed.' Here, two sentences before what is traditionally taken as the first articulation of the Cogito, we have the first articulation of the Cogito, not in terms of intellection but in terms of willing: *if I convince (persuade) myself of something then I certainly exist.* The experience of passivity cannot be our ultimate state of being simply because, when I entertain this experience as my reality, it is an experience which I have created through my act of will. If I persuade myself, then I am as a persuading, willing being. If focusing on the *res cogitans* expressing itself in 'the perception of the intellect' leads us to *cogito ergo sum*, focusing on the *res cogitans* expressing itself in 'the operation of the will' leads us to *volo ergo sum.*[20]

Thus we may take the attempt at universal doubt as a necessary step in revealing the truth about the essence of a human being and in actualizing that essence as completely as possible. This strategy forces the confrontation with the omnipotent deceiver which results in optimally active human presence, destroying the habitual acceptance of those beliefs which routinely are taken not as customary beliefs but as obvious truths (I mean the beliefs which express trust in the existence and veracity of the senses and their objects, and trust in the existence and veracity of reason and its objects). But in addition, through this strategy we reveal to ourselves the important point about our nature that there is no passivity of which we are or can not be aware, no passivity to which we need be subject if we do not want such subjection.[21] This strategy reveals that we can work at being as free, as active, as fully human as we choose to be.[22]

Earlier I mentioned Descartes's response to Regius that 'no actions can be reckoned human unless they depend on reason'. There is, as well, his statement from the *Discourse* that it is only 'our thoughts' which lie 'entirely within our power' (AT VI 25; CSM I 123). My reading now suggests that the question of the First Meditation is not just whether reason (either 'pure' or in its validation of and conjunction with the senses) is ever to be trusted; that question concerns the *intellectual* aspect of the *res cogitans*. There is also the question

[20] I owe this formulation to Anthony Kenny, who offered it during the discussion of this chapter at the University of Reading conference.

[21] I am speaking here of what is usually the case in the course of human life, and not about unusual situations like that of being bound and tortured.

[22] Free development of the sciences of mechanics, medicine, and morals may be seen as ways to overcome the passivity of involuntary subjection to afflictions of a physical, mental, or social kind. A fruit expected from the science of medicine was that human beings would become less and less passive because able to do away with involuntary submission to death (which would itself no longer be predictable in its inevitability). For himself, Descartes optimistically expected death already to have lost its three-score-and-ten inevitability; and the *philosophes* who followed in his footsteps anticipated only the passivity of death through the statistically-inevitable accident.

concerning the *volitional* aspect; one way of stating it is whether anything ever 'lies entirely within our power'. Certainty on the impossibility of the existence of an omnipotent deceiver answers both questions affirmatively.

My reading of the *Meditations* is one in which we reach certainty through an argument in which reason disqualifies sense and then attempts to disqualify itself, an argument forced to its radical conclusion through the operation of the will imposing doubt on sense and on reason—*a doubt which then comes to be applied to the will itself.* This reading, which involves both aspects of the *res cogitans*, finds support in Descartes's language of what are traditionally taken as the 'Cogito passages' in the Second and Third Meditations.

In the first of these, Descartes gives both will and intellect their place: '*I am, I exist*, is necessarily true whenever it is put forward by me [through an act of will] or conceived in my mind [through its impression on the intellect]' (AT VII 25; CSM II 17). And when a few paragraphs later the *res cogitans* is more fully characterized, three of its eight characteristics are in terms of intellect ('understands', 'imagines', 'has sensory perceptions') and the rest in terms of will ('doubts', 'affirms', 'denies', 'is willing', 'is unwilling'). Descartes offers a near-identical list in the opening paragraph of the Third Meditation. The fact that in both these passages will is mentioned before intellect indicates a parallel with the argument I have elucidated in Section I of this chapter. There, that which was doubted last (the ability to understand items known *per se*), is shown to be indubitable first, while in this case our experience of free will is doubted after reason and is pronounced validated before reason.

When in part I of the *Principles* Descartes restates the first two of the Meditations, the same order of argument presents itself. In principles 4 and 5 reason offers grounds which are to disqualify sense and imagination as well as reason. Principles 6 and 7 then turn to 'free will' and articulate the Cogito. Since we here get further support for my reading of the *Meditations*, it is instructive to focus on these latter two principles for a moment.

Although in these two principles we meet the traditionally recognized formulation of the Cogito in Principle 7, it is principle 6 in which bounds are set to the omnipotent deceiver through the experience of freedom. It reads as follows:

But whoever turns out to have created us, and however powerful and however deceitful he may be, in the meantime we nonetheless experience within us the kind of freedom which enables us always to refrain from believing things which are not completely certain and thoroughly examined. Hence we are able to take precautions against going wrong on any occasion.

Thus we now possess the certainty that (in the words of the heading of Principle 6) 'We have free will, enabling us to withhold our assent in doubtful matters and hence avoid error.' This is knowledge of what we 'experience' as ultimately valid (it withstands the force of the one who has 'created us', 'however powerful and however deceitful he may be') and useful ('we are able to take precautions against going wrong on any occasion'). At this point one might say—but, I believe, mistakenly so—that the *next* 'piece of knowledge' is that of Principle 7. There Descartes writes: because 'it is a contradiction to suppose that what thinks does not ... exist', it follows that '*I am thinking, therefore I exist* ... is the first and most certain of all to occur to anyone who philosophizes in an orderly way.' And one might add—again, I believe, mistakenly—that, since the knowledge of Principle 6 is stated before that of Principle 7, Descartes is confused when he calls the latter's knowledge 'the first of all to occur ...'. I believe it would be wrong to charge Descartes with confusion here, because these two principles express different aspects of the same thing. In the face of the presumed existence of an omnipotent deceiver, both express the achievement of certainty, both state the existence of the *res cogitans*, the first in terms of the will and the second in terms of the intellect. And they do so in an order which is not peculiar to the *Principles*; we found the same order in the *Meditations*.

If we now return to the *Meditations*, we can see that this co-presence of will and intellect, with the will preceding the intellect in an order of exposition which reflects the structure of the argument, is typical of the first three of the *Meditations*. There is, in fact, a primacy of free will over reason in that the willing aspect of the *res cogitans* is the driving force which leads to each epistemically differently qualified presence of the intellect.[23] Since I have dealt with this in detail

[23] C. Wilson and C. Schildknecht ('The Cogito Meant "No More Philosophy"') suggest that the nineteenth-century poet and critic Paul Valéry was the first to maintain that 'Descartes' was first and foremost a will' (p. 49). That position led him to the conclusion that 'Descartes' doubt ... [is] directed in the main not against the "knowledge" proferred by the outer world, but against that making its appearance from within. It reflects an effort to contain and suppress a radical uncertainty: was the revelation of unlimited intellectual power truly a vision sent by God? Or was it a fantasy generated by the dreaming idea-producing self which generates such other realistic fantasies, or even a temptation staged by a demon?' Though congenial to me, the

elsewhere,[24] I shall not repeat the argument but only indicate the points at which this primacy is very clear.

It is very clear in the introduction of the omnipotent deceiver, which on my present reading is the ultimate tool enabling us to doubt all our beliefs, whether about sense, reason, or will. It is not just the submission to this test which is self-willed. Also the subsequent awareness of the truth so basic that it can function as Archimedean point comes about through an act of will. It is only through the act of willing expressed in 'paying attention' that we have the assurance of the truth of the Cogito and, later on, of the truth that in the awareness of the Cogito we are necessarily aware of the existence of a veracious God.[25]

From that point on, will and intellect continue to function in tandem, but it remains the case that in all the moves of the argument, both in the ones that constitute progress and in those that do not,[26] the will is primary to the intellect. Once we have established the existence of the *res cogitans* as characterized by will and intellect, we know that ideas or thoughts exist, but we also know that nothing will get us beyond this point unless we *will* to use 'thoughts'. And before the full powers of reason have been validated and all of reason has been shown to be autonomous, we already know that the will is autonomous, that we really are active when we experience ourselves to be so, and that we will not have such experiences unless we will to

statement goes both too far and not far enough. I would be able to support it fully were the phrase 'was the revelation of unlimited intellectual power truly . . .' replaced by 'was the experience of limited intellectual and unlimited volitional power truly . . .'.

[24] See Schouls, *Descartes and the Enlightenment*, ch. II, pt. 1.

[25] See the Third Meditation's statements on this paying attention to the Cogito: 'If one concentrates carefully [*Quod diligenter attenditi*], all this is quite evident by the natural light. But when I relax my attention [*Sed quia, cum minus attendo*] . . . it is not so easy . . .' (AT VII 47; CSM II 32); and 'the more carefully I concentrate . . . [*quo diligentius attendo*]' (AT VII 45; CSM II 31). See as well Descartes's letter to Gibieuf, written one year after the publication of the *Meditations* (AT III 474–6; CSMK 201–2); and note his statement in the Fourth Set of Replies (AT VII 246; CSM II 171). That 'paying attention' is an act of will Descartes states explicitly, for example, in a letter to Mesland (AT IV 116; CSMK 233–4). On this role of 'attention' and its relation to the will, see as well Schouls, *Descartes and the Enlightenment*, ch. IV, pt. 2.

[26] There are several moves in the *Meditations* which do not so much constitute progress in the answering of Descartes's basic questions, but which primarily prepare the ground for such progress through their breaking of the habits of trusting sense and trusting reason. For the relevant passages, see the Second Meditation's paragraphs 10–16 (which are meant to break trust in the senses) and the Third Meditation's paragraphs 7–12 (which are meant to break trust in the compositive function of reason).

have them.[27] Hence, when we will to use our thoughts, we know that we are not externally determined to such willing by either omnipotent deceiver or veracious God. We can, *if we will*, 'start again right from the foundations' and 'establish' 'sciences' which are 'stable and likely to last'.

Autonomous human nature therefore dictates, for both theoretical work and practical experience, that activity precede passivity. As the Fourth Meditation makes explicit, that is how God has made human beings: on their own capable to pursue truth and continue activity through implementation of the dicta of reason, but equally capable to avoid truth and commit themselves to error and so bind themselves into the passivity which characterizes the mechanistic behaviour which such non-rational deeds entail.[28] When the Fourth Meditation states this relationship between activity and passivity, between will and intellect, it lends further support for my reading of the first three Meditations:

> God could easily have brought it about that without losing my freedom, and despite the limitations in my knowledge, I should nevertheless never make a mistake. He could, for example, have endowed my intellect with a clear and distinct perception of everything about which I was ever likely to deliberate; or he could simply have impressed it unforgettably on my memory that I should never make a judgment about anything which I did not clearly and distinctly understand. (AT VII 61; CSM II 42)

God has not imposed on me in either of these ways. Had he done so that would have been 'without losing my freedom' in the sense that it would still have required willingness to act in accordance with my intellect's clear and distinct ideas or with my memory's forceful impression. Nevertheless, there would have been loss of autonomy at a different level, passivity where now there is activity. Instead of making me inescapably aware of ideas in my understanding or

---

[27] Which, of course, is not to say that we really are passive when we experience ourselves to be passive. That matter will not be settled until the Sixth Meditation.

[28] If they follow the latter course of action, this is a 'misuse' of 'freedom' resulting in the 'privation' which constitutes 'the essential definition of falsity and wrong' (AT VII 60–1; CSM II 42). It results in a 'privation' because, for Descartes, ignorance and error are not 'real' just as blindness is not 'real'. Both error and blindness indicate a lack of power as distinct from the actualization of a human faculty. This 'misuse' of freedom becomes compounded when action ensues on that of which one is ignorant or with respect to which one is in error, for such action is then really no more than non-rational hence non-human behaviour; it tends to incorporate one into the mechanism of nature.

impressions in my memory, God has given me the power to 'avoid error in the second way, which depends merely on my remembering to withhold judgment on any occasion when the truth of the matter is not clear'. It is, then, my own activity which creates in me 'the habit of avoiding error', a critically acquired habit which supplants the uncritical habits suspended in the First Meditation and in the opening paragraph of the Second—those of unquestioning trust in the validity of sense and reason and in the efficacy of will and, consequently, in the existence of these faculties and their objects. It is, then, no wonder to see Descartes stating at this point that it is in the exercise of this power that my 'greatest and most important perfection is to be found' (AT VII 62; CSM II 43).

This 'perfection' consists in being true to my nature through the right use of freedom. It is a 'perfection' which allows for more than keeping from error; it is in fact one of the conditions necessary for the pursuit of truth. This is because of Descartes's position—again exemplified in the structure of the argument of the first three Meditations—that we would not reason except through acts of will like those involved in suspending judgement, implementing doubt, determining the imagination to propose hypotheses, and determining the intellect to be attentive. Reason performs none of these tasks as it were automatically; strictly speaking, reason cannot perform any of them on its own, for to each it has to be determined by the will. No action can be called human unless it be rational, but there can be no action called 'reasoning' except it be willed. Thus it is not God who has 'endowed my intellect with a clear and distinct perception of everything about which I was ever likely to deliberate', but it is I who give myself such perceptions wherever they are possible through willing attentive awareness. Hence the *res cogitans'* passive cognition of truth depends not on the action of God on its intellect but on that of its own will on its intellect.

We can now see that it makes sense to say about the opening paragraph of the *Meditations* that 'everything' in the phrase 'it was necessary . . . to demolish everything completely' covers whatever in which we are or perhaps might be passive. We are passive in sensory perception but also in intellection when the mind is confronted with a truth which is clear and distinct to it. And with the presumed presence of an omnipotent deceiver we are, for all we know, passive in what we experience as acts of self-determination when we exercise doubt, suspend judgement, and focus attention on what appears as given in the intellect. This necessary demolition, as well as the necessity and nature of the new starting-point, are determined by Descartes's doctrine of human essence and its two aspects of freedom and reason. Both are traditionally assumed to be autonomous but, given the questioning of all tradition, Descartes asks whether they are in fact autonomous. Descartes's most fundamental question then becomes: does anything ever lie 'entirely within our power'? Once he knows that he really is active when he experiences himself to be so, and knows that he will not have such experiences unless he wills to have them, he turns to the next question, to the other aspect of human essence: can reason ever be trusted?, and through exercise of a will now known to be autonomous he shows that reason is absolutely trustworthy. Once that point has been established, he is ready to show the (extent of the) trustworthiness of the senses. With these three items of knowledge secured, the question of the First Meditation is fully answered: human beings are indeed capable of the requisite activity which allows their achievement of absolutely certain knowledge.

9

Descartes's Compatibilism

VERE CHAPPELL

Compatibilism is the doctrine that determinism is logically consistent with libertarianism. Determinism is the doctrine that every being and event is brought about by causes other than itself. Libertarianism is the doctrine that some human actions are free.

Was Descartes a compatibilist? There is no doubt that he was a libertarian: his works are full of professions of freedom, human as well as divine. And, though he held that God has no cause other than himself, Descartes thought that everything apart from God is externally caused: he was a determinist with respect to the created universe. So it appears, assuming him consistent with himself, that Descartes must have been a compatibilist. And, indeed, there are passages in his writings in which he appears explicitly to affirm that he is. Since both Descartes's libertarianism and his determinism are complex doctrines, however, his view of the relation between them is complex as well.

Descartes's position is best seen in the light of his basic ontology. Among the things that are, he distinguishes God from created beings, substances from attributes, minds from bodies, and persisting features from events. Events attributed to minds are thoughts, those to bodies motions, and events of both kinds are subdivided into actions and passions. Mental actions for Descartes are volitions; some of these 'terminate' in the mind itself, others in the body. Mental passions are perceptions, among which some are caused by the mind, some by the body. Those caused by the mind are perceptions of volitions and perceptions which depend on volitions, for example, the perceptions we have when we 'imagine something non-existent' or 'consider something purely intelligble'. Perceptions caused by the body include sense impressions, bodily sensations, and emotions such as love and sadness (*Principles*, pt. I, arts. 48–56: AT VIIIA 22–6, CSM I 208–12; *Passions*, arts. 1–25: AT XI 327–48, CSM I 328–38).[1]

In stating his libertarian view, Descartes applies the term 'free' not only to actions but also to the agents who perform actions—the substances of which the actions are attributes. (Sometimes it is the performance that is said to be free, whence the agent is said to act or to do something freely). An agent may be called free with respect to a particular action, in which case she is free if and only if the action is free. Or she may be called free without qualification, in which case her being free consists in her ability to perform free actions. It is in this latter sense that Descartes speaks, as he sometimes does, of freedom as a power or faculty of agents (Fourth Meditation: AT VII 56, CSM II 39; *Principles*, pt. I, art. 39: AT VIIIA 19, CSM I 205; letter to [Mesland] of 2 May 1644: AT IV 116, CSMK 234).

Descartes frequently characterizes the actions and the agents which have freedom as 'human'—they are 'human actions' and 'human beings', or 'men'. But this is a loose way of speaking. A man on the Cartesian view is not a single agent or substance but a composite of two distinct substances, a mind and a body. As for the actions ascribed to a man, these fall into three distinct groups. First are those that the mind performs by itself: these are volitions. Second are the purely corporeal operations which belong to the body: these are mere bodily motions, such as the free fall of one's arm, or the beating of one's heart. And third is a class of mixed or composite actions each of which has both a mental and a corporeal part, a volition followed by one or more bodily motions: examples are the voluntary raising of a man's arm and his running in order to catch the bus. It is only the actions in this third category that can properly be said to belong to the whole man, the composite of body and mind.

Sometimes Descartes says that volitions are actions, not of the mind, but of the will, and in this vein he ascribes freedom to the will as well. This is also loose talk on his part. His position is not, as critics have charged, that the will is a substance or agent distinct from the mind. Rather, the will is one of the mind's powers, one of its two principal capacities—the other being the intellect or power of perceiving. Volitions are the will's actualizations, not its attributes: they are in fact occasional or episodic attributes of the mind, the very mind to which

---

[1] In quoting Descartes, I have followed CSM or CSMK, except in the case of the *Passions of the Soul*, where I have used the translation of Stephen Voss.

the will itself belongs as a permanent attribute. So when Descartes says that the will acts, what he means is that the mind exercises its power of willing, thereby performing volitions; it is the mind that is the agent of these performances.

In strict speech, the only actions that are free for Descartes are volitions, and the only free agents are the minds that perform these volitions. Not only is no purely corporeal action ever free; but no composite action is properly said to be free either, even if its mental component—the volition that prompts one to run for the bus, for example—is free, strictly speaking.

But volitions are not merely the only free actions for Descartes. It is also his view that every volition is free, and that it is so, furthermore, of necessity. For it is the essence of the will, as he puts it, to act freely: willing is free by nature (Second Replies: AT VII 166, CSM II 117; *Passions*, art. 41: AT XI 359, CSM I 343). Indeed, at several places in his text Descartes uses the expression 'free decision' (*liberum arbitrium*) as the name of the faculty of will (Fourth Meditation: AT VII 56, 57, 59; CSM II 39, 40, 41; *Passions*, art. 152: AT XI 445, CSM I 384; letter to Christina of 20 November 1647: AT V 85, CSMK 326). It is not that men have the power of willing, some of whose exercises are free and some not. Rather they have just the power of free-willing, or willing-freely. Given merely that a man has a will, it follows logically that he has the capacity for free action.

The scope of freedom, however, is not as narrow for Descartes as this restriction of it to volitions might suggest. According to the traditional view, there are only two things that the will does (or rather two things that the mind does by willing). It either determines in favour or it determines against some action distinct from its own action of willing—it wills to perform or wills not to perform the action in question. For Descartes, by contrast, willing is a general type of mental activity of which there are a number of different species: 'desire, aversion, assertion, denial and doubt are various modes of willing', he says in one place, noting that judging too, since it just consists in affirming or denying, is an act of the will (*Principles*, pt. I, arts. 32–4: AT VIIIA 17–18, CSM I 204; cf. *Comments on a Certain Broadsheet* AT VIIIB 363, CSM I 307). Elsewhere he says that all of the soul's 'appetites' are volitions (*Passions*, art. 47: AT XI 364; CSM I 346), although other passages make it clear that he wants to distinguish volition not only from bodily appetite but also from that desire which is one of the six primitive 'passions of the soul' (*Principles*, pt. IV, art.

190: AT VIIIA 317–18, CSM I 281; *Passions*, art. 80: AT XI 387, CSM I 356). On the traditional view, a man can will to affirm some proposition or to deny it (or will not to do either), and his affirming and his denying are actions—actions, indeed, on the part of the intellect—which are distinct from the action of willing itself: as some scholastic philosophers put it, the affirming and so forth are acts 'commanded' by the will, whereas the willing is an act 'elicited' from it. Descartes's position, however, is that affirming and denying and such are among the will's elicited acts; they are its very performances and not merely distinct actions commanded by it. Indeed, for Descartes, there is no generic action of willing, no action that is merely a volition and not also something more specific such as a judgement or appetite. The variety of actions, therefore, that count as free on his view is actually quite wide.

What *is* freedom as Descartes conceives it: wherein does it consist? In several passages, he equates being free with being voluntary (Third Replies: AT VII 191, CSM II 134; *Principles*, pt. I, art. 37: AT VIIIA 18, CSM I 205; letter to [Mesland] of 2 May 1644: AT IV 116, CSMK 234). To be voluntary is simply to depend on the will; and depending on the will is usually taken to mean being caused by it— that is, being caused by a volition or action of willing. This cannot be Descartes's understanding of voluntariness, however, since on his view it is volitions themselves that are free. Not only are volitions not caused by volitions, but the only things that are caused by volitions are perceptions and motions of bodies, and none of these is free. Hence, when Descartes says (by implication—he never does so directly) that a volition is voluntary, he must mean that it depends on the will, not as one event depends on a second event by which it is caused to occur, but as an attribute depends on the substance to which it belongs, or in this case, more specifically, as an action depends on its agent. Volitions are voluntary in the sense that they are the will's, or rather the mind's, own performances.

That this is indeed Descartes's meaning is confirmed by the fact that he also identifies freedom, on occasion, with spontaneity (Fourth Meditation: AT VII 59, CSM II 41, letter to [Mesland] of 9 February 1645: AT IV 175, CSMK 246). An action is spontaneous if it is performed by its agent entirely on his own, without being forced or helped or affected by any external factor, or by anything other than his very self. By this definition, to be sure, only the actions of God are spontaneous, properly speaking. So, when Descartes attributes spontaneity to the actions of created agents, he must be using the word in a qualified or restricted sense, in the way that he uses the word 'substance' when he says that not only God but certain creatures are substances (*Principles*, pt. I, art. 51: AT VIIIA 24, CSM I 210). The actions of creatures, therefore, are spontaneous if they depend on no created entity apart from the agent who performs them. Now the agent by which a human volition is performed is just the human mind; there is neither any need nor any room for any other agent or cause (other than God) to take part in the action of willing. Furthermore, in performing volitions the mind uses only its own power of willing. Whatever, therefore, depends on the will in the way that a volition must do, is bound to depend on the mind to which that will also belongs. In the case of volitions, voluntariness and spontaneity coincide.

Unfortunately, there is a third notion that Descartes appeals to in his efforts to explicate freedom, namely, indifference (*Principles*, pt. I, art. 41: AT VIIIA 20, CSM I 206; letter to [Mesland] of 9 February 1645: AT IV 173, CSMK 245). An action is indifferent if its agent is able, on the point of performing it, not to perform it, or to perform some other action instead. It is understandable that Descartes should refer to this notion, as well as to spontancity, in his discussions of freedom. Spontaneity is the essence of freedom according to certain Oratorian thinkers of his time, whereas the Jesuits chose to define freedom in terms of indifference.[2] Since Descartes wished to find favour with both groups, he often stressed the similarity of his views to theirs, to the point of using their preferred language when he felt it appropriate to do so. The difficulty is that the notions of spontaneity and indifference appear to yield two different conceptions of freedom.

The situation is complicated by the fact that Descartes uses the word 'indifference' with two distinct meanings. Besides indifference in the Jesuits' sense, he introduces his own sense, according to which an action is indifferent only if its agent has no reason to perform it, or the reasons for and against it are evenly balanced (Fourth Meditation: AT VII 58, CSM II 40; AT VII 59, CSM II 41; Sixth Replies: AT VII 432–3, CSM II 292; letter to [Mesland] of 9 February 1645: AT IV 173, CSMK 245). It is obvious that an action may be

---

[2] An Oratorian thinker of Descartes's acquaintance was Guillaume Gibieuf; Descartes refers to his *De libertate Dei et Creaturae* (1630) in a letter to Mersenne of 21 April 1641 (AT III 360; CSMK 179). A Jesuit with whom Descartes corresponded on the subject of freedom was Denis Mesland: see Descartes's letters dated 2 May 1644 (AT IV 111 ff.; CSMK 23 ff.) and 9 February 1645 (AT IV 173 ff.; CSMK 244 ff.).

indifferent in the one sense without being indifferent in the other; and Descartes says explicitly that a free action need not be indifferent as *he* uses the word (Fourth Meditation: AT VII 58, CSM II 40; Sixth Replies: AT VII 433, CSM II 292; letter to [Mesland] of 2 May 1644: AT IV 118, CSMK 234). But there are also passages in which Descartes maintains that actions that are not indifferent in the Jesuits' sense are none the less free, because of their spontaneity. Such actions are those by which a proposition clearly and distinctly perceived is affirmed or assented to; for it is impossible, Descartes contends, for the mind not to assent in such cases, and yet its action is free. In speaking of the Cogito, for example, he declares that he 'could not but judge that something so clearly understood was true' (Fourth Meditation: AT VII 58, CSM II 41). And more generally he says, 'if we see very clearly that a thing is good for us, it is very difficult—and, on my view, impossible, as long as one continues in the same thought—to stop the course of our desire' (letter to [Mesland] of 2 May 1644: AT IV 116, CSMK 233). This is not a point of minor significance in Descartes's philosophy; on the contrary, it is crucial to his epistemological project. For the inability of the mind to be mistaken when it affirms what it clearly and distinctly perceives is the ultimate basis of secure human knowledge.

There are free actions, therefore, which are not indifferent: in their case spontaneity is sufficient for freedom.[3] On the other hand, in one of his last pronouncements on the nature of freedom (in a letter addressed, it is true, to a Jesuit), Descartes explicitly says that the free mind is always indifferent in the sense of being able not to perform any action that it does perform.

[3] Besides citing actions which are free and yet not indifferent, Descartes may actually assert that indifference (in the Jesuits' sense) is not required for freedom. That he does assert this is argued, *inter alia*, by Michelle Beyssade in 'Descartes's Doctrine of Freedom' (Ch. 10, this volume). At issue is the meaning of Descartes's statement in the Fourth Meditation *'Neque enim opus est me in utramque partem ferri posse, ut sit liber'* (AT VII 57, ll. 27 f.). According to the usual interpretation, Descartes is saying here: 'In order to be free, there is no need for me to be inclined both ways'—which is indeed how his words are translated in CSM. Beyssade claims, however, that the statement ought to be rendered: 'In order to be free, it is not necessary that I should be able to go both ways', giving the verb *ferri* active force. On the usual reading, Descartes is referring to (what I have called) Cartesian indifference, which he then goes on to characterize. On Beyssade's interpretation, the reference is to the 'two-way power' or 'positive faculty of determining oneself to one or other of two contraries' (letter to [Mesland] of 9 February 1645: AT IV 173; CSMK 245) which constitutes indifference in the Jesuits' sense. Beyssade's reasoning on this point is persuasive, and I am inclined to accept her conclusion—although doing so does raise some further problems (see below, n. 5).

I do not deny [he declares] that the will has this positive faculty [and that] it has it . . . with respect to all . . . actions; so that [even] when a very evident reason moves us in one direction, although morally speaking we can hardly move in the contrary direction, absolutely speaking we can. For it is always open to us to hold back from pursuing a clearly known good, or from admitting a clearly perceived truth, provided we consider it a good thing to demonstrate the freedom of our will by so doing. (Letter to [Mesland] of 9 February 1645: AT IV 173; CSMK 245)[4]

There is no consensus among Cartesian scholars as to how this difficulty ought to be dealt with. One obvious strategy is to read the qualification expressed by the phrase 'morally speaking' back into Descartes's earlier statements. The trick is to do this without undermining his entire epistemology. I do not know if this strategy can be made to succeed, but to pursue it would take me away from my chief business in this chapter.[5] In any case, the remaining main tenets of the Cartesian view of freedom are clear: that all and only volitions are free actions, that (apart from God) all and only minds are free agents, and that actions and agents are free if and only if they are spontaneous.

Descartes's libertarianism is a specific position, and he is fairly explicit in setting forth his understanding of freedom. Not so his determinism, or how he conceives of causation. He does affirm a number of quite general propositions about causal relationships: that 'something cannot arise from nothing' (Third Meditation: AT VII 40; CSM II 28); that 'there must be at least as much [reality] in the efficient and total cause as in the effect of that cause' (ibid.); that everything depends on God (letter to Elizabeth of 3 November 1645:

---

[4] According to Michelle Beyssade (Ch. 10), the view stated here represents a 'change in Descartes's thought' from the position he had taken in the Fourth Meditation, where (as she interprets him) he denies that a free agent must have the power of going in either of two contrary directions. She also argues that the same change is expressed in—and accounts for—the difference between Descartes's original Latin statement of this point and its later translation (which he is supposed to have supervised) into French, which reads: '*Car, afin que je sois libre, il n'est pas nécessaire que je sois indifférent à choisir l'un ou l'autre des deux contraires*' (AT IXA 46). Beyssade's claim is that the indifference referred to in the French statement is that of the Cartesian kind, so that Descartes is now *not* denying that every free action is indifferent in the Jesuits' sense.

[5] It is worth noting that the difficulty here mentioned is compounded if Michelle Beyssade's reading of Descartes (see above, nn. 3, 4) is correct. On her view, the doctrine of the letter to Mesland is opposed to that of the Fourth Meditation: what he says in the one place contradicts what he says in the other. The problem for the interpreter is then not to make the apparent conflict between the two passages disappear, but to explain the real change in Descartes's thinking from the one to the other, and to assess its impact on the rest of his system.

AT IV 332; CSMK 277); that corporeal events are governed by laws (*Principles*, pt. ii, art. 36: AT VIIIA 61–3; CSM I 240–1); that souls and bodies act on one another (*Passions*, art. 34: AT XI 354; CSM I 341); and that some of our actions depend on our free will (*Passions*, art. 152: AT XI 445; CSM I 384). But, though it seems clear that causation is not the same thing in all of these relationships, Descartes says almost nothing about the differences between them. Nor does he do much to explain what causing, or being the cause or a cause of something, or depending on, amounts to in any one of these cases. So an account of Descartes's determinism must of necessity be somewhat speculative.

Since the precise subjects of Cartesian freedom are actions of willing, it is the causal relationships involving these in particular that pertain to the concerns of this chapter—that is, the relationships in which volitions are determined by or depend upon something other than themselves. Volitions, according to Descartes, are subject to three sorts of causes.

First, they are caused by God, in common with everything else in the universe. Descartes distinguishes two aspects of God's causation of things. On the one hand, God is the original creator of substances, and thus of the minds possessing the wills from which volitions are elicited. On the other hand, God concurs in all the operations of substances, including those ascribed to the will. Thus, not only is God the cause of 'all effects', including those that 'depend on human free will', but 'the slightest thought could not enter into a person's mind without God's willing, and having willed from all eternity, that it should so enter' (letter to Elizabeth of 6 October 1645: AT IV 314; CSMK 272). So God is causally responsible for every mind with its power of willing by having created it; and he is responsible for every volition by concurring in all of the actions of minds.

Secondly, volitions depend on the minds whose actions they are. This dependence is partly a matter of simply belonging to a substance, in the way that any attribute does. Since volitions, however, are not merely attributes but actions, and therefore events, there is more to their dependence than this. They owe not only their being but their occurrence at particular times to the minds they belong to: minds produce or perform their volitions as agents, besides possessing them as substances. Furthermore, each volition is produced solely by its own mind (leaving God out of account): this is what makes it a spontaneous and hence a free action. This means not only that no other (created)

agent takes part in performing it, but that no (created) factor outside
its own mind even affects it. Cartesian minds are thus (God aside)
wholly autonomous in performing their volitions. Descartes puts this
by saying that the will has 'a real and positive power to determine
[it]self' (letter to [Mesland] of 2 May 1644: AT IV 116; CSMK 234).

Finally, volitions are determined by other thoughts that occur in the
minds that perform them. The thoughts in question are perceptions,
since Descartes does not allow volitions to be caused by other volitions.
But not all perceptions are equally effective in causing volitions. Those
that are perfectly clear and distinct make it impossible (at least 'morally
speaking') for the minds in which they occur not to assent to what they
contain, assent being an act of the will. Obscure perceptions, by
contrast, may have no effect on the will whatsoever; or if they do affect
it they merely incline or dispose the will in one direction or the other,
without necessitating its movement (even morally speaking) in either.
In both of these cases the causal factor, the perception, is an event,
whereas the causes of the other two sorts we have noted, God and the
mind, are agents. It is not merely the content of a perception I have,
it is also my having it, that either makes me perform a volition or
inclines me to do so. But Descartes shows no reluctance in general to
count events, as well as agents, as causes. It is true that he never
explicitly calls a perception the 'cause' of a free volition. But he
regularly uses causal locutions in characterizing this relationship.
Thus, clear perceptions are said to 'impel' us or the will to perform
volitions (Sixth Replies: AT VII 433, CSM II 292; letter to [Mesland]
of 9 February 1645: AT IV 173, CSMK 245), as well as to make us
incapable of not doing so. And even the passions, which are obscure
perceptions and hence merely 'incline' the will without necessitating
it, are said to 'incite' and to 'dispose' the soul to this or that action of
willing (letter to Elizabeth of 15 September 1645: AT IV 295, CSMK
267; *Passions*, art. 40: AT XI 359, CSM I 343; *Passions*, art. 86: AT
XI 392, CSM I 358).

It might seem perplexing that perceptions should have causal roles
in willing for Descartes, given his doctrine that volitions are spontaneous actions on the part of the minds they belong to. A spontaneous
action is one that its agent performs all by itself, and a volition is
spontaneous just because the mind that produces it is not only not
compelled to do so by any external agent, it is not even assisted by
anything other than its very self. Such perplexity, however, can be
dispelled by recalling that Cartesian perceptions are attributes of

minds, just as volitions are; and that, while no perception is identical with the mind in which it occurs—it is not that very thing—neither is it really distinct from it. In every case in which a perception has any effect on a volition, the perception and the volition are attributes of the same mind, and their interaction takes place entirely within it. Neither, therefore, is an external factor with respect to the other, let alone with respect to the one mind in which both occur.

It is true that minds are not fully responsible, causally, for all their perceptions, in the way that they are for all their volitions. Perceptions are passive states, not actions; and though perceptions need minds to possess and sustain them as attributes, they often owe their occurrence to the actions of entities outside the mind, to corporeal agents. But a perception that is caused by an external agent is an obscure perception, and at best it merely inclines the mind in which it occurs to perform a volition. If such a perception were to cause a volition in the sense of (morally) necessitating its occurrence, then Descartes might have to grant that the external cause of the perception was the cause—or at least a partial or contributing cause—of the resulting volition, owing to the transitivity of this kind of causal relation; in that case the volition would not be spontaneous. But no such perception does cause a volition in this sense. And the perceptions that do cause volitions in the sense of (morally) necessitating their occurrence—namely, the ones that are clear and distinct—are none of them caused, even partly, by any external or corporeal factor. They are the productions wholly and solely of the minds they belong to: and that is why the volitions they cause, even though necessitated, are none the less spontaneous, and so free.

More needs to be said about how the mind works, on the Cartesian theory, when it performs a volition because of some perception it has, whether clear or obscure. Not much of this, unfortunately, is made explicit by Descartes himself, at least not in any systematic way. But the main lines of what he would or ought to have said on this subject can be worked out from some of his scattered remarks, especially in his last major work, *The Passions of the Soul.*

It is a fundamental principle for Descartes that the human will is naturally oriented towards goodness and truth: the mind has a natural tendency to perform a positive volition when presented with an instance of goodness or truth (letter to Mersenne of May 1637: AT I 366, CSMK 56; Second Replies: AT VII 166, CSM II 117; Sixth Replies: AT VII 432, CSM II 292; *Passions*, art. 177: AT XI 464,

CSM I 392). This is part of the 'institution of nature' which Descartes appeals to on several occasions (Sixth Meditation: AT VII 87, CSM II 60; *Passions*, art. 44: AT XI 361–2, CSM I 344; *Passions*, art. 50: AT XI 368–70, CSM I 348; *Passions*, art. 94: AT XI 399–400, CSM I 362; *Passions*, art. 137: AT XI 430, CSM I 376). What I call an instance of truth is provided by any proposition which is represented to the mind: the positive volition is one to affirm or assent to the proposition in question. An instance of goodness is provided by any proposition in which an object or situation is represented as being good in some way: the positive volition is one to pursue the object or to realize the situation in question. Mental representations are just perceptions in Descartes's ontology, whether or not they take the form of propositions; and they are formed in the mind by the intellect, which is its perceptive faculty. Perceptions may be generated by corporeal objects outside the mind, including the body with which the mind is united; or they may be produced by the mind itself acting alone, merely in consequence of an act of willing (so that we have one volition causing a perception which in turn causes another volition, even though Descartes does not permit one volition to be caused by another directly (*Passions*, art. 20: AT XI 344, CSM I 336). It is another one of Descartes's fundamental principles that the will cannot act except in response to an exercise of the intellect—some perception or representation or idea—so that willing presupposes perceiving: no volition without representation (Fourth Meditation: AT VII 60, CSM II 41; Fifth Replies: AT VII 377, CSM II 259; *Comments on a Certain Broadsheet*: AT VIIIB 363, CSM I 307).

When any (propositional) perception is clear and distinct, then the institution of nature is such that the will moves immediately to affirm— that is, to judge to be true—the perception in question. We then say that the perception makes the will act (although strictly speaking, of course, it is the mind that acts). It is, however, only in conjunction with the will's (or the mind's) natural tendency to act, when presented with an instance of truth, that the perception is able to bring about the action of willing. So the institution of nature has to be recognized as a causal factor in such situations as well, a factor deriving ultimately, no doubt, from the creative or concurring action of God.

The situation is more complicated when the perception which 'incites' a volition is obscure. Here the most interesting case to consider is that in which the obscure perception is a 'passion of the soul', in Descartes's special use of that term. These passions are powerful motivators of human actions, especially those having to do with our bodies: it is their function, Descartes says, 'to dispose the soul to will the things that nature tells us are useful, and to persist in this volition' (*Passions*, art. 52: AT XI 372; CSM I 349). 'Useful' here means 'useful for the purpose of preserving our bodies' (*Passions*, art. 137: AT XI 430; CSM I 376), usefulness in this sense being one species of goodness. And nature tells us that something is useful by representing it as good in this way, by arranging for us to perceive it as good. Because this perception is obscure, the soul does not respond immediately by willing to pursue the thing perceived as good. What happens rather is that a passion is produced in the soul, the passion of desire in particular: though other passions such as love and joy and hope and courage may be aroused as well (*Passions*, arts. 56–67: AT XI 374–8; CSM I 350–2), these are effective in moving the will only 'by means of the desire they produce' (*Passions*, art. 144: AT XI 436; CSM I 379). It is then this passion that causes the appropriate volition, not by necessitating its occurrence, but by disposing the soul to perform it.

Note that the institution of nature is invoked by Descartes at two points in the process just sketched. Nature first operates by causing a perception of a thing's usefuless to be produced in the soul. And it is by nature's doing again that the passion roused by this perception influences the will. Of course nature is at work also in the intervening process by which the perception gives rise to the passion, for this involves actions on the part of corporeal agents—sense organs, nerves, and brain—all of which are governed by natural laws, the laws of physics in fact. This part of the story is told by Descartes in considerable detail (*Passions*, arts. 7–16 *et passim*: AT XI 331–42 *et seq.*; CSM I 330–5 *et seq.*), more detail, certainly, than he provides in the case of the parts dealing specifically with volitions.

We can now address the question of Descartes's compatibilism, the logical consistency of his position that volitions are free with each of his claims regarding their determination by causes. Since he explicitly makes each of these claims—that volitions are caused by God, by the minds in which they occur, and by clear perceptions—while remaining committed to the freedom of every volition, it *follows* that Descartes is a compatibilist with respect to each of these relationships. But his compatibilism is not merely implicit in his writings, as a logical consequence of his explicit statements. Descartes also explicitly says, with respect to two of the three ways in question, that there is no conflict between a volition's being free and its being caused. With respect to God, there is, for example, his statement to Elizabeth that 'the free will [or] the independence which we experience and feel in ourselves . . . is not incompatible with a dependence of quite another kind, whereby all things are subject to God' (letter to Elizabeth of 3 November 1645: AT IV 333; CSMK 277). With respect to clear perception, we have the testimony of the Fourth Meditation that 'neither divine grace nor natural knowledge [sc. both of which are sources of clear perception] ever diminishes freedom; on the contrary, they increase and strengthen it' (Fourth Meditation: AT VII 58; CSM II 40); and Descartes's declaration in the Sixth Replies that 'not only are we free when ignorance of what is right makes us indifferent [sc. in the Cartesian sense of the word], but we are also free—indeed at our freest—when a clear perception impels us to pursue some object' (Sixth Replies: AT VII 433; CSM II 292). As for the remaining way in which volitions are caused, namely by depending on a mind, being so caused is not only not in conflict with, it actually constitutes the freedom of volitions, according to Descartes's equation of freedom with spontaneity: being free entails being caused in this way. In this case, therefore, that freedom is compatible with causal dependence is a consequence a fortiori.

Of course it is one thing for a philosopher to say that there is no incompatibility between two apparently contrary claims in his system, and quite another for his saying this to be justified, or even intelligible. Two problems remain in connection with Descartes's professions of compatibilism in the two cases just noted. How can a volition be free if a clear perception *impels* its performance? And how can a volition be free if, as Descartes says in another letter to Elizabeth, everything that happens comes *entirely* from God, and God is not just the 'universal cause' but 'the *total* cause of everything' (letter to Elizabeth of 6 October 1645: AT IV 314; CSMK 272; emphasis added)?

The first of these problems is solved if we understand clear perceptions to impel volitions only 'morally speaking' and not absolutely. Alternatively, we could define freedom wholly in terms of spontaneity and give up the requirement of (Jesuitical) indifference. There are difficulties consequent upon both of these alternatives: the one places Descartes's epistemology in jeopardy, the other flies in the face of clear textual evidence. But either or both of these difficulties could, perhaps, be resolved, without doing major damage to the Cartesian system.

The second problem, however, is harder to deal with. Even if we identify freedom with spontaneity, eschewing indifference, we still have to understand how a volition which depends wholly on the mind that performs it can also come entirely from God. Earlier, we set God aside, and defined spontaneity in terms solely of created agents; but now it looks as if that stipulation was illegitimate. It now looks as if we have two distinct conditions for the performance of any volition, each of which is sufficient as well as necessary: on the one hand, that some created mind produce it; on the other, that it come from God. Furthermore, it must have looked so to Descartes himself on occasion, for in the *Principles* he notes the 'great difficulties' we get ourselves into 'if we attempt to reconcile . . . divine preordination with the freedom of our will', and suggests that the proper response to these difficulties is simply to give up the attempt (*Principles*, pt. I, arts. 40–1: AT VIIIA 20; CSM I 206).

A more satisfactory response, however, would be to consider the action of God to be not sufficient for the performance of any volition, but only necessary therefor. There is some textual basis for thinking that this was in fact Descartes's considered position. For example, in the letter to Elizabeth just cited, he immediately glosses his remarks that everything comes 'entirely from' God and that God is 'the total cause of everything' by saying, in the one case, that 'the slightest thought could not enter into a person's mind *without* God's willing . . . that it should so enter'; and, in the other, that 'nothing can happen *without* His will' (letter to Elizabeth of 6 October 1645: AT IV 314; CSMK 272; emphasis added). In both instances the original remark connotes sufficiency on the part of God's action, but the gloss implies only its necessity. On the other side, however, these are not the only passages in which Descartes uses the language of sufficiency in speaking of God's causal relation to created things, including free human volitions (Third Replies: AT VII 191, CSM II 134; *Principles*, pt. I, art. 24: AT VIIIA 14, CSM I 201; *Principles*, pt. I, art. 41: AT VIIIA 20, CSM I 206). It may be that such usages can all be dismissed as rhetorical exaggerations, which Descartes in general was not loath to indulge in. But this would have to be shown in detail before this way of solving the problem could be adopted with confidence.[6]

---

[6] I am grateful to John Carriero, Jack Davidson, Robert Sleigh, Kenneth Winkler, and especially Paul Hoffman and Stephen Voss, for helpful comments on an earlier version of this chapter.

10

Descartes's Doctrine of Freedom: Differences between the French and Latin Texts of the Fourth Meditation

MICHELLE BEYSSADE

It is a well-known fact that the French text of *Les Méditations métaphysiques*, published in 1647, is not an exact and strict translation of the Latin *Meditationes de prima philosophia* published in 1641 (in Paris) and in 1642 (in Amsterdam). One of the reasons for this is that Descartes, when he revised Duc de Luynes's fine French translation of his original Latin, introduced, as the publisher lets the reader know, 'some minute changes' or modifications, in order to 'correct himself rather than his translator' and 'to make his own thoughts clearer' (AT IX 2-3).[1]

In the case of most of the differences we observe between the Latin original text and the French version, it is impossible to say whether they should be attributed to Descartes himself or to his translator—and in no case can there be any absolute certainty. But there is at least one passage in the *Meditations* in which some of the discrepancies between the two texts are very likely the result of changes or modifications due to Descartes himself. Some of these discrepancies are minute, others less so, but in any event their significance turns out to be substantial. The passage in question is from the Fourth Meditation (AT VII 57-8, IX 46) where Descartes explains what free will will consists in, and where he gives two successive definitions, the second being introduced with *vel potius/ou plutôt* ('or rather'). In the

---

[1] '*pour se corriger plutôt qu'eux [les traducteurs] et pour éclaircir . . . ses propres pensées . . .*' (from the short preface, 'Le libraire au lecteur', printed at the start of the first French edition of the *Meditations* (1647)).

TABLE 10.1 *Fourth Meditation* (AT VII 57–8, IX 46)

Latin text (1641–2)	*French text (1647)*
Voluntas sive arbitrii libertas . . . tantum in eo consistit quod idem, vel facere vel non facere (hoc est affirmare vel negare, prosequi vel fugere) possimus, vel potius in eo tantum quod ad id quod nobis ab intellectu proponitur affirmandum vel negandum, sive prosequendum vel fugiendum, [1] *ita feramur ut a nulla vi externa nos ad id determinari sentiamus.* Neque enim opus est [2] *me in utramque partem ferri posse* ut sim liber, [3] *sed contra,* quo magis in unam propendeo, sive quia rationem veri et boni in ea evidenter intelligo, sive quia Deus intima cogitationis meae ita disponit, tanto liberius illam eligo; nec sane divina gratia, nec naturalis cognitio unquam imminuunt libertatem, sed potius augent & corroborant. [4] *Indifferentia autem illa,* quam experior, cum nulla me ratio in unam partem magis quam in alteram impellit, est infimus gradus libertatis, & [5] *nullam in ea perfectionem, sed tantummodo in cognitione defectum, sive negationem quandam, testatur;* nam si semper quid verum & bonum sit clare viderem, numquam de eo quod esset judicandum vel eligendum deliberarem; atque ita, quamvis plane liber, numquam tamen indifferens esse possem.	La volonté . . . consiste seulement en ce que nous pouvons faire une chose, ou ne la faire pas (c'est à dire affirmer ou nier, poursuivre ou fuir), ou plutôt seulement en ce que, pour affirmer ou nier, poursuivre ou fuir les choses que l'entendement nous propose, [1] *nous agissons en telle sorte que nous ne sentons point qu'aucune force extérieure nous y contraigne.* Car, afin que je sois libre, il n'est pas nécessaire [2] *que je sois indifférent à choisir l'un ou l'autre des deux contraires;* [3] *mais plutôt,* d'autant plus que je penche vers l'un, soit que je connaisse évidemment que le bien et le vrai s'y rencontrent, soit que Dieu dispose ainsi l'intérieur de ma pensée, d'autant plus librement j'en fais choix et je l'embrasse. Et certes la grâce divine et la connaissance naturelle, bien loin de diminuer ma liberté, l'augmentent plutôt et la fortifient. [4] *De façon que cette indifférence* que je sens, lorsque je ne suis point emporté vers un côte plutôt que vers un autre par le poids d'aucune raison, est le plus bas degré de la liberté, et [5] *fait plutôt paraître un défaut dans la connaissance, qu'une perfection dans la volonté;* car si je connaissais toujours clairement ce qui est vrai et ce qui est bon, je ne serais jamais en peine de délibérer quel jugement et quel choix je devrais faire; et ainsi je serais entièrement libre, sans jamais être indifférent.
[1] we move (go) in such a manner that we do not feel we are	[1] we act in such a manner that we do not feel any external force is

TABLE 10.1 *Continued*

Latin text (1641-2)	French text (1647)
<u>determined</u> by any external force	<u>constraining us</u>
[2] <u>I can move</u> (<u>go</u>) both ways	[2] <u>I am indifferent as to the choice</u> of one or the other of two contraries
[3] but <u>on the contrary</u>	[3] but <u>rather</u>
[4] <u>As for</u> that indifference	[4] <u>So that</u> this indifference
[5] does <u>not</u> reveal <u>any perfection</u> in it	[5] reveals . . . <u>rather than a perfection</u> of will

quotation given in Table 10.1, I note five discrepancies between the Latin and French texts. I shall argue that these changes originate from a change of mind by Descartes (and it will also emerge that the *ou plutôt* in the French text may not, after all, have exactly the same meaning as the *vel potius* in the Latin).

I. The Main Discrepancy: The Sense of 'Indifference'

The most conspicuous discrepancy is the second one in the text: the word *indifférent* appears in the French text in a place where, in the Latin text, the word *indifferens* does not appear (see Table 10.1, item number 2). The French text asserts that, 'in order to be free, there is no need for me to be *indifferent* as to the choice of one or the other of two contraries'. The Latin, by contrast, says that 'in order to be free, there is no need for me to be able to go both ways'. In other words, the Latin text deals with the *power of choosing* between two opposing alternatives (let us call this a two-way power), while the French text deals with the *indifference as to the choice* between two opposite ways. What is meant by indifference? There is no definition of the word where it appears in this sentence. But it cannot have any other meaning than that explained a few lines later, where the word *indifférence* renders the Latin word *indifferentia*.

I quote in English: 'this indifference I feel when I am not pushed to one side rather than to another by the weight of any reason . . .' Indifference means the *state* of hesitation or wavering because of ignorance or insufficient knowledge. The letter Descartes wrote to Mesland on 9 February 1645 confirms that this is, according to

Descartes, the proper meaning of the word *indifférence* and that Descartes did not give it any other meaning when he wrote the *Meditations*: 'Indifference seems to me to mean properly the *state* of the will when it is not impelled one way rather than another by any perception of truth or goodness. This was the sense in which I took it when I wrote that the lowest degree of freedom was that by which we determine ourselves to things to which we are indifferent' (AT IV 173; CSMK 245).

The state or condition referred to here (*je sois indifférent* ('I am indifferent')) is quite distinct from the *power* (*ferri posse*. 'I can move or go, I am able to move or go), the *power* or the *ability* of going both ways. What is meant by *ferri posse*? The translation of the phrase *in utramque partem ferri posse* is, as Anthony Kenny has noted, far from easy.[2] My own view is that *ferri* is not here used in a passive sense, but is employed in a manner corresponding to the middle voice in Greek: 'middle', because, despite its grammatically passive form, it has an active sense, which corresponds to the reflexive form in French. Thus the correct French rendering would be *se porter* as distinct from *être porté*, that is, 'to bring oneself' as distinct from 'to be brought', i.e. 'to move', not 'to be moved'. So I do not agree with Anthony Kenny's view that *ferri* should be rendered passively as 'to be impelled both ways'; in my view, 'there is no need for me to be able to go both ways' would be a better translation of the Latin phrase in this context.

Accordingly, what Descartes regards, in the Latin text, as not necessary for human freedom, i.e. as not constitutive of the essence of freedom, is the power of choosing between two contraries. *In utramque partem ferri posse* reformulates and repeats in different words *idem vel facere vel non facere posse*—a phrase from the preceding sentence. It means the power of doing or not doing something, the power or ability of choosing one or the other of two alternatives. Freedom then, in 1641, does not require a two-way power, but consists merely in being unconstrained: it is the spontaneous movement towards something.

By contrast, what Descartes, in the French text, regards as not necessary for human freedom, that is as not constitutive of its essence, what he dissociates from freedom, *is the state of indifference or wavering or balance* due to ignorance. In making this move, the French text, published in 1647, leaves it open for the reader to think that the two-

---

[2] A. Kenny, 'Descartes on the Will', 18.

way power *is* necessary for freedom—something which the original Latin had explicitly denied.

The two texts express different claims. *Être indifférent à choisir* is not a translation of *ferri posse*. Here we have an important discrepancy. It is, of course, illuminated in its full significance when we place the two successive texts within the context of Descartes's other writings; but it is quite conspicuous by itself, for our attention is called to it by an apparent clumsiness in the French version and also by a certain reticence in it.

To begin with, the word *indifférent* is not defined when it first occurs. Is this not clumsy? Actually, in the corresponding Latin sentence, the word *indifferens* does not appear. But in the original Latin text, the word *indifferentia* is defined when it first occurs. So what might possibly seem a clumsiness in the French version is an indication that Descartes had reworked his text in order to convey a different view. In altering the text, Descartes anticipates a notion, that of indifference, which is explained a little further on, but which, in the original Latin, does not appear so early.

So much for the apparent clumsiness. Now for the reticence. As we have seen, the French version omits reference to the two-way power and substitutes the state of indifference. But on the question of whether the two-way power is required for freedom it remains silent, thus leaving open a question that the Latin text resolved in the negative. Is the power of choosing between two alternatives still required as a necessary part of the highest grade of freedom—a spontaneous, because perfectly illuminated, assent to the clearly known truth or goodness? According to the Latin text, the answer is no; this power is not necessary in order to be free. The French text does not give either a negative or an affirmative answer. It alters the phrase which implied this denial. It does not go so far as to say yes, but makes it possible to say yes.

Now we know that Descartes, in a letter written to Mesland on 9 February 1645, in which he explains and settles his thoughts on freedom after his discussion with the Jesuits, claims explicitly that the two-way power holds even in the full light of evidence. I quote, in Kenny's translation: 'When a very evident reason moves us in one direction, although, morally speaking, we can hardly move in the contrary direction, absolutely speaking we can' (AT IV 174; CSMK 245).[3]

---

[3] Notice that 'we can move' renders *possimus ferri*. As for the restrictive clause which follows, introduced with *modo* ('provided'), I think it does not deny what has just been said, but specifies the condition and the means for the exercise of this power.

So this letter sheds some light on the difference we noted between the two texts of the *Meditations* and gives it its full significance—there has been *an evolution in Descartes's view on freedom*; or perhaps we should simply say that *his thought has become more explicit.* Descartes, who had originally distinguished freedom from the two-way power, was led, in the course of his discussion with the Jesuits, to recognize and make more explicit the importance and the continuous presence of this power in freedom. When he came to revise the French translation of the *Meditations*, a few years after writing the Latin text, Descartes had probably already changed his mind. So I take it that he used the opportunity of the revision to withdraw from the new text the distinction that the original Latin text established between freedom and the two-way power; in the new revised version he dissociated freedom only from the state of indifference. In short, the conspicuous discrepancy between the two versions is highly significant and marks a definite change in Descartes's thought.

II. Two Objections Considered

There are other discrepancies to be observed in our passage, but, before I exhibit them in order to strengthen my claim that Descartes retouched and reworked his text, I have to examine two objections which can be raised against my view first of the Latin text, and secondly of the French text.

(*a*) It can be asked, first, concerning the Latin text, whether it is so clear that Descartes dissociates the power of choosing from the definition of freedom. Throughout the passage, even after the *vel potius* which rectifies the first definition, Descartes keeps the verb *eligere*, translated 'to choose' (*sed tanto liberius eligo . . . judicandum vel eligendum*); this is in accordance with the definition of free will as *facultas eligendi*. Must we not, therefore, say that the fullest freedom, in the full light of evidence, is still, for Descartes, a choice—a choice without hesitation, without wavering, but nevertheless a choice?

But is it right to use the term *choice*? What does *choice* mean? If it is not necessary in order to be free, as the Latin text unambiguously says, that I am able to go both ways, then the verb *eligere* which occurs in the following lines cannot mean 'to choose between two opposite ways'. The highest freedom consists in going spontaneously one way without being able to choose the opposite way. Perhaps, then, we have to distinguish in French between *choisir* ('to choose') and *élire* ('to elect' or 'to embrace'), and it is better to translate *eligere* by *élire* as the duc de Luynes above did when he translated *facultas eligendi* by *puissance d'élire*. *Eligere* means an unconstrained assent or acquiescence, which *does not necessarily involve the power of choosing between two alternatives*. Thus, *eligere* does not involve choice, or, if we use the word 'choice', if we continue, as it is usual, to translate *eligere* by *choisir* in French and 'to choose' in English, we have to remember that *choice* is not necessarily choice between two alternatives; conversely, when we think of a choice between two alternatives, we ought to say explicitly 'choice between two contraries or alternatives', and not merely *choice*. This is what I have done in this chapter.

To conclude on this first difficulty: Descartes, in the original Latin text, after he said that the two-way power is not necessary for freedom, maintains that free will is *facultas eligendi*. Hence, *eligere, élire*, is not necessarily *choisir* 'to choose', or at least it does not necessarily mean the choice between two opposite ways. Freedom or free will, *facultas eligendi*, is not necessarily a power of choosing between two alternatives.

Let us note that, in the French version, since it has not dissociated freedom from the power of choosing between two opposite ways, as the Latin text did, there is no problem in talking of *choisir* or *faire choix de* where the Latin text said *eligere* (*tanto liberius . . . eligo/d'autant plus librement j'en fais choix*). The idea of choice, in the context of the French version which is silent on the question of a two-way power, does not prevent any awkwardness. None the less, *faire choix de* is perhaps not an exact translation for *eligere*, and maybe the translation adds *et je l'embrasse* ('and I embrace it') in order to lead the reader towards the idea of something different from the idea of choice between two opposite ways, namely the notion of 'electing' or 'embracing' (in French, *élection*).

(*b*) The second difficulty concerns the French text. Another occurrence of the verb *choisir* in the French version can be advanced as an objection against my view. In the sentence in which I mentioned a discrepancy between the two texts, the French text says, '*il n'est pas nécessaire que je sois indifférent <u>à choisir</u> l'un ou l'autre des deux contraires* ('there is no need for me to be indifferent as <u>to the choice</u> of one or the other of two contraries'). One could thus deny the discrepancy I noted between the two texts, and object that the same idea of (two-way) choice occurs in both texts.

The reply to this objection is first that the state of indifference is indeed an indifference as to choice. This state makes the choice uneasy and sometimes for ever unrealized, but it does not abolish the power of choice (that is the reason why Descartes, at the end of this passage, recognizes a degree of freedom in it—albeit a low one). Secondly, what Descartes explicitly underlines about the state in question, in order to dissociate it from freedom, is precisely the *indifference* as to choice, and not the power of choosing which is present in this state. The idea of choice is, admittedly, present in the words 'indifferent as to the choice', but only in so far as the difficulty and even the impossibility of choosing is meant. What is dissociated here from the essence of freedom is really the state of indifference, the state of indifference as to choice, of course, but *not* the power of choice itself, in contrast with the Latin.

With these two objections—the first one concerning the Latin text, the second one concerning the French text—dispelled, we can proceed to examine the other discrepancies noted between the two texts. What has emerged so far is that the French text does not translate the Latin one: it formulates a different view. Let us now look at the other discrepancies.

III. The Four Remaining Discrepancies

Discrepancy Number 3

Just after the words discussed above, we find in Latin *sed contra* ('but on the contrary') and in French *mais plutôt* ('but rather'). The difference is perhaps not very important in itself, but it is connected to the difference between the two contexts, and, to that extent, is significant.

I say 'perhaps not very important in itself' because—we cannot but acknowledge it—the French text might have contained *mais au contraire* ('but on the contrary') without losing its coherence, and the Latin text, without losing its coherence, might have followed the *vel potius* ('or rather') we find in the preceding sentence with *sed potius* ('but rather'), as it in fact does, four lines further on.

However, *sed contra* expresses more precisely what the original text intends to say: the denial of holding the two-way power as essential for freedom. In the Latin text, when Descartes elucidates (in the sentence beginning with *neque enim*) the reason why he prefers the second definition given in the preceding sentence, that is the definition introduced with *vel potius*, he withdraws, or downgrades, the first definition, the two-way power (*idem vel facere vel non facere posse*, repeated with *in utramque partem ferri posse*). So the *vel potius* of the preceding sentence is reformulated as *sed contra*, which emphasizes that withdrawal, and shows that *vel potius* introduced not an elucidation, but a correction. *Sed contra* restricts the meaning of *vel potius* and introduces a corrective effect.

The French text expresses a different view. Since it dissociates freedom only from the state of indifference ('to be indifferent as to the choice of one or the other of two contraries' does not repeat 'to be able to do a thing or not to do it' but means something different), Descartes, here, has no reason to emphasize this dissociation. *Mais plutôt* ('but rather') is sufficient.

As I have said, this modification is, in one sense, insignificant, since it is possible to invert the expressions, but, in another sense, it is significant: each text, the Latin and the French, is more satisfactory as it is. And this modification is obviously consistent with the first one we noted.

Discrepancy Number 4

The Latin text says: *Indifferentia autem illa quam experior* ('as for that indifference I experience'); the French text says *De façon que* cette indifférence que je sens ('So that this indifference I feel').

In the Latin phrase *Indifferentia autem illa, autem* underlines the fact that the notion introduced here is another notion, a new one in the analysis. Descartes previously considered the two-way power. He now considers the state of indifference. These are two distinct notions. Neither the power nor the state is the same as freedom, but they have to be distinguished from one another. The particle *autem* here juxtaposes and distinguishes the items it governs. Moreover, Descartes says: *indifferentia autem illa. Illa* lays the stress on the difference, on the distance from what came before. (Hence, in my view, *illa* should be translated into English by '*that*' rather than by '*this*'.)

De façon que cette indifférence, in the French text, sets in place of the juxtaposition a consecutive clause which closely links what follows with what precedes. The notion of indifference, in the French text, is not a new one. We have already been told that indifference is not required for freedom. This claim is then explained and illustrated with some examples. Afterwards we arrive at the conclusion that (*de façon que* ('so that')) this indifference, this very indifference we mentioned two sentences earlier, is the lowest degree of freedom. 'So that' (*de façon que*) in the French text implies a continuity which we do not find in the Latin text.

We see that this discrepancy is consistent with the two preceding ones. It confirms our contention that the text has been intentionally retouched by the author. The discrepancy could not possibly be attributed merely to a lack of accuracy in the translation. Nobody would translate *autem* by *de façon que* through lack of attention. It is a purposeful modification in order to bring the end of the passage into harmony with a first essential change.

Discrepancy Number 5

There is in the French text a *plutôt* which does not correspond to anything in the Latin text, neither a *potius* nor a *contra*: *fait <u>plutôt</u> paraître un défaut dans la connaissance qu'une perfection dans la volonté* ('reveals a defect of knowledge <u>rather</u> than a perfection of will'). In the Latin we have: <u>*nullam*</u> *in ea perfectionem, sed tantummodo in cognitione defectum, sive negationem quamdam, testatur* ('does <u>not</u> reveal <u>any</u> perfection in it, but only a defect or some negation in knowledge').

Both sentences deal with the state of indifference, but the original Latin text denies that this state exhibits any perfection of freedom or free will (*nullam in ea perfectionem*). The French text, by contrast, does not deny this; it does not rule out that some perfection of free will is exhibited in that state, but it down-plays this idea, and stresses the lack of knowledge this state contains and exhibits ('reveals a defect of knowledge <u>rather</u> than a perfection of will').[4]

Well, what is this perfection of the will, which the French text, unlike the Latin, does not deny of the state of indifference? It cannot be anything other than the two-way power, which can be exercised in the state of indifference. But the two texts do not consider its relationship to freedom in the same manner.

The Latin text presents it as inessential to freedom: it is not at all a perfection of the will. Since the perfection of freedom is merely in the spontaneous assent to the clearly known truth or goodness, the

---

[4] We can note in both texts the relationship between *perfectio/perfection/*perfection and *defectus/défaut/*defect: *defectus* is the absence, the lack, the negation; *perfectio* is the presence, the reality or actuality.

ignorance and the lack of inclination one way or the other, characteristic of the state of indifference, are incompatible with the perfection
of freedom. But later on, the French version ceases to regard the two-
way power as inessential; this power, so far from being dissociated
from freedom, is affirmed as the reality of freedom, a perfection, and
one that exists even in the state of indifference. This latter state, of
course, mainly reveals a lack of knowledge, but, within this lack of
knowledge, it allows the reality or perfection of free will to remain—
that is, the power of choosing between two alternatives. Even if I am
indifferent, even in the same situation as Buridan's ass, I can choose
one side or the other; I can decide, determine myself, and this is a
perfection.

We see that this difference between the two texts is important in
itself. It relates to a change of mind. And it is perfectly consistent with
the main discrepancy discussed at the start of this chapter: the two-
way power is no longer excluded from the definition of freedom; it is
no longer alien to the perfection of free will.

Like the first discrepancy discussed, this one has to be directly
linked with what Descartes wrote to Mesland, in the letter quoted
above. In this letter, the faculty of determining oneself to one or to
the other of two contraries is termed a positive power. It is held as
one of the criteria or tests by which to measure freedom. Descartes
makes plain that it can be found in all the actions of the will and that
it is one and the same, always equally positive, regardless of whether
knowledge is lacking or the understanding is fully illuminated.

So it appears that Descartes became even more aware of the
presence and the essential place in freedom of that power of choice
between two alternatives (a power that others, though not Descartes
himself, sometimes also call indifference, but in *a sense which is distinct
from the first and proper sense*: a positive *power* of indifference, distinct
from the negative *state* of indifference; some commentators speak of
'positive indifference' for this power, and of 'negative indifference' for
the state[5]). The French version of the *Meditations* bears witness to this
evolution. In the first discrepancy we noted, Descartes ceases to
exclude the two-way power from his definition of freedom. In the case
of the present discrepancy, Descartes ceases to deny that this two-way
power constitutes a genuine perfection of the will.

---

[5] For the term 'negative indifference', see F. Alquié, *La Découverte métaphysique de
l'homme chez Descartes*, 288.

Discrepancy Number 1

The remarks I have to make here are more tentative than the preceding ones. They occurred to me when I looked at the *Meditations* after having read the whole letter to Mesland, and it may be that they are only a retrospective projection of one text on the other.

The difference is in the first sentence of our passage. The Latin version reads: *vel potius in eo tantum quod . . . ita feramur ut a nulla vi externa nos ad id determinari sentiamus* ('or rather simply in that we move towards . . . in such a manner that we do not feel *we are determined* to do so by any external force'). The French version reads: *ou plutôt seulement en ce que . . . nous agissons en telle sorte que nous ne sentons point qu'aucune force extérieure nous y contraigne* ('or rather simply in that . . . we act in such a manner that we do not feel any external force is constraining us to do so').

I shall not spend much time on the difference between *nos determinari* and *nous contraigne*. The notion of 'constraint' automatically implies determination by external force. However, we notice that the Latin text uses the more neutral word *determinari*, applicable to internal as well as external determination; and this suggests, or at least allows for, the possibility of an internal determination, which might pertain to freedom and maybe constitutes its essence.

What strikes me here is the difference between *feramur* and *nous agissons*. Perhaps *nous agissons* was employed simply and solely to render the 'middle voice'—the sense of *feramur*, which means *nous nous portons* ('we move') and not *nous sommes portés* ('we are moved').[6] But if we pay attention to the exact meaning of *agir* ('to act'), one may ask what exactly it means, when it is distinguished from *pouvoir faire* ('to *be able to do* or not to do'), which is in the first definition of free will, a definition Descartes intends to alter after *ou plutôt* ('or rather'). Is not the *action* what comes after the *choice*? Can we not distinguish between freedom before the action and freedom during the action?

If it is possible to say that freedom before the action consists in our ability to choose between two contraries (to do or not to do), the situation is not the same during the action. Once the action has been undertaken, it is no longer possible to choose. 'To do or not to do' is no longer the question. A free action, at this subsequent stage, is merely an unconstrained action. We no longer have to be able to do the contrary of what we are doing; we merely have to do what

---

[6] For this distinction, see above, Sect. I.

we are doing spontaneously, willingly moving ourselves and not being moved.

From this standpoint, *ou plutôt* (or rather), in the French sentence, might signify that Descartes is passing from one moment of freedom to another one, in order to attain a complete view of freedom, a view which is not restricted to what precedes the action. What Descartes might have intended in the phrase introduced by *ou plutôt* is not to correct the first definition (will as a two-way power) in order to lead the reader towards the idea of an internal determination, but to prevent an incomplete idea of freedom. The two-way power is not abandoned but only put in its proper place, or rather limited to its proper time. In fact the next sentence of the French version does not exclude it, as the Latin text does, from the definition of freedom; it excludes only the state of indifference.

We know that this distinction of two moments in the analysis of freedom is developed in the letter to Mesland on 9 February 1645, after Descartes recognized, even when there is no indifference, the persistence of the two-way power, explicated as a positive faculty of determining oneself to one or the other of two contraries. Descartes explains in the letter that, if we consider the actions of the will before their performance, freedom entails the positive power of choice between two contraries and not the negative state of indifference; but that, considered in the actions of the will during this performance, freedom does not entail indifference either in the proper sense (the negative state) or in the second one that is sometimes used (the positive power).

In this letter, which gives a very precise account of his doctrine of freedom, Descartes is in a certain manner reasserting his original statement, that of 1641, which dissociated freedom from a two-way power; he is, moreover, reasserting that he does not contradict himself when he recognizes, as he does in the first paragraph of the letter, that the two-way power exists even in the case of a clearly perceived truth, since he holds that the two-way power is not present the whole time, during the entire course of the free action. In this letter Descartes strives to expound his doctrine by going as far as possible in recognizing the presence in free will of the two-way power, without contradicting the original Latin text of the *Meditations* which dissociated it from freedom.

But this distinction of moments, which gives a coherence to the different states of the development of his thought, is *perhaps* also what

he suggests in the French version of the *Meditations*, without insisting
on it, so that the *ou plutôt* ('or rather') does not appear as a *mais au
contraire* ('but on the contrary'), but introduces a restriction on the two-
way power, putting it in its place—or rather its time. It seems to me
likely that this modification is intentional, though I am not as sure of
this as I am in the case of the other changes I have discussed. At all
events, if it is intentional, it is connected, like the four other changes,
to Descartes's main purpose, which is to retract his earlier denial that
the two-way power is necessary for freedom.

    We thus see that all of these discrepancies, more or less conspicuous,
more or less important by themselves, relate to a systematic shift in
Descartes's thought. They all cohere, and, from their coherence,
acquire additional force and significance.

IV. A Final Objection and Concluding Comments

A possible objection, based on what comes after our passage, has to
be examined before concluding. On the following page of the Fourth
Meditation, in the French version (AT IX 47), Descartes maintains
that, in the face of the evidence of the Cogito, I cannot but judge it
to be true: *je ne pouvais pas m'empêcher de juger . . . que cela était vrai*—
a phrase which exactly translates the Latin *non potui non judicare* (AT
VII 58, l. 29). *I cannot but judge*: Descartes, here, denies the two-way
power, in the French text as well as in the Latin text.

    In order to reply to this objection, let us notice that the example of
the Cogito is given, as the first one in a series of three examples, within
the scope of the exploration of error, and that this exploration takes
place in accordance with the essential aim of the search for truth which
characterizes the *Meditations*. Now, from this standpoint, the power of
saying *no* to something evident in effect vanishes. It is when 'I
examined whether anything exists in the world' that, confronted by the
evidence of my own existence, I could not but judge it to be true. This
inability is the reverse side of my will and search for truth, to which
all is at the moment subordinated. This inability is not an absolute
one. The letter to Mesland quoted above dispels any semblance of
contradiction with what we have said before: morally speaking, I
cannot say no; absolutely speaking, I can.

    It is worth noting in passing that, in the same paragraph, shortly
afterwards, the French version omits the word *sponte* which the Latin

text conjoins as a synonym to the word *libere* (AT VII 59, l. 3). Freedom is no longer identified with spontaneity—a change which was probably deliberate, and connected to those we have observed in our passage.

In conclusion let me say a word about the aims of this chapter as they bear on the general treatment of Descartes's doctrine of freedom. It seems to me that Descartes became more and more aware of the importance of the two-way power in freedom—that is, of its essential role in freedom; of the perfection it evinces in freedom; of its continuous presence in freedom. The divergence between the two texts of the *Meditations* bears witness to this change of mind. That is the thesis of this chapter. I do not, however, intend to deny that, according to Descartes, the essence of freedom does not amount to the two-way power; that the greatest freedom consists in the spontaneous assent to the clearly known truth, and that, at the time of perceiving clearly and distinctly the truth, and as long as we pay attention to a clearly and distinctly known truth, we cannot resist it. Notice in connection with this last proposition (which I am not denying) that our ability to distract our attention from something evident amounts to the two-way power. Of course, the fact that we cannot fix our attention constantly on the same thing is a weakness; but the fact we can distract our attention from something, and from something evident, is a power. Compare the letter to Mesland of 2 May 1644: 'We can call up before our mind some other reason to make us doubt of it, and so suspend our judgement, or perhaps even make a contrary judgement' (AT IV 116; CSMK 234). But that is another story.

Thus we can conclude that the two texts, the Latin one and the French one, do not express the same view. The Latin text denies that the two-way power is a part of the definition of freedom and excludes it from the highest grade of freedom; it does not recognize any perfection in it. The French text does not exclude it from the definition of freedom (though it does not explicitly include it), and it does hold it to be a perfection.

If we speak of an evolution in Descartes's doctrine of freedom (from the *Rules for the Direction of our Native Intelligence* to the *Passions of the Soul*, through not only the Latin and French texts of the *Meditations* but also the Latin and French texts of the *Principles*—an evolution which I cannot follow up here), the French version of the *Meditations* might be considered to be a stage in this development. But the letter to

Mesland, which provides us with a very detailed account of Descartes's thought on freedom, leads us to regard this 'evolution' as a more and more accurate explanation (or even a qualification) of a doctrine which became increasingly precise, but does not contradict itself. What remains non-explicit in the French version of the *Meditations* leads us to think that this French text is rather a recasting, or a reworking, made *after* the doctrine has been made plain and explicit, a moderate recasting in order to allow the reader to think something different from the original text, without expounding it explicitly.

For we must not forget that the French text is offered as a translation of the Latin text, and that the modifications the publisher mentions are not presented as exceeding its function of translation; described as minute, these changes are not meant to draw attention to themselves—and perhaps the more substantial they are, the less Descartes meant to draw attention to them. They are covered up rather than emphasized, so that the French text may still appear as a mere translation. Even when it is extremely probable that the changes it contains were initiated by Descartes, as is the case with our passage, the French text is ambiguous.

Such is the ambiguity in the French phrase *ou plutôt* in the first sentence, which corresponds with the Latin *vel potius*. It is on the one hand an exact translation of *vel potius*, but, on the other hand, it has another meaning which is revealed in the following line: *vel potius*, in the Latin text, introduces a correction and withdraws what precedes; *ou plutôt*, in the French text, introduces a more precise explanation which completes what precedes without withdrawing it. The elusiveness of these subtle shifts and differences is no accident. The French version of 1647 is at the same time a translation, and a new text.[7]

[7] I am deeply indebted to Wayne Waxman and to John Cottingham for their many suggestions for improvements to my English translation of the original French version of this chapter.

PART FOUR

The Senses and the Body

Descartes on Sense and 'Resemblance'

MARGARET D. WILSON o

Descartes begins the *Meditations* with the stated purpose of over-throwing those of his 'former beliefs' that allow of doubt, in the hope of erecting in their place a 'firm and permanent' scientific structure. His first step is to withdraw his 'trust' from the senses, on the grounds that they have sometimes 'deceived' him. 'Whatever I have up to now accepted as most true, I have received either from the senses or through the senses; however, I have sometimes found these to deceive; and it is prudent never to trust completely those who have deceived us even once' (AT VII 18).[1] In the Sixth Meditation, tracing his progress from naïve 'faith' in the senses to scepticism concerning their deliverances, he writes:

afterwards many experiences gradually destroyed all the faith that I had in my senses; for I from time to time observed that towers which from a distance looked round, appeared square from close up, and that enormous statues standing on their pediments did not seem large when viewed from the ground; and in these and countless other such cases I found that judgements of the external senses were mistaken. (AT VII 76)

Readers of the *Meditations*, focusing on passages such as these, have often concluded that Descartes's basic 'sceptical' point concerning the senses' inadequacy is grounded on ordinary daily experience: dis-crepancies that arise among our 'perceptions' when we perceive the same thing under different circumstances—at small and at great distances, for example—show that we cannot regard a judgement as certain beyond any doubt, merely because we take it to express what

---

[1] I take responsibility for the translations in this paper; but at the same time I wish to acknowledge that my readings have to some degree been influenced by both CSM and Haldane and Ross.

we have seen or otherwise perceived by sense. According to this point of view, Descartes introduces 'sensory ideas' as the indubitable residue that remains when judgements about external objects are called into question. In fact, though (as is now widely recognized), Descartes is aiming at a broader and more radical form of 'detachment from sense'—one that seems to carry with it the postulation of sensory ideas quite apart from any issues about 'certainty'. He wants to establish that sense experiences actually work *against* a true or reliable conception of what there is: that we cannot *in general* rely on our senses to reveal to us the nature of things.

One reason Descartes regards sense experience as an inadequate means for achieving knowledge of reality is that he holds that the real does not reduce to the physical or corporeal, but includes incorporeal and hence absolutely non-sensible entities: God and the thinking self. More to the point here, though, is his contention that the senses generally fail to provide us with an accurate or reliable conception of the nature or qualities of *physical things themselves*, of the bodies around us. True, our knowledge that such things *exist* ultimately depends on their having some effect on our sense organs and brain—and through the latter some effect on our minds. Also he takes it that variations in our sense experience correspond with *some kind* of differences in external things. Beyond that, however, the ordinary sense-based conception of the physical world (which, Descartes implies, gains its hold on us in unwary childhood) is inherently and broadly mistaken and confused: it amounts to a constant and pervasive 'deception of sense'.

Descartes asserts this position particularly insistently and directly in the *Principles of Philosophy*. The following passage is representative:

the perceptions of sense . . . do not, except occasionally and accidentally, teach us what external bodies are like in themselves. Thus . . . we may easily set aside the prejudices of the senses, and in this matter rely on the intellect alone, attending carefully to the ideas with which it is endowed by nature. (*Principles*, pt. II, art. 3: AT VIIIA 41–2)

Many familiar passages in the *Meditations* convey a similar message. Apart from providing the basis of our knowledge of the *existence* of a physical world, and of the legitimate claim that this world includes a variety of material states, the senses seem to be limited to the role of preserving the mind–body union, by alerting us to what is good or bad for us—considered as embodied beings—in the environment. In the

Sixth Meditation Descartes particularly insists that one must not rely on the senses beyond this appointed role, 'as though they were certain rules for immediately discerning the essence of bodies located outside us'; for about this 'they only indicate what is most obscure and confused' (AT VII 83). Knowledge of the truth about bodies pertains to 'mind alone', and not mind and body in conjunction (AT VII 82–3).

Of course the supposed deliverance of 'the mind' concerning the nature of matter and bodies coincides with the basic concepts of Descartes's mechanistic science. To understand and explain what goes on in the physical world, Descartes holds, we must clearly realize that bodies are merely bits of extension, with their particular figures, and particular motions relative to each other. This insight requires firmly grasping the distinction between manifest perceptual experience and the scientific reality: between mere sensory ideas in the mind, on the one hand, and the quantities in bodies, on the other hand. (But the global contrast between perceptual phenomenology and 'real' physical things is not necessarily dependent on the more naïve and obsolete features of the Cartesian theory of matter.)

Descartes characteristically expresses this distinction by denying that his sensory ideas—which, he says, are present to his mind, and 'immediately sensed'—'resemble' bodies, or are 'similar' to them. For example, he notes in the Third Meditation that the 'principal and most common error' that is found in his judgements consists in 'the fact that I judge that the ideas [of sense] which are in me are similar or conformable to certain things located outside me' (AT VII 37). The following passage (which occurs a little earlier in the Third Meditation) presents this view a bit more expansively:

I have before received and admitted many things to be very certain and manifest, which yet afterwards I found to be doubtful. What then were these things? They were the earth, sky, stars and all other things which I apprehended by the senses. But what did I clearly perceive of them? Just that the ideas or thoughts of such things appeared before my mind. [*Nempe ipsas talium rerum ideas, sive cogitationes, menti meae obversari.*] But even now I do not deny that these ideas are in me. But there was something else which I used to affirm, and which, because of the habit of believing, I judged that I perceived clearly, which nevertheless I did not perceive, that there were certain things outside of me from which these ideas proceeded, and to which they were entirely similar. (AT VII 35)

Here Descartes ascribes to himself (and by implication to others) *the views that*, first, sense experience involves the presence of such 'ideas' to the mind; and, secondly, that the ideas 'resemble' external objects from which they also 'proceed'. The former view is said to be genuinely 'clearly perceived'—i.e. (one may here gloss) evidently and reliably apprehended to be so. The latter view, however, is only speciously 'clear', is not genuinely evident, or reliably apprehended. A few pages later Descartes suggests that the unfortunate habit of belief in the 'resemblance' of our ideas to external objects that produce them arises from nothing more than 'blind impulse' (AT VII 40). A slightly more rationalized view of the origin of this erroneous assumption about perceptual experience emerges in the Sixth Meditation, where Descartes comments:

> Outside me, besides the extension, figure, and movements of bodies, I also sensed in them hardness, heat, and other tactile qualities, and further, light, and colours, and odours, and tastes and sounds, from the variety of which I distinguished the sky, the earth, the sea, and generally all the other bodies from each other. And surely it was not without reason that, from the ideas of all these qualities which offered themselves to thought, and which alone I properly and immediately sensed, I believed that I sensed certain things completely different from my thought, namely bodies from which these ideas proceeded . . . [*Nec sane absque ratione, ob ideas istarum omnium qualitatum quae cogitationi meae se offerebant, & quas solas proprie & immediate sentiebam, putabam me sentire res quasdam a mea cogitatione plane diversas, nempe corpora a quibus ideae istae procederent . . .*] (AT VII 74–5)

The first 'reason' Descartes mentions here is that he is not able to bring about or prevent the occurrence of such ideas. He continues:

> And since the ideas perceived by sense were much more vivid and lively, and even in their own way more distinct than any of those which I formed by knowing meditation . . . it did not seem possible that they proceeded from myself; and thus it had to be the case that they came from some other things. And since I had no other knowledge of such things except from these very ideas, nothing else could come to my mind than that the things were similar to the ideas. (AT VII 75)

But even if the belief in 'resemblance' is to this extent natural and understandable, further critical reflection will establish that it is simply not rationally tenable: there is simply *no good* reason to suppose that there is in a white or green body 'the same whiteness or greenness that I sense'; or that there exists in fire 'anything resembling heat' (any more than there is reason to suppose that there exists in fire something similar to the pain that I experience if I approach too closely) (AT VII

82–3). With respect to the fire all I have *reason* to believe is that 'there is something in it, whatever it may be', which excites the sensations of heat (or pain) in me. Closely parallel passages occur in the *Principles*. For example, in pt. I, art. 66, Descartes remarks that, 'when we saw a certain colour, we thought we saw some thing which was located outside of us and completely similar to the idea of colour that we were then experiencing in ourselves . . .' (AT VIIIA 32).

Jonathan Bennett has popularized the expression 'veil-of-perception theory' as a characterization of conceptions of sense perception which turn on the notion that (mental) 'ideas', and not bodies or their qualities, are the immediate or direct objects of awareness in sense experience.[2] Statements such as those I have just quoted from Descartes certainly appear to put him in the veil-of-perception camp. It is only ideas or thoughts that are present to his mind in sense experience. In so far as he relies on sense, these ideas seem to provide all the information he has to go on in trying to size up (what he assumes to be) the things around him. And while the ideas are taken to give him some contact with an independent physical world, they do not enable him to apprehend the actual qualities (or 'essence') of bodies.

In fact these passages, and others found almost up to the end of the *Meditations*, seem to convey a largely *negative and purgative* approach to sense experience: only when we have accepted the view of the senses as thoroughly and systematically 'deceptive' are we in a position to make advances in physics, by replacing theories cast in terms of the old sensory, qualitative, 'confused' ideas of body with explanations formulated entirely in terms of the 'distinct', intellectual, Cartesian geometrical ones. For this reason I once suggested that the *Meditations* seems hardly to present a theory of sense perception at all, 'in the ordinary philosophical sense'.[3] (I observed in a note that of course Descartes does develop a scientific theory of perception, in the *Dioptrics* and elsewhere). I particularly mentioned that it would be misleading to label the position sketched in the Sixth Meditation a form of representative or causal realism. Certainly this observation was in no way based on a denial that Descartes's mind, in the *Meditations*, is ensconced behind a veil of (mental) ideas. I took it as obvious that passages such as those just quoted established that this was in fact his

---

[2] See J. Bennett, *Locke, Berkeley, Hume: Central Themes,* 68 ff. (Bennett had already introduced this terminology in an earlier paper.)   [3] M. Wilson, *Descartes,* 203.

position. My point, on the contrary, was that Descartes allowed too little range for our *piercing* the veil, on the purely empirical level, to count as a 'realist' about sense perception ('representational' or otherwise).

Today, 'veil-of-perception' theories are widely regarded as absurd. (And indeed Bennett intended his designation as derogatory: it was meant, as he says, to 'express what is wrong with the theory'.[4]) Perhaps partly for this reason, there has developed a certain following for the notion that Descartes is not, after all, accurately interpreted as postulating (mental) ideas as intermediates between the mind and physical objects in sense perception. In 1983 both Ronald Arbini and Michael J. Costa published articles opposing the interpretation of Descartes as postulating mental intermediates in our perception of bodies.[5] Arbini focuses on Descartes's accounts of perception of size, shape, distance, and position in the *Dioptrics* and the Sixth Replies. He suggests that in these works Descartes explains '*how* the understanding operates together with the senses to dispel scepticism concerning the observed properties of matter'.[6] Thus, he says, they show us how to fill out Descartes's sketchy indication, at the end of the *Meditations*, that we can reliably determine the particular sizes, shapes, and so on of bodies, by utilizing all the resources of memory and intellect, joined to sense (AT VII 89). Mental 'ideas', Arbini points out, do not significantly figure in these accounts. Costa holds that, when Descartes talks of ideas being immediately present to the mind, he means corporeal ideas in the brain—not some kind of mental 'image-like entity' or 'phenomenal object'. (This may still count as a *physical* veil of ideas account—an issue I will not further pursue.) John Yolton, in a 1975 paper (cited by Costa as supporting his interpretive position) and in his later book, *Perceptual Acquaintance*, maintains that for Descartes to have an idea is just *to perceive*—and I take it he means to perceive *a physical object, directly*.[7] More recently, Ann Wilbur MacKenzie has suggested that (for cases *other than* sensations of colour and so forth) Descartes's conception of representation provides 'the raw materials for an interesting conception of direct sensory

---

[4] Bennett, *Locke, Berkeley, Hume*, 69.

[5] R. Arbini, 'Did Descartes have a Philosophical Theory of Sense Perception?', and M. J. Costa, 'What Cartesian Ideas are not'.

[6] Arbini, 'Did Descartes have a Philosophical Theory of Sense Perception?', 319.

[7] J. Yolton, 'Ideas and Knowledge in Seventeenth-Century Philosophy'; *Perceptual Acquaintance from Descartes to Reid* (see e.g. p. 15).

access to the world, according to which nothing sensed or cognized in the sensory process mediates sensory awareness of the physical object'.[8]

All of these treatments of Descartes's position on sense perception are quite complex, and cover a wide range of Cartesian material. I am not going to attempt a point-by-point discussion of them here.[9] I only want to reconsider, in the light of some of the points made in this debate, the claim that Descartes's conception of 'ideas of sense' carries with it the assumption that we do not perceive physical entities 'directly' in ordinary sense experience. I have to confess in advance that my motivation for this effort is not so much that I find that the works cited above have ultimately caused very much change in my views about sense perception in the *Meditations*. But they have caused me to re-examine them, with the result that I can attempt to offer a few observations that may be helpful in further clarifying some of the issues.

Of course it would be nice, in undertaking a discussion of this interpretive problem, to have before us a precise statement of what is being disputed. Shortly I will suggest that the question whether mental ideas function as 'intermediaries' in Descartes's conception of sense perception admits of varying interpretations. But for a start I will simply invoke Yolton's formulations. He denies that mental ideas are 'entities' that intervene between the mind and perceived bodies. He holds, on the contrary, that ideas are simply 'acts' of perception.[10]

I used to think that the Sixth Meditation passage, in which Descartes says that only ideas of colours and so forth are 'properly and immediately sensed', counted conclusively in favour of a veil-of-perception interpretation. And, indeed, the translations both of Haldane

---

[8] A. W. MacKenzie, 'Descartes on Life and Sense', 178. MacKenzie cites Yolton's 'more sweeping interpretation', in his article and his book, as an encouraging example for her own. See also B. O'Neil, *Epistemological Direct Realism in Descartes' Philosophy*, which Yolton discusses at some length, though critically.

[9] For more detailed discussion, see my reviews of Yolton and O'Neil.

[10] Yolton, *Perceptual Acquaintance*, 34–9. Yolton notes (p. 36) that in the Preface to the Reader (of the *Meditations*) Descartes indicates that 'idea' can be used in two senses: as an operation of understanding, or 'for the thing represented by that operation of the understanding'. It appears to be Yolton's position that, except in the case of God, for a thing to 'be in the understanding' is just for it to be understood: i.e. that the second sense of 'idea' involves, in general, no 'ontic' commitment. I do not find his position on this point very clearly explained or defended (see my review cited in the previous note). For a fuller discussion of the concept of 'idea' in Descartes see V. Chappell, 'The Theory of Ideas'.

216   *Margaret D. Wilson*

and Ross and of Cottingham tend to enforce this impression. The former have Descartes saying 'considering the ideas of all these qualities which presented themselves to my mind, and *which alone I perceived properly or immediately* . . .'; and the latter can be read as going even further in the direction of commitment: 'Considering the ideas of all these qualities which presented themselves to my thought, although the ideas were, strictly speaking, *the only immediate objects* of my sensory awareness . . .' (emphases added).[11] (I should add, though, that, if Cottingham's insertion of 'object' seems peculiarly tendentious, he at least keeps the term 'sense' in the picture. In this respect his translation is not only closer to the text, but preserves a feature that may be crucial, for a reason I am about to mention.) I now realize, however, that I was probably misunderstanding an aspect of this passage. Descartes's account of the 'levels of sense' in the Sixth Replies gives reason to think that behind this passage from the Sixth Meditation may lie a distinction between what 'properly' belongs to *sense* (basically, the old 'special sensibles') and *perceptual states that involve intellectual or computational processes* (as do determinations of size and situation, for example, according to both the *Dioptrics* and the Sixth Replies). In the Sixth Replies, the latter forms of perception are said not strictly to belong to *sense*—even though, in deference to common ways of speaking, Descartes there classifies them as belonging to 'the third level of sense' (AT VII 437). Thus (I now think) Descartes may *not* be explicitly making the point, in the Sixth Meditation passage, that we *directly perceive ideas of sense, as opposed to physical things*. Rather, he may just be isolating what is 'properly and immediately sensed', according to terminological assumptions which distinguish what is 'proper to sense' from perception involving active intellectual processes. This reading would help to leave open the question of whether or not *physical objects or bodies* actually are (immediately or directly) 'perceived', in circumstances that *we* would count as sense perception.

Further, I think Arbini is right in asserting that Descartes's accounts of our perception of bodies' size, shape, and distance in the *Dioptrics* and the Sixth Replies to a considerable degree avoid the veil-of-perception view of external world perception as mediated by sensory ideas. In the *Dioptrics*, it is true, Descartes appeals to various 'sensations' (such as those involved in awareness of the position of the head or eyes) in explaining our ability to 'judge' such physical features as

[11] Haldane and Ross (eds.), *The Philosophical Works of Descartes*, i 187–8; CSM II 52.

position and distance. But such sensations are treated as subliminal informational inputs, rather than as providing an intermediate, strictly 'mental' set of perceptual *objects* which our minds use as stepping stones in working outward to the actual *physical* things.[12]

Descartes's rejection of 'replica' accounts of perception in the *Dioptrics* and elsewhere may provide additional ammunition for the view that he *rejects* accounts of perception of external objects that appeal to awareness of intermediate entities. As he writes in the *Dioptrics*:

one must be careful not to suppose that, in order to sense, the mind needs to contemplate certain images which are sent by the objects to the brain, as our Philosophers commonly do; or, at least, one must conceive the nature of these images quite differently than they do. For, besides the fact that they do not consider anything about [the images] except that they ought to resemble the objects they represent, it is impossible for [the Philosophers] to show us how [the images] can be formed by these objects, received by the external sense organs, and transmitted by the nerves to the brain. (AT VI 112)

According to Descartes, the only reason philosophers have for assuming that sense perception of objects requires resembling images in the brain is the assumption that vision must be modelled on the bringing to mind of originals by means of their pictorial representations: 'seeing that our thought can easily be excited by a picture to conceive the object painted there, it seemed to them that it must be excited in the same way to conceive those objects that touch our senses by some little pictures that are formed in our head ...' (AT VI 112). 'The Philosophers' suppose that perception of external objects can and must be explained by postulating images or pictures, transmitted from the objects to the brain, which resemble the objects, and are then perceived, 'as if there were yet other eyes in our brain with which we could perceive them' (AT VI 130).[13] In his ridicule of this type of theory Descartes seems to suggest both (*a*) that it is futile to try to explain the perception of objects by postulating the perception of some stand-ins for the objects; and (*b*) that processes invoked in the explanation of perception need not be interpreted as being themselves *perceived*. Although he does not deny that images formed in the brain play a role in the causal explanation of perception, he says that the

---

[12] See especially the Sixth Discourse.
[13] Descartes's satirical characterization of his predecessors' views is historically questionable. See G. Hatfield, 'Descartes' Physiology and its Relation to his Psychology'.

only question to be raised with respect to such images is 'how they can give the mind the means to sense all the different qualities of the objects to which they relate, and not at all how they carry resemblance to them' (AT VI 113).[14] And—according to at least one line of thought which he advocates—the fact that brain-states of whatever type regularly excite a certain type of 'thought' or sensation in the mind is due merely to a divinely ordained concomitance or 'natural institution' (AT VI 130).[15]

Of course, Descartes's objections to the replica theory have to do with the *physical* conditions of sense perception, not with the issue of whether some kind of *mental* entities serve as intermediaries between the mind and the 'objects'. But one can see the temptation to generalize this point to the view that he would reject *any* stand-ins, within the human being, for the external things in theorizing about perception. If not, would he not say so? But, in fact, he does not—in the *Dioptrics*, *The Treatise on Light*, the Sixth Replies, and other works concerned with theoretical accounts of sense experience—treat perception as involving the problematic inferences from mental to physical entities that are characteristic of veil-of-perception views.

I think it is important to insist, though, that Descartes's objectives in the *Dioptrics* and related works are really quite different, for the most part, from the concerns of the *Meditations*. Arbini seems to scoff at the distinction, implied in my earlier remarks, between 'philosophical' and 'scientific' theories of perception.[16] I agree that the distinction between 'philosophical' and 'scientific' concerns is often made too glibly—and that I took it too much for granted in my earlier remarks on Descartes's views on perception. I am certainly a great believer in the importance of Descartes's commitments as a mechanistic scientist for the interpretation of the *Meditations* in general; and I think the increased interest in the whole range of Descartes's writings—including, particularly, the 'scientific' ones—is one of the greatest improvements in Cartesian scholarship in recent decades. I

[14] He notes that the mind can be stimulated to think of an object by words or signs that do not at all resemble it, as well as by resembling pictures (AT VI 112). See also the *Treatise on Light* (AT XI 3–6), and below, pp. 222–3.

[15] See also the Sixth Meditation (AT VII 87–8). For additional references and more detailed, critical discussion of Descartes's views about the causation of sensation, see M. Wilson, 'Descartes on the Origin of Sensation'. In 'Descartes on Life and Sense', Ann MacKenzie discusses in detail, from a somewhat different point of view, the quoted passages from the *Dioptrics*, and many related texts concerned with perception.

[16] Arbini, 'Did Descartes have a Philosophical Theory of Sense Perception?', 330.

even agree with Arbini that consideration of the *Dioptrics* and the Sixth
Replies helps to shed a little light on Descartes's comments, towards
the end of the Sixth Meditation, about the possibilities of arriving at
truth concerning 'things that are particular only', such as that the sun
is of a certain size (AT VII 80).

All that said, it seems to me that the sceptical issues that pervade
the *Meditations* really are correctly distinguished as specifically 'philosophical'. Today, people attempting to explain the physical and
physiological basis of our perceptual experience generally do not have
much time for such issues as whether there really is anything 'out
there' for us *to* perceive (even though one does often find more-
or-less casual mention of the appearance/reality distinction at the
beginning of psychological texts on perception). I see no good reason
for denying to Descartes, the scientist, a similar kind of abstraction
from the sceptical and scientific realist commitments addressed in the
Meditations and certain parts of the *Principles*.

This line of thought, I suggest, leads to a delineation of grounds
for a veil-of-perception reading of the Meditations which, as far as I
can see, are wholly untouched by both considerations drawn from
Descartes's treatment of perception in works such as the *Dioptrics* and
by Yolton's discussion in *Perceptual Acquaintance* (which ultimately
centres more on the *Meditations*). I do not see how there can be any
legitimate question that in the *Meditations* Descartes treats knowledge
of physical existence as secondary to, and inferentially derivative from,
knowledge of mental ideas. Thus, in the Second Meditation he asserts
(however problematically) that the indubitability of the existence of
ideas is established through the indubitability of the meditator's
existence as a thinking thing—while the existence of *any* physical entity
is still in doubt (AT VII 27–9). Of course Descartes eventually affirms
that sensory ideas depend on the mind–body union, but knowledge of
their 'presence in me' is prior to any well-grounded knowledge of that
union. These familiar considerations, it seems to me, establish a clear
sense in which Descartes does hold a veil-of-ideas theory with respect
to the perception of bodies—i.e. our knowledge that we actually perceive
any bodies is dependent upon, and derived from, the epistemologically
prior affirmation that we have in our minds ideas 'of them'.

A similar point can be made with respect to Descartes's conception
of the 'objective reality' of ideas (prominent in the Third Meditation),
on which Yolton places particular stress. Yolton holds, with some
textual basis, that the objective reality of an idea for Descartes is just

the (immediate) presence to the mind of an object: thus, he interprets, 'to have an idea is just to perceive'.[17] In one sense this may be true, and it may well provide a basis (as Yolton holds) for distinguishing Descartes's conception of the idea–object relation from Malebranche's, helping to give one legitimate sense to the claim that awareness of objects is 'immediate' for Descartes. Nevertheless, in whatever sense Descartes wishes to maintain that the objective reality of his ideas involves the presence of objects to his mind, it *has* to be compatible with another sense in which it does not. That is, Descartes can know all about the objective as well as the formal aspects of his ideas, *without yet knowing whether any extra-mental entities exist.*

Perhaps another sense can be given to the claim that Descartes holds a veil-of-perception theory, apart from issues of epistemic priority and inference. The proposal I have in mind depends on how we answer the question whether or not he takes colour sensations (and the others on the list quoted above) in any way to *represent* physical qualities (in the sense of presenting them, or having objective content). Some have held that he does *not*: Ann MacKenzie, for instance, who regards as decisive Descartes's remark in the *Principles* that such sensations 'represent nothing outside thought'.[18] Now Descartes seems to indicate in a passage I have quoted from the Sixth Meditation (AT VII 74–5) that such sensations are necessary for our perceptually distinguishing physical things from each other. Well, one may reason, if colour sensations, and the others, do not even represent anything outside the mind, yet are essential to our distinguishing of bodies in sense perception, then here is *another* sense, apparently distinct from issues about the order of certainty, in which perception of physical things is strictly mediated by purely mental entities. That is, our ability to perceive the diversity of bodies around us is mediated (on this view) by our awareness of mere mental modes with a strictly external, causal relation to the bodies they somehow help us discriminate. In still other words, because of the nature and role of sensations, Cartesian ideas of bodies cannot after all be fully understood merely as acts of perception in which bodies are immediately grasped, or 'present to the mind'.

(Yolton summarizes the role of sensation in discrimination at the end of his chapter on Descartes in the following way:

[17] Yolton, *Perceptual Acquaintance*, 38.
[18] See MacKenzie, 'Descartes on Life and Sense', 180. MacKenzie also offers other texts, and some detailed argument, in support of this interpretive position.

Perceptual discriminations (*a*) do not require any entities (particles or images) to be transmitted from object to perceiver; (*b*) do not require any similarities between idea and object; (*c*) are made on the basis of sensations felt by the perceiver; and (*d*) those sensations are a response to or an interpretation of natural signs, i.e. motions in the environment that are duplicated in nerves and brain.[19]

This is an accurate, concise statement of Descartes's general position in the *Dioptrics* and elsewhere. But the observation that, for Descartes, discrimination of bodies depends on 'sensations felt by the perceiver' seems to raise serious questions for Yolton's interpretive claim that perception of physical things is not supposed to involve intermediate mental entities.)

I am not sure how much emphasis I want to put on this argument. For one thing, Descartes's conception of the role of mere sensation in perceptual discrimination of bodies is not very clearly developed.[20] For another, I myself have come to doubt whether Descartes ever intends strictly to deny that sensations do in some limited sense represent (in the sense of 'present') the physical qualities that are their external causes (spinning of particles, in the case of colour). My main reason for this reservation (which involves a change in view from what I say in my book) is that even in the *Principles* he continues to talk of sensations as 'confused images'; and to me this terminology strongly suggests some kind of objective presentation.[21] Even so, I think the argument helps to articulate somewhat precisely the intuition— expressed, for instance, by John Mackie in *Problems from Locke*—that the mechanists' insistence on a pervasive difference and contrast between sensory ideas and bodies as they really are implies a denial that sensory awareness of bodies is 'direct'.[22] To put the point briefly, the contrast between sensory experience and real qualities drives the mechanists to an understanding of sensations ('ideas of secondary qualities') as purely mental entities, without objective content. To the extent that sensations are still ascribed an important role in the

---

[19] Yolton, *Perceptual Acquaintance*, 39.

[20] One of the most detailed discussions of this issue, in the Sixth Replies, presents plenty of problems of its own. (See M. Wilson, 'Descartes on the Perception of Primary Qualities', and C. Wolf-Devine, *Descartes on Seeing*, 84–8).

[21] See M. Wilson, 'Descartes on the Representationality of Sensation'.

[22] J. L. Mackie, *Problems from Locke*, 7, 16, 28; ch. 2. Mackie does not deny that ideas of secondary qualities are 'representative' for Locke (p. 16), but I think he means only that the idea-types are (as Locke says) correlated in some causal way with types of mechanical states of objects.

discrimination of bodies, however, we are left indeed with mental intermediaries between our perceiving minds and the external physical things.

Finally, I want to turn briefly to the question how, exactly, Descartes's denial that sensory ideas 'resemble' qualities in bodies should be understood. As we have partly seen, Descartes, in analysing the perceptual process, emphatically denies 'resemblance' at more than one point: in fact, he denies it at three. Sensory ideas do not resemble either their 'objects', or the brain states that are the immediate causes of the ideas in thought; and the brain states do not resemble the bodies that are their (more-or-less) remote causes.

Today it may seem odd enough even to enquire whether a *brain state*—physical entity though it may be—'resembles' an external physical object such as a tree. But we know that Descartes took himself to be opposing the view that when we see trees there are fairly exact pictorial duplications of trees in our brains (to which the mind somehow has access). In any case, I am not particularly concerned here with the question whether physical things as diverse as trees and brain states can be meaningfully affirmed or denied to 'resemble' each other. Rather, I want to ask what sense can be made of the sober denial that certain mental entities or 'thoughts' 'resemble' physical qualities or states. And for the sake of brevity I will deal only with the denial that sensory ideas resemble the *objects* to which they are normally 'referred'.

As early as the *Treatise on Light* Descartes emphasizes that it is a common error to suppose that sensations 'resemble' the objects that are their (distal) physical causes: 'For although everyone is commonly persuaded that the ideas that we have in our thought are entirely similar to the objects from which they proceed, I do not at all see any reason that assures us that this is so . . .' (AT XI 3). He goes on to mention several examples of ordinary phenomena—beginning with the fact that words, while 'having no resemblance to the things that they signify do not fail to make us conceive them' (AT XI 4). Similar examples occur in the *Dioptrics* and the *Principles*, again in support of the point that what 'makes us conceive' certain objects need not resemble the objects conceived (*Principles*, pt. IV, art. 197: AT VI 112–13; VIIIA 320–1). In both the *Treatise on Light* and the *Principles* Descartes notes that the reader might object that the analogy is imperfect: when we understand the meaning of words, the mind or understanding interprets the purely sensuous apprehension (but does not contribute in the same way to sense itself). In the *Treatise on Light* Descartes says this objection is not really sound: 'in just the same way it is our mind which represents to us the idea of light each time the action that signifies it touches our eye' (AT XI 4). In all three works, Descartes moves on to other examples, which I will not consider here. The observation I want to make with respect to the remarks in the *Treatise* is just that Descartes suggests that the denial of resemblance between mental and physical entities is illuminated by considering alleged non-resemblance between cause and effect *within* the realm of the mental: the thought of a tree is not at all like the experience of hearing the word 'tree', which brings it to mind. The implicit contrast, I take it, is between hearing the word, and actually seeing a picture of a tree.

Consider, then, the contrast Descartes goes on to draw in the *Treatise* between the sensation of sound and the 'true image' of the 'object' of that sensation:

most Philosophers maintain that sound is nothing but a certain trembling (vibration) of air which comes to strike our ears; so that if the sense of hearing conveyed to our thought the true image of its object, it would have to be the case that, instead of making us conceive sound, it made us conceive the movement of the parts of air which tremble against our ears at the time. (AT XI 5)

Similarly, a gendarme whose buckle or strap is pressing him under his armour may think he has suffered a wound. No such error would be possible if 'his touch, in making him sense [*sentir*] this strap, had imprinted its image on his thought' (AT XI 6). Again, Descartes writes in the *Principles*:

such is the nature of our mind that from the fact alone that certain motions occur in the body, it can be stimulated to have all sorts of thoughts, *carrying no image of these motions* . . . and especially those confused thoughts called sensings or sensations. (*Principles*, pt. IV, art. 197: AT VIIIA 320; emphasis added)[23]

---

[23] Cf. the Sixth Meditation (AT VII 88) 'when the nerves in the foot are moved in a strong and unusual manner, this motion, reaching through the spinal cord to the inner parts of the brain, there gives the mind a signal to sense something, namely pain as if existing in the foot. . . . It is true that the nature of man could have been so constituted by God that this same motion in the brain would exhibit something else to the mind: either itself [the motion] as it is in the brain, or as it is in the foot, or in any of the intermediate locations . . .'

What I want to propose is, first, that Descartes's denial of 'resemblance' between his sensory ideas and the qualities of bodies after all relies to some extent on comparing mental awarenesses. Against the experience of the sensation of sound, we place the (mental) 'image' of motions of air particles. The two, phenomenally, do not 'resemble' each other. Thus, strictly, the denial of resemblance between mental and physical entities is mediated by the denial of resemblance between two *mental* entities: the *sensation*, and the mechanistic *imaging* of such physical qualities as light and sound. Yet of course, Descartes, in denying that sensations resemble their objects, is not principally maintaining that they fail to resemble other mental states. He is implicitly making the further point that sensations are not 'true' to their objects, in the way that mechanistic images of bodies in motion may be.

Underlying this way of understanding the resemblance issue is the assumption that physical reality *is imageable*: that it can be presented to us as it is by our imagination. Descartes does clearly to some degree maintain this view: for instance, he stresses his ability distinctly to imagine *res extensa* at the beginning of the Fifth Meditation (AT VII 63). Yet a number of passages—particularly in the *Meditations*—indicate that not all aspects even of *physical* reality can be grasped by imagination: the *understanding* is required in order for us to grasp the indefinite variability of the single piece of wax (Second Meditation); and the imagination is unable to present even specific determinate shapes if they are quite complex (in which case they can only be *understood*) (Sixth Meditation: AT VII 72–3).

Again, though Descartes does speak of distinctly *imagining*, he most commonly associates distinct (as opposed to confused) ideas or perception with the *understanding*. Thus sensations are accounted 'confused' not merely because they fail to present or exhibit to us 'true images' of external occurrences; but also because they fail to present *anything intelligible*. This view lies behind Descartes's remark in the Third Meditation, in the context of a discussion of the 'objective reality' of his various ideas, that his sensations 'exhibit so little reality' to him that he 'can scarcely distinguish it from non-being' (AT VII 44). But he particularly stresses this point in the *Principles*:

in order that we may here distinguish that which is clear from that which is obscure we must very carefully note that we have a clear or distinct knowledge of pain, colour, and other things of the sort when we view them simply as sensations or thoughts. But when we judge these to be some sort of things existing outside of our minds, in no way are we able át all to understand what sort of things they are, but it is just the same, when someone says that he sees a colour in some body, or feels a pain in some limb, as if he said that he there saw or felt something but was completely ignorant of what is was, that is, that he did not know what he saw or felt. (*Principles*, pt. I, art. 68: AT VIIIA 33)

This point is quickly combined with the usual observations about erroneous beliefs in 'resemblance':

For even though, when he is less attentive, he may easily persuade himself that he has some notion of it, because he supposes that it is something similar to this sensation of colour or pain which he experiences in himself, yet if he examines what it is, that is presented by this sensation of colour or pain, as if existing in a coloured body or suffering part, he will notice that he is totally ignorant of it. (ibid.)

In the next Principle (art. 69) he observes that 'we know [*cognoscere*] in a very different way' 'what size, or shape, or motion . . . or position, or duration, or number and the like are in a body that we see' (qualities that he says are 'clearly perceived'), than we know what may be, in the same body, 'colour, or pain, or odour, or taste, or any of the other things that I have said should be referred to sense'. In article 70 he reiterates the point that our sensations do not enable us to *understand* anything about bodies:

It is therefore evident that it is really the same, when we say that we perceive colours in objects, as if we said that we perceived something in the objects of which we are ignorant what it is, but by which is caused [*a quo efficitur*] in us this particular (*ipsis . . . quidam*) very manifest and perspicuous sensation, which is called the sensation of colour. (AT VIIIA 34)

As long as we restrict ourselves to noncommittal causal judgement, we will not go astray:

But when we think we perceive colours in objects, although we do not know what this might be, that we are calling by the name of 'colour', and we are not able *to understand* any similarity between the colour which we suppose to be in objects and what we experience to be in sense: because we nevertheless do not notice this, and [because] there are many other [things] such as magnitude, figure, number, etc., which we clearly perceive are not otherwise sensed or *understood* by us, than they are or at least can be in objects: it is easy for us to fall into the error of judging that that, which we call colour in the objects, is something entirely similar to the colour we sense, and thus to judge that that, which we in no way perceive, is clearly perceived by us. (AT VII 34–5; emphasis added)

To say that sensations are 'confused' or 'obscure' is to say that they fail to provide a distinct *understanding* of real qualities of bodies, not merely that they fail to provide *images* of the right sort. We cannot tell by having them, or by inspecting them, what sort of configurations of parts of extension, transferring motion, give rise to them—or even that they have such a cause. Our ideas of figure, size, etc., by contrast, do afford distinct understanding of qualities as they may exist in nature.

Given the close association, in Descartes's writings, between saying sensations are 'confused' or 'obscure', and insisting that they fail to 'resemble' external things, it seems reasonable to assume that the concept of 'resemblance' should be understood partly metaphorically, and not merely pictorially. A 'non-resembling' idea, that is, should be construed as one that fails to yield intelligibility—and this may not be entirely a matter of failing to present a 'true image' of a physical cause. Conversely, on this reading, a geometer's idea of a chiliagon may 'resemble' external reality, even though (according to Descartes) we are unable to provide ourselves through imagination with a clear mental picture of a chiliagon.

And, indeed, Descartes's one *positive* statement (that I know of) about an idea resembling something physical appears to concern an *intellectual* idea: 'We clearly understand this [matter] as a thing entirely different from ourselves, or from our mind; and we also seem to see clearly that the idea of it comes to us from things located outside ourselves, to which it is entirely similar' (*Principles*, pt. II, art. 1: AT VIIIA 41).[24]

---

[24] This remark contrasts, though, with the remark quoted above from the beginning of the Fifth Meditation in which Descartes seems to stress the distinct *imaginability* of *res extensa* (AT VII 63). Descartes observes in the Third Meditation that he finds in himself 'two different ideas of the sun' which (respectively) present it as small or large. He says that the former is acquired 'as if' from the senses, while the latter is derived from 'certain notions innate in me, or made by me in some other manner'. These remarks perhaps suggest by implication that the favoured idea (the second) resembles the sun: 'certainly both cannot be similar to the same sun existing outside me.' But what he mainly stresses is, again, that the idea derived 'as if' from sense does *not* resemble the sun (see AT VII 39–40).
Note that Descartes hedges in this passage with regard to the origin of both ideas: he does not say straightforwardly that the former comes from sense, nor that the latter is derived from innate ideas. Thus the passage does not really tell against the suggestion I made earlier that Descartes may understand 'ideas of sense' in a quite peculiar and restricted way, relating to the 'special sensibles'; further it is compatible with his suggestion towards the end of the *Meditations* that the true determination of the sun's size requires the resources of sense and memory as well as intellect. I want to thank John Nelson for a comment that caused me to look at the passage again, with a question about its implications for some of what I have said here.

Still, it would be a mistake to *under*estimate the importance of imagination and images in Descartes's conception of nature: and, correspondingly, in his conception of distinct and resembling, as opposed to confused and non-resembling ideas. Both the prominence of imagistic thinking, and the tendency to insist also on the understanding as a different and superior factor in our grasp of the world, are evident in the following revealing remark from the end of the *Principles*:

who has ever doubted that bodies move and have various sizes and shapes, according to which diversity their motions also vary; or that from inter-collision larger bodies are divided into many smaller ones and change their shapes? We find this out not just by one sense but several—sight, touch and hearing; *and we also distinctly imagine and understand it.* But the same cannot be said of the rest, such as colour, sound and so forth, which are perceived not by several senses but by one alone; *for their images in our thought are always confused, nor do we know what they are.* (*Principles*, pt. IV, art. 200: AT VIIIA 323–4; emphasis added)[25]

I conclude, then, that Descartes's talk of (non-)resemblance between ideas and bodies can *partly* be interpreted in terms of the issue of a comparison between *mental* entities (sensations, images of motion); and can *partly* be interpreted metaphorically, in terms of the question whether sensations afford an *intelligible* conception of the physical objects or qualities that give rise to them. An intelligible conception of something physical may not necessarily involve a 'true image'; and, even when there is such an image, its 'truth' may involve an intellectual element that does not reduce to phenomenal presentation. I do not say that these observations are fully sufficient to counter Berkeley's riposte to the 'resemblance' terminology of his scientific realist opponents: that an idea can be 'like' nothing but an idea. But I do think that they help to place the talk of resemblance in a philosophically serious context.

In summary, I have tried here to defend the attribution of a 'veil-of-perception' theory to Descartes. In part this defence has involved distinguishing the objectives and concerns of the Meditations from

---

[25] The emphasis in this passage on the tradition between 'special' and 'common sensibles' is atypical for Descartes. But it occurs in a context where he is expressly concerned to argue that he has not employed any principle not accepted by Aristotle and 'other philosophers of every age'.

those of the more 'scientifically' oriented writings on perception; in part on emphasizing the role of colour and other sensations in discriminating bodies. And, finally, I have tried to help make some sense of the talk of (non-)resemblance between ideas and bodies, which is so prominent a feature of the classic scientific realist veil-of-perception views.

Sensory Ideas, Objective Reality, and Material Falsity

LILLI ALANEN

I. Introduction

This chapter deals with the problematic notion of material falsity introduced by Descartes in the Third Meditation to account for the unreliability of a subclass of ideas: sense perceptions or sensory ideas. It is one of Descartes's professed doctrines that ideas, when considered in themselves, without being referred to anything else, cannot be false. Falsity occurs in judgements, and a judgement depends on an independent act of the will: there can be no falsity properly speaking in ideas as such.[1] Material falsity, however, seems to be an exception to this rule—it is described as another kind of falsity, intrinsic to some adventitious ideas, notably those of sensory qualities, like heat and cold, of which there is no telling whether they are true or false (AT VII 43; CSM II 30). Is Descartes, as Arnauld worried, confusing idea with judgement, or worse, is this to be seen as another instance of the inconsistency of his theory of ideas, for which Descartes has been so often charged? The brief account in the Third Meditation is very unsatisfactory indeed—yet I think it is possible to make perfectly good sense of the view there introduced, once all the statements and scattered comments Descartes makes on this obscure topic are put together. It takes some good will though, because Descartes's notion of ideas, and the metaphors he offers in accounting for it, are far from constituting a clear and distinct theory. It takes some interpretation too, and it may be just a matter of taste which one ends up favouring.

[1] '*Jam quod ad ideas attinet, si solae in se spectentur, nec ad aliud quid illas referam, falsae proprie esse non possunt*' (AT VII 37; CSM II 26).

The one I will defend here agrees on many points with those recently presented by Jean-Marie Beyssade and Margaret Wilson. Both readings are based on a distinction between two different ways in which Cartesian ideas can refer to or represent things, although they state it in quite different terms.[2] Differently from Beyssade and Wilson, I take materially false ideas to be complex ideas involving unnoticed judgements. I also want to suggest that there are more than two ways in which ideas can represent, that to represent, for Descartes, is another general term which can be put to various uses, and that the relation or function for which it stands can be spelled out in different contexts in different ways. To show this I want first to look at Descartes's use of the term idea and the notion of objective reality in terms of which it is defined.

II. Two Senses of 'Idea'

Descartes's redefinition of the notion of mind or intellect in terms of thought also involves a redefinition of mental acts and their objects. *Thought*, in Descartes's wide sense of the word, covers any conscious mental states, including emotions, feelings, and sense perceptions, and it is also used coextensively with *idea* and *perception* as general terms to cover both the acts and the objects of awareness.[3] There is thus a sense of idea in which sensations, feelings, and passions, although in so far as they depend on the mind–body union they are said to be confused and obscure thoughts, can be called ideas.[4] *Idea*, however, is also defined more restrictedly, in the *Meditations*, and the first question I

[2] J.-M. Beyssade, 'Descartes on Material Falsity', and M. Wilson, 'Descartes on the Representationality of Sensation'. I am grateful to Jean-Marie Beyssade for letting me read the manuscript of his paper, which I have found very helpful, even if I differ from Beyssade concerning the role of judgement in material falsity (see below, Section V). Margaret Wilson's paper, which marks a change of position from her earlier readings of Descartes's view on this topic, came to my notice when this chapter was already written.

[3] Traditionally referred to as different kinds of faculties or psychic capacities, the intellect, the will, the imagination, the emotions, and sense perceptions become, within the Cartesian framework, different modes of one capacity, thought. What sets them apart, as modes of thought, from other, non-mental, things and phenomena is the awareness accompanying them: they qualify as thoughts, for Descartes, in so far as they are or can be consciously perceived (AT VIII 7, CSM I 195; AT VII 160, 176, CSM II 113, 124).

[4] It is not difficult to document such a use of idea throughout the Cartesian opus (cf. Beyssade, 'Descartes on Material Falsity').

want to address is which of the two, the wide or the narrow sense of idea, is applicable to sensations.

Descartes notes, in the preface to the *Meditations*, the ambiguity of the word idea: it can be taken materially, as an operation of the intellect, or it can be taken objectively, as the thing represented by that operation (AT VII 8; CSM II 7).[5] In the Third Meditation, where Descartes offers his most extensive account of ideas, idea is taken in the latter, and as Descartes describes it, proper sense. Idea here is restricted to a subclass of thoughts, which are 'as it were [*tanquam*] images of things', because they are said to include some kind of 'likeness' of their object, as when thinking, for instance, 'of a man, or a chimera, or the sky, or an angel, or God' (AT VII, 37, CSM II 25–6). There is more to thoughts, however, than what they represent: namely the occurrent act of thinking itself, which has a distinctive form of its own that, in so far as it is immediately perceived, deserves also to be called *idea* (AT VII 8; CSM II 7).[6]

Descartes has been accused of a systematic ambiguity in the use of idea as between act and object.[7] Descartes surely does not make things easy for us by his wide use of 'idea' and 'perception' as umbrella terms for all the various modes of thinking—acts as well as objects of different kinds of thought. There is no inconsistency, however, as long as one remembers that occurrent thinkings or 'ideas' in the wide sense are complex mental phenomena or processes of which act and object are merely different aspects which, though they can, for the purposes of analysis, be identified separately, always occur together. Like Husserl's acts of consciousness, Descartes's thinkings have a complex structure—*qua* conscious they are, on the one hand, acts of a kind, having a distinctive form as acts, and they have, on the other hand, also a specific content or object, by which they can, once their act-form is given, be individuated.[8]

Thoughts, hence, are representational acts, and, *qua* representational, they are necessarily about or of something: what they are of or

---

[5] This distinction, it can be noted, parallels the distinction between what in contemporary philosophy of mind is described sometimes as propositional attitudes and propositional contents, sometimes also as mental or intentional acts and contents.

[6] See the observation made in the Third Replies: 'I use the term idea for whatever is immediately perceived by the mind, so that when I will and fear, since I at the same time perceive that I will and fear, the same volition and fear are numbered among my ideas' (AT VII 181; CSM II 127).   [7] See e.g. A. Kenny, *Descartes*, 110–14.

[8] I discuss this more extensively in L. Alanen, 'Cartesian Ideas and Intentionality', 345–9.

about distinguishes them from any other acts of the same kind. I may be unable to tell what the object of my perception is in having a sensation of cold, but I surely can tell the difference between feeling cold and feeling warm, and what makes the difference is the quality of my feeling—that is, the idea of cold or warmth qualifying my present sensory state.

But are sensations ideas on a par with the ideas listed above as examples of ideas taken objectively, like those of God, of the sky, or of a chimera? What about sensations of pain or pleasure, or of feelings of uneasiness, moods, melodies, etc.—do they always have an object individuating them? In short, are sensations really ideas in the strict and primary sense of the word, for Descartes? The question is pressing—only ideas in the strict sense are representations of external, mind-independent things—only ideas in the strict sense can have cognitive value. If sensations do not have a representational content or object, what role, if any, do they play for our knowledge of reality?

The paradigm for representation that Descartes uses in defining ideas in the strict sense is that of pictorial representation: ideas, in representing, are said to be *as it were* images of things. If taken literally, this metaphor is highly misleading. Ideas do not, like images, represent by pictorial likeness, and they are not, like images, separable entities interposed between the perceiver and the model. Yet ideas, like images, are actual presentations of their objects—the idea makes an object present to the mind. But what is presented to the mind by the confused and more-or-less obscure sensory and emotional states?

The metaphor of images or likeness is particularly inadequate when talking of sensory ideas: Cartesian sensations, as we all know, have nothing in common with, for instance, the *eidola* or 'intentional forms' of the scholastic theory, described in the *Optics* as 'little images flitting through the air' (AT VI 85–6; CSM I 153–4). Descartes's mechanistic account of sense perception in combination with his dualistic metaphysics has, it seems, once and for all rendered any attempts to build the relation between mental (including sensory) representations and physical reality on likenesses vain.[9]

III. Objective Reality

If Descartes's notion of representation is not to be explicated by that of pictorial representation, how should it be understood? What

[9] See the *Optics* (AT VI 130; CSM I 167), and *The World* (AT XI 4–5; CSM I 81).

is the objective being of the thing by which the idea is said to represent the latter to the mind, if it is *not* a mental image or copy of it?

By objective reality Descartes means 'the being of the thing which is represented by an idea, in so far as this exists in the idea' (AT VII 161; CSM II 113–14). The idea, taken objectively, is (or has) a kind of being, *esse*: without being real in the sense of an actually and formally existing mind-independent thing (as e.g. the sun or the people out there), it has *some* degree of reality *qua* represented or conceived by an intellect (the reality of the sun as actually perceived or conceived of by my mind).

In attributing being to ideas taken objectively, Descartes ascribes a certain independence to them with respect to the mind. An idea, *qua* form of thought, has a given real nature which is not arbitrary, the being or reality of which cannot be reduced to the (material) reality of the occurrent thought-act, or of the mind which actually perceives it. Ideas in Descartes's sense of representational forms in the mind have, although this may sound queer, some kind of thought-independent *reality*. The being or reality of the idea taken objectively is thus to be distinguished both from the formal reality of the idea taken materially as an occurrent mode or act of thinking, and from the formal or actual reality of the thing represented. While the objective reality of the idea is independent of the former—that is, of the material or formal reality of the act of thinking—it is somehow dependent on the thing represented, the (formal) reality of which it is supposed to reflect or mirror.

Without being able to argue for it in this context, I want to follow Calvin Normore's bold suggestion, that the similarity or likeness between the idea and the thing it represents can be taken straightforwardly in the sense of identity or sameness of the *res* or thing represented and the idea, qualified only by a difference in their ontological status. This suggestion, as I understand it, applies in the first hand to those clear and distinct ideas of things that the human mind has a natural capacity to discover, and that are sometimes described as innate. The idea of a particular thing, say a horse, should in this approach be considered as identical with the particular, but having another kind of *esse* or reality. We would have, on the one hand, this particular horse running on the nearby field with *esse actualem* or *formalem*, and, on the other hand, the very same horse *qua* conceived, with *esse objectivum*.[10] This intentional or objective reality of ideas, because it is independent of the mind that conceives it, requires as its cause some external thing or being possessing at least as much reality formally (or eminently) as is contained in the idea objectively.[11] Any idea, in so far as it is distinctly conceivable, has some degree of objective reality which must be caused, even when the thing conceived is not existing actually or formally, like the sun in the heavens, but is merely possible, like a yet unrealized machine of highly intricate design (AT VII 103; CSM II 75). Ideas, in this strict sense, are things thought of, *res cogitata* (AT VI 599), and as such they have a mode of being of their own which is less than the actual, formal, or material reality of the things conceived but nevertheless greater than pure non-being. Differently from Normore, I take this to be a general feature of Cartesian ideas: ideas are representative—that is, they have objective being by their very nature—and as such they are always about or of something even when, as is the case with sensory ideas, there is no telling what thing they are of or about. Sensory ideas, as I understand it, hence also belong to the class of ideas in the restricted, proper sense of the term.

IV. Degrees of Reality

All ideas, I want to argue, are, however, not representative in the same way or to the same degree—they are not all, even though they may be taken to be, of real, that is, of clearly and distinctly conceivable,

---

[10] See C. Normore, 'Meaning and Objective Being', 235–8, and L. Alanen, 'Cartesian Ideas and Intentionality'. The identity, in fact, according to Normore's suggestion, holds between the ideas as divine exemplars, and the particulars which instantiate them in actual reality. The suggestion is extremely interesting but needs to be elaborated, as I hope to do in a longer study on 'Descartes's Philosophy of Mind', presently under work. See also L. Alanen, 'Some Questions Concerning Objective Reality and Possible Being in Descartes and his Predecessors'.

[11] For Descartes, who regards God as the efficient cause not only of actual but also of possible beings and, indeed, of possible and necessary truths as well, there is nothing odd in assuming that ideas have some kind of being which requires a cause. It should be noted, however, that the notion of causality invoked here is very far from the causality invoked in contemporary theories of meaning or reference—it is, among other things, broad enough to include that of eminent causation, whatever that is. Descartes insists in the Third Meditation that the (efficient) cause of the objective being of ideas need not be actually (formally) instantiated, but can be eminently contained in some formally existing substance having *at least* as much or more reality or perfection actually and in fact as the idea possesses objectively (AT VII 41–2; CSM II 28–9).

actually or possibly existing things. Though all ideas taken materially, *qua* modes of thought, have the same amount of formal reality, ideas taken objectively, as representations, differ: some contain more and some less reality or objective being depending on the nature of the thing they represent. Ideas representing substances are said to contain, 'so to speak', more objective reality than ideas representing mere modes or accident. Modes, in fact, can neither exist nor be clearly conceived independently of the substance in which they inhere and of which they are modifications.[12] In the Cartesian ontological hierarchy modes occupy the lowest degree of reality or perfection (AT VII 166, CSM II 117; AT VIII 25 ff., CSM I 210 ff.).

There is also, as Calvin Normore points out, a close connection between Descartes's use of the notion of objective reality and his theory of modality. The objective reality of a clear and distinct idea entails the possible existence of the thing it represents. Possible existence, for Descartes, 'is contained in the concept or idea of everything that we clearly and distinctly understand' (AT VII 116–17; CSM II 83). A clear and distinct idea of a thing shows whether the thing is real—i.e. whether it is possible. The reality or possibility of things which are not clearly and distinctly conceived, by contrast, remains doubtful. Their ideas, to the extent that they are obscure and confused, do not represent or display the objective reality required for any reliable inferences about the formal nature of their object.

Calvin Normore thinks with Margaret Wilson that 'we must distinguish the representive character of Cartesian ideas from their objective reality'. All ideas purport to be or are taken to be about something and hence have a representative character. All ideas, however, would not in fact have objective reality: materially false ideas are ideas of non-things that lack objective reality altogether and hence fail, in spite of their representative character, to represent anything real.[13] This distinction seems to create more problems than it solves. It leaves us,

---

[12] There is a difference also in the idea of a created, finite substance, and that of a necessary, infinite substance: the idea of a perfect, self-subsisting being has more objective reality than ideas representing finite substances (AT VII 40; CSM II 27–8). The notion of degrees of reality applies to natures, and is connected to that of ontological dependence (see Normore, 'Meaning and Objective Being', 226).

[13] Normore, 'Meaning and Objective Being', 226. Cf. the discussion in M. Wilson, *Descartes*, 102–19. Margaret Wilson, however, defends a more nuanced position in 'Descartes on the Representationality of Sensations', 13 ff. Wilson now distinguishes two senses of *represent* and argues that those thoughts, like sensations, which do not represent presentationally can nevertheless be said to represent referentially.

among other things, with two sets of representative ideas—those having, and those lacking, objective reality, in which case the representative character and function of the former remain unexplained. It also leaves us with two notions of falsity, and the task to explain the relation between the two. Material falsity, I contend, is not due to a lack of objective reality. How then should it be explained, and how is this material falsity related to formal falsity?

V. Truth and Falsity

Ideas, as we saw, cannot be false when considered solely in themselves, without referring them to anything else (AT VII 37; CSM II 25–6). Merely perceiving or entertaining an idea—say of a goat, a chimera, a feeling of pain, of wanting or desiring something—cannot involve any falsity. Falsity comes with judgement, that Descartes takes to involve an additional act of volition affirming or denying something about the thing represented by the idea. The most common mistake consists in judging, without sufficient evidence, that 'the ideas which are in me resemble, or conform to, things located outside me'. But there is an interesting qualification to this doctrine right from the start: 'If I considered just the ideas themselves simply as modes of thought without referring them to anything else, they could scarcely [*vix*] give me material for error' (AT VII 37; CSM II 26).

This *vix*, as Beyssade rightly stresses, introduces the topic of material falsity. Before discussing it, something must be said about Descartes's view of the relation of the will and the intellect in judging. It has been much criticized, notably by Spinoza, who denies any free power of assenting to or denying what is perceived by the intellect. Not only does Spinoza deny this: he would not allow for any distinction between the will and the intellect, or in contemporary terms, between propositions and propositional attitudes, in the context of belief. Ideas or propositions, for Spinoza, come to the mind as *beliefs*, that is, as affirmations or denials. Suspension of judgement, for Spinoza, is not an act of the will, but an inadequate or imperfect perception of the intellect. A true idea, say the idea of a triangle, involves the affirmation that its three angles are equal to two right-angles, and this idea can neither be nor be conceived without this affirmation.[14]

[14] I am here following the account in J. Bennett, *A Study of Spinoza's Ethics*, 162, and A. Donagan, *Spinoza*, 46.

In spite of his distinction between will and perception, and in spite of his view that the attitude (assent or denial) taken to an idea or its propositional counterpart *can* be freely chosen, Descartes, I take it, would not disagree with Spinoza that ideas (or propositions) come to the mind as beliefs (involving affirmations), and also that they are, as such, either true or false. But he does not hold, like Spinoza, that perceiving or entertaining an idea is the *same* as explicitly affirming that the idea or its propositional counterpart is true. Merely having a false belief without endorsing it—i.e. without affirming that it is a true belief—need not in itself involve any error.

Take my sensory idea of the sun: the sun, as I see it with my eyes, is not much bigger than a football. This idea, if spelled out in an affirmative proposition about the size of the sun, would clearly be false. Merely seeing the sun, or thinking the propositional counterpart of the idea of the sun as given in visual perception, does not, according to Descartes, entail any falsity or error: it is true that the sun, as I see or imagine it, does not appear bigger than so. Error arises when I, by using my will, affirm that this sensory idea represents the sun in its true nature, and that the sun in the heavens has the size it appears to have. What is important here is to distinguish between merely entertaining a belief, and accepting it, or claiming it to be true. Only the latter is a matter of judgement in the proper sense of the word, and a true judgement, for Descartes, requires an analysis or clarification of what evidence for accepting or denying a belief presently entertained consists in. This evidence, ultimately, comes down to the agreement or disagreement of the content of the idea or belief in question with other clear and distinct ideas.[15]

Descartes does not think of ideas primarily as propositions or propositional contents. It should be stressed that the truth or falsity of ideas with which we are here concerned relates to ideas of things (*res*), not to conceptual or eternal truths, of which Descartes says that they have no existence outside the mind. We know that they are true as soon as we conceive them clearly and distinctly, because so to conceive them is to see that their denial involves contradiction and is, hence, impossible (AT VIII 23–4; CSM I 208–9). Ideas of things, on the contrary, represent particulars or individual essences, which may or may

---

[15] See A. Gewirth, 'Clearness and Distinctness in Descartes'. See also the discussion in Donagan, *Spinoza*, 45.

not exist in the mind-independent reality.[16] The judgements, the truth of which is to be ascertained, are about their nature and existence. It is one thing to conceive a particular clearly and distinctly—another to affirm that the particular exists actually or that its true nature is such and such. To conceive a particular clearly and distinctly is to see that existence is not incompatible with it. One can think of a particular realizing that it is real—i.e. that its existence is possible—without affirming that it exists. It follows that all ideas, separately considered, are true in themselves, when not referred to anything else—that is, when taken exactly for what they clearly and distinctly represent. That is, they are true to the extent that they are clear enough to represent some possibly existing entity, either a substance or some mode of a substance. A clear and distinct idea displays, by its degree of objective reality, the degree of reality that the thing it represents would have formally: the idea of a substance, as we have seen, has more reality objectively than that of a mode. The idea of a mode or property, on the other hand, is clear and distinct only to the extent that it contains or is somehow connected with the idea of the kind of substance of which it is a modification. Shape, for instance, cannot be clearly and distinctly understood without extension, because shape, as a mode, is in itself an incomplete entity (*Principles*, pt. I, art. 53: AT VIIIA 25; CSM I 210–11).

VI. Material Falsity

So far we have been concerned with clear and distinct ideas, and the claim has been that clear and distinct ideas of particular things or entities, when considered separately, just as they are in themselves, are true. They are, we could say, 'materially' true (though Descartes, for all I know, does not use this expression), because they do not, *in se praecise spectantur*, give material for error. The objective being contained in the true idea adequately reflects the formal or actual being of the thing represented. Ideas, however, as they normally occur, are far from being clear and distinct, nor do they come to the mind one by one, for separate inspection—rather, they are presented in the context of other ideas and beliefs involving mostly unnoticed, spontaneous, or habitual judgements. Such is the case, notably, of sensory

[16] See above, Section III.

ideas: as adventitious, they are immediately referred to external things, and yet, because of their intrinsically confused character as accidental modes of the mind caused by the body and depending on the mind–body union, they can easily be misleading.

Thus, in examining his various ideas representing corporeal things with respect to their differing degrees of objective reality, Descartes notices that his ideas of sensory qualities (the list includes: light and colours, sounds, smells, tastes, heat and cold, and the other tactile qualities) are so confused and obscure that, he writes:

I do not even know whether they are true or false, that is, whether the ideas I have of them are ideas of things or of non-things. For although, as I have noted before, falsity in the strict sense or formal falsity can occur only in judgements, there is another kind of falsity, material falsity, which occurs in ideas *when they represent non-things as things*. For example, the ideas which I have of heat and cold contain so little clarity and distinctness that they do not enable me to tell whether cold is merely the absence of heat or vice versa or whether both of them are real qualities or neither is. And since there can be no ideas which are not as it were of things, if it is true that cold is nothing but the absence of heat, the idea which represents it to me as something real and positive deserves to be called false; and the same goes for other ideas of this kind. (AT VII 43–4; CSM II 30; emphasis added)

Material falsity hence is connected with obscurity and confusion: the idea of God, for instance, cannot be materially false because it is 'utterly clear and distinct and contains in itself more objective reality than any other idea'. It is, indeed, 'the truest and most clear and distinct of all my ideas' (AT VII 46; CSM II 31–2).

Objective reality comes in degrees—can truth also come in degrees? This is hardly conceivable. Arnauld points out the inconsistency in speaking of truth and falsity of ideas when falsity (and truth) in the strict sense can occur only in judgements. If the idea of cold is a positive idea, it represents something real; if, on the other hand, it is just an absence (of heat), then it cannot exist objectively—that is, there can be no idea having objective being of what formally is an absence of being or non-being.[17]

Arnauld's charge against Descartes, briefly, is that Descartes

---

[17] Arnauld writes: 'For an idea is called "positive" not in virtue of the existence it has as a mode of thinking (for in that sense all ideas would be positive) but in virtue of the objective existence which it contains and which it exhibits to our mind. Hence the idea in question may perhaps not be the idea of cold but it cannot be false' (AT VII 207; CSM II 145).

confuses judgement with an idea: the idea of cold is false because it is not the idea of cold—i.e. the *judgement* that it is the idea of cold is false, but the idea within you is 'completely true' (AT VII 207; CSM II 145).

Descartes, in answering, repeats his point that ideas taken materially— i.e. as mere operations of the intellect—can have no reference to the truth or falsity of their objects. Arnauld's objection turns on taking ideas not materially but in the *formal* sense (*formaliter*). To the great perplexity of the reader, ideas taken in the formal sense or formally, here, turn out to be ideas taken objectively: 'Since ideas are forms of a kind, and are not composed of any matter, when we think of them as representing something we are taking them not *materially* but *formally*' (AT VII 231–2; CSM II 163).[18] Descartes's remark that he had found the word 'materially' used in a sense identical with his own in the first scholastic author he came across (in Suárez's *Metaphysical Disputations*) is not very helpful. If material falsity applies to ideas, as Descartes says, in the 'formal sense', and the idea taken formally here is the idea taken objectively, it is not easy to see how he could avoid inconsistency. For does not he claim *both* that *no* ideas can involve falsity when considered solely in themselves (AT VII 37; CSM II 26), *and* that among the ideas taken objectively some are false in themselves—that is, 'materially false'?

To say that an idea can be materially false is to say, Descartes explains, that it 'can provide subject-matter for error'. To provide subject-matter for error is the same as to provide subject-matter for (give occasion to) false *judgements* (AT VII 233; CSM II 163). Now any idea which is not sufficiently clear and distinct can in principle be the subject-matter of false judgements. Hence any idea can be in this sense materially false: some give greater, some lesser scope for error, although those that 'give the judgement little or no scope for error do not seem to deserve to be called materially false as much as those that give great scope for error', like sensory ideas do.[19] But if it is only a

---

[18] The contrast made earlier was, on the one hand, between ideas taken materially (or formally), as actual modes of thought, and ideas taken objectively as representing something (AT VII 41; CSM II 28), and, on the other hand, between the objective being of ideas and the actual or formal being or reality of their causes (AT VII 41–2; CSM II 29). On this terminological inconsistency see the comments of M. Grene, *Descartes*, 177, 189.

[19] Descartes writes: 'Confused ideas which are made up at will by the mind such as the ideas of false gods do not provide as much scope for error [*erroris occasione*] as the confused ideas arriving from the senses such as the ideas of colour and cold (if it is

matter of degree, of more or less confusion, one does indeed wonder, with Arnauld, whether Descartes is not after all confusing a judgement with an idea? His answer seems to concede the point: ideas are materially false if and in so far as they give occasion to false judgements, which is to say that they are not false in themselves.

But what should we say about the *vix* qualifying Descartes's claims that ideas do not give material for error, when considered in themselves, without referring them to something else? (AT VII 37, quoted above). By this reservation, Descartes seems to admit exceptions to the rule, and the exceptions, as we saw, are to be found among the confused ideas of sensory qualities. What is it about ideas of senses or feelings that renders them particularly prone to give material for error?

Such ideas are confused partly because they are commonly taken to represent real qualities of external things, which according to Cartesian science they cannot do, for the simple reason that external things have no such properties (AT VII 43; CSM II 29–30). It is, however, not, as the answer to Arnauld makes clear, merely a question of whether what they are taken to represent *is* real or not, but a question, instead, of how they *appear* to us, how they are immediately perceived (AT VII 234, ll. 18–24; CSM II 164). What renders them problematic is that it is impossible, because of their obscurity and confusion, to judge whether what they represent is some positive (real) entity outside the sensation or not.[20] I do not see, as Beyssade does, a change of emphasis or position here, but take this as a mere repetition of the point made in the Third Meditation: the obscurity and confusion of the ideas of sensory qualities hinder me from seeing whether they are true or false, that is, whether they are of things or not (AT VII 43, ll. 23–6). The reality they exhibit, Descartes there explains, is so slight that I cannot even distinguish it from a non-thing (AT VII 44, l. 15; CSM II 30). This, as Beyssade rightly stresses, is a phenomenological problem—not a scientific one: phenomenologically, the reality they

---

true as I have said that these ideas do not represent anything real). The greatest scope for error is provided by the ideas which arise from the sensations of appetite. Thus the idea of thirst which the patient with dropsy has does indeed give him subject-matter for error since it can lead him to judge that a drink will do him good when in fact it will do him harm' (AT VII 234; CSM II 163–4).

[20] '*illam materialiter falsam appello, quod, cum sit obscura & confusa, non possim dijudicare an mihi quid exhibeat quod extra sensum sit positivum, necne . . .*' (AT VII 234, ll. 14–17; CSM II 164).

contain objectively, whatever it is, tends to be confounded with their material or formal reality as modes of thought.[21]

Material falsity, hence, is a property of obscure and of confused sensory ideas. An idea is obscure when it is not clear in the sense of being fully present to the mind, and it is confused, as opposed to being distinct, when it is not possible to tell or spell out exactly (analytically) what the idea contains objectively and how its content is delimited from ideas of other things. The most confused sensory ideas and emotions or feelings like thirst or pain can be very clear, in the sense of being manifest states, and yet at the same time inherently and irremediably confused (*Principles*, pt. I, arts. 45–6: AT VIIIA 21–2; CSM I 207–8). Not only are they subject to constant change (cf. the wax-analysis) and cannot, therefore, be present to the mind for a very long time, but their connection to the things causing them (external bodies and their movements) is and remains unintelligible.[22] Because they are adventitious, and hence out of our control, because, moreover, of their unstable, evanescent, and unintelligible nature as body-dependent mental states, their content, that is, the reality that they represent, which is that of a mode of the mind, cannot be distinctly spelled out or specified. In this they are radically different from the clear and distinct ideas of the intellect (the wax as a piece of extended matter), which are transparent to anyone who bothers to examine them with sufficient care. The content of sensory ideas, on the contrary, is and remains opaque, no matter how much we try to analyse or specify it.[23]

Yet—and this, I take it, is part of the problem of material falsity—there are contexts in which these 'opaque' sensory perceptions can be both clear and distinct: when they are taken *not* to resemble or picture real properties of external things causing them, but are considered in themselves, as mere sensations, that is, as inherently confused and accidental, body-dependent modes of thought. In spite of their opacity, which makes them completely useless as means of discerning or discovering the true nature of the things causing them, they still have an important pragmatic function: they function as natural signs indicating both the presence of and variations in external things and also their import with respect to the mind–body union on which they

---

[21] Beyssade, 'Descartes on Material Falsity', fos. 13–14.

[22] See e.g. *Principles*, pt. IV, arts. 197–8 (AT VIII 321–2; CSM I 284–5).

[23] Cf. Beyssade, 'Descartes on Material Falsity', See also L. Alanen, 'Descartes's Dualism and the Philosophy of Mind', and the references there given.

depend. Thus we learn from the Sixth Meditation that they are, more often than not, reliable for pragmatic purposes, even when they are *not* to be relied upon or used as rules for judgements about the nature of external bodies. Thirst indicates the need of water or refreshments, tiredness that it is time for rest, etc.[24] Now, if sensations or sensory ideas, as Descartes admits, can be used as (mostly) reliable signs instituted by nature for pragmatic (biological) purposes, they can hardly be inherently *false*. Obscurity and confusion are hence not for Descartes, as they may be for Spinoza, the same as falsity. The opacity of sensations may be irremediable, and yet sensations, in the strictest sense of the word, are true in themselves, as is confirmed in the famous passage analysing grades of certainty in the senses in the Sixth Replies (AT VII 438). Falsity, here again, is said to require judgement, which is an act of the intellect and belongs to the third grade of sensory perception. But this is not *sensation* properly speaking, because *sensation* in the very restricted sense here introduced belongs to the second grade.[25] There is no falsity in sensations *stricto sensu*, at the second grade of sensory response (AT VII 438; CSM II 296). This category comprises all the 'immediate effects produced in the mind' by the motion of the particles of the bodily organ to which it is united. The list includes the very same perceptions (pain, pleasure, thirst, colours, heat, cold, and the like) which in the Third Meditation are discussed as instances of materially false ideas.

Does this mean that Descartes does not, after all, regard sensations as an exception to his view that all ideas, when viewed solely in

---

[24] 'For the proper purpose of the sensory perceptions given me by nature is simply to inform [*ad menti significandum*] the mind of what is beneficial or harmful for the composite of which the mind is a part; and to the extent they are sufficiently clear and distinct. But I misuse them by treating them as reliable rules for immediate judgements about the essential nature of the bodies outside us, about which they give nothing but very obscure and confused indications' (AT VII 83, ll. 15–23; CSM II 57–8).

[25] The distinction suggested here seems to be one between the sensation as a pure experience [*qualia?*] and sense perception in a broader and more familiar sense of the term. The former is the directly experienced sensory response to external or internal stimulation; the latter involves beliefs immediately and automatically generated by that response, and beliefs which are not, but which can be made subject for criticism. For a similar account of sensations see Wilfrid Sellars, 'Lectures'. Descartes's account is *not*, though it is often taken in that way, a genetic or descriptive one, but an epistemological distinction, the purpose of which is to determine the scope and certainty of sensory knowledge. The sensations, I take it, are *not* given as such—rather, they are identified or categorized as sensations or sensory states only as an outcome of a critical analysis of what exactly is given in sensory perception in the broader, common sense of the word.

themselves, are true? There are indications, in the *Principles* too, that Descartes holds that even sensations, in spite of their inherent lack of distinctness, can be true when considered *strictly* as sensations, i.e. as confused thoughts (*Principles*, pt. I, arts. 65, 70: AT VIIIA 32, 34). But this seems to render the problem of material falsity even more mysterious.

The only way I can make sense of this, without charging Descartes of inconsistency or a change of mind,[26] is by concluding that material falsity pertains not to the simple sensations in the strict sense as such, but rather to unanalysed, confused, complex sensory ideas, the components of which turn out, on closer scrutiny, to be incompatible and contradictory. Material falsity hence occurs in the ideas not of the second but of the third level of sensory perception, which involves unnoticed or unconscious judgements. To think, for instance, of sounds, or colours, or sensations of temperature, not to speak of pain, thirst, etc., as mind-independent things, for instance, as properties (modes) of external, extended substances, as our spontaneous judgements incline us to do, involves contradiction, because there is no common measure between those sensory qualities and extension. It is to form complex ideas presenting things as non-things: the things they purportedly represent turn out, on closer scrutiny, to be contradictory entities that cannot possibly exist. Such complex ideas are composed of confused sensations and unnoticed judgements about their origin or nature. Differently from ideas of size, shape, etc., that Locke called 'primary qualities', which, in so far as they can be clearly and distinctly perceived, are, for Descartes, ideas of the intellect, the sensory, 'secondary' qualities cannot, because they are incommensurable with the former, be distinctly conceived as properties of real, extended things.

Descartes does not say very much about how the habitual, unnoticed judgements which are associated, by habit or nature, with sensory ideas come about—and what he says is not, as Margaret Wilson has shown, too helpful.[27] What is clear, I think, is that sensations are not primarily perceived as such; they do not present themselves as isolated, discrete impressions or sense-data; instead, they come to the mind in connection with other ideas, against a background of other 'ideas', beliefs, or attitudes in terms of which they are, automatically, or

---

[26] See the discussion in Wilson, *Descartes*, 100–19, and Kenny, *Descartes*, 117–25. But see also Wilson, 'Descartes on the Representationality of Sensation'.

[27] M. Wilson, 'Descartes on the Perception of Primary Qualities'.

instinctively as it were, interpreted. I see a bent stick in water, not light, colour, shapes, etc. The various visual sensations of light, colour, etc. that compose my idea of the stick are not given as such, but, rather, they are identified as such only after reflection on the purported object of perception—they are, we could say, the outcome of a pheno-menological reduction of a kind. What is perceived, what our sensory ideas are of, primarily, are external things with certain characteristic appearances.

If the sensations involved in ordinary perceptual ideas are thus not primarily given as such, as sensations of various kinds, they can, like the habitual judgements of the third grade of sensory perception, be separated and sorted out, by the attentive mind, and be subjected to closer, critical analysis. This, indeed, is what the Cartesian method prescribes us to do, and it is only by such a method that real and true, that is, clear and distinct, ideas can be distinguished from materially false and confused ones. The extent to which sensory perceptions can be trusted at all depends on the beliefs connected with them. What makes us go wrong is not the sensations themselves, but the unnoticed beliefs in terms of which they are spontaneously interpreted. By reflecting on and analysing, critically, our sensory experience, we are, Descartes thinks, able to distinguish our actual perceptions—that is, what is directly or immediately perceived by the senses—from the beliefs which are added on to the actual perceptions. An essential part of Descartes's method of clarification consists, precisely, in rendering the unnoticed, habitual, and mostly precipitate judgements and beliefs involved in sensory perception explicit and thereby subject to critical evaluation.[28]

The sensory idea of the bent stick in the water is a case of a confused, compound idea that is materially false in so far as it is spontaneously taken to present the stick in its true nature. Borrowing the terminology used by Alan Gewirth, we could say that material falsity belongs to compound ideas, the interpretive content of which goes, as it were, beyond their direct content: ideas to which we have, without noticing it, added something we do not immediately perceive. Materially false ideas have also been described as 'formally suspect', and what renders them suspect in this sense, I contend, is the fact that we have added to them, without noticing it, more reality than what they contain objectively.[29]

[28] See G. Hatfield, 'The Senses and the Fleshless Eye', 56 ff.
[29] Gewirth, 'Clearness and Distinctness in Descartes'; cf. Grene, *Descartes*, 177.

If this is granted, material falsity would differ from formal falsity not because no judgements are involved, but because the judgements involved are implicit and unnoticed, and therefore difficult to distinguish from the actual sensations, giving us thus material for error.[30] Material falsity hence arises from, but is not the same as the obscurity and confusion of, an idea: a confused idea, in order to be materially false, involves, in addition, implicit unnoticed false judgements about what it contains or presents, confusedly, to the mind. Because of the opaque character of sensory ideas, *any* judgement about their content other than that it is caused by something external, the nature of which we ignore, is bound to be false or unjustified (*Principles*, pt. I, art. 70: AT VIII 34; CSM I 218).

The way material falsity has been understood here does not commit Descartes to the view that sensations are non-representational and hence without any cognitive value. This is obviously not something Descartes could commit himself to: sensations function as signs, and as such they point to or evoke something that it imports us to be aware of. It does commit him, however, to the view that the objective reality or representativeness of sensations is problematic, because of their intrinsic opacity, or confusion, which hinders us from determining what formal reality they represent objectively or are ideas of. They are, one could say, indeterminate by their very nature. For all their indeterminacy, sensations are still extensional, in so far as they are caused by and evoke some mind-independent, external things. Different sensations make us think of different things and point to different causes—there is systematic variation in sensations which, presumably, corresponds to a variation in the external things causing them: they represent whatever they represent in virtue of a contingent quasi-causal connection. But they have no determinate, distinctly conceivable content that could be further analysed or specified. There is, hence, no way of reading off or deducing, from the sensations

---

[30] Gewirth does not think that this interpretation makes the idea or perceptive act judgmental, because there is no volitional act involved ('Clearness and Distinctness', 264). I agree there is no conscious voluntary act of assent or denial involved in these implicit judgements, but I still think we can talk of unnoticed judgements or beliefs, involving assent or denial, which, though they depend on the will, can be made by spontaneous or habitual inclination or impulse as well, rather than deliberately performed. We are, one could say, programmed or trained to respond to certain perceptual situations by certain beliefs or judgements, as when granting, for instance, that the stick immersed in water is bent, that the pain is in my foot, or that it is good for me to drink, whenever I feel thirsty.

themselves, what they point to, what they signify or indicate to the mind, because there is no internal connection between a sensation and its cause, between the sign and its signification. Whatever meaning they evoke, it is associated or assigned to them by natural institution or by habit. The framework within which they function as signs is the union of the mind and the body as instituted by nature: they have no meaning outside the context of the union, the preservation of which they are supposed to serve. They do not display, objectively, the thing causing them in its formal reality, but they indicate something, the nature (formal reality) of which we ignore, and of which we do, therefore, not know whether it can exist or not apart from the act of thinking itself.

Because of the slight degree of reality of the things (mental modes caused by the body) presented objectively by sensory ideas, they can be said to belong to the bottom level of represented perfections—representations of what is such that, to speak in Platonist terms, we do not know if it is or is not. But, I want to insist, even though they can be said to have, in this sense, their share of non-being or nothingness—they are *not* nothing—they are not non-ideas. There is a clear difference between a non-idea—that is, a contradictory idea—and a sensory idea. The latter is of something, though we know not what; the former of a non-thing, that is, of a thing so specified that we see, as soon as we try to conceive or think of it, that it is unthinkable. The sensory idea, *qua* mode of the mind, is real; moreover it indicates something that may be real though we do not know what kind of reality that thing might possess (substance, mode; mental, material). A contradictory idea, on the other hand, represents nothing at all, since it is the idea of a thing, the existence of which is impossible. A contradictory idea—the idea of a non-thing—excludes the reality of its object, because its object is inconceivable: it can neither be represented nor exist. A sensory idea, by contrast, does not by itself exclude all objective reality: it may or may not have one, but the possibility of its having an object is not excluded by the idea itself. We need other ideas to determine what, if any, formal reality it contains objectively. Whenever their content is determined spontaneously, by unnoticed judgements, we are likely to end up with a materially false sensory idea—one to which we have added more objective reality than what our immediate perceptions contain or present. By contrast, it suffices to try to contemplate the idea of some contradictory entity, like a valley without a mountain, or the idea of a round square, to know that they are inconceivable and cannot possibly exist, i.e. that they are non-things.[31]

VII. Concluding Remarks

Material falsity, I have argued, pertains primarily to obscure and confused complex sensory ideas and differs from formal falsity not because no judgements are involved, but because the judgements involved are implicit and therefore not recognized as such. Ideas, normally, present themselves in a context of other ideas and beliefs, and involve explicit or implicit judgements. The sensory ideas which deserve to be called materially false are complex ideas composed of inherently confused sensations and implicit, false judgements. In themselves, however, when disentangled from the judgements or beliefs unconsciously associated with them, no ideas (not even sensations in the strict sense) are false. It follows that the distinction between ideas taken objectively and judgements is far from being as clear-cut or unproblematic as Descartes's account of error in the Fourth Meditation seems to suggest. It also follows that the class of primary ideas—ideas taken objectively—includes many different kinds of representations ranging from clear and distinct ideas of the intellect to obscure and confused sensory ideas: the first are picture-like in the sense that they show or display the thing represented in its true nature; the latter are more like signs, in the sense that they evoke a signification without displaying it. All sorts of gradations, between the two extremes, are possible.[32] It is not, as we have seen, because they

---

[31] The case of chimeras is interesting. As Descartes understands it, they are fictitious beings, which, in so far as they are composed of elements that can be clearly and distinctly conceived, are possible, and hence real (although unexistent) beings. The idea of a chimera, in itself, is thus a true idea (see AT VII 362, CSM II 250; *Conversation with Burman* : AT V 160, CSMK 343; letter to Clerselier of 23 April 1649: AT V 354, CSMK 376). Spinoza, however, takes 'Chimera' to mean something that 'of its own nature, cannot exist', and which as such is a contradictory entity, on the par with the (non) idea of a round square, which is inconceivable (appendix to Descartes's 'Principles of Philosophy', in *The Collected Works of Spinoza*, ed. and trans. E. Curley, 299, 307).

[32] See the interesting analysis of J.-C. Pariente, *L'Analyse du langage à Port-Royal*, 72–7. Arnauld, Pariente argues, takes the correspondence between the idea and its *ideatum* in a strong sense, which means that Arnauld, when objecting to Descartes, like Spinoza, assumed a complete correspondence or agreement between the two. Later, in the *Art of Thinking* (1662), he seems to have adopted the Cartesian doctrine, that complex ideas can be false because they contain (unnoticed) judgements (without, however, using the term 'material falsity'). What Arnauld has realized, according to

lack objective being that sensory ideas fail to represent the true nature of their object—rather, it is because their function as representations is different from that of clear and distinct ideas of the intellect. The latter, as instruments or means of knowledge, display their object by themselves—there is no question of whether or what they represent: we know immediately what their object is, and the more distinct the idea, the more properties of the thing represented can be inferred from it. There is no gap between the represented and the formal reality here; all the properties of the thing are contained, as it were, in the idea, and can, although they are not all actually represented, be deduced from it. The idea coincides with the thing, the formal nature or reality of which it presents, objectively. It is, as stated before, the thing thought of. Sensory ideas, on the other hand, because of their opaque, indeterminate nature, point to or evoke real things, but they do not present, objectively, a fully or uniquely specified particular. The way they represent is different, because they function as signs, for pragmatic purposes, and for those purposes they are clear and distinct enough: they inform us of the presence and importance of external things—not of their true nature. True knowledge of external bodies depends for Descartes on the intellect anyway, and not on the senses.[33] But if this is granted, and if, as has been here argued, the clear and distinct ideas of the intellect present things themselves, objectively, in their true nature, then the attribution of the veil-of-ideas theory to Descartes seems inappropriate. Ideas, of course, can form a veil of ignorance, when they are misused, or, like materially false ideas, mixed up with precipitated, unnoticed judgements. But when taken for what they are, namely as signs for action, and not as copies of real entities, not even the most confused sensations need to be construed as forming a veil obscuring the true nature of the things

Pariente, is that 'the level of the idea and that of judgement should not be opposed as two rigid levels', and that one must admit, in between them, 'relations which are not reducible to the simple anteriority of the idea before the judgement' (p. 73). The judgements involved are not to be understood as actual, explicit judgements, but rather as prejudices—beliefs or opinions already formed which are, as it were, deposited or incorporated within the materially false idea (pp. 76–8).

[33] See e.g. Hatfield, 'The Senses and the Fleshless Eye', and Wilson, 'Descartes on the Perception of Primary Qualities'. Wilson's careful discussion also shows that Descartes's view of the relation of sense perception and the intellect in the knowledge of external bodies is ambiguous and remains, ultimately, problematic. See also her 'Descartes on the Representationality of Sensation'.

that cause them. Designed as they are not to give us insight in the
metaphysical structure of the world, but merely to 'help us to get
around', the ontological mistakes that the uncritical perceptual beliefs
generate can, on the contrary, be pragmatically useful.[34]

---

[34] Cf. Sellars, 'Lectures', 133–4.

13

The Reconfiguration of Sensory Experience

ANN WILBUR MACKENZIE

I. Introduction

There is no question that Descartes's philosophy makes provision for the *intellectual* apprehension of the object of geometry, and, given the identification (in his mature writings) of this object with the object studied by physics, none that Descartes's philosophy makes provision for the *intellectual* apprehension of the geometrical structure of physical reality. There *is* question, however, about what provision it makes for *sense perception* of determinate geometrical properties of middle-sized local portions of matter: their determinate size and shape, their spatial location with respect to the perceiver and each other, and their change in location (i.e. motion). The project here is to ascertain how Descartes construes *sense perception* of primary properties.[1]

This study is motivated by a very attractive interpretation of Descartes's philosophy of science which maintains, in broad terms, that Descartes envisioned a science which would be both certain and experimental.[2] This coupling of certainty with experiment in science places reasonably heavy epistemic demands on the senses. Daniel Garber puts the point as follows:

---

[1] Descartes himself does not use the expressions 'primary qualities' and 'secondary qualities'; nor does he provide any covering labels whatever. Instead, he uses *lists* to indicate what he has in mind. List (*a*) usually includes: size, shape, position, motion; list (*b*) usually includes light and colour, sounds, tastes, smells, heat, hardness, and other tactile qualities. With some risk of pernicious anachronism, I shall use the expressions 'geometrical properties' and 'primary properties' interchangeably in place of Descartes's list (*a*) and 'secondary qualities' in place of Descartes's list (*b*).

[2] For recent advocates of this view, see B. Williams, *Descartes*, ch. 9, D. Garber, 'Science and Certainty in Descartes'.

The fact that sensory knowledge is admitted, under appropriate circumstances, is crucial to reconciling Descartes' demand for certainty in science with his frequent claims to being an experimentalist ... The breakdown in certainty comes ... not with experiment, which can, if used properly, under the control of reason, lead to certain knowledge, but with the use of something like hypothetico-deductive method, which can never lead to certainty.[3]

Variants of this interpretation of Descartes's philosophy of science differ on important questions about how certainty is to be preserved through levels of enquiry which require observation and experiment. But Garber's interpretation (in 'Science and Certainty in Descartes') of what confers certainty seems to imply that, if it is to be preserved through levels importantly using experiment, then the scientist must be able to achieve *clear and distinct sensory knowledge of determinate primary properties of middle-sized objects*. Such sensory knowledge would be important at two points in what we now take to be the observation level: first in the formulation of a clear statement of the specific explanandum (phenomenon to be explained), and, secondly, for interpreting the *results* of those experiments conducted to discover the correct explanation.

I shall try to show here that Descartes provides a treatment of sense perception of primary properties which is consistent with the idea that, under appropriate circumstances including the governance of reason, the required clear and distinct sensory knowledge can be achieved. This will enable me to draw the conclusion that, appearances to the contrary notwithstanding, Descartes's writings specifically on the senses[4] are consistent with a philosophy of science which maintains that science can be both certain and empirical.

This may seem implausible given that Descartes's mature epistemological writings (the *Meditations* and part I of the *Principles*) leave the impression of a *deeply negative assessment* of the cognitive role of the senses in the search after truth. Some preliminary comments are in order here.

[3] D. Garber, '*Semel in vita*', 115–16.
[4] I have in mind here both the scientific, technical treatments of the senses (which are also deeply conceptual) in Descartes's *Optics* and the *Treatise of Man*, and the more heavily epistemological studies in the *Meditations* and part I of the *Principles of Philosophy*, both of which assess the cognitive role of the senses in the search after truth. The *Passions of the Soul*, and, it might be added, the second part of the Sixth Meditation, both of which contain an assessment of the cognitive role of the senses in a different context, namely in the context of the practical affairs of embodied minds, are not directly related to the task at hand.

When the context is the search after truth, there can be no question that Descartes is concerned to bring the senses under the supervision of reason. One main reason for the introduction of hyperbolical doubt is that it provides 'the easiest route by which the mind may be led away from the senses' (Synopsis: AT VII 12; CSM II 9), and the application of this doubt, at least through the end of the Third Meditation, involves an attempt to undercut the readers' confidence in *all* the testimony of the senses. This is, to be sure, a very heavy-handed treatment of the senses. However, recent commentators have provided convincing support for the claim that this mauling of the senses needs to be interpreted in the context of Descartes's general project to promote the new (mechanical) science. Thus, one main project in the *Meditations* is to reject the empiricist epistemology of common sense (which Descartes takes to underwrite Aristotelian-scholastic science) and to replace it with an epistemology more suitable for the new science.[5]

The question then becomes whether Descartes's positive episte-mology, developed in large part to underwrite the new science, accords any status to the senses in the search after truth. Posing the question this way makes it quite natural to raise the further question whether, in his thinking about the senses, Descartes *distinguishes*, in any important way, between sense perception of primary properties and sense perception apparently of secondary qualities. I shall be arguing here that he does.

The core of my argument is that Descartes subjects what he takes to be the common-sense understanding of *sensory experience* to intense philosophical scrutiny. The common-sense understanding of sensory experience (what we today would call 'sensory awareness' or 'the sensory given') fails to discriminate between primary properties and secondary qualities which fall within experience. Descartes acknow-ledges that sensory experience, thus understood, provides us with only a very obscure and confused grasp of (extramental) reality. However, Descartes's philosophical reflection on this undiscriminating under-standing of sensory experience involves the gradual paring apart of the primary-property and secondary-quality components, so that these components are distinguished both ontologically and

---

[5] Recent advocates of this view include: Garber, '*Semel in vita*'; G. Hatfield, 'The Senses and the Fleshless Eye'; J. Carriero, 'The First Meditation'. For related interpretations, see: M. Wilson, *Descartes*, and C. L. Larmore, 'Descartes' Empirical Epistemology'.

epistemologically. The result is (i) that it is only the secondary-quality component of sensory experience which Descartes takes to provide an obstacle to the search after truth, and (ii) that sense perception does provide the mind with rather direct cognitive access to *primary properties* of middle-sized objects, which, when suitably regulated by reason, yields the raw materials for clear and distinct sensory knowledge of the kind needed for a science which is both experimental and certain.

Of central philosophical interest here is that achieving a more discriminating understanding of sensory experience forces Descartes to abandon a *uniform* conceptual analysis of sensory perception in general, and to replace it with two *separate* analyses, one of *sense perception of primary properties*, the other of *sense perception apparently of secondary qualities*. To understand the pressure on Descartes, we need to note the two main elements in his metaphysics which, together, constrain his thought about sense perception (in the search after truth).

First, Descartes's geometrical conception of matter implies that determinate primary properties (size, shape, motion, etc.) are real properties of material objects, but secondary qualities (*per se*) are not. Secondly, Descartes's theory of mental representation seems to involve an act–object construal at least of the paradigm cases of mental representation—namely, clear and distinct ideas. The constraints on 'objects' of clear and distinct ideas (outlined in the Third Meditation) when applied to sensory ideas imply that (*a*) determinate primary properties of middle-sized chunks of matter can serve as objects of clear and distinct sensory ideas, but secondary qualities cannot, and therefore that (*b*) sensory ideas can represent primary properties but not secondary qualities.

Descartes's dual analyses of 'sense perception' satisfy these two metaphysical constraints: the analysis of *sense perception of primary properties* renders it genuinely representational (though not invariably veridical), and the *different* analysis of *sense perception apparently of secondary qualities* renders it non-representational (and consequently not 'of' anything outside the mind). This segregated analysis underwrites Descartes's more nuanced epistemological treatment of sense perception in the search after truth.

The argument to follow is complicated enough to want overview. Sections II and III concentrate on the two main stages in Descartes's attempts to clarify the concept of sense perception. Section II outlines

Descartes's attempt (in the Fourth, Fifth, and Sixth Discourses of his *Optics*) to provide a single uniform analysis of sense perception in general, using the notion of representation as the key to his analysis. Section III outlines Descartes's general views about representation (in the Third Meditation) and studies an objection by Arnauld together with Descartes's response (Fourth Objections and Replies), which displays Descartes's recognition of the fact that sense perception apparently of secondary qualities cannot be analysed as involving representation. The end result is Descartes's reconfigured understanding of sensory experience. Section IV concentrates on Descartes's positive epistemological assessment of the role of sensory experience in the search after truth. There is a brief discussion of the treatment in the Sixth Meditation, and a more extensive discussion of part I of the *Principles of Philosophy*. The aim is to show that Descartes's reconfigured understanding of sensory experience informs his answer to the methodological question of how the senses should be used in the search after truth, and results in his more nuanced epistemological assessment of the cognitive value of the senses in the search after truth.

II. Sensory Representation in the *Optics*

The central discussion of sense in the Fourth, Fifth, and Sixth Discourses of the *Optics* is very ambitious.[6] It attempts both to *refute* the Aristotelian–scholastic theory of perception (which is not consistent with the new mechanical world-view) and *replace* it with a new theory (which is). The discussion also develops, within the framework of the new theory, a uniform (scientific) treatment of both perception and misperception, which identifies some of the 'fidelity conditions' for accurate perception and some of the factors which lead to misperception.

Descartes takes the basic explanatory concept in the traditional theory to be the concept of a *resembling image* (which he refers to variously as 'form', 'image', and 'intentional species'). He interprets this theory to be committed to the claim that little images are formed in our brains and that these images stimulate our minds to perceive the object *by virtue of* the resemblance which the image has to the

---

[6] For detailed discussion and textual support of the interpretation I am about to outline, see A. W. MacKenzie, 'Descartes on Sensory Representation'.

object sensed (*Optics*, Fourth Discourse: AT VI 112.[7] Descartes argues that, although *physical images* ('corporeal images') *are* formed in our brains in the sensory process, these images do not resemble the environmental object sensed in the way required by the traditional theory. Even in those cases where corporeal images *do* bear some (imperfect) resemblance to the object sensed, it is *not by virtue of this resemblance* that we are able to sense the object: 'Now although this picture, in being so transmitted into our head, always retains some resemblance to the objects from which it proceeds, nevertheless, as I have already shown, we must not hold that it is by means of this resemblance that the picture causes us to perceive the objects, as if there were yet other eyes in our brain with which we could apprehend it' (Sixth Discourse: AT VI 130).[8]

It is important to recognize that Descartes is rejecting the notion of resembling image in the analysis of sense perception in general, not just for sense perception as it relates to secondary qualities. The major focus of attention in the *Optics* is on (visual) perception of primary properties, and Descartes's best (scientific) arguments against the notion of resembling image occur in his treatment of distance and direction perception.

Descartes proposes to replace the notion of resembling image with the notion of representation, and he seems to be advocating a version of natural sign theory. He outlines his new theory with the help of two key analogies,[9] the result of which is in Table 13.1 (the column headings are mine). The basic idea here (reading row by row) is that what links words (X) with what words signify (Y) is the rules of language (S); what links figures in two-dimensional engravings (X) with three-dimensional objects (Y) is the rules of perspective (S); what links corporeal images in the brain (X) to objects and properties of objects (Y) is the whole causal nexus (S). The common logical structure here is: X represents Y to mind Z by virtue of S, and Descartes is claiming, in the abstract, that: the vehicle of representation need not resemble the object of representation in order to enable a mind to conceive/perceive the object because the *background system* links the object to the vehicle. The overall view seems to be that the whole

---

[7] P. J. Olscamp (trans.), *Discourse on Method, Optics, Geometry and Meteorology*, 89.
[8] Olscamp (trans.), 101.
[9] The word analogy (Fourth Discourse: AT VI 112; Olscamp (trans.), *Discourse*, 89), and the two-dimensional engraving analogy (Fourth Discourse: AT VI 113; Olscamp (trans.), 90).

TABLE 13.1 *Representational situations*

Background system (S)	Vehicle of representation (X)	What gets represented (Y)
Human convention	Words	What the words signify
Rules of perspective	Two-dimensional engravings	Three-dimensional objects
The whole causal nexus	Corporeal brain images	Objects, properties of objects

causal nexus will play the same functional role (linking objects with vehicles of sensory representation) in the new science that the notion of resemblance played in the old.

The emerging conception of the role played by the brain in sense perception (within the context of the general natural sign theory) is that the brain acts as a multifaceted natural indicator differing in complexity, but not kind, from simple single-faceted natural indicators like thermometers, delivering its 'measurements' (i.e. the environmental correlates) to consciousness. Evidently, the *vehicle of representation* (the relevant 'measuring' brain event) need not resemble its environmental correlate in order to make it present to consciousness, just as the word 'apple' need not resemble any apple in order to make an apple present to consciousness.

The reason why sensory representation of objects and their properties is normally accurate is that, under normal conditions, the presence of an environmental object with the relevant property is a major part of the cause of the brain event doing the representing. This general model provides Descartes with the wherewithal to give a uniform account of sensory representation and misrepresentation, and he offers this fact as further support for the theory.[10] The basic idea is that under normal circumstances, when the complex brain event is caused in the normal way, there really will be an object at the particular location, having the relevant size and shape. But if the brain event is abnormally caused, in any of the ways Descartes attempts to identify, then *none the less* it will exhibit in consciousness the *usual* environmental correlate.

I noted earlier that, in his *Optics*, Descartes seems to be proposing a uniform analysis of sensory perception (i.e 'of' both primary properties and secondary qualities). It is now time to recognize that the two

[10] *Optics*, Sixth Discourse (AT VI 141; Olscamp (trans.), 107).

key ideas in the theory sketched in the Fourth, Fifth, and Sixth Discourses create an unresolved tension when they are applied to perception 'of' secondary qualities. On the one hand, we have Descartes's general notion of representation which involves a vehicle making an object *present to the mind* (I have taken this to mean 'present to consciousness'). On the other hand, we have the specific *kind* of representation at work in sense perception (i.e. natural representation rather than e.g. conventional representation) which requires that there *be* a usual environmental correlate of a brain event if that brain event is to serve as a vehicle of sensory representation. Now, with respect to secondary qualities (e.g. light and colour), the only *real* environmental correlates of brain events are (unknown) micro-mechanical properties of matter outside the head. And Descartes seems to have had these in mind when he wrote the *Optics*, since, when he uses colour words (and the word 'light') in the First, Fifth, and Sixth Discourses, he reminds his reader that he means the micro-mechanical basis.[11] But such micro-mechanical properties are *not* made present to consciousness when one, for example, sees a red apple. Either Descartes must abandon the general idea that representation involves making something present to consciousness, or he must give up the idea that sense perception apparently of secondary properties is a kind of representation.

III. Representation in the Third Meditation

Descartes sketches a general theory of mental representation in the Third Meditation, using clear and distinct ideas as paradigm examples of mental representation and contrasting them with obscure and confused ideas.[12]

The definition of 'idea' in the Second Replies indicates that Descartes intends not (any longer) to use 'idea' to refer to corporeal brain images or brain events. Ideas henceforth are modes of thought. This marks a departure from the way Descartes viewed sensory representation (in the *Optics*), but I do not think it marks a change in

[11] *Optics*, Fifth Discourse (AT VI 118; Olscamp (trans.), 94); Sixth Discourse (AT VII 132; Olscamp (trans.), 102).
[12] My thinking is influenced by K. Clatterbaugh, 'Descartes' Causal Likeness Principle', and Margaret Wilson's discussion of the Third Meditation in *Descartes*, ch. 3. However, neither of these writers adopts the act–object interpretation of clear and distinct ideas I here begin to develop.

logical structure: the *vehicles of representation* will now be modifications in the mind (rather than some being modifications in the brain).[13] Probably 'mental acts' is the best way to view the vehicles of representation in the case of *occurrent* ideas. (Perhaps 'inferential structures' would be the best way to view vehicles of representation in the case of *innate* ideas).[14] The task now is to get straight on what Descartes takes the *objects* of representation to be. To do this, I will need to develop an interpretation of the obscure notion of 'the objective reality of ideas'. Some preliminaries are in order.

First, when Descartes talks about 'reality', he has in mind properties, qualities, modes, accidents, or attributes of substances, though occasionally he talks also of substances as realities.[15]

Secondly, Descartes distinguishes the 'formal reality' of a property from its 'objective reality'. The point of this distinction in Descartes's thought is to emphasize the difference between a substance actually having (exemplifying) a property—then the property has *formal* reality in the substance—on the one hand, and a mind thinking of, or sensing, the property—then the property has *objective* reality in the thought or sensory idea.

'Formal reality' ('reality simpliciter' as Margaret Wilson puts it), can be defined:

D1 A property P has formal reality in a substance x at t iff x actually exemplifies P at t.

Thirdly, one of Descartes's formulations of what I shall call 'the objective-reality principle' in the Third Meditation is: 'in order for a given idea to contain such and such objective reality, it must surely derive it from some cause which contains at least as much formal reality as there is objective reality in the idea' (AT VII 41; CSM II 28–9). Two points of clarification are in order here.

First, Descartes cannot be talking about occasioning causes of occurrent ideas, because innate ideas have objective reality, and they

[13] Descartes emphasizes the point that ideas are not just modes of thought but also vehicles of representation. See the Third Meditation (AT VII 40; CSM II 27–8), and the corresponding passage in the *Principles*, pt. I, art. 17 (AT VIIIA 11; V. R. Miller and R. P. Miller (eds.), *Descartes, Principles of Philosophy*, 9). He is making the same point, in different language, in his Fourth Replies (to Arnauld) (AT VII 232; CSM II 163).

[14] A full defence of the act–object interpretation I advocate requires careful study of innate ideas in Descartes's thought. This must be saved for another occasion, however, and my attention here will be fixed on occurrent ideas.

[15] See Clatterbaugh, 'Descartes' Causal Likeness Principle', 382–4.

need have no occasioning causes. More generally, it is evident that Descartes is not interested in explaining why an idea comes to mind at a particular time; he is interested in understanding the constraints on what an idea can be about, no matter when (or whether) the idea 'comes to mind'.

Secondly, Descartes has what we might call a 'componential' theory of ideas, though the syntax is never developed. The objective reality principle is intended to apply only to the *basic components* (or 'simple notions'). Thus, the idea of a chimera, for example, is a composite idea, only the basic components of which would be expected to satisfy the objective reality principle. Descartes's analogy in the First Meditation (AT VII 19–20; CSM II 13–14) that visions which come in sleep are like paintings alludes to this theory, and part I of the *Principles* lists 'all the simple notions of which our thought is composed' (*Principles*, pt. I, arts. 47–8: AT VIIIA 22–3).[16]

The objective–reality principle entails:

Only those properties which can exist formally in some substance can exist objectively in an idea.

'Can exist formally' in this formulation is too weak, however, since it suggests that merely possible properties will suffice. Descartes explicitly *rejects* this suggestion in the Third Meditation: 'the objective being of an idea cannot be produced merely by a potential being, which strictly speaking is nothing, but only by an actual or formal being' (AT VII 47; CSM II 32). And, in a letter dated 29 July 1648, Descartes says: 'I . . . am convinced that there is no such quality [as heaviness] in nature, and that *consequently* there is no real idea of it in the intellect . . . '(AT V 222; CSMK 358). Thus the objective-reality principle entails:

Only those properties which exist formally in some substance can be included in the objective reality of an idea.

I do not mean to suggest that Descartes thinks that the property must exist formally at the same time as it is included in the objective reality of an occurrent idea. Descartes is explicit about this in his formulation of the a posteriori proof in part I of the *Principles*: 'And because we in no way find in ourselves those supreme perfections of which we have the idea; from that fact alone we rightly conclude that they exist, *or certainly once existed*, in something different from us; that is, in God:

---

[16] Miller and Miller (eds.), *Principles*, 21.

and from this ... it most evidently follows that they still exist' (*Principles*, pt. I, art. 18: AT VIIIA 12; emphasis added).[17] This is a puzzling point, but it is an instance of the same general principle underlying Descartes's treatment of misperception in the *Optics*.

I can now provide the first approximation of a definition of 'objective reality'. Let z be any thinking substance, and Q be the name of one of her ideas:

A property P *is the* (or part of the) *objective reality of z's idea* Q at t iff:

z has an idea Q at t such that P is the (or part of the) formal reality represented by Q.

A reformulation is required, however, in the light of Descartes's definition of 'objective reality' in the Second Replies: '*Objective Reality of an Idea*. By this I mean the being of the thing which is represented by an idea, in so far as this exists in the idea ... For whatever we perceive as being in the objects of our ideas exists objectively in the ideas themselves' (AT VII 161; CSM II 113–14). I suggest the following reading of this difficult passage: take as an example of one of the objects of our ideas an extramental object like the sun. Not all properties formally existing in the sun need to be represented by the idea of the sun, and Descartes's definition insists that only those properties which are exhibited in consciousness by the idea are included in the objective reality of that idea. Given this reading, I thus propose:

D2 *A property* P *is the* (or part of the) *objective reality of z's occurrent idea* Q at t iff:

z has an occurrent idea Q such that:

(*a*) P is the (or part of the) formal reality represented by Q, and

(*b*) P is exhibited in z's consciousness at t by Q.[18]

Given this definition, we can see that the scientific and conceptual work in the *Optics* as it applies to sense perception of *primary properties* fits neatly into the general theory of representation outlined in the Third Meditation. Primary properties of middle-sized local portions of matter can satisfy both clauses (*a*) and (*b*), so they can be included in the objective reality of sensory ideas.

A failure of fit does arise in the case of secondary qualities, however. Given Descartes's definition of 'the objective reality of an idea', the

---

[17] Ibid. 10.

[18] I will leave for another occasion the task of defining objective reality of innate ideas.

suggestion left hanging in the *Optics* that sensory ideas might represent the micromechanical bases in environmental objects has been ruled out, since these are not exhibited in consciousness (clause (*b*) in my definition is violated).[19] The question then is whether ideas apparently 'of' secondary qualities represent anything.

Descartes raises the question as he surveys the ideas he has of corporeal things. He classifies these ideas in the taxonomical tree in Fig. 13.1. Descartes directs attention to the right-hand branch of the tree. *These are secondary qualities.* Descartes asserts that he can think of these in 'only a very obscure way' and that he does not even know whether the ideas he has of them 'are ideas of real things or of non-things'. He illustrates his points using the then-familiar positive–privative contrast, and introduces the notion of material falsity of ideas. This adds complexity which can be ignored here.

IDEAS OF CORPOREAL THINGS

'Things' which I perceive very clearly in 'them'		'Things' thought of in only a very confused and obscure way
[ ]	[ ]*	light and colour
		sounds
size	substance	smells
shape	duration	tastes
position	number	heat and cold
motion		other tactile qualities

F I G . 1 3 . 1 *Third Meditation* (AT VII 43; CSM II 30)
* Empty square brackets indicate that Descartes provides no covering label.

Arnauld, in the Fourth Objections, subjects the whole passage to probing critical scrutiny. Ignoring subtleties, Arnauld's question is: supposing that cold has no formal reality, how can we have the idea of cold? One of Arnauld's arguments (again ignoring subtleties) might

---

[19] I do not mean to suggest that Descartes is committed to denying that the micromechanical bases of colours (etc.) can be represented at all; just not at the level of sense. This matter is discussed in A. W. MacKenzie, 'Descartes on Life and Sense'.

be reconstructed as follows.[20] Given that, first, the idea of cold is coldness itself as it exists in the intellect, and secondly, that the objective-reality principle is true, and assuming that cold has no formal reality,[21] it follows that there is no idea of cold. Therefore, if someone takes one of his ideas to be the idea of cold, he has misjudged the object of his idea.[22]

Descartes, in the Fourth Replies, *accepts* the basic thrust of this argument:

When my critic says that the idea of cold 'is coldness itself in so far as it exists objectively in the intellect', I think we need to make a distinction. For it often happens in the case of obscure and confused ideas—and the ideas of heat and cold fall into this category—that *an idea is referred to something other than that of which it is in fact the idea.* Thus if cold is simply an absence, the idea of cold is not coldness itself as it exists objectively in the intellect, *but something else, which I erroneously mistake for this absence, namely a sensation* which in fact has no existence outside the intellect. (AT VII 233; CSM II 163; emphasis added)

The overall logic of Descartes's response here should be noted. Descartes *does not deny* the general principles Arnauld ascribes to him. He does not deny (in the abstract) that the idea of x is x-ness itself as it exists in the understanding; nor does he retract the objective-reality principle, which implies that, if x exists (objectively) in the understanding, then x exists formally in some substance. Confronted with the given that x does not exist formally, Descartes directs Modus Tollens upon the only remaining degree of freedom: what I *took to be* an idea of x is not, in fact, an idea of x; rather, there is some y (different from x) which I have mistaken for x, and what I took to be the idea of x is, in fact, the idea of y. Descartes emphasizes that we are prone to this kind of mistake when the original idea is obscure and confused, as is the case with ideas of secondary qualities.

Although the general logic here is straightforward, it is not clear whether Descartes has in mind *concepts* of secondary qualities or *occurrent sensory ideas* 'of' secondary qualities (i.e. sensations themselves). Furthermore, the same general logic has different applications in the two cases, because the objective-reality principle can be satisfied in one but not in the other. I shall discuss these cases in turn, starting with concepts.

[20] Arnauld's version in the Fourth Objections is at AT VII 206–7; CSM II 145–6.
[21] There is an important clarification here which will be discussed below.
[22] My justification for streamlining Arnauld's argument as I have is that it is the version to which Descartes responds.

Descartes's point applied to *concepts* of secondary qualities is reasonably straightforward. We misidentify the objects of such concepts ('[a concept] is referred to something other than that of which it is in fact the [concept]'), mistakenly taking these objects to be properties of matter, whereas in fact the objects of such concepts are sensations. It is important to be straight on the logic here. Sensations are modes of thinking, so sensations have formal reality: they inhere formally in the mind.[23] Thus the objective-reality principle is satisfied in the case of concepts of secondary qualities: there is something with formal reality for these concepts to be concepts of—namely, the relevant sensation. Thus *concepts* of secondary qualities can have objective reality, and the concept of red differs from that of cold in that the former has a red-sensation as its object whereas the latter has a cold-sensation as its object. In short, *concepts* of secondary qualities represent *sensations*.

Sensations (occurrent sensory ideas apparently 'of' secondary qualities), however, *have no objective reality*. There is no property P which satisfies both constraints in the definition of 'objective reality' (D2 above). A red-sensation differs from a cold-sensation, to be sure, since these are qualitatively distinct states of sensory awareness. But this difference consists in the fact that they have different *formal* reality; it does not consist in the fact that they differ in *objective* reality, for they have none. Thus, in the case of sensations themselves, it would be misleading to suggest that we mistake their objects, since they have no objects. The only mistake we may be inclined to make in the case of sensations is to take them as having objects—that is, as representing something.

Let me draw together the threads of this discussion. The general theory of representation outlined in the Third Meditation implies that sensations apparently of secondary qualities do not represent anything, and Descartes seems to acknowledge this explicitly in the Fourth Replies. He thus abandons *part* of the theory of sense perception as a

---

[23] Or they inhere formally in the union of mind and body. Descartes is very unsure of the exact ontological status of sensations. In the Sixth Meditation he treats them as confused *modes of thinking* (which makes it appear that they inhere formally in the mind) but he adds that they arise from the union of mind and body (AT VII 81; CSM II 56). In *Principles*, pt. I, art. 48, Descartes refuses to ascribe them either solely to the mind or solely to the body, making it appear that they inhere formally in the union of mind and body. This discomfort on Descartes's part does not affect my point here, which is that sensations do have formal reality, inhering either in the mind or in the union of mind and body.

kind of representation developed in the *Optics*. However, the *other part* of the theory accords nicely with Third Meditation views about representation, and there is no indication that Descartes ever abandons a representational analysis of sense perception of primary properties.[24]

It is worth pausing to reflect on what all this means in relation to a common-sense understanding of sensory experience which fails to discriminate between primary properties and secondary qualities within experience. Descartes's conceptual work constitutes a transformation— or reconfiguration—of this common-sense understanding because it emphasizes the fundamental difference between these two components within sensory experience. In language closer to Descartes's own, the reconfigured view would be that sensory ideas have some objective reality, namely the primary properties they represent, but they also have a purely subjective (or sensational) component, namely, the modifications of the mind normally caused (or occasioned) by the relevant micromechanical properties of corporeal objects, and that this subjective (sensational) component does not represent anything outside the mind.

I am suggesting that Descartes has achieved this more discriminating understanding of sensory experience at least by the time he wrote his Replies to the Fourth Objections. Perhaps he had already achieved it by the time he wrote the *Meditations*. (The discussion of material falsity in the Third Meditation suggests it, and there are hints in the Sixth Meditation as well.) In any event, this reconfigured understanding of sensory experience pervades part I of the *Principles of Philosophy*, and it is clearly articulated in *Principles*, pt. I, art. 71.

IV. The Role of Sensory Experience in the Search after Truth

In the Sixth Meditation Descartes indicates that sensory experience may have some positive role to play in the search after truth: 'But now,

[24] In *Descartes*, ch. III, Margaret Wilson outlines an interpretation similar in some respects to my own, and I am deeply indebted to her discussion. But her interpretation is more extreme than mine: she argues that Descartes, under pressure from Arnauld, abandons a representational construal of all ideas of sense (p. 105). However, once one takes seriously the idea that Descartes provides a *segregated* analysis of 'sense perception', one needs textual support for the claims both that (*a*) Descartes abandons a representational construal of sense perception apparently of secondary qualities and that (*b*) Descartes abandons a representational construal of sense perception of primary properties. Although there is ample support for (*a*), I find none for (*b*).

when I am beginning to achieve a better knowledge of myself and the author of my being, although I do not think I should heedlessly accept everything I seem to have acquired from the senses, neither do I think that everything should be called into doubt' (AT VII 77–8; CSM II 54).[25] Descartes then provides his final argument for the real distinction of mind and body, acknowledges that he does in fact have faculties of imagination and sense perception, and uses sensory experience as a key element in his proof for the existence of corporeal things.

At the end of this proof, Descartes offers the following preliminary assessment of the role of the senses in science:

It follows that corporeal things exist. They may not exist in a way which exactly corresponds with my sensory grasp of them, for in many cases the grasp of the senses is very obscure and confused. But at least they possess all the properties which I clearly and distinctly understand, that is, all those which, when viewed in general terms, are comprised within the subject matter of pure mathematics. (AT VII 80; CSM II 55)

This passage is certainly consistent with the reconfigured understanding of sensory experience outlined above, although it does not explicitly affirm it. Descartes immediately introduces questions about sense perception in relation to determinate primary properties of physical objects and to secondary qualities, reminding his reader that secondary qualities are less clearly understood than the determinate ('particular') primary properties:

What of the other aspects of corporeal things which are either particular (for example that the sun is of such and such size or shape), or less clearly understood, such as light or sound or pain, and so on? Despite the high degree of doubt and uncertainty here, the very fact that God is not a deceiver, and the consequent impossibility of there being any falsity in my opinions which cannot be corrected by some other faculty supplied by God, offers me a sure hope that I can attain the truth even in these matters. (AT VII 80; CSM II 55–6)

Descartes then turns his attention to sensations of pain, hunger, thirst, etc., using the fact that he has such sensations to establish that there is a more intimate union between minds and (human) bodies than might be expected given the clear and distinct conception of thinking substance and of extended substance (AT VII 81; CSM II 56).

---

[25] The interpretation I am about to develop is influenced by Martial Gueroult's reading of the structure of the Sixth Meditation, in *Descartes' Philosophy Interpreted According to the Order of Reasons*, chs. 12, 14.

As I read the Sixth Meditation, this completes Descartes's preliminary assessment of the cognitive role of sensory experience in the search after truth. The focus of the remaining discussion (AT VII 81–9; CSM II 56–61) is on the cognitive role of sensation in the practical affairs of embodied minds, and the new theodicy there developed (AT VII 83–9; CSM II 58–61)—which is explicitly distinguished from the one in the Fourth Meditation—attempts to deal with the fact that sensations appear occasionally to deceive us about what is harmful or beneficial to the body (or to the union of mind and body).

To summarize: Descartes identifies two points in his metaphysics at which sense experience plays key roles. First, sense experience is required in establishing with certainty that the external world exists.[26] Secondly, the fact that we have sensations establishes a more intimate union of mind and body than might have been expected. Furthermore, Descartes expresses the conviction that sense perception will be able to play a positive role in science, but he provides no account of the details. For a treatment of the details, we must look to the *Principles of Philosophy*, to which I now turn.

Part I of the *Principles* outlines the metaphysical and epistemological foundations of the new science. Within this general framework, Descartes develops his assessment of the cognitive role of the sensory experience in science. In what follows, I will rivet attention on this aspect of Descartes's discussion, extracting it from his more general epistemological treatment. The focal question in this aspect of Descartes's treatment is his answer to the methodological question: how ought the senses to be used in the new science? I will provide an overview of the five main steps in Descartes's answer to this question.

STEP ONE (*Principles*, pt. I, art. 30) is Descartes's assessment of what follows from the assertion that God exists and is not the cause of human error. Descartes draws three conclusions from this: first, that our God-given faculty of knowledge cannot encompass any object which is not true in so far as it is clearly and distinctly perceived; and, secondly, that mathematical truths are no longer suspect, since they are utterly clear to us. Descartes then turns his attention to the senses: 'And if we notice something which is clear and distinct in our senses (either while we are awake or while we are asleep), and we distinguish it from what is confused and obscure; we shall easily recognize, in

---

[26] This point is emphasized by Garber, '*Semel in vita*', 103–7.

anything whatever, what should be taken to be true' (AT VIIIA 17).[27] The third conclusion, then, is a conditional claim: *if* sensory experi- ence includes aspects which are clear and distinct, and *if* we can distinguish what is clear and distinct from what is confused and obscure, *then* we can use the senses in the search after truth.

STEP TWO is the implication of the theory of error outlined in *Principles*, pt. I, arts. 33–42. The upshot of this theory is that we never go wrong when we assent only to what we clearly and distinctly perceive (art. 43). The methodological implication of this for the use of the senses in science is that we should assent only to what is clearly and distinctly perceived within the senses. The methodological ques- tion then becomes: what can be clearly and distinctly perceived within sensory experience?

This question is addressed within the context of a much more general study which involves identifying the basic components of human thought and indicating, with respect to each of these, what can be perceived clearly and what can be perceived only obscurely. Descartes introduces this general study as a way of eliminating the prejudices formed in early childhood: 'in order that we may free ourselves from these, I shall here briefly enumerate all the simple notions of which our thought is composed; and in each one, I shall distinguish what is clear, from what is unclear or misleading' (*Principles*, pt. I, art. 47: AT VIIIA 22).[28]

STEP THREE is Descartes's answer to the question: what are the basic components of human thought? He answers this question by providing a classification of 'all the objects which come within our perception' (art. 48). Although Descartes's taxonomy is fascinating, and rewards careful study, I shall not discuss it here. Suffice it to say for the present overview that, in order to classify 'all the objects which come within our perception', Descartes creates a subcategory of what I shall call 'anomalous states' which includes bodily appetites, emo- tions, and secondary qualities.[29] This subcategory does not include any primary properties (they show up elsewhere in the taxonomy), nor does it make any reference to sensations of primary properties.

---

[27] Miller and Miller (eds.), *Principles*, 15.   [28] Ibid. 21.

[29] The label is apt. These states are 'anomalous' because, although they must be states of something, Descartes refuses to categorize them together with states of either of the two main kinds of (created) substances in his ontology. Instead, these anomalous states 'should be attributed neither solely to the mind nor solely to the body', but rather they 'originate from the close and profound union of our mind with the body' (*Principles*, pt. I, art. 48: AT VIIIA 23; Miller and Miller (eds.), *Principles*, 21).

The general classification of 'all the objects which come within our perception' structures the remainder of the discussion in part I of the *Principles*. The aim is to distinguish the clear elements from the obscure and confused elements within these basic components of human thought.

STEP FOUR (*Principles*, pt. I, arts. 65–9) provides Descartes's indication of how the primary properties and the anomalous states can be clearly known.

The discussion of how primary properties—the diverse modes of extension, or modes which belong to extension (such as all shapes, the positions of parts, and the motions of the parts)—can be clearly known is brief and direct: 'we shall best understand [all these items] if we regard them only as modes of the things in which they are' (*Principles*, pt. I, art. 65: AT VIIIA 32).[30]

The discussion of the anomalous states (sensations, emotions, and appetites) is more elaborate. Descartes indicates how these states can be clearly known, and how to distinguish what is clear from what is obscure and confused in such matters (arts. 66–9). Descartes uses pain and colour as his main examples. He makes two important points. First, pain and colour (etc.) can be clearly and distinctly perceived '*when they are regarded only as sensations or thoughts*' (Principles, pt. I, art. 68: AT VIIIA 33; emphasis added).[31] That is, these states can be clearly and distinctly perceived when they are taken simply as *subjective states* or, in Descartes's words, as 'what we are inwardly conscious of' (Principles, pt. I, art. 66: AT VIIIA 32).[32] Secondly, these anomalous states become obscure and confused when we try to take them as representing something outside thought. The *reason* why they become obscure and confused when we try to take them as representational is that *we have no conception of their objects*:

when someone says that he sees colour in some body, or feels pain in some limb, it is exactly as if he were to say that he sees or feels there something of whose nature he is completely ignorant, that is, that *he does not know what he is seeing or feeling* . . . [I]f however he examines what it is that this sensation of colour or pain (considered as if existing in the coloured body, or in the painful part) represents, he will certainly notice that *he is entirely ignorant of it* (art. 68, AT VIIIA 33; emphasis added).[33]

Descartes completes this discussion by explicitly contrasting the way we know primary properties in objects with the way we know secondary

[30] Miller and Miller (eds.), *Principles*, 30. [31] Ibid. 31.
[32] Ibid. 30. [33] Ibid. 31.

qualities (art. 69). The text, although somewhat obscure, leaves no doubt that it is sense perception which Descartes has in mind. There is a wide gap, he tells us, between our knowledge of those features of bodies that we clearly perceive (that is, the size, in a body which has been observed, or figure, or motion), on the one hand, and our knowledge of those features like colour in a body, as well as pain, smell, taste, etc., on the other.

STEP FIVE (*Principles*, pt. I, art. 70) provides Descartes's answer to the methodological question of how sensory experience ought to be used in making judgements concerning perceptible things. It is the logical outcome of applying the results of Step Four (the assessment of what can and cannot be clearly and distinctly perceived within sensory experience) to the general principle articulated in Step Two (we never go wrong when we assent only to what we clearly and distinctly perceive). Descartes is most concerned about getting straight on the use of sensory experience as a basis for judgements about secondary qualities in objects, and the use of sensory experience as a basis for judgements about primary properties is presented by way of contrast.

Descartes begins article 70 by reminding his reader that, 'when we say that we perceive colours in objects, this is in fact as if we were to say that we perceive something in objects of whose nature we are ignorant, but by means of which a certain very manifest and evident sensation is created in us, which is called the sensation of colour' (AT VIIIA 34).[34] It is quite appropriate to use such sensations as a basis for the judgement that there is something in the object from which the sensation comes *the nature of which we do not know*: 'as long as we merely judge that there is something in objects (that is, in the things from which a sensation comes to us, of whatever exact kind those things may be) the nature of which we do not know; we will . . . avoid error . . . ' (AT VIIIA 34).[35] If, on the other hand, we use our sensory experience as a basis of attributing secondary qualities to objects, we fall into error:

But when we think that we perceive colours in objects, although in fact we do not know what it is that we are calling by the name 'colour', and cannot understand any similarity between the colour which we are supposing to be in objects and that which we experience to be in our sensation . . . we easily fall into the error of judging that which we call colour in objects, is something

---

[34] Ibid. 31–2.   [35] Ibid. 32.

entirely similar to our sensation of colour; and thus of believing we clearly perceive something which we do not perceive in any way. (AT VIIIA 34–5)[36]

The source of the temptation to fall into this kind of error, Descartes asserts, is due to the contrasting situation with respect to primary properties. It is 'because there are many other things, like size, figure, number, etc. which we clearly perceive to be felt or understood by us in a manner which does not differ from that in which they are, or at least can be in objects' (AT VIIIA 34)[37] that we fall into the error of ascribing secondary qualities to objects.

The methodological upshot of this more nuanced treatment of role of sense perception in science is that sensory experience may be used in science as a basis for judgements about the primary properties of middle-sized physical objects, but that we must refrain from using it as a basis for judgements attributing colours, sounds, tastes, etc. to them.

This completes my discussion of Descartes's positive account of the role of sensory experience in the new science. I believe that extracting this theme from the more general epistemological discussion in part I of the *Principles* provides ample evidence for the conclusion that Descartes is using his reconfigured understanding of sensory experience as the basis for his more nuanced epistemological assessment. The potential obstacle in using sensory experience in science is the fact that it contains sensations of secondary qualities; but once we recognize, by means of philosophical reflection, that these sensations cannot be taken as representing anything outside of thought, we can then use the remaining genuinely representational component of sensory experience to access the determinate primary properties of middle-sized objects. This is what we need, at the observation level, in the new science.

It is worth remarking that Descartes follows his methodological pronouncements with an explicit articulation of the reconfigured understanding of sensory experience which he expects his readers to have achieved. The context is the claim that the principal cause of error arises from the preconceived opinions of childhood, and Descartes is describing the youthful mind still immersed in its body:

the mind had certain diverse sensations, namely those which we call the sensations of taste, of odour, of sound, of heat, of cold, of light, of colour,

[36] Ibid.   [37] Ibid.

and of similar things; which represent nothing situated outside thought. At the same time, the mind also perceived sizes, figures, motions and such; which were not presented to it as sensations, but as certain things or modes of things, existing or at least capable of existing outside thought: even if it did not yet note this distinction between those things. (AT VIIIA 35)[38]

What Descartes calls 'sensations' here are, of course, secondary qualities, and he explicitly asserts that they do not represent anything outside thought. He distinguishes this non-representational component of sense experience from primary properties which the mind perceives, yet which are presented to the mind *not as sensations*, but rather as modes of things existing (or capable of existing) outside thought. The fact that the youthful mind did not yet note the difference indicates that Descartes takes the common-sense understanding of sensory experience to fail to distinguish between the objects of representation and (subjective) sensations within experience.

[38] Ibid. 32–3.

14

Descartes: The End of Anthropology

STEPHEN VOSS

I. The Varieties of Cartesian Platonism: Stage 1

What is a human being? Any systematic philosophy ought to offer an
answer to that question. You would think that Descartes's philosophy
would; it is natural to think that his new vision of souls and bodies
provides a new way to do anthropology—a new way to conceive human
beings. His first intuition, indeed, is that a human being is a *compound*
of a Cartesian *soul* and a Cartesian human *body*. But I believe that,
when all is said and done, he concludes that he has no answer at all
to this question.

In the following pages I will display Descartes's failure to incorporate human beings into his new universe as the culmination of a
historical process discernible in his writings. I will argue that he had
good metaphysical reasons to conclude that no Cartesian anthropology
is possible. Appreciating the story requires attention to shifting patterns within his writings, and to passages absent from as well as present
in the text. The story clearly has large philosophical implications, but
we cannot examine them now.

Descartes's writings about man (*homo*, *l'homme*) undergo two dra-
matic shifts, in 1641 and 1642–3, separating them into three stages.[1]
The first shift is obvious but unimportant, the second covert but
critical. The first is easily seen, in language characteristic of 1641–2.
The second is nearly invisible, marked only by a new absence within
the philosopher's customary language. The first shift expresses little
interesting new theory. The second shift is decisive: placed in the

---

[1] 'Man' is the most accurate translation of Descartes's terminology, and for the sake
of fidelity to his text I shall follow him in this unhappy usage.

framework of the *Principles*, the dualism of the *Meditations* suddenly seems deeply inhospitable to the thesis that man exists at all.

These developmental theses are inspired by a Leibnizian herme-neutic. Time for Leibniz is God's way of allowing contradictory propositions to be true: *p* can be true at one time and not-*p* at another. And the appearance of conflict among Descartes's statements can often be alleviated by supposing that he sometimes changed his mind.

The first stage in Descartes's writing presents a moderate Platonism; the second, a scholastic Platonism; the third, an extreme Platonism, which, following Maritain, we may also call angelism: 'Cartesian dualism breaks man up into two complete substances, joined to one another no one knows how: on the one hand, the body which is only geometric extension; on the other, the soul which is only thought—an angel inhabiting a machine and directing it by means of the pineal gland.'[2] Not that there is anything very 'moderate' about his original position—it is only the surprising final position that can justify assigning it that title.

Descartes's final position is to be found not in the *Meditations*, but in later works like the *Principles* and the *Passions of the Soul*. Never-theless, there are philosophical reasons why the final position was the extreme one, and these reasons reflect forces generated by his continuing cogitation upon the doctrines of the *Meditations*. That leads me to think that it is the final position that reveals most about Descartes's doctrines. I shall argue that Descartes came to believe that the metaphysical framework of the *Principles* cannot accommodate the doctrine of the *Meditations* that there exists an entity composed of soul and body, and that his final position is that there is no such thing as man.[3]

Here it is necessary to tread cautiously. Descartes never asserts that there are no men, and perhaps he never comes to believe it. But on the evidence he did cease to believe that there are men. I shall mean phrases like 'Descartes believes that there are no men' to allow the milder possibility that he merely ceases to believe that there are.

[2] J. Maritain, 'The Cartesian Heritage', in *The Dream of Descartes*, 179.

[3] This chapter pursues the logic of several recent works, systematically examining the *difficulties* Descartes's dualism generates for his doctrine of man, notably L. Alanen, 'Descartes's Dualism and the Philosophy of Mind'; J. Cottingham, 'Cartesian Trialism'; M. Grene, *Descartes among the Scholastics*; P. Hoffman, 'The Unity of Descartes's Man'; G. Rodis-Lewis, 'La Conception de *L'Homme* dans le cartésianisme', 'Le Domaine propre de l'homme chez les cartésiens', and 'Le Paradoxe cartésien', in *L'Anthropologie cartésienne*; and G. A. Wilson, 'Henry of Ghent and René Descartes on the Unity of Man'.

Perhaps Descartes's final position should not be surprising. In general, the compound of two things need not be a thing. Consider five analogies a philosopher might use to advertise Platonism. Soul and body resemble, respectively:

(*a*) a prisoner and a prison (cf. *Cratylus* 400c, *Phaedrus* 250c);
(*b*) a worker and a tool (*Theaetetus* 184e);
(*c*) an aspirant and an impediment (*Phaedo* 66a);
(*d*) a traveller and a vehicle (*Timaeus* 69c–d);
(*e*) a human being and a set of clothing (*Phaedo* 87b–e).

You would probably not include the compound of the worker and her tool in your ontology. The two items do not compose yet a third item. Indeed, for most sensible ontologies, the two items mentioned in *each* of (*a*)–(*e*) do not constitute a thing to be taken seriously.[4]

Platonists proposing these analogies typically care first of all about the *nature* of soul and body and the *relation* between them. They may have little interest in the existence and nature of the soul–body *compound*. But Descartes is no mere Platonist. His Sixth Meditation hope is also to allow room for that compound. Still, as pairs (*a*)–(*e*) suggest, that may not be easy.

Moderate Platonism is presented during Stage 1 in the *Regulae*, the *Treatise on Man*, the *Discourse*, and the *Meditations*. The following theses define that position. We may lump the first three of them together: they are Platonist theses Descartes never questioned, common to all three of his stages.

MP1 I am a soul, a substance whose whole essence or nature is to think.

MP2 The body is a substance whose whole essence is to be extended; more particularly, it is a machine, which accomplishes all human activities or functions other than thinking.

MP3 There is an intimate union between the soul and the body of a man, evidenced by the fact that when the body is affected the soul receives not simply a thought but a sensation.

MP4 The soul and the body compose a man; the man is a whole or compound, whose parts or components are soul and body.

---

[4] I say 'most' because there are exceptions, most notably N. Goodman's ontology in *The Structure of Appearance*, according to which, if a speck of sand in the Sahara and the Arctic Ocean are individuals, so is their sum. Goodman's principle may be a necessity for a nominalist, but making a virtue of it is another matter.

The first two theses present Platonism; the last two moderate it. MP4 is presented during Stage 1 in eleven texts, culminating in the Sixth Meditation, Descartes's central anthropological text. They are enumerated in the Appendix as texts P1–P11.[5] When I say that Descartes's Platonism later becomes extreme, I mean that he ceases to accept MP4. Stage 2 begins when Descartes sends the *Meditations* out to generate objections. Stage 3 visibly gestates for months, then begins definitively in mid-1643.

II. The Attacks on Moderate Platonism

This anthropology is subjected to two politico-philosophical shocks in 1641. Antoine Arnauld attacks, and Henricus Regius praises, what each takes to be its implications.

Here is Arnauld's disagreement, in the Fourth Objections, with the Sixth Meditation argument for the real distinction between soul and body: 'It seems . . . that the argument proves too much, and takes us back to the Platonic view (which M. Descartes nonetheless rejects) that nothing corporeal belongs to our essence, so that man is merely a rational soul and the body merely a vehicle for the soul—a view which gives rise to the definition of man as "a soul which makes use of a body"' (AT VII 203; CSM II 143). Arnauld draws three conclusions from Descartes's argument. Do they really follow from the position taken in the Sixth Meditation? Does it really prove too much? Let me label them C1, C2, and C3, and consider whether Descartes must accept them.

C1 Nothing corporeal belongs to our essence.

Moderate Platonism indeed entails that nothing corporeal belongs to my essence. I am a soul and my soul's whole essence is to think and nothing corporeal belongs to thought.

C2 Man is merely a rational soul.

Moderate Platonism does entail that I am a rational soul. If it entailed that I am a man, it would entail C2. But it actually entails the negation of C2, by conceiving man as the compound of soul and body. Still, the Sixth Meditation can deny that man is a soul only because it

---

[5] The Appendix gathers certain texts crucial to the argument, and I refer to them in the body of this chapter in this style.

is committed to the position that I am not a man.[6] This position, though Arnauld does not notice it, is damaging enough, and deserves a title of its own:

C2* I am not a man.

C3 The body is merely a vehicle for the soul.

The content of C3 is vague. Descartes consistently seeks to disown it by arguing that soul and body are closely united, so answering Arnauld at AT VII 227–8; CSM II 160. We will be better placed to assess Arnauld's third accusation by the end of the chapter.

C1, C2*, and C3 express in three ways the worry that Cartesian anthropology creates gaps within our conception of man. C1 expresses the worry that there is a gap between me and my body; C2* that there is a gap between me and the man; C3 that there is a gap between my soul and my body.

Meanwhile Descartes's disciple Regius was at work in Utrecht, deriving further corollaries. In theses sustained on 8 December 1641 he proclaimed:

C4 Man is an *ens per accidens*.

C5 It is the soul that is an *ens per se*.

Descartes accepts C5; must he accept C4? This question must also wait.

III. Descartes's Scholastic Counter-attack: Stage 2

Descartes's response to these two shocks constitutes Stage 2. It includes a specific approach to defending moderate Platonism involving a small number of scholastic formulas characteristic of this brief period. They are displayed mainly in the 1641 Responses to the Objections to the *Meditations* and letters of 1641 and 1642 to Regius. I have two aims in examining Stage 2: to see what alteration the new language signals in Descartes's understanding of man, and to pave the way to examine the more profound Stage 3, by ascertaining the condition in which moderate Platonism emerges from these defensive labours.

Geneviève Rodis-Lewis says that the objections of Elisabeth, Arnauld, and others 'drove Descartes to choose between Aristotle's and Plato's

---

[6] As G. E. M. Anscombe has seen ('The First Person').

perspectives'.[7] I believe that that is exactly right. I add a little detail:
Descartes's first response is not to choose, but to try to have both
(Stage 2); then, when he does choose, his choice is extreme indeed
(Stage 3).

A. Substantial Union

Stage 2 is marked by four new uses of metaphysical language. In the
first one, Descartes speaks in six passages (SU) of a 'substantial union'
between soul and body. He never explains what this amounts to; he
even counsels Regius that he need *not* explain it (AT III 493; CSMK
206)! Is it simply a real union between substances? Is it a union that
generates a new substance—the man constituted by that union? Both
of those readings generate difficulties. Descartes does not say once
that a substantial union brings about a new substance. The simplest
and most conservative interpretation of the phrase is that it has just
the content that his Sixth Meditation phrase did—'I am very closely
joined and, as it were, intermingled with [the body], to such an extent
that I compose one thing with it' (P5); and Descartes indeed tells
Arnauld that what he proved in the Sixth Meditation was precisely that
the mind 'is substantially united with the body' (SU2).

What is implied in Descartes's statement that there is a 'substantial
union' between soul and body? A reminder and two hints help answer
the question.

The reminder is this. A word like 'union' might mean either the
state of being joined or a *thing* constituted or brought into existence
because such a state holds. In Descartes's standard usage the union
between body and soul is the state of being joined, not its product.
Categorically, it is a relation, not a thing generated by a relation.
Consider what the phrase 'that union' at the end of this passage refers
to: 'even though this matter changes and its quantity increases or
decreases, we nevertheless believe that it is the same body, numerically
the same, while it remains joined and substantially united to the same
soul; and we believe that this body is completely whole while it has
within it all the dispositions needed to preserve that union'.[8] It must

---

    [7] G. Rodis-Lewis, *L'Œuvre de Descartes*, I, 354.
    [8] From text SU6. For other texts displaying the distinction between the union and
its product, see SU3; SU4; SU5; AT III 692–3, CSMK 227. Descartes often uses a
verb or an adjective in alluding to the soul–body union, again treating it as a relational
state: see such central texts as SU1; SU2; AT XI 119–20, CSM I 99; AT VI 59, CSM

stand for the condition of being united, not for a product of that condition. It is one thing to hold that two things are united, another to infer that they constitute a composite object. In this case, as will emerge, that is something Descartes seems to have changed his mind about.

The hints are the ones already mentioned. First, Descartes tells Regius that he need not explain the nature of the union. If he thought that the union constituted man a substance, he would have had every political reason to urge Regius to proclaim that consequence. The second hint is Descartes's own statement to Arnauld that what he had proved in the Sixth Meditation was that the mind is substantially united with the body. Now the point of the Sixth Meditation argument is that the union is an extremely strict and intimate one; it is not that the union renders the soul–body compound a substance. The most sensible inference is that this new language is nothing but new language. It signals no new doctrine. Descartes will stress in Stage 2, and for that matter to the end of his life, the extraordinarily intimate character of the union between soul and body.[9] But that is something he had already stressed in the *Discourse* and the *Meditations*. All that is new, I think, is the adjective 'substantial' and the adverb 'substantially'.[10]

I 141; AT VII 81, 354, 442, CSM II 56, 245, 297–8; AT III 124, CSMK 149; *Principles*, pt. II, art. 2; AT IV 347, CSMK 279; *Passions*, arts. 30 and 137. And when he uses a noun to speak of the union he can typically be read most naturally again as speaking of the state of being united: see such central texts as AT VII 389–90, CSM II 266; AT III 665–6, CSMK 218; *Principles*, pt. I, art. 48; AT V 85, CSMK 326.

[9] H. Gouhier, *La Pensée métaphysique de Descartes*, chs. 12 and 13.

[10] Janet Broughton and Ruth Mattern argue plausibly against the view that substantially united entities are simply entities with substances as parts, on the basis of texts like SU3 (they might equally have adduced SU1 and SU2). They adduce Descartes's statement that mind and body are united '*realiter et substantialiter*': 'here it is clear that substantiality modifies neither the mind alone nor the body alone, but rather the mind and the body united' ('Reinterpreting Descartes on the Notion of the Union of Mind and Body', 27 n. 20). The three uses of the adverb '*substantialiter*' suggest that Descartes aims to pick out a type of union. That seems right, but it is not necessary to suppose, as they do, that substantial union is union resulting in a compound *substance*. That is fortunate if Descartes continues to speak of the substantial union even when he no longer believes that it results in a compound entity.

Before he hits on the notion of being substantially united, Descartes infers that soul and body constitute a single being because they are united '*étroitement*' (*Discourse*, text U2), '*arctissime*' (Sixth Meditation, text U3). Afterwards he infers it from their '*veram unionem substantialem*' (SU4). Might his premiss in the latter case amount to no more than it had earlier—a particularly close union between two substances? That is what the argument of this section inclines me to believe.

B. Ens per se

The second prong of Descartes's response involves another piece of scholastic jargon. He tells Regius in December 1641 and January 1642 to proclaim that man is an *ens per se* (EPS1–EPS3). In the specific sense that the human body and soul make up such a being—and only in that sense—he grants that body and soul can be regarded as 'incomplete substances'.[11] We need to notice two things: first, how seldom Descartes is willing to speak of man as *ens per se* or of body and soul as incomplete; secondly, how constantly he affirms that soul and body remain substances in their own right (for a characteristic example, see P12).

What does Descartes mean by his talk of man as *ens per se*? The phrase was a standard synonym for 'substance', and Descartes accepts the equivalence in the Fourth Responses (AT VII 222; CSM II 156–7). Yet for several reasons the obvious conclusion—that man is a substance—is too strong. In the Fourth Responses Descartes did not tell Arnauld that man was an *ens per se*, and could not have anticipated that on 8 December 1641 Regius would force his hand by publicly using the phrase himself. Secondly, Descartes speaks of man as *ens per se* only four times, and never once *asserts* the doctrine—he only counsels Regius to do so, and reports Regius' words to Dinet.[12] Thirdly, there are passages that seem to cry out for a simple assertion that man is a substance and yet Descartes evidently consciously abstains. Texts P12 and P22 are good cases: there man is classed respectively as a 'unity' and as a 'subject'. Even in Stage 2 Descartes does not maintain that man is a substance.

If his aim is not to proclaim that man is a substance, what is it? His political hope is to deflect the heat Regius had generated. His philosophical hope is to shore up the doctrine that soul and body constitute a whole with a theoretical groundwork that will make man's status intelligible and credible. Thus text EPS2 is buttressed by the same reasoning that Descartes used in the *Discourse* and the *Meditations* to show that the soul is not a sailor in a ship;[13] EPS1 is buttressed by the new point that the body's dispositions are appropriate to its being joined to the soul; and EPS3 is buttressed by the new language of

[11] Fourth Responses (AT VII 222; CSM II 156–7); EPS1.
[12] I owe this point to Vere Chappell, who has developed it in 'L'Homme cartésien'. Chappell's discussions on this entire area have been consistently illuminating.
[13] On this comparison see Rodis-Lewis, *L'Œuvre de Descartes*, II, 500 n. 43; Gouhier, *Pensée métaphysique*, 345–6; and M. Grene, 'Die Einheit des Menschen', 310.

substantial union between body and soul. The new language is an element in a well-defined campaign, whose immediate aim is to barricade the doctrine of man against the assaults of Utrecht.

C. Man's Essence or Nature

Descartes makes a third friendly gesture towards scholasticism. The scholastics attributed a nature or essence to man, regarding that as required by their doctrine that man is a substance. This language, too, is fleetingly adopted. Descartes tells Arnauld that the mind is part of the 'essence' of man;[14] and he proposes that Regius defend the claim that man is an *ens per se* by saying that 'the union which joins a human body and soul to each other is not accidental to a man, but essential, since a man without it is not a man' (E2). One thing that is essential to a man—if there are others they are never identified—is man's union-generated composition out of soul and body.

This doctrine is marshalled opportunistically and fleetingly. It is not expressed after January 1642. It is maintained alongside the doctrine that soul and body each have a nature or essence of their own. Text E2 is meant to help show that man is no mere *ens per accidens*, but, as I argue in Section VII, this will require more than a specification of man's components. To recall some traditional favourites, Descartes might identify man's specific good or man's specific function.

Descartes persistently argues for the union which is essential to man by adducing a fundamental fact: when a human body is harmed, the soul may feel sensations (P4, P5). An adequate account of man's *essence* should make that possibility intelligible; it should explain how the soul–body union engenders a capacity for sensations. Providing such an account is not part of the project in Stage 2.

That fundamental fact is not a fact about man, but about body, soul, and their relation. In stating it one predicates nothing of man. To be told that man's essence includes being constituted of soul and body by an intimate linkage is to learn, thanks to our knowledge of the essence of soul and body, a great deal about man's components and

---

[14] E1; cf. AT VII 228; CSM II 160: even the arm 'belongs to the nature of the whole man', though (AT IV 167; CSMK 243) Descartes surely cannot mean to make an essentialist point with that remark. One wonders whether we can be sure that text E2 itself is meant to make an essentialist point. Both texts have a suspiciously *de dicto*, even cavalier, aroma about them; cf. the clearly *de dicto* point about a clock's 'nature and essence' at AT II 367; CSMK 121–2.

their optimal fit. But when Descartes speaks of man's essence, it is no part of his purpose to clarify or explain the characteristics of the composite being itself.

D. Form

There is, finally, a fourth gesture. Descartes comes to speak of the soul as a form, sometimes a substantial form—language that was customary among scholastics, and an object of suspicion among Platonists. In metaphysically immature days, he had spoken in a single breath both Platonically of the composite whole of mind and body and scholastically of the body as informed by the mind (F1). That use of 'form' and 'inform' had lain entirely dormant, awaiting its opportunity, throughout the 1630s. Could the early syncretism help solve the problem that arose in 1641?

When opportunity knocks, Descartes first answers in another's voice, cagily, in the Fifth Responses: 'If we are to take "soul" in its specific sense, as meaning the "first actuality" or "principal form of man", then the term must be understood to apply only to the principle in virtue of which we think . . . ' (F2). Then, in January 1642, he advises Regius to say that the soul is a 'substantial form' (F3)—the substantial form of the man (F4). In the same year he mentions Regius' woes to Dinet (F5). This, however, is the high-water mark for the new terminology. It crops up in two letters to Mesland, of 1645 and 1645 or 1646 (F7, F8), and a 1646 letter to Clerselier (F9), all in defence of a new picture of transubstantiation. The language appears just one other time: Descartes says in the *Principles* that 'the human soul, while informing the whole body, nevertheless has its principal seat in the brain . . . ' (F6). But this was a dying gasp. When, three years later in 1647, the *Principles* was translated into French, Descartes made sure that his manual did not contain the scholastic phrase. The clause now ran 'although our soul is united to the whole body . . . '.

It is significant that the purely *anthropological* use of 'form' ceases in January 1642 with F3 and F4, when Descartes speaks for the last time of the form of *man*. Thereafter, in F5–F9, the soul is classed as the form of the body or of its matter. This shift coincides with and reflects Descartes's incipient dissatisfaction with the very idea of man.

Does this language express hylomorphic doctrine? 'In scholastic Aristotelianism', says Gilson, 'the form of a body—even if substantial— is but an abstraction: the mind may conceive it by itself, but it cannot, except in the unique case of the rational soul, subsist by itself. So for a scholastic the true reality is never either form or matter but the physical composite, born from the union of form and matter, which alone deserves the name of substance."[15] On a true hylomorphic account, form is an abstraction from a substance, and not literally a part of it; form is not itself a substance; and truths about substances are prior to truths about form or matter. In none of these ways is Descartes's talk of the soul as form an expression of hylomorphism: the Cartesian soul always remains a substance; it is always this substance that thinks and wills, feels and acts; and truths about souls and bodies are always prior to truths about men.

On a true hylomorphic account, moreover, form has the power to produce a unity or a substance by informing body or matter, but Descartes never attributes that capacity to the human soul; for that matter, he never conceives the scholastic physicists who populate nature with substantial forms to attribute that function to them.[16] It is significant that the task of making a *unity* out of mind and body is assigned to the mind–body union, centrally in P4 and P5, during a period when Descartes does not speak of the soul as form.

Gilson has seen why Descartes's talk of the soul as form does not express hylomorphic doctrine. When Descartes speaks of substantial forms, his intention is typically to reject the scholastic thesis that such things attach to extended things. But what is the content of the rejected thesis? Here is his own answer: 'when we deny substantial forms, we mean by the expression a certain substance joined to matter, making up with it a merely corporeal whole, and which, no less than matter and even more than matter . . . is *a true substance, or thing subsisting per se*' (AT III 502; CSMK 207; emphasis added). When Descartes *denies* that there are substantial forms in nature, what he denies is that there are Cartesian souls there.[17] Equally, when he *affirms* that the soul is a substantial form, he affirms only that it is a Cartesian soul. That is why he can tell Regius, just after he has instructed him to deny substantial forms in nature,

[15] É. Gilson, *Études sur le rôle de la pensée médiévale dans la formation du système cartésien*, 162.
[16] Contrary to Marjorie Grene's suggestion: 'This single surviving substantial form [the Cartesian soul], it appears, has the power to produce a unity out of two independent substances, the unity that *is* this or that existing human being' (*Descartes among the Scholastics*, 24). None of texts F implies that a form is needed to play this role.
[17] Similarly for 'real qualities': 'I do not suppose there are in nature any *real qualities*, which are attached to substances, like so many little souls to their bodies . . .' (AT III 648; CSMK 216). See also AT III 667, CSMK 219; AT V 222-3, CSMK 358.

if the soul is recognised as merely a substantial form, while other such forms consist in the configuration and motion of parts, this very privileged status it has compared with other forms shows that its nature is quite different from theirs. And this difference in nature opens the easiest route to demonstrating its *non-materiality* and *immortality* . . .

the soul . . . is the true substantial form of man. For the soul is thought to be immediately created by God for no other reason than that it is a *substance*. (emphasis added)[18]

Gilson provides a plausible explanation why, under Descartes's pen, the term 'form' is reinterpreted in a characteristic non-hylomorphic manner: 'the scholastic conception of a distinct notion to which no separable reality corresponds has no meaning in Cartesianism, and this is why Descartes always criticizes substantial forms as though forms were substances.'[19] So it is that the Stage 2 language of soul as form commits Descartes, unspectacularly, to nothing more than his old belief in Cartesian souls.

An epicycle complicates this nice picture. For the most part Stage 2 ceases to exist in 1642, but three texts written after that year speak of the soul as a form, and another affirms the substantial union between soul and body; to that extent, one aspect of Stage 2 persists as late as the letter of 2 March 1646 to Clerselier. Moreover, all four of texts SU6 and F7–F9 occur in presentations of Descartes's distinctive account of transubstantiation. And, even though a (substantial) form is nothing but the Cartesian soul familiar from the *Discourse* and the *Meditations*, the soul now begins to play a genuinely scholastic role. Descartes tells Mesland that the human body or the body of Jesus Christ in the Eucharist retains its identity not in virtue of its matter but in virtue of its form: in virtue of being united to a particular soul (F7, F8). But he downplays any such criterion of identity in the 1649 *Passions*, remarking that death is the body's fault, not the soul's (art. 6), and that the body is 'one, and in a way indivisible, in proportion to[20] the disposition of its organs' (art. 30). At last, in 1645–6, Descartes is prepared to add a characteristic to the soul—one it *lacked* in the heart of Stage 2 proper, when Descartes counselled Regius that 'when we consider the body alone we perceive

---

[18] From F3 and F4. Cf. F2, F5, and F6.

[19] Gilson, *Études*, 162–3. On Descartes's revision of Aquinas' conception of substantial form, see also Gilson's comments on AT VI 59, l. 15, in *René Descartes, Discours de la méthode, texte et commentaire*, 431–2.   [20] *A raison de*: not 'because of'.

nothing in it demanding union with the soul . . . ', that 'the soul and body
. . . each can subsist apart . . . ' (AT III 461, 508; CSMK 200, 209).
Aristotle and Aquinas held that matter is the principle of individuation. But works by Toledo (1583) and Suárez (1597) mark an altered
landscape.[21] Geneviève Rodis-Lewis has shown that for the scholastics
whom Descartes read at La Flèche,

even if form alone is judged insufficient to ground individuation, it retains a
preponderant role. And no scholastics at the beginning of the 17th century
accepted the Thomist solution in terms of matter. When Descartes declares
that unity and numerical identity do not derive from matter, but from form,
he is therefore using current notions, without betraying opposition with
respect to scholasticism.[22]

Not simply current language, then, but 'current notions'. In this quite
remarkable and unique context, Descartes indeed learns to think as
well as speak with the scholastics. He does so, not in Stage 2 proper,
but in a kind of extension of Stage 2 which sprang up after its other
remnants had vanished from the scene.

In my view the important alteration in Descartes's anthropology is
associated with Stage 3, however, not with Stage 2, and it is well to
place Descartes's new theory of identity for the body back into that
framework. True, it would have been opportune for Descartes to
borrow the theory from seventeenth-century scholasticism. All the
same, this theory is perfectly compatible with extreme Platonism. To
say that union with a soul constitutes the criterion for a human body's
identity is not to commit oneself to the existence of a soul–body
compound. The criterion is part of a philosophical account of the
human body; it is not necessarily part of an account of the human
being. By the time he espoused the criterion, Descartes had long since
ceased to propose an anthropology.

IV. The Limits of Descartes's Scholasticism

One fundamental anthropological text from Stage 2 contains positive
documentation for the modesty of Descartes's scholastic shift. The

---

[21] Francisco Toledo, *Commentaria una cum quaestionibus in tres libros Aristotelis De anima*; Francisco Suárez, *Disputationes metaphysicae*. See G. Rodis-Lewis, *L'Individualité selon Descartes*, 30–4, and J.-R. Armogathe, *Theologia Cartesiana: L'Explication physique de l'Eucharistie chez Descartes et dom Desgabets*, 74.
[22] Rodis-Lewis, *L'Individualité selon Descartes*, 34. This passage summarizes her account in ch. 1 of the Scotist triumph in seventeenth-century scholasticism.

second difficulty posed by Mersenne in the Sixth Objections had been that thought might simply be a corporeal motion (AT VII 413; CSM II 278). In his response Descartes sets explicit limits to his new hylomorphic talk.

The gist of his point is this. Since we are used to attributing different properties to the same subject, we might suppose that it is the same being that thinks and moves. But there are two ways in which we can take two things to be one and the same—by a unity of their nature or by a unity of composition. It had in fact been a 'unity of nature' that the scholastics affirmed between soul and body, for they held that the thing that thinks *is* the thing that is extended. Now, Descartes says, there is indeed such an affinity between understanding and willing that the thing that understands and the thing that wills are the same in virtue of a unity of nature. That is, the willing and the understanding are modes of the same thing. By contrast, there is a diversity between bone and flesh which entails that the thing that is bone and the thing that is flesh are the same only in virtue of a 'unity of composition'. That is, the thing that is bone is distinct from the thing that is flesh, and the two together help to compose one thing. Similarly, the thing that thinks is not identical with the thing that moves. Thinking and moving exclude one another, at least as strictly as flesh and bone do; they lack the compatibility of nature which understanding and willing possess. 'I observe a distinction or difference in every respect between the nature of an extended thing and that of a thinking thing, which is no less than that to be found between bones and flesh' (AT VII 424; CSM II 286).

Mersenne added a postscript to the Sixth Objections, a note from some philosophers and geometers who had said they saw that some bodies think. That gave Descartes an opportunity to refine his response—and think harder about its implications. He denies that he has ever seen that human bodies think; all he has seen is that there are human beings, who have both bodies and thought. How can that be? 'This occurs by a thinking thing's being combined with a corporeal thing' (AT VII 444; CSM II 299).

Even in Stage 2 Descartes holds the scholastic doctrine of a unity of nature between the thinking thing and the extended thing hostage to the doctrine of the real distinction. His response to Mersenne erects a barrier to scholastic reading of Stage 2 language.

It also prepares Descartes for the leap to Stage 3. Once he rules out thinking bodies it is natural for him to raise the same question about his own compound man that he has just settled in the case of the scholastic non-compound man. If he is inclined to think that a man *thinks and is extended*, to be sure 'by a thinking thing's being combined with a corporeal thing', then precisely the same scrutiny can be turned on *this* man—'I observe a distinction or difference in every respect between the nature of an extended thing and that of a thinking thing ... '. If Descartes does not do the scrutinizing as he writes this passage, I think he does it soon. See Section VII for the details.[23]

During 1641–2 Descartes learns to speak as he had been spoken to at La Flèche. He gives up none of his own characteristic doctrines in order to do it; the earlier Platonism persists. He appears to espouse just one scholastic anthropological thesis—that man has an essence or a nature, which includes being composed of soul and body.[24] He surely thinks that it can consistently and usefully be grafted on to the earlier position. My argument for the modesty of the alteration in doctrine has stressed the opportunistic and fleeting character of Descartes's new way of speaking of man, his avoidance of the stronger scholastic language he might naturally have deployed, and his persistent and active commitment to Platonist principles.

As Stage 2 comes to a close, man remains a composite of soul and body, so closely united as to constitute a whole. The body's dispositions fit it for the familiar Cartesian soul. Though it is of the essence of man to be so composed, that essence reveals little about man's own characteristics. Soul and body are still really distinct, 'one and the same' only by a unity of composition.

V. A Halt to Mereological Anthropology: Stage 3

By April 1642 (the time of EPS4) Descartes ceases to speak scholastically of man. In fact, if we chart his scholastic anthropological *assertions* (as opposed to advice and reportage), we discover that these cease by August 1641 (N2).

But I am more interested in the shifts in doctrine presaged by such

---

[23] See Fred Sommers's *logical* argument that if minds and bodies are of ontologically different types then their composite cannot be an individual, and must be a heterotypical entity, like Italy seen as the composite of a society and a peninsula: 'Dualism in Descartes'.

[24] Annie Bitbol-Hespériès has suggested in conversation that even this doctrine may be present earlier, expressed in Descartes's talk of our 'nature' in the Sixth Meditation.

shifts in language. Perhaps the act of writing the Sixth Responses had sparked the suspicion that moderate Platonism shared some of the flaws of scholastic anthropology. By mid-1643 (the time of U8) Descartes drops MP4. This shift was a sea-change, and it had taken time. These things are difficult to judge, but after the Sixth Responses Descartes asserts the existence of Cartesian man perhaps only three times: in N2 = P15 (August 1641), P19 (probably written early in 1642), and U8 (28 June 1643). Such a meagre production during April 1641–February 1650, weighted so heavily towards its early terminus, is impossible to ignore, dwarfed as it is by the Sixth Meditation alone and encapsulated as it is within voluminous writings during that period on every aspect of the soul, the body, and their relations.

In this section I examine the demise of Descartes's specifically mereological language about man. Before mid-1642 I find eighteen passages in which Descartes speaks of a compound whose parts are soul and body (P1–P18). I find just two theoretically significant passages later than that (P19, P22).[25]

P19 is found in *Principles*, part II, article 3. It paraphrases a passage from the Sixth Meditation: compare its language with P9's. According to the heading, sense perception shows 'what benefits or harms the human composite [*humano composito*]'. The body of the article elaborates: 'sensory perceptions are exclusively related to this conjunction [*conjunctionem*] of the human body with the mind, and normally show us what benefit or harm external bodies can do it ... '. Strikingly, the references to the human composite and the conjunction of body and mind are dropped entirely in the 1647 French translation; it speaks only of what is useful or harmful 'to us', and speaks of sense perceptions as having reference to the soul's strict union with the body. While the Latin '*conjunctionem*' clearly refers to the soul–body composite, the French refers only to the soul–body relation, and does not mention man at all.

The passage was probably written early in 1642, possibly late in 1641. Descartes was sufficiently content with it late in 1643 to send

---

[25] Otherwise there is only this mereological language in Stage 3: Descartes accepts Sixth Meditation language about the soul–body compound when he approves the 1647 French translation of the *Meditations* (P5–P11), in the same year he accepts a mereological translation of a non-mereological passage from *Principles*, pt. I, art. 60 (P21), and in three absolutely non-theoretical passages (P20, P23, P24) he speaks of the mind as our principal or better 'part'.

it to the publisher.[26] Yet if the question concerns Descartes's belief in 1642–3, I think it sensible to put somewhat more weight on the new material in part I that was actively engaging him than on older material he was passively repeating. In the light of the letter to Elisabeth of 28 June 1643, I believe that the entire period between August 1641 and that letter was one of transition, when he could neither stand on the bottom nor swim to the top. Fairly early in this interval he writes the major text in part I of the *Principles* that virtually banishes man; at the very conclusion of the interval, before that text is published, he remains capable of expressing belief in man. At that terminus, I think, Stage 3 definitively begins. We shall examine all the material just alluded to in Sections VI–VIII; let us return now to the mereological texts.

P22 is from the 1648 *Comments on a Certain Broadsheet*, directed against Regius. It begins with the statement 'But that which we consider as having at the same time both extension and thought is a composite: namely a man, consisting of a soul and a body [*Illud autem, in quo extensionem & cogitantionem simul consideramus, esse compositum: hominem scilicet, constantem anima & corpore*] . . . '. Does not Descartes speak straightforwardly here of man as composed of soul and body? The matter is not so simple. Descartes had already spoken to Regius of man as composed of parts (P16), soul and body (P17), and this passage, whose language this late in Descartes's career is unparalleled, is perhaps a simple continuation of the earlier conversation. But more needs to be said about the passage if we are to understand Descartes's viewpoint in 1647–8.

Descartes's topic is not man, but the soul. His aim is to defend the Platonic doctrine that the soul is a substance distinct from the body, against Regius' insinuation that the soul might be a mode of the body (AT VIIIB 342–3; CSM I 294–5). Like the Platonists we considered earlier, he defends dualism with an analogy—body is to soul as person is to clothing; like them, he does not aim (as he had in the Sixth Meditation) to defend any doctrine about a composite object. Here is the core of P22:

The last thing we note is that in subjects composed of several substances, one often stands out, which is considered by us to be such that the remaining

[26] The work was published in Amsterdam on 10 July 1644. Descartes could have edited the passage any time up to the final months of 1643, when most of the manuscript was sent to Elzevier. See AT XII 356–7, III 646–7, IV 72–3; and Gouhier, *Pensée métaphysique*, 329 n. 23.

things joined to it are nothing but modes. Thus a man who is dressed can be considered as a compound [*compositum*] of man and clothing, but being clothed [*vestitum esse*] in relation to the man is just a mode. *In the same way*, in the case of man, who is composed [*compositus*] of soul and body, our author [Regius] may be considering the body as standing out, in relation to which being ensouled [*animatum esse*] or having thought is nothing but a mode. But it is foolish to infer from this that the soul itself, or that by which the body thinks, is not a substance distinct from the body. (emphasis added)

Descartes speaks of man as composed of soul and body. Does he mean this text to support moderate Platonism? It seems to me that he does not: his polemic intent runs in quite another direction, and if his words suggest anything about man to a philosophical mind, it is this: just as person and clothing do *not* make up a single thing, neither do soul and body. The analogy allows that the body may be instituted by nature for a close and intimate union with the soul: clothing may be fitted by artifice, even fitted *étroitement* to a single wearer, without for all that forming 'one thing' with her. We can put the point the other way round: a person who takes P22 to support MP4 should also take it to support an ontology on which a person and her clothing make up a compound thing. It is difficult to believe that Descartes means to express any friendliness to such enterprises in this passage.[27]

Some readers will take P19 and P22 otherwise, or take passages I have slighted, like P20–P21 and P23–P24, or overlooked, like the letter to Chanut of 15 June 1646 (AT IV 441; CSMK 289), to show Descartes committed in Stage 3 to the soul–body compound. But one must not miss the forest for the trees: any reader who systematically examines the letters to Elizabeth, for example, or the *Passions of the Soul*, cannot fail to be struck by Descartes's resolute consistency in attributing human features not to human beings but to souls or bodies. After the Sixth Meditation Descartes writes often and at length about the soul and the body and their relations; what he does not write is

---

[27] According to Grene, 'Descartes does explicitly (e.g. AT VIIIB, 350–1) distinguish between simple and complex substances, the latter consisting of more than one substance. According to him, we can take a man and his suit, for example, as two substances, or we can count the man and his suit as one substance, namely, as a man who has the property of being dressed in such and such a way' (*Descartes among the Scholastics*, 38). But there is nothing in this passage to support the counter-intuitive view that a person wearing a suit is a complex substance of which one component is the suit. Both here and in the discussion of incomplete substances at AT VII 222–3; CSM II 156–7, Descartes carefully avoids speaking of complex *substances* consisting of more than one substance.

anything like the Sixth Meditation. We now examine the passages in the 1644 *Principles of Philosophy* in which he lays the metaphysical groundwork for the end to anthropology.

VI. The Project of the *Principles*

During 1642–3 Descartes brings to a virtual halt his MP4-style talk of man as a soul–body compound. With the memories of Arnauld's criticism and Utrecht's controversy fresh in his mind, why on earth would he turn his back on man?

I suggest that the catalyst was the project of the *Principles*. I suggest that Stage 3 is generated by Descartes's attempt to confine the doctrine of the *Meditations* within the metaphysical framework he elaborates in the *Principles*. I believe that Descartes came to realize that the man of the Sixth Meditation has no place in that metaphysics.

We may be inclined to see a metaphysics of man in the *Principles*. Perhaps we take man to be the home of the sensations, appetites, and passions sheltered under the primitive notion of the mind–body union. Or perhaps we see a newly genial Descartes ready to assign to man all the modes of mind and body. But the text leads in exactly the opposite direction, for plausible philosophical reasons.

Principles, part I, article 48, is metaphysics in the service of epistemology It enumerates the objects of human knowledge, and serves as an outline for the rest of part I, which is devoted to a survey of how knowledge and error are possible. Now Cartesian enumeration is meant to be exhaustive: Descartes's primary enumerative maxim is to be 'sure of leaving nothing out' (AT VI 19; CSM I 120). And this enumeration and part I's subsequent survey contain no mention of man whatever, save the resolutely uncommittal U9. This portion of the *Principles* offers the most straightforward and direct evidence that Descartes no longer believes in man.

Article 48 sketches a theory of types, a taxonomy of the characteristics (*res*) predicable of objects. It licenses the schema shown in Table 14.1. Descartes presents no taxonomy of the modes or characteristics that *man* can possess. He enumerates only two kinds of objects—minds and bodies. He does not specify here the objects to which appetites, passions, and sensations pertain, but he makes it absolutely clear throughout his work that these characteristics are thoughts, hence

TABLE 14.1 *The metaphysics of* Principles, *pt. I, art. 48*

Kind of characteristic	Examples of each	Objects each pertains to
The most general things	Substance, duration	All kinds of things
Intellectual or thinking things	Perception, volition	Mind
Material things	Extension, shape, motion	Body
Things which originate from the Union and must not be referred to the mind alone or the body alone	Appetites, passions, and sensations	—

modes of the mind.[28] Thus the characteristics at the fourth line are a subcategory of those at the second.

Again, *Principles*, part I, article 53, gives a general procedure for determining what kinds of characteristics a substance is metaphysically capable of possessing.[29] The procedure makes use of the idea of a *principal attribute* which constitutes the *nature* of a substance: it is a substance's principal attribute that makes possible its other characteristics (save its most general ones, no doubt).

Now the only principal attributes Descartes mentions are thought and extension, and the only substances minds and bodies. The *Principles* is wholly silent on the question of a principal attribute for *man*, or of a procedure for determining what characteristics man can possess once characteristics have been parcelled out to mind and body.

VII. Philosophical Reasons for Extreme Platonism

How are we to interpret the anthropological silence of the *Principles*? Two kinds of reflections are useful, one on the difficulties and the other on the dangers inherent in a Cartesian metaphysics of man.

A. Difficult Tasks

Descartes is not one to take joy in a difficult and complex metaphysics, and the trials of incorporating the desired principles and procedures

[28] AT VII 78, CSM II 54; AT III 85, 479, 665, CSMK 148, 203, 218; *Principles*, pt. I, arts. 9, 32, 53, 66–8; pt. IV, arts. 189–91, 196–8; AT IV 310–11, 602–5, CSMK 270–1, 306–8; AT V 192, CSMK 354; *Passions*, arts. 17, 24; etc.
[29] The procedure is developed elsewhere, too, e.g. in AT VII 176, 444, CSM II 124, 299; AT III 475–6, 665, CSMK 202, 218; AT V 221, CSMK 357.

into the theory of the *Principles* must have repelled him. I examine only two issues: the taxonomy of man in the light of article 48 and the ground of man's unity.

There are many type-theoretic questions a serious metaphysician will wish to ask about this interesting compound—fundamentally, what characteristics it is metaphysically possible to predicate of men, but also what kinds of procedures can determine which ones a particular man actually has. It helps to start with the latter. How, rationally, can we answer questions like these?

Are men rational animals?

This seems straightforward enough, but even in Stage 1 Descartes had recoiled from it: 'What is a man? Shall I say "a rational animal"? No . . .'[30] What then of the rest?

> Is the man sad whenever the soul is sad? Is a man *ever* sad?[31]
> Is man a thinking thing?
> Is man a mind? ('*res cogitans, id est, mens*' (AT VII 27, ll. 13–14; CSM II 18))
> How much does a man weigh?
> Where is a man located?
> Do men even *have* weight and location?
> Is man an extended thing?
> Is man a body? ('*corporis, quatenus est tantum res extensa*' (AT VII 78, l. 18; CSM II 54))
> Is man corruptible?
> Is man immortal?

Principles, part I, article 48, may appear to preserve a place for man in the Cartesian theory of types. Henri Gouhier takes the word 'union' to designate man's principal attribute,[32] and Tad M. Schmaltz argues that the appetites, passions, and sensations arising from the union are to be attributed to man. In a 'broad sense', he writes, sensations are modes of mind, but 'strictly speaking only purely intellectual thoughts can be modes of mind'.[33] Sensations are instead modes of the union,

---

[30] AT VII 25; CSM II 17; see also AT X 515–17; CSM II 410–12.

[31] I have in mind the dolt of *Passions*, art. 147, with heart constricted by funeral trappings and soul so touched by his wife's death as to draw 'genuine tears from his eyes', who 'at the same time feels a secret [uppercase] Joy in the innermost depths of his soul'. Given these facts about body and soul, is the *man* happy or sad?

[32] Gouhier, *Pensée métaphysique*, 329–30.

[33] T. Schmaltz, 'Descartes and Malebranche on Mind and the Mind–Body Union', 293.

and pertain to man. Consider then this taxonomic rule, which I name in honour of Gouhier and Schmaltz:

> Rule GS. The things that arise from the union (namely, sensations, appetites, and passions) are the characteristics of man.

There are a number of difficulties in this attempt to locate man in the schematism of article 48. Descartes never describes the union as man's principal attribute. He explains that sensations, appetites, and passions are *thoughts* the *soul* has—see again the texts cited in note 28—which arise, as he says here, from its union with the body. He never says that it is only in a broad sense but not strictly speaking that sensations are modes of the soul. The notion that sensations and intellectual thoughts are to be parcelled out to different owners runs squarely into the Second Meditation, according to which it is the same I that understands, imagines, and has sensory perceptions (AT VII 28–9; CSM II 19), and the Sixth Meditation, according to which it is one and the same mind that wills and understands and has sensory perceptions (AT VII 86; CSM II 59). Men who retain only thoughts caused by their soul's union with the body are bloodless and nearly thoughtless abstractions. Descartes does not mention such beings in part I of the *Principles* or anywhere else.[34]

Alternatively, perhaps it is reasonable to attribute all the features of souls and bodies indifferently to the man. When we become good Cartesians we parcel those features out to the soul or the body. Can we reverse the procedure, and hold that the features of soul or body may also be attributed to the man?

In many cases our childhood prejudices or Aristotelian habits incline us to say Yes. The rule that fuels our intuitions might be this one; let us name it in honour of those prejudices and habits.

> Rule PH. If either the soul or the body has a certain property, the man has it.

There is a good reason why Rule PH should be intuitively attractive. The reason does not recommend it to a good Cartesian. Our habit is to suppose we are only men (to deny C2*), and so to suppose that we already possess all those properties that Descartes wants to apportion here to our soul and there to our body. The rule gets its original persuasiveness from a period in our lives when we were pre-philosophical

---

[34] See Cottingham, 'Cartesian Trialism', 228–9, and Alanen, 'Descartes's Dualism', 407–8.

monists, before Cartesian method made us dualists. The rule simply restores our prejudices.[35]

Anyway, this rule is too crude to be Cartesian. We might suppose that we can pile all of the modes proper to minds and all of the modes proper to bodies on to a single thing naturally and without contradiction. But in one curious and absolutely fundamental case these two sets of modes come into contradiction with one another: 'there is a great difference between the mind and the body, inasmuch as the body is by its very nature always divisible, while the mind is utterly indivisible ... This one argument would be enough to show me that the mind is completely different from the body, even if I did not already know as much from other considerations.'[36] The rule yields a contradiction when we apply it to discover whether man is divisible or not. Descartes never discusses whether man is divisible.[37] I take this singularity in his talk of man to signal a structural weakness in moderate Platonism: in general there are no sufficient grounds for judgements about the modes of man. From that conclusion it is a very short step indeed to deleting man from one's ontology.

Perhaps Descartes made a gesture in the direction of a metaphysics of man when he told Regius to say that the union joining mind and body is essential to a man (E2). Perhaps that suggests that man's principal attribute is to be composed of mind and body in virtue of the union. That attribute would license a little progress in discovering the truth about man: 'a human being, because composite, is by his nature corruptible ...' (P15). But we falter quickly; we find no way to make similar progress on the range of questions whose surface is scratched in the paragraphs above. Such helplessness suggests that it is metaphysically inadequate to specify the essence of a thing in purely compositional terms.

[35] 'The experience of the first years suggests the idea of a body that thinks. In other words, I spontaneously conceive the union of soul and body as a unity of nature. When methodically elaborated science puts each notion in its place ... I then cease to take my experience to say more than it really says, and my language becomes exactly adapted to what I know ... *Hocque fieri per compositionem rei cogitantis cum corporea ex eo perpexi*: the fact that the same beings have a body and a faculty of thought signifies a union constituting a unity of composition' (Gouhier, *Pensée métaphysique*, 359).

[36] AT VII 85–6; CSM II 59; fundamental: AT VII 520; CSM II 354.

[37] Of course prior to Stage 3 Descartes frequently says that man is *composite*, or has *parts* (P). But *divisibility* is another matter: it is an attribute, like shape and motion, that bodies possess in virtue of the principal attribute *extension*. See e.g. AT XI 34, CSM I 91; AT VI 36, CSM I 129; AT VII 63, 223, CSM II 44, 157; *Principles*, pt. I, arts. 26, 48; pt. II, arts. 20, 23.

Marjorie Grene argues that Descartes was able to maintain the unity of man only by breaking down the classic distinction between substance and mode. Taking her cue from Descartes's apparent admission that the mind can be considered a quality or accident of the body, as clothing of the clothed person,[38] she takes Descartes to provide for human unity by making mind at once a substance and a property or mode of the body.[39] Grene builds on Paul Hoffman's similar reading that 'the mind inheres in the body as form inheres in matter'.[40] Hoffman argues with great care and ingenuity that Descartes may be able to maintain such a thesis, but Grene sees disaster in it for the idea of substance. I think that is closer to the truth, and that Descartes himself could not have viewed such a position as an option. It is important to see that Hoffman and Grene are working to solve a *problem* that confronts Descartes—the preservation of man in a Cartesian metaphysics of substance and mode, as one being and not simply a pair made for each other. If Descartes cannot solve this problem, he is left with another philosophical reason, perhaps the most basic one of all, to drop man from his ontology.

Here, briefly, is why I doubt that Descartes can regard mind as a quality, mode, or property inhering in the body. (1) Descartes himself interprets the puzzling passages that seem to conflate substance and accident: it is not mind, but having a mind, not clothing, but being clothed, that is the accident or mode. (2) It would be self-contradictory for a substance to be a mode, since a mode cannot be understood apart from its substance. (3) In particular, mind can be understood apart from body. (4) After proclaiming that man is an *ens per accidens*, Regius wrote that the mind is only a mode of the body; 'the latter error', responded Descartes, 'is far worse than the former'. (5) Active qualities and modes have less reality than, hence cannot be, substances. (6) All of a body's properties are referred to extension, but mind can be understood apart from extension. (7) What inheres in a substance is a characteristic of it, but mind is not a characteristic of body.[41]

---

[38] AT VII 441–2, CSM II 297–8; AT III 460, CSMK 200.

[39] Grene, *Descartes among the Scholastics*, 36–40.

[40] Hoffman, 'The Unity of Descartes's Man', 351.

[41] (1) AT VIIIB 351, CSM I 299; AT VII 435, CSM II 293. (2) AT VIIIB 352, CSM I 299–300; AT V 163, CSMK 345; *Principles*, pt. I, art. 61. (3) AT VIIIB 350; CSM I 298. (4) AT IV 250; CSMK 255. (5) AT III 503; CSMK 208. (6) *Principles*, pt. I, art. 53; AT VII 223, CSM II 157. (7) See AT II 223, CSMK 111; AT VII 176, CSM II 124; *Principles*, pt. I, art. 61.

Descartes has yet to provide for mind and body a *unity* that is more than an accidental and vehicular *union*.[42]

B. Hazards

The metaphysics of man may have struck Descartes not only as onerous but also as hazardous. One difficulty with Rule PH, for example, is that it appears inconsistent with the principle that no thinking thing can be an extended thing. I have pointed out in Sections III and IV that in Stage 2 Descartes not only maintained that principle but used it to deflect overly scholastic readings of his scholastic language. If he became convinced that a man would have to be a thinking and extended thing, it should not be surprising that he would again do what he had to in order to safeguard the principle.

Descartes's commitment to MP1–MP3 gave him good philosophical reasons to drop his commitment to MP4. Probably for such reasons, Stage 2 was man's last gasp. From late 1641 to mid-1643 Descartes prepared to get by with the far more austere, and far more faithfully Platonic, ontology of souls and bodies. That is what he sets out to do in the great metaphysical schema of *Principles*, part I, articles 48–76, and that is what he consistently carries out from mid-1643 to the end of his life.

VIII. A Close and Intimate Union

I have drawn up a rough picture of Stage 3 by temporally charting *two* of Descartes's ways of speaking of man—as the bearer of a form and as the composite of soul and body (Sections IIID, VI). Of course, even though both those forms of language virtually cease by 1642, Descartes continues to use terms like '*l'homme*'. Not all such usages carry ontological implications; many are, we might say, ontologically innocent— he may say '*l'âme de l'homme*' where he could as easily say '*l'âme humaine*'. To make the case airtight it would perhaps be necessary to chart all non-innocent language about man. For example, one might investigate whether the transition from 'harmful to *the composite*' (P9; 1641) to 'harmful to *the body*' and 'bad with respect to *the soul*'

---

[42] Gilson arrives at a similar conclusion by a somewhat different route in 'Anthropologie thomiste et anthropologie cartésienne', in *Études*, 245–55; corrections by Gouhier, *Pensée métaphysique*, 360–2.

(*Passions*, arts. 138, 141; 1649) signals a pattern like the ones that texts F and texts P exemplify.

But I shall close by charting one aspect of Descartes's talk of the union between soul and body. It would be an error to infer that Descartes believed at time *t* that there are men from the premiss that he asserted at *t* that soul and body are united. Nevertheless, in certain absolutely central passages Descartes does conclude, in the phrases I italicize here, that the union is strict enough to constitute a thing of soul and body:

And I showed how it is not sufficient for [the rational soul] to be lodged in the human body like a sailor in his ship, except perhaps to move its limbs, but that it must be more closely joined and united with the body in order to have, besides this power of movement, feelings and appetites like ours *and so constitute a true man* [*un vrai homme*]. (U2)

Nature also teaches, by these sensations of pain, hunger, thirst, etc., that I am not merely present in my body as a sailor is present in a ship, but that I am very closely joined and, as it were, intermingled with it, *to such an extent that I compose one thing* [*unum quid*] with it. (U3)

If anything, Descartes is more concerned in his later years to stress the intimate character of the union. What happens when we chart his commitment to the *inference* that the union is intimate enough to constitute an entity of the linked elements?

Texts U1–U9 appear to endorse the inference from union to thing thereby generated. The last two manifest the hesitancy over man during the transitional period 1642–3 already noted in Section V in connection with P19. U9, from the *Principles* of 1644, was the last to see the light of day, but was probably written around the beginning of 1642. It speaks subjunctively of God joining some corporeal substance to a thinking substance to produce 'one thing [*unum quid*]', the Latin phrase reproducing the language of U3 as P19 had reproduced that of P9. 'And even if we should suppose that God had joined': this is as close as the metaphysical schema of articles 48–76 comes to a commitment to man.

The text written last, U8, dates from mid-1643. By then moderate Platonism was moribund; it had been over a year since Descartes had written the important letters to Regius and Hyperaspistes and drafted the position paper that begins with article 48 of part I of the *Principles*; it had been as long since he had even appeared to license the inference to union-generated entity (U7, U9). The last apparent endorsement (the letter can be variously read) occurs in the letter to Elisabeth of 28 June 1643, in his final attempt to answer her questions about the union; here he says that 'to conceive the union between two things is to conceive them as a single thing' (U8: AT III 692; CSMK 227). That puzzling letter is probably Cartesian man's swan song.

Henri Gouhier and Ferdinand Alquié have shown that in his later years (the ones I have labelled Stage 3) Descartes was increasingly attentive to the concerns of the 'concrete man', the 'free man'.[43] But one must not be misled by the quoted phrases. Descartes's theoretical foundation for his thought about the human concerns of the incarnated soul does not involve a commitment to the *existence* of the concrete man. His thought is founded on a commitment to the close and intimate union of body and soul.

Earlier, in U2 and U3, he had argued for such a union from our bodily sensations, and then immediately inferred that this union was so intimate as to constitute of soul and body a single thing. That had been his defence, before the fact, against the charges that he was committed to C3 and angelism. Later he argued for the union with the doctrine of a divine institution of Nature between body and soul.[44] But he no longer inferred that the union gave rise to the man.

IX. 'I normally say that I see the men themselves'

'And finally when the *rational soul* is in this machine,' the *Treatise on Man* had run, 'it will have its principal seat in the brain, and reside there like the fountain-keeper' who regulates waters setting automata into motion (AT XI 131-2; CSM I 101). The *Discourse* and the *Meditations* had disowned the image of an angelic soul 'inhabiting a machine and directing it'. But when Gassendi asks how he as a soul can experience pain (by which Nature teaches that he is not merely present in the body as a sailor in a ship), and how he could be compounded with matter so as to make up one thing with it, Descartes gives no

[43] See Gouhier, *Essais sur Descartes*, essay 6: 'La Philosophie de l'homme concret'; and Alquié, *La Découverte métaphysique de l'homme chez Descartes*, pt. 4: 'L'Amour de l'être: La Nature et l'homme libre'.
[44] AT VII 88, CSM II 60–1; *Principles*, pt. IV, arts. 189, 196–8; AT III 460–1, 508, CSMK 200, 209; AT IV 166–8, 346–7, 603–6, CSMK 243–4, 279, 307–8; AT V 223, CSMK 358; *Passions*, arts. 36, 50, 90, 94, 137.

answer.[45] Instead, a few pages earlier, he smiles beneficently upon C3 and angelism: 'It is true that the mind does not work so perfectly when it is in the body of an infant as it does when in an adult's body, and that its actions can often be slowed down by wine and other corporeal things. But all that follows from this is that the mind, so long as it is joined to the body, uses it like an instrument to perform the operations which take up most of its time' (AT VII 354; CSM II 245).

Is the close and intimate union between mind and body sufficient to constitute of them 'one thing', 'a true man'? Before 1642 Descartes's answer was Yes. After 1643 his answer was No. He left 'the mark of the craftsman stamped on his work' to help us fix the image of the path he had taken: before 1642 he named a book *Treatise on Man*; after 1643 he wrote two books on similar topics but dropped 'man' from their titles—*Description of the Human Body, Passions of the Soul.*

Unwilling to make of man an *ens per accidens*, unable to make of man an *ens per se*, Descartes ceases to regard man as an *ens* at all. In the absence of a composite being that might have housed both body and soul, the gaps which the Fourth Objections had recorded between my body and 'my soul, by which I am what I am' now definitively exile me from all that is corporeal. Arnauld and Regius are finally vindicated: man has disappeared from the Cartesian universe.[46]

[45] AT VII 343–5; CSM II 238–9. For Descartes's responses, see AT VII 390; CSM II 266–7.
    [46] Research for this chapter was partially carried out during a seminar in the summer of 1991 sponsored by the National Endowment for the Humanities and directed by Willis Doney. I benefited a great deal from discussion at the seminar and at the conference at Reading later that fall, organized by John Cottingham. Jean-Marie Beyssade graciously provided a forum to present my interpretation of *Principles*, pt. I, art. 48, at his seminar on part I of the *Principles* at the Sorbonne in spring 1992. I gratefully acknowledge the support of NEH and the valuable contributions made by Jean-Marie Beyssade, Vere Chappell, John Cottingham, Frederick Crosson, Willis Doney, Daniel Garber, Paul Hoffman, Pauline Phemister, Marleen Rozemond, Karen-Claire Voss, and Kenneth Winkler.

APPENDIX

I list two categories of text, the first characteristic of Stage 2, the second of Stage 1. To my knowledge the lists are exhaustive. For writings published in Descartes's lifetime the date of publication is given; for others, the date of writing or mailing. It would be nice to know when the published works were completed, or at least when they were dispatched to be published. What follows is about right. The *Discourse* was sent to the publisher in spring 1637 and appeared in June. The text of the *Meditations* was sent off in November 1640 and the Responses in April 1641, and the first edition published in August 1641. The letter to Dinet was composed during March and April 1642 and published in May. The *Principles* was sent off in batches starting in the final months of 1643 and published in July 1644. The Letter-Preface to its French translation was sent off in June 1647 and published the same month. The *Comments on a Certain Broadsheet* was sent off at the end of 1647 and published at the start of 1648. The *Passions* was given to the publisher in September 1649, and came out in November.

I. Scholastic Formulas Concerning Soul, Body, and Man

SU. Texts in which Descartes speaks of a substantial union *between body and soul.* Dates: 1641 (2), 1642 (3), 1645.

Clarification: 'the mind is really and substantially united to the body . . . by a true mode of union, as everyone agrees, though nobody explains what this is, so you need not do so either' (SU3).

SU1   Fourth Responses (AT VII 219, ll. 17–20, IX 171; CSM II 154–5): '*mentem . . . corpus . . . esse substantialiter unitam . . .*' (For both of SU1 and SU2, the language of substantial union is retained in the 1647 French translation.)

SU2   Ibid. (AT VII 228, ll. 12–16, IX 177; CSM II 160): '*nec etiam nimis parum, dicendo illam esse corpori substantialiter unitam, quia unio illa substantialis non impedit quominus clarus & distinctus solius mentis tanquam rei completae conceptus habeatur.*'

SU3   Second letter to Regius of January 1642 (AT III 493, ll. 1–10; CSMK 206): '*debes profiteri te credere . . . mentem corpori realiter & substantialiter esse unitam . . .*'

SU4   Ibid. (AT III 508, ll. 3–13; CSMK 209): '*Afferimus enim hominem ex Corpore & Anima componi . . . per veram unionem substantialem . . .*'

SU5   Letter to Dinet (At VII 585m l. 2; E. S. Haldane and G. R. T. Ross (eds.), *The Philosophical Works of Descartes*, II 362: '*unionem substantialem qua mens corpori conjungitur . . .*'

SU6   French letter to Mesland of 9 February 1645 (AT IV 166, ll. 11–22;
      CSMK 243): *'joint & uny substantiellement ...'*

EPS. Texts in which Descartes speaks of man as an ens per se. Dates:
1641, 1642 (3).

Clarification 1: 'substances, that is, things which subsist on their own ...
   [*substantiae, hoc est, res per se subsistentes*]' (Fourth Responses: AT VII 222;
   CSM II 156–7).
Clarification 2: 'the notion of a <u>substance</u> is just this—that it can exist by itself,
   that is without the aid of any other substance [*notio <u>substantiae</u>, quod per se,
   hoc est absque ope ullius alterius substantiae possit existere*]' (Ibid.: AT VII 226;
   CSM II 159).

EPS1 Letter to Regius of mid-December 1641 (AT III 460, ll. 16–25;
      CSMK 200).
EPS2 Second letter to Regius of January 1642 (AT III 493, ll. 1–4; CSMK
      206).
EPS3 Ibid. (AT III 508, l. 13–509, l. 2; CSMK 209).
EPS4 Letter to Dinet (AT VII 585, l. 17–586, l. 2; Haldane and Ross (eds.),
      Philosophical Works, II 362) [= SU5].

E. Texts in which Descartes speaks of man as having an essence. Dates:
1641, 1642 (and 1647: see N1).

E1   Fourth Responses (AT VII 219, ll. 17–24, IX 171; CSM II 155).
E2   Second letter to Regius of January 1642 (AT III 508, ll. 19–22; CSMK
      209).

N. Texts in which Descartes speaks of man as having a nature. Dates: 1641
(2).

N1   Fourth Responses (AT VII 228, ll. 5–12; CSM II 160). (*'Essence'* is
      used in the 1647 French translation (AT IX 177).)
N2   Letter to Hyperaspistes of August 1641 (AT III 422, ll. 9–13; CSMK
      189): 'a human being, because composite, is by his nature corruptible
      [*quod compositum humanum sit ex natura sua corruptibile*] ...'

F. Texts in which Descartes says that the mind informs (F*1*, F*6*, F*7*, F*9*) *or* is the form of (F*2*, F*8*) *or* the substantial form of (F*3*, F*4*, F*5*) *the body* (F*1*, F*5*, F*6*, F*8*) *or its matter* (F*7*, F*9*) *or the man* (F*2*, F*3*, F*4*). Dates: 1628, 1641, 1642 (3), 1644, 1645, 1645 or 1646, 1646.

Clarification: 'To prevent any ambiguity of expression, it must be observed that when we deny substantial forms, we mean by the expression a certain substance joined to matter, making up with it a merely corporeal whole, and which, no less than matter and even more than matter—since it is called an actuality and matter only a potentiality—is a true substance, or self-subsistent thing' (second letter to Regius of January 1642: AT III 502; CSMK 207).

F1   *Regulae* (AT X 411, ll. 17–23; CSM I 39–40).
F2   Fifth Responses (AT VII 356, ll. 17–21; CSM II 246).
F3   Second letter to Regius of January 1642 (AT III 503, ll. 1–17; CSMK 207–8).
F4   Ibid. (AT III 505, ll. 16–22; CSMK 208).
F5   Letter to Dinet (AT VII 587, ll. 8–16; Haldane and Ross (eds.), *Philosophical Works*, II 363): The Rector at Utrecht published certain theses, 'the principal of which was *concerning the substantial forms of material things*, all of which had been denied by the physician [Regius] with the exception of the rational soul . . .'
F6   *Principles*, pt. IV, art. 189 (AT VIII 315 ll. 23–5; CSM I 279). (The 1647 French translation drops the language of form (AT IXB 310).)
F7   French letter to Mesland of 9 February 1645 (AT IV 168, l. 9–169, l. 24; CSMK 243–4).
F8   Letter to Mesland of 1645 or 1646 (AT IV 346, ll. 15–22; CSMK 278–9).
F9   Letter to Clerselier of 2 March 1646 (AT IV 373, ll. 1–4; CSMK 284).

II. Formulas Expressing a Moderate Platonist Position

P. Texts in which Descartes speaks of soul and body as parts *or* components *of the man, or of man as a* composite *of soul and body.* Dates: 1628, 1633, 1637 (2), 1641 (12), 1642 (2), 1644, 1647 (2), 1648 (2), 1649.

P1   *Regulae* (AT X 411, ll. 17–23; CSM I 39–40) [= F1].
P2   *Treatise on Man* (AT XI 119, l. 4–120, l. 3; CSM I 99).
P3   *Discourse*, pt. V (AT VI 46, ll. 12–23; CSM I 134). (The language of part and whole is accepted in the 1644 Latin translation (AT VI 566).)
P4   Ibid. (AT VI 59, ll. 12–18; CSM I 141): '*& ainsi composer un vray homme.*' (The language of part and whole is accepted in the Latin translation (AT VI 573).)
P5   Sixth Meditation (AT VII 81, ll. 1–5; CSM II 56): 'Nature also teaches, by these sensations of pain, hunger, thirst, etc., that I am not merely

present in my body as a sailor is present in a ship, but that I am very closely joined and, as it were, intermingled with it, to such an extent that I compose one thing with it [*unum quid cum illo componam*].' French translation, 1647 (AT IX 64): '*tellement confondu & meslé, que je compose comme un seul tout avec luy.*'

P6   Ibid. (AT VII 81, ll. 24–5; CSM II 56): 'Also the fact that some of those perceptions are pleasing to me and others unpleasant makes it very certain that my body, or rather my whole self in so far as I am composed of a mind and a body [*me totum, quatenus ex corpore & mente sum compositus*], can be affected by the various beneficial and harmful bodies which surround it.' French (AT IX 65): '*mon corps (ou plutost moy-mesme tout entier, en tant que je suis composé du corps & de l'ame) . . .*'

P7   Ibid. (AT VII 82, ll. 23–5; CSM II 57): '[I am speaking here] only of that which is bestowed on me, as a composite of mind and body, by God.' French (AT IX 65): '*comme estant composé de l'esprit & du corps.*'

P8   Ibid. (AT VII 82, l. 30–83, l. 2; CSM II 57): 'knowledge of the truth about such things appears to belong to the mind alone, and not to the composite [*de iis verum scire ad mentem solam, non autem ad compositum, videtur pertinere*].' French (AT IX 66): '*au composé de l'esprit et du corps . . .*'

P9   Ibid. (AT VII 83, ll. 17–18; CSM II 57): 'For the perceptions of the senses given by nature have as their purpose to signify to the mind what is beneficial or harmful to the composite of which it is a part [*composito, cujus pars est*], and to this extent they are sufficiently clear and distinct.' French (AT IX 66): '*au composé dont il est partie . . .*'

P10   Ibid. (AT VII 85, ll. 21–3; CSM II 59): 'with respect to the composite, or the mind united to this body . . . [*ad compositum, sive ad mentem tali corpori unitam*].' French (AT IX 68): '*au regard de tout le composé, c'est à dire de l'esprit ou de l'ame unie a ce corps . . .*'

P11   Ibid. (AT VII 88, ll. 20–2; CSM II 61): 'the nature of man as composed of mind and body [*naturam hominis ut ex mente & corpore compositi*] cannot but mislead from time to time.' French (AT IX 70): '*la nature de l'homme, en tant qu'il est composé de l'esprit & du corps . . .*'

P12   Fourth Responses (AT VII 222, ll. 20–30, IX 173; CSM II 157): '*substantiam, cum qua unum per se componunt . . . mens & corpus sunt substantiae incompletae, cum referuntur ad hominem quem componunt . . .*'

P13   Sixth Responses (AT VII 423, l. 2–424, l. 6, IX 226; CSM II 285–6).

P14   Ibid. (AT VII 444, ll. 10–14 + 25–445, ll. 2 + 17–19, IX 242; CSM II 299–300).

P15   Letter to Hyperaspistes of August 1641 (AT III 422, ll. 9–13; CSMK 189) [= N2].

P16   Letter to Regius of mid-December 1641 (AT III 460, ll. 5–9; CSMK 200).

P17   Second letter to Regius of January 1642 (AT III 508, l. 3–509, l. 2; CSMK 209).

P18   Letter to Dinet (AT VII 585, l. 17–586, l. 2; Haldane and Ross (eds.), *Philosophical Works*, II 362 [= SU5]).

P19   *Principles*, pt. II, art. 3 (AT VIII 41, ll. 24–7; CSM I 224): 'Sensory perceptions teach, not what is really in things, but what benefits or harms the human composite [*humano composito*]. It will be enough if we note that sensory perceptions are exclusively related to this conjunction of the human body with the mind [*corporis humani cum mente conjunctionem*], and normally show us what benefit or harm external bodies can do to it . . .' French, 1647 (AT IXB 64–5): '*Que nos sens ne nous enseignent pas la nature des choses, mais seulement ce en quoy elles nous sont utiles ou nuisibles. Il suffira que nous remarquions seulement que tout ce que nous appercevons par l'entremise de nos sens se rapporte à l'estroite union qu'a l'ame avec le corps, & que nous connoissons ordinairement par leur moyen ce en quoy les corps de dehors nous peuvent profiter ou nuire . . .*'

P20   Letter-preface to French translation of *Principles* (AT IXB 4, ll. 3–4; CSM I 180): '*les hommes, dont la principale partie est l'esprit . . .*'

P21   French translation of *Principles*, pt. I, art. 60 (AT IXB 51, ll. 33–7): 'And even if God were to join a body and a soul so closely that it would be impossible to unite them further, and were to make a composite of these two substances thus united [*et feroit un composé de ces deux substances ainsi unies*], we also conceive that the two would remain really distinct, in spite of this union . . .'

P22   *Comments on a Certain Broadsheet* (AT VIIIB 351, ll. 5–23; CSM I 299).

P23   Letter for [Arnauld] of 4 June 1648 (AT V 192, ll. 2–3; CSMK 354): 'the better part of him, his mind . . . [*ea tamen parte, quae melior est, nempe ingenio*].'

P24   *Passions*, art. 139 (AT XI 432, ll. 4–5; CSM I 377) '*Ce qui suffiroit, si nous n'avions en nous que le corps, ou qu'il fut nostre meilleure partie; mais d'autant qu'il n'est que la moindre . . .*'

U. Texts in which Descartes appears to suggest that the union *between soul and body generates a thing from them.* Dates: 1633, 1637, 1641 (3), 1642 (2), 1643, 1644.

U1   *Treatise on Man* (AT XI 119, l. 4–120, l. 3; CSM I 99) [= P2].

U2   *Discourse*, pt. V (AT VI 59, ll. 12–18; CSM I 141) [= P4].

U3   Sixth Meditation (AT VII 81, ll. 4–5; CSM II 56) [= P5].

U4   Sixth Responses (AT VII 444, ll. 10–18; CSM II 299): 'In fact I have never seen or perceived human bodies think; all I have seen is that there are human beings, who possess both thought and a body. This occurs by the composition of a thinking thing with a physical thing [*Hocque fieri per compositionem rei cogitantis cum corporea*] . . .'

U5   Letter to Regius of mid-December 1641 (AT III 460, ll. 9–13; CSMK 200): 'Say too that in your ninth you said that a human being comes into being *per accidens* out of body and soul in order to indicate that it can be said in a sense to be accidental for the body to be joined to the soul, and for the soul to be joined to the body, since the body can exist without the soul and the soul can exist without the body.'

U6   Second letter to Regius of January 1642 (AT III 508, l. 3–509, l. 2; CSMK 209), e.g.: 'We affirm that human beings are composed [*componi*] of body and soul . . . by a true substantial union [*per veram unionem substantialem*] . . . the union which joins a human body and soul to each other is not accidental to a human being, but essential, since a human being without it is not a human being . . . I thought I would please the theologians more by saying that a human being is an *ens per accidens* . . . than if I said that he is an *ens per se*, in reference to the union of the parts' [= P17].

U7 Letter to Dinet (AT VII 585, ll. 17–28; Haldane and Ross (eds.), *Philosophical Works*, II 362): 'it was affirmed in some thesis that from the union of the mind and the body there is not produced [*fieri*] an ens per se but per accidens . . . it was immediately added that these substances were called incomplete with regard to the composite that results from their union [*ratione compositi quod ex earum unione oritur*] . . .'

U8 Letter to Elisabeth of 28 June 1643 (AT III 692, l. 7–694, l. 6; CSMK 227–8): 'to conceive the union between two things is to conceive them as a single thing [*comme une seule*]. . . . it does not seem to me that the human mind is capable of conceiving very distinctly and at the same time the distinction between the soul and the body and their union, because to do this one must conceive them as a single thing [*comme une seule chose*] and at the same time conceive them as two, which is in opposition [*se contrarie*] . . .'

U9 *Principles*, pt. I, art. 60 (AT VIII 29, ll. 6–10; CSM I 213): 'And even if we should suppose that God had joined some corporeal substance to such a thinking substance so closely that they could not be joined more closely, and in this way had produced one thing from these two, they will nevertheless remain really distinct [*Ac etiamsi supponamus, Deum alicui tali substantiae cogitanti substantiam aliquam corpoream tam arcte conjunxisse, ut arctius jungi non possint, et ita ex illis duabus unum quid conflavisse, manent nihilominus realiter distinctae*] . . .' (The idea of the inference from such a union to a thing thereby constituted is absent in the 1647 French translation, which renders '*et ita*' simply by '*et*'. See P21.)

Bibliography

I. Texts and Editions: Descartes

Adam, C., and Milhaud, G. (eds.), *Descartes, Correspondence* (Paris: Presses Universitaires de France, 1936–63).

—— and Tannery, P. (eds.), *Œuvres de Descartes* (rev. edn., 12 vols., Paris: Vrin/CNRS, 1964–76) [abbreviated as AT].

Alquié, F. (ed.), *Descartes, Œuvres philosophiques* (3 vols., Paris: Garnier, 1963).

Buzon, F. (ed.), *Descartes, Abrégé de musique, avec présentation et notes* (Paris: Presses Universitaires de France, 1987).

Cottingham, J. (ed.), *Descartes' Conversation with Burman* (Oxford: Clarendon Press, 1976).

—— Stoothoff, R., and Murdoch, D. (eds.), *The Philosophical Writings of Descartes*, i–ii (Cambridge: Cambridge University Press, 1985) [abbreviated as CSM]; volume iii of the preceding, by the same translators and A. Kenny (Cambridge: Cambridge University Press, 1991) [abbreviated as CSMK].

Crapulli, G. (ed.), *Descartes: Regulae ad directionem ingenii* (The Hague: Nijhoff, 1966).

Gilson, É. (ed.), *René Descartes, Discours de la méthode, texte et commentaire* (Paris: Vrin, 1925; 4th edn., 1967).

Haldane, E. S., and Ross, G. R. T. (eds.), *The Philosophical Works of Descartes* (2 vols., Cambridge: Cambridge University Press, 1911).

Hall, T. S. (ed.), *Descartes, Treatise on Man* (Cambridge, Mass.: Harvard University Press, 1972).

Kenny, A. (trans.), *Descartes, Philosophical Letters* (Oxford: Oxford University Press, 1970).

Mahoney, M. S. (trans.), *Descartes, The World* (New York: Abaris, 1979).

Marion, J.-L. (ed. and trans.), *Règles utiles et claires pour la direction de l'esprit* (The Hague: Nijhoff, 1977).

Miller, V. R., and Miller, R. P. (eds.), *Descartes, Principles of Philosophy* (Dordrecht: Reidel, 1983).

Olscamp, P. J. (trans.), *Discourse on Method, Optics, Geometry and Meteorology* (Indianapolis: Bobbs-Merrill, 1965).

Rodis-Lewis, G. (ed. and trans.), *Lettres à Regius et remarques sur l'explication de l'esprit humain* (Paris: Vrin, 1959).

Verbeek, T. (ed. and trans.), *René Descartes et Martin Schook, la querelle d'Utrecht* (Paris: Les Impressions Nouvelles, 1988).

Voss, S. (ed. and trans.), *The Passions of the Soul* (Indianapolis: Hackett, 1989).

II. Texts and Editions: Other Pre-Twentieth-Century Writers

Aristotle, *Metaphysics*, ed. W. D. Ross (Oxford: Oxford University Press, 1924).
—— *Posterior Analytics*, in *Prior and Posterior Analytics*, ed. W. D. Ross (Oxford University Press, 1949).
Arnauld, A., *La logique, ou l'art de penser* (Paris, 1662).
Baillet, A., *La Vie de M. Des-Cartes* (2 vols., Paris: Horthemels, 1691; photographic reprint, Hildesheim: Olms, 1972; New York: Garland, 1987).
Cobos, C., *Expositio in libros Metaphysicae* (1583).
Gibieuf, G., *De libertate Dei et Creaturae* (Paris, 1630).
Leibniz, G. W., *New Essays Concerning Human Understanding*, trans. and ed. P. Remnant and J. Bennett (Cambridge: Cambridge University Press, 1981).
—— *Philosophical Papers and Letters*, ed. L. E. Loemker (2nd edn., Dordrecht: Reidel, 1969).
Mas, D., *Disputatio Metaphysicae* (1587).
Nietzsche, F., *Unmodern Observations*, ed. W. Arrowsmith (New Haven, Conn.: Yale University Press, 1990).
Nifo, A., *In librum Destructio destructionum Averrois commentarii* (Lyons, 1529).
Pomponazzi, P., *Tractatus de immortalitate animae* (1516; ed. G. Morra, Bologna, 1954).
Spinoza, B., *The Collected Works of Spinoza*, ed. and trans. E. Curley (Princeton, NJ: Princeton University Press, 1985).
Suárez, F., *Disputationes metaphysicae* (Salmanticae, 1597).
Toledo, F., *Commentaria una cum quaestionibus in tres libros Aristotelis De anima* (Cologne, 1583).
Zúñiga, D., *Philosophiae prima pars* (1597).

III. Books and Articles Published after 1900

Adams, R. M., 'Where do our Ideas Come from?'—Descartes vs. Locke', in S. Stich (ed.), *Innate Ideas* (Berkeley, Calif.: University of California Press, 1975), 71–87.
Alanen, L., 'Descartes' Dualism and the Philosophy of Mind', *Revue de métaphysique et de morale* (1989), 391–413.
—— 'Cartesian Ideas and Intentionality', *Acta Philosophica Fennica*, 49 (1990), 344–69.
—— 'Some Questions Concerning Objective Reality and Possible Being in Descartes and his Predecessors', *Annals of the Finnish Society for Missiologics and Ecumenics*, 55 (1990), 553–65.
Alquié, F., *La Découverte métaphysique de l'homme chez Descartes* (Paris: Presses Universitaires de France, 1950; 2nd edn., 1966).

Amaral, P. (ed.), *The Metaphysics of Epistemology* (Atascadero, Calif.: Ridgeview, 1989).

Anscombe, G. E. M., 'Substance', *Proceedings of the Aristotelian Society*, suppl. vol. 38 (1964), 7–78.

—— 'The First Person', in S. Guttenplan (ed.), *Metaphysics and the Philosophy of Mind* (Minneapolis: University of Minnesota Press, 1981).

Arbini, R., 'Did Descartes have a Philosophical Theory of Sense Perception?', *Journal of the History of Philosophy*, 21 (1983), 317–37.

Armogathe, J.-R., *Theologia Cartesiana: L'Explication physique de l'Eucharistie chez Descartes et dom Desgabets* (La Haye: Nijhoff, 1977).

Baier, A., 'The Idea of the True God in Descartes', in A. O. Rorty (ed.), *Essays on Descartes' Meditations* (Berkeley, Calif.: University of California Press, 1986), 358–87.

Bennett, J., *Locke, Berkeley, Hume: Central Themes* (Oxford: Oxford University Press, 1971).

—— *A Study of Spinoza's Ethics* (Indianapolis: Hackett, 1984).

Beyssade, J.-M., 'Descartes on Material Falsity', in P. D. Cummins and G. Zoeller (eds.), *Essays on the Theory of Perception in Modern Philosophy* (North American Kant Society Studies in Philosophy, 2; Atascadero, Calif.: Ridgeview, 1992).

Broughton, J., and Mattern, R., 'Reinterpreting Descartes on the Notion of the Union of Mind and Body', *Journal of the History of Philosophy*, 16 (1978), 23–32.

Butler, R. J. (ed.), *Cartesian Studies* (Oxford: Blackwell, 1972).

Carriero, J., 'The First Meditation', *Pacific Philosophical Quarterly*, 68 (1987), 222–48.

Chappell, V., 'The Theory of Ideas', in A. O. Rorty (ed.), *Essays on Descartes' Meditations* (Berkeley, Calif.: University of California Press, 1986), 177–98.

—— 'L'Homme cartésien', in J.-L. Marion and J.-M. Beyssade (eds.), *Méditer et répondre* (Paris: Presses Universitaires de France, 1994).

Clarke, D. M., *Descartes' Philosophy of Science* (Manchester: Manchester University Press, 1982).

Clatterbaugh, K., 'Descartes' Causal Likeness Principle', *Philosophical Review*, 89 (1980), 379–402.

Costa, M. J., 'What Cartesian Ideas are not', *Journal of the History of Philosophy*, 21 (1983), 537–49.

Cottingham, J., 'Cartesian Trialism', *Mind* (1985), 218–30.

—— *Descartes* (Oxford: Blackwell, 1986).

—— *The Rationalists* (Oxford: Oxford University Press), 1988.

—— 'The Cartesian Legacy', *Proceedings of the Aristotelian Society*, suppl. vol. 66 (1992), 1–22.

—— (ed.), *The Cambridge Companion to Descartes* (New York: Cambridge University Press, 1992).

—— *A Descartes Dictionary* (Oxford: Blackwell, 1993).

—— 'A New Start? Cartesian Metaphysics and the Emergence of Modern Philosophy', in T. Sorell (ed.), *The Rise of Modern Philosophy* (Oxford: Clarendon Press, 1993), 145–66.

Cover, J. A., and Kulstad, M. (eds.), *Central Themes in Early Modern Philosophy* (Indianapolis: Hackett, 1990).

Cress, D., 'Creation *De Nihilo* & St. Augustine's Account of Evil in *Contra Secundum Juliani Responsionem Imperfectum Opus*, Book V', in J. C. Schnaubelt and F. van Fleteren (eds.), *Miscellanea Augustiniana* (New York: Lang, 1989).

Curley, E. M., *Descartes against the Skeptics* (Oxford: Blackwell, 1978).

Dicker, G., *Descartes: An Analytical and Historical Introduction* (Oxford: Oxford University Press, 1992).

Donagan, A., *Spinoza* (Brighton: Harvester Press, 1988).

Doney, W., 'The Cartesian Circle', *Journal of the History of Ideas*, 16 (1955), 324–38.

—— (ed.), *Descartes: A Collection of Critical Essays* (New York: Doubleday, 1967).

Feldman, F., 'Epistemic Appraisal and the Cartesian Circle', *Philosophical Studies*, 31 (1977), 429–32.

Fletcher, G., and Scheute, M. B. (eds.), *Paradosis* (New York: Fordham University Press, 1976).

Frankfurt, H. G., 'Descartes' Validation of Reason', in W. Doney (ed.), *Descartes: A Collection of Critical Essays* (New York: Doubleday, 1967), 209–26.

—— *Demons, Dreamers and Madmen: The Defence of Reason in Descartes' Meditations* (Indianapolis: Bobbs-Merrill, 1970).

—— 'Descartes on the Creation of the Eternal Truths', *Philosophical Review*, 86 (1977), 36–57.

—— 'Descartes on the Consistency of Reason', in M. Hooker (ed.), *Descartes: Critical and Interpretive Essays* (Baltimore: Johns Hopkins University Press, 1978), 26–39.

Garber, D., 'Science and Certainty in Descartes', in M. Hooker (ed.), *Descartes: Critical and Interpretive Essays* (Baltimore: Johns Hopkins University Press, 1978), 114–51.

—— '*Semel in vita*: The Scientific Background to Descartes' Meditations', in A. O. Rorty (ed.), *Essays on Descartes' Meditations* (Berkeley, Calif.: University of California Press, 1986), 81–116.

—— 'Descartes, the Aristotelians, and the Revolution that did not Happen in 1637', *Monist*, 71 (1988), 471–86.

—— 'Descartes and Experiment in the *Discourse* and *Essays*', in S. Voss (ed.), *Essays on the Philosophy and Science of René Descartes* (Oxford: Oxford University Press, 1993).

Gaukroger, S., (ed.), *Descartes: Philosophy, Mathematics and Physics* (Sussex: Harvester, 1980).

—— *Cartesian Logic: An Essay on Descartes' Conception of Inference* (Oxford: Clarendon Press, 1989).

—— 'Descartes: Methodology', in G. H. R. Parkinson (ed.), *Routledge History of Philosophy*, iv. *The Renaissance and Seventeenth Century Rationalism* (London: Routledge, 1993).

Gewirth, A., 'The Cartesian Circle', *Philosophical Review*, 50 (1941), 370–95.

—— 'Clearness and Distinctness in Descartes' (1943), repr. in W. Doney (ed.), *Descartes: A Collection of Critical Essays* (New York: Doubleday, 1967), 250–77.

Gilson, É. *La Liberté chez Descartes et la théologie* (Paris: Alcan, 1913).

—— *Études sur le rôle de la pensée médiévale dans la formation du système cartésien* (4th edn., Paris: Vrin, 1975).

—— 'Autour de Pomponazzi: Problématique de l'immortalité de l'âme en Italie au début du XVIe siècle', *Archives d'histoire doctrinale et littéraire du moyen âge*, 18 (1961), 163–279.

Gómez, J., 'Pedro da Fonseca: Sixteenth Century Portuguese Philosopher', *International Philosophy Quarterly*, 4 (1966), 632–44.

Goodman, N., *The Structure of Appearance* (3rd edn., Dordrecht: Reidel, 1977).

Gouhier, H., *La Pensée réligieuse de Descartes* (Paris: Vrin, 1924).

—— *La Pensée métaphysique de Descartes* (3rd edn., Paris: Vrin, 1978).

—— *Essais sur Descartes* (3rd edn., Paris: Vrin, 1973).

Greenblatt, S., *Renaissance Self-Fashioning* (Chicago: University of Chicago Press, 1980).

Grene, M., *Descartes* (Minneapolis: University of Minnesota Press, 1985).

—— 'Die Einheit des Menschen: Descartes unter den Scholastikern', *Dialectica* (1986), 309–22.

—— *Descartes among the Scholastics: The Aquinas Lecture 1991*, (Milwaukee: Marquette University Press, 1991).

Gueroult, M., *Descartes selon l'ordre des raisons* (Paris: Montaigne, 1953; 2nd edn., 1968). English trans. R. Ariew, *Descartes' Philosophy Interpreted According to the Order of Reasons* (Minneapolis: University of Minnesota Press, 1984).

Guttenplan, S. (ed.), *Mind and Language: Wolfson College Lectures 1974* (Oxford: Clarendon Press, 1975).

Hatfield, G., 'The Senses and the Fleshless Eye: The Meditations as Cognitive Exercises', in A. O. Rorty (ed.), *Essays on Descartes' Meditations* (Berkeley, Calif.: University of California Press, 1986), 45–80.

—— 'Descartes' Physiology and its Relation to his Psychology', in J. Cottingham (ed.), *The Cambridge Companion to Descartes* (New York: Cambridge University Press, 1992), 335–70.

Hoffman, P., 'The Unity of Descartes' Man', *Philosophical Review*, 95 (1986), 339–70.

Hooker, M. (ed.), *Descartes: Critical and Interpretive Essays* (Baltimore: Johns Hopkins University Press, 1978).

Jones, R. F., *Ancients and Moderns* (St Louis: Washington University Studies, 1936; repr. New York: Dover, 1961).

Kelley, D. R., and Popkin, R. H. (eds.), *The Shapes of Knowledge from the Renaissance to the English Enlightenment* (Norwell, Mass.: Kluwer, 1991).

Kenny, A., *Descartes: A Study of his Philosophy* (New York: Random House, 1968).

—— 'Descartes on the Will', in R. J. Butler (ed.), *Cartesian Studies* (Oxford: Blackwell, 1972), 1–31.

Kulstad, M., and Cover, J. (eds.), *Central Themes in Early Modern Philosophy* (Indianapolis: Hackett, 1990).

Laporte, J., *Le Rationalisme de Descartes* (Paris: Presses Universitaires de France, 1945; 3rd edn. 1988).

Larmore, C. L., 'Descartes' Empirical Epistemology', in S. Gaukroger (ed.), *Descartes: Philosophy, Mathematics and Physics* (Sussex: Harvester, 1980).

—— 'Descartes' Psychologistic Theory of Assent', *History of Philosophy Quarterly*, 1 (1984), 61–74.

Loeb, L. E., *From Descartes to Hume: Continental Metaphysics and the Development of Modern Philosophy* (Ithaca, NY: Cornell University Press, 1981).

—— 'The Cartesian Circle', in J. Cottingham (ed.), *The Cambridge Companion to Descartes* (New York: Cambridge University Press, 1992), 200–35.

Lohr, C. H., 'Jesuit Aristotelianism and Sixteenth-Century Metaphysics', in G. Fletcher and M. B. Scheute (eds.), *Paradosis* (New York: Fordham University Press, 1976), 203–20.

—— 'Metaphysics', in C. B. Schmitt and Q. Skinner (eds.), *The Cambridge History of Renaissance Philosophy* (Cambridge: Cambridge University Press, 1988), 537–638.

—— 'The Sixteenth-Century Transformation of the Aristotelian Division of the Speculative Sciences', in D. R. Kelley and R. H. Popkin (eds.), *The Shapes of Knowledge from the Renaissance to the English Enlightenment* (Norwell, Mass: Kluwer, 1991), 49–58.

MacKenzie, A. W., 'Descartes on Life and Sense', *Canadian Journal of Philosophy*, 19 (1989), 178–92.

—— 'Descartes on Sensory Representation', *Canadian Journal of Philosophy*, suppl. vol. 16 (1990), 127–46.

Mackie, J. L., *Problems from Locke* (Oxford: Clarendon Press, 1976).

Marion, J.-L., *Sur la théologie blanche de Descartes* (Paris: Presses Universitaires de France, 1981).

Maritain, J., *The Dream of Descartes*, trans. M. Andison (New York: Philosophical Library, 1944; originally published as *Le Songe de Descartes* (Paris: Corêa, 1932)).

Markie, P. J., *Descartes's Gambit* (Ithaca, NY: Cornell University Press, 1986).

Morris, J., 'Descartes' Natural Light', *Journal of the History of Philosophy*, 11 (1973), 169–87.

Normore, C., 'Meaning and Objective Being: Descartes and his Sources', in A. O. Rorty (ed.), *Essays on Descartes'* Meditations (Berkeley, Calif.: University of California Press, 1986), 223–41.

Olson, M. A., 'Descartes' First Meditation: Mathematics and the Laws of Logic', *Journal of the History of Philosophy*, 26 (1988), 407–38.

O'Neil, B., *Epistemological Direct Realism in Descartes' Philosophy* (Albuquerque, N. Mex.: University of New Mexico Press, 1974).

Pariente, J.-C., *L'Analyse du langage à Port-Royal* (Paris: Les Editions de Minuit, 1985).

Parkinson, G. H. R. (ed.), *Routledge History of Philosophy, iv. The Renaissance and Seventeenth Century Rationalism* (London: Routledge, 1993).

Reif, P., 'The Textbook Tradition in Natural Philosophy, 1600–1650', *Journal of the History of Ideas*, 30 (1969), 17–32.

Rodis-Lewis, G., *L'Individualité selon Descartes* (Paris: Vrin, 1950).

—— *L'Œuvre de Descartes* (2 vols., Paris: Vrin, 1971).

—— *L'Anthropologie cartésienne* (Paris: Presses Universitaires de France, 1991).

Rorty, A. O. (ed.), *Essays on Descartes'* Meditations (Berkeley, Calif.: University of California Press, 1986).

Rossi, P., 'The Legacy of Ramon Lull in Sixteenth-Century Thought', *Medieval and Renaissance Studies*, 5 (1961), 182–231.

Rubidge, B., 'Descartes' *Meditations* and Devotional Meditations', *Journal of the History of Ideas*, 51 (1990), 27–49.

Rubin, R., 'Descartes' Validation of Clear and Distinct Apprehension', *Philosophical Review*, 86 (1977), 197–208.

Ryle, G., *The Concept of Mind* (London: Hutchinson, 1949).

Schmaltz, T., 'Descartes and Malebranche on Mind and the Mind–Body Union', *Philosophical Review* (1992), 281–325.

Schmitt, C. B., 'Toward an Assessment of Renaissance Aristotelianism', *History of Science*, 9 (1973), 159–93.

—— *Aristotle and the Renaissance* (Cambridge, Mass.: Harvard University Press, 1983).

—— and Skinner, Q. (eds.), *The Cambridge History of Renaissance Philosophy* (Cambridge: Cambridge University Press, 1988).

Schnaubelt, J. C., and Fleteren, F. van (eds.), *Miscellanea Augustiniana* (New York: Lang, 1989).

Schouls, P. A., 'Descartes and the Autonomy of Reason', *Journal of the History of Philosophy*, 10 (1972), 307–22.

—— *The Imposition of Method, A Study of Descartes and Locke* (Oxford: Oxford University Press, 1980).

—— *Descartes and the Enlightenment* (Edinburgh: Edinburgh University Press, 1989).

Sellars, W., 'Lectures', in P. Amaral (ed.), *The Metaphysics of Epistemology* (Atascadero, Calif.: Ridgeview, 1989), 95–120.

Shea, W. R., 'Descartes and the Rosicrucian Enlightenment', in R. S. Woolhouse (ed.), *Metaphysics and Philosophy of Science in the Seventeenth and Eighteenth Centuries* (Dordrecht: Reidel, 1988), 73–99.

Sirven, J., *Les Années d'apprentissage de Descartes* (Albi: Imprimerie Coopérative du Sud Ouest, 1928).

Smyth, R., 'A Metaphysical Reading of the First Meditation', *Philosophical Quarterly*, 36 (1986), 283–303.

Sommers, F., 'Dualism in Descartes: The Logical Ground', in M. Hooker (ed.), *Descartes: Critical and Interpretive Essays* (Baltimore: Johns Hopkins University Press, 1978), 223–33.

Sorell, T., 'Morals and Modernity in Descartes', in T. Sorell (ed.), *The Rise of Modern Philosophy* (Oxford: Clarendon Press, 1993), 273–88.

—— (ed.), *The Rise of Modern Philosophy* (Oxford: Clarendon Press, 1993).

Stich, S. (ed.), *Innate Ideas* (Berkeley, Calif.: University of California Press, 1975).

Stoothoff, R., 'Descartes' Dilemma', *Philosophical Quarterly*, 39 (1989), 294–307.

Van de Pitte, F., 'Some of Descartes' Debts to Eustachius a Sancto Paulo', *Monist*, 71 (1988), 487–97.

Voss, S. (ed.), *Essays on the Philosophy and Science of René Descartes* (Oxford: Oxford University Press, 1993).

Williams, B., *Descartes: The Project of Pure Enquiry* (Harmondsworth: Penguin, 1978).

—— *Shame and Necessity* (Berkeley, Calif.: University of California Press, 1993).

Wilson, C., and Schildknecht, C., 'The Cogito Meant "No More Philosophy": Valéry's Descartes', *History of European Ideas*, 9 (1988), 47–62.

Wilson, G. A., 'Henry of Ghent and Rene Descartes on the Unity of Man', *Franziskanische Studien* (1982), 97–110.

Wilson, M. D., 'Leibniz: Self-Consciousness and Immortality in the Paris Notes and After' (Sonderheft for Hans Wagner), *Archiv für Geschichte der Philosophie*, 58/4 1976, 335–52.

—— 'Review of O'Neil, *Epistemological Direct Realism in Descartes' Philosophy*', *Philosophical Review*, 85 (1976), 408–10.

—— *Descartes* (London: Routledge & Kegan Paul, 1978).

—— 'Review of Yolton, *Perceptual Acquaintance from Descartes to Reid*', *Times Literary Supplement*, 16 August 1985.

—— 'Can I be the Cause of my Idea of the World? (Descartes on the Infinite and the Indefinite)', in A. O. Rorty (ed.), *Essays on Descartes' Meditations* (Berkeley, Calif.: University of California Press, 1986).

—— 'Descartes on the Representationality of Sensation', in M. Kulstad and J. Cover (eds.), *Central Themes in Early Modern Philosophy* (Indianapolis: Hackett, 1990), 1–22.

—— 'Descartes on the Origin of Sensation', *Philosophical Topics*, 19 (1991), 293–323.

—— 'Descartes on the Perception of Primary Qualities', in S. Voss (ed.), *Essays on the Philosophy and Science of René Descartes* (Oxford: Oxford University Press, 1993), 162–76.

Wolf-Devine, C., *Descartes on Seeing: Epistemology and Visual Perception* (Carbondale and Edwardsville: Southern University Press, 1993. (Journal of the History of Philosophy Monograph Series)).

Woolhouse, R. S. (ed.), *Metaphysics and Philosophy of Science in the Seventeenth and Eighteenth Centuries* (Dordrecht: Reidel, 1988).

Yolton, J., 'Ideas and Knowledge in Seventeenth-Century Philosophy', *Journal of the History of Ideas*, 13 (1975), 145–65.

—— *Perceptual Acquaintance from Descartes to Reid* (Minneapolis: University of Minnesota Press, 1984).

Table of Citations of Descartes's Works

Comments on a Certain Broadsheet

	AT VIIIB	CSM I	
	342–3	294–5	289
	350	298	232, 289 n.
	363	307	179, 187

Conversation with Burman

	AT V	CSMK	
	154–5	339	76
	156	339–40	76, 121 n.
	160	343	248 n.

Correspondence

	AT	page	CSMK	book
To Arnauld	AT V	222	358	260, 283 n.
To Chanut	AT IV	144	289	290
To Christina	AT V	85	326	179, 279 n.
To Clerselier	AT V	354	376	284 n.
To Elizabeth	AT III	665–6	218	279 n.
		667	219	283 n.
		692–3	227–8	278 n., 299
	AT IV	295	267	185
		314	272	184, 189, 190
		332	277	183–4
		333	277	189
To Froidmont	AT I	402	—	33
		413–24	61–6	33–4
To Gibieuf	AT III	474–6	201–2	173 n.
To Hogeland	AT III	722	144	39
To Hyperaspistes	AT III	425–6	190–1	139 n.
		429	193	68–9
To Mersenne	AT I	81	13	50
		135–54	20–6	117 n.
		144	22	111
		145	22–3	118
		150	24–5	118, 119
		152	25	118, 119
		153	26	119
		182	—	111
		366	56	186
	AT II	597	139	115, 122–3, 125, 130
		598	139–40	125

To Mersenne (cont.)		622	141	141
	AT III	124	149	279 n.
		126–7	149–50	141
		183–4	153	141
		265–7	163–4	141
		268	164	141
		271–2	165	141
		298	173	120 n.
		334–5	175	143–4
		360	179	181 n.
		648	216	383 n.
To Mesland	AT IV	116	233–4	173 n., 178,180, 182, 185, 205
		118	234	182
		166	242–3	67
		167	243	281 n.
		173	244–5	126 n., 181, 182 n., 183, 185, 193–4
		174	245	195
		175	246	180
To Morin	AT I	537	—	33
		539	—	33
		541	—	32
		557	—	33
	AT II	199–200	107	116–17
		201–2	108	33
		210	—	33
		367	121–2	281 n.
To Regius	AT III	64–5	147–8	136
		64	147	99, 128
		371	182	160
		454–5	199	160
		461	200	283 n.
		493	206	278
		502	207	283
		508	209	283 n.
To Vatier	AT I	559–60	85	52
Discourse on the Method				
Part I	AT VI	4	CSM I 113	42
		7	114	42
		13	117	163
		15	118	162, 167

	19	120	291
Part II	25	123	170
Part III	27	124	162 n.
	28	125	162, 167
Part V	46	134	161 n.
	58–9	140–1	161 n., 278 n.–279 n.
Part VI	70	147	31, 39
	77	150	163 n.

Meditations on First Philosophy

	AT VII	CSM II	
Dedication	2	2	151
Preface	3	4	55
	8	7	231
Synopsis	12	9	253
	13	9	81, 82, 144
	15	11	143, 155
First	18	17–18	209
	19–20	13–14	260
	21	14	142 n., 165
	22	15	168
Second	23–4	16	169
	25	17	171
	27–9	18–20	219, 294
	27	18	74, 293
	30–2	20–2	91
	30	20	67 n.
Third	34–5	24–5	137 n., 225
	35–6	24–5	142, 211
	36	25	113, 115 n., 124, 127, 129, 134–5
	37	25–6	211, 229 n., 231 n., 236, 240, 241
	38	26	124, 125
	39	27	91–2, 124, 169, 226 n.
	40	27–8	89, 121 n., 125, 183, 212, 259 n.
	41–2	28–9	89–90
	41	28	240 n., 259
	43	29–30	93, 239

Meditations (cont.)			
Third (cont.)	44	30	65, 77, 224, 229, 239, 241, 262
	45	31	94, 106–7, 121 n., 173 n.
	46	31–2	103–4, 106, 239
	47	32	173 n., 260
	48	33	66 n., 73, 77
	50	34	107 n.
	51	35	121, 142
	52	35–6	121, 142, 167 n., 216
Fourth	53–4	37–8	142, 146
	53	37	167 n.
	56	39	178, 179
	57	40	121 n., 179, 191, 192
	58	41	181, 182, 189, 191, 192
	59–60	41	146
	59	41	179, 180, 181, 205
	60–1	42	145, 174 n.
	60	41	187
	61	42	174
	62	43	175
Fifth	63	44	224, 226 n.
	69	106	124, 144 n.
	70	48–9	130
Sixth	72–3	50–1	224
	74–5	51–2	212, 220
	76	52–3	209
	77	54	266
	78	54	78 n., 145, 151, 293
	79	55	169
	80	55	219, 266
	81–9	56–61	267
	81	56	264 n., 266, 279 n.
	82–3	56–7	211, 212–13
	83–9	58–61	267
	83	58	145, 151, 212, 243 n.

86	59	294
87	60	187, 218 n.
89	61–2	214

Objections and Replies

First Set

103	75	234
116–17	83	235

Second

124	88–9	150 n., 154
128	91	85
140	100	166
144–5	103	133
145–6	103–4	124
146	104	127
147–8	105–6	139
147	105	124
148–9	106	144, 145 n.
153–4	108–9	85–6
160	113	70, 230 n.
161	113–4	75, 233
162	114	65 n.
165	116	77 n.
166	117	179, 186, 235
168	118	77
169	119	78

Third

176	124	230 n.
181	127	231 n.
191	134	180, 190
195	136–7	165 n.

Fourth

203	143	276
206–7	145–6	263 n.
207	145	239 n., 240
222	156–7	65, 156–7, 280, 289 n.
226	159	65
227–8	160	276
228	160	65, 281 n.
231–2	163	240
232	163	259
233	163	240, 263
234	164	241
246	171	173 n.

Fifth

271–2	189–90	79 n.
276	192	81 n.
354	245	279 n., 300
355	245	74

Objections (cont.)	359	248	79
Fifth (cont.)	362	250	248 n.
	365	252	98
	377	259	187
	389–90	266	279 n.
Sixth	413	278	286
	424	286	286
	431–3	291	121 n.
	432–3	292	181
	432	292	186
	433	292	121 n., 182, 185, 189
	435	293–4	121 n.
	437	294–5	216
	438	295–6	243
	442	297–8	279 n.
	444	299	286
Seventh	550	375	164
	580	392	31
Optics			
First Discourse	AT VI 85–6	CSM I 153–4	232
Fourth Discourse	112	165	217, 256
	113	166	218, 256 n.
	118	—	258 n.
Sixth Discourse	130	167	217, 218 232 n., 258 n.
	132	168	258 n.
	141	172	257 n.
Passions of the Soul			
Part I, Art. 1	AT XI 327–8	CSM I 328	32, 41, 162 n.
1–26	327–48	328–38	162 n., 178
7–17	331–42	330–5	188
20	344	336	187
30	351	339	279 n.
34	354	341	184
41	359	343	179, 185
47	364	346	179
50	368–70	348	187
Part II 52	372	349	188
56–67	374–8	350–2	188
80	387	356	180
86	392	358	185
94	399–400	362	187

	137	430	376	187, 188, 279 n.
	144	436	379	188
Part III	152	445	384	179, 184
	177	464	392	186–7

Principles of Philosophy

French Preface	AT IXB	5	CSM I 181	31
		7–8	182	40
		14	186	41, 42
		15	186	41
Part I, Art. 1	AT VIIIA	327–8	328	32, 41, 162 n.
5		6	194	166
6		6	194	171–2
7		7	194–5	74, 171–2
8		7	195	161 n., 230 n.
9		7	195	292 n.
17		11	198–9	259 n.
18		12	199	74, 261
20		12	200	74, 77 n.
24		14	201	190
27		15	202	97
30		16–17	203	124, 267
32–4		17–18	204	179
33–42		17–21	204–7	268
37		18	205	180
39		19	205	178
41		20	206	181, 190
45–6		21–2	207–8	242
45		21–2	207–8	123 n., 163 n.
47		22	208	72 n., 260, 268
48–56		22–6	208–12	178
48		23	208–9	72 n., 237, 260, 264 n., 268, 279 n., 291–3
51–2		24	210	64–5, 181
53		25	210–11	70–1, 71–2, 73, 235, 238, 292
60		28–9	213	64–5
63		30–1	215	76 n.
65–9		32–5	216–18	269
65		32	216	269
66		32	216	213, 244, 269
68		33	217	224–5, 244, 269
69		33–4	217–18	225, 246, 270

Principles (cont.)

	70	34–5	218	270–2
Part II	1	41	223	226
	2	41	224	279 n.
	3	41–2	224	210
	6	43	225	67 n.
	9	45	226–7	78–9
	18	50	231	85 n.
	20	51	231	83
	36	61–3	240–1	184
Part IV	190	317–18	281	180
	196	320	283	223
	197–8	321–2	284–5	242 n.

Rules for the Direction of the Mind

Rule 3	AT X	367	CSM I	13	38
		368		14	115
Rule 4		376–7		19	49
Rule 11		406		36	50
		410		39	122
Rule 12		415		42	161 n.
		420		45	163 n.
		421–2		46	161 n.

The Search for Truth

	AT X	502–3	CSM II	403	38
		509		406–7	162 n.

Treatise on Man

	AT XI	131–2	CSM I	101	299

The World or *Treatise on Light*

Chapter 1	AT XI	3–6	CSM I	81–2	218 n.
		3		81	222
		4		81	222, 223, 232 n.
		5		82	223
		6		82	223
Chapter 6		33		90–1	116
		34–5		91–2	116 n.
		35		91–2	116
Chapter 7		38		93	115
		39-40		93–4	116
		43		95–6	115
		44		96	115
		47		97	116

Index

a posteriori reasoning (from effect to cause) 138
absolute knowledge 112, 113, 114, 117, 120, 127, 128, 136, 137, 139
activity and passivity 160, 161, 167, 168, 169, 170, 174, 175, 186
Agricola, Rudolfus 50
Agrippa, Henricus Cornelius 50–1
air, and sound 223, 224
Alexandrian reading of Aristotle 55
Amsterdam 279 n.
analogies:
  Archimedean point (Cogito) 173
  blind man in a cellar (mediocre minds) 39
  child and mathematics (wisdom) 147
  engraving (objects of sensation) 256–8
  fountain keeper (rational soul) 299
  hand (substance) 65
  mark of the craftsman on his work (idea of God) 300
  paintings (visions in sleep) 260
  tree (sciences) 42
  whirlpool (doubt) 169
  words and meaning (objects and sensations) 256–8
angel 127, 133
anger 188
anthropology, Cartesian 273–300
Aquinas, Saint Thomas 40, 55, 56, 152 n., 285
  Summa theologiae 145
Archimedean point (the Cogito) 173
Ariadne 159
Aristotelian 34, 35, 36, 55, 164 n.
  theory of perception 253, 354
Aristotle 29, 31, 33, 34, 36, 38, 40, 41, 43, 47, 54–5, 56, 57, 60, 277, 285
  De Anima 55, 285
  humanism 55
  Jesuit commentators of 56, 60
  Metaphysics 56 n.
  Posterior Analytics 136 n.
  Topics 50
arithmetic, *see* mathematics
Arnauld, Antoine 143, 229, 241, 276, 277, 278, 281, 291

Art of Thinking 248
Fourth Set of Objections to the *Meditations* 65, 156–7, 173 n., 239–40, 241, 259, 262–3, 265 n., 276, 280, 281 n., 289 n.
  letter to 260, 283 n.
art 40, 42
  of all arts (rhetoric) 54
assent, commanded by truth 124–6, 127–8, 129–30, 131, 144 n., 160, 182, 186–7, 200
atheism 139
atoms 34
  impossibility of 83
attribute(s) 64, 66, 68
  definition of 68
  nothingness lacks 71–2
  see also substance
Augustine, Saint 22, 29, 37, 150, 152, 153, 154
Ausonius 22
autonomy:
  of human nature 174, 176
  of reason 111–40, 162–7
  of will 167–76
Averroistic reading of Aristotle 55
axioms:
  'no less is required to preserve something than to create it' 77 n.
  'nothing possesses no attributes' 71–2
  in proofs of God's existence 136

Bacon, Francis, 30, 42
Baconian idea of science 41
Baillet, Adrien 111 n.
Berkeley, George 43, 227
body/bodies:
  as extended substance 64, 161–2, 224, 226 n.
  motion of 116
  and space 97, 99, 100, 101, 102, 108
body, human 63
  compared with machine 299
  as extended in space 70–1
  and mind (dualism) 58, 273, 274, 275–300 *passim*
  numerical identity of 67

body, human (*cont.*):
  parts of 82–3
  really distinct from the soul/mind
    64–5, 161
  union with the soul/mind 65, 66, 67,
    70, 71, 210, 211, 219, 242–3, 247,
    264 n., 266–7, 273–305
Bourdin, Pierre, *see* Seventh Set of
  Objections to the *Meditations*
Buridan's ass 201
Burman, Frans, see *Conversation with
  Burman*

Caterus (Johan de Kater), *see* First Set of
  Objections to the *Meditations*
cause:
  causal reality principle 89–109 *passim*,
    125, 183, 234 n., 259–65
  demonstrated/proved from effects
    (reasoning *a posteriori*) 138
  efficient 89, 119, 125, 234 n.
  of error 135
  final 119
  and God 89–110, 119, 183
  total 89, 119, 125
certainty 127–30, 172
Chanut, Hector-Pierre 290
chiliagon 226
chimera(s) 248 n., 260
Christian(s) 50, 139
Christianity, Aristotelian foundation
  of 55, 56
Christina, Queen of Sweden 179, 279 n.
clarity and distinctness:
  as criterion of truth 182
  and God 175
  and memory 174
  regarding ideas/notions 103–4, 105,
    112, 235, 238, 242
  regarding perception/
    understanding 112–13, 114–15,
    122, 123, 124–7, 144–5, 146, 147,
    148, 150–1, 155, 163, 174, 175, 182,
    186–7, 251–2, 254, 266, 267
Clavius, Christopher 36–7 n.
clear perceptions(s), *see* clarity and
  distinctness
Clerselier, Claude 248 n., 282, 284
Cobos, Cristóbal de los 56 n.
Cogito, the 48, 52, 120, 128, 134, 137 n.,
  169–70, 182, 204
  not a syllogism 166 n., 171
cogito ergo sum 124, 127, 166, 170, 171, 172

Coimbra commentators 47, 56
cold, idea of 103, 262–3
Collegio Romano, *see* Jesuits
colour:
  ideas of 224–5, 228
  see also secondary vs. primary qualities
Comments on a Certain Broadsheet 71, 179,
  187, 232, 289
common notion(s)/principles/ideas, *see*
  axioms
compatibilism 177, 182–3, 188–90
concurrence of God 64, 66, 68–9, 118,
  184, 187
Conversation with Burman 76, 121 n.,
  167 n., 248 n.
Copernicus, Nicolaus 44
cosmogony 115, 116
cosmos 116, 149, 150
courage 188
creation 153

darkness, conception of 94
deceiving God hypothesis 70, 78, 80–1,
  134–5
  see also evil/malicious demon
deduction 38
degrees of reality 89–90, 234–6
Democritus 33–4
demolition and knowledge 159–60, 163,
  164, 165, 175–6
demon, malicious, *see* evil/malicious
  demon
demonstration(s), deductive 47–60
Descartes, René, as 'father of modern
  philosophy' 19–27 *passim*, 29–46
  passim, 91
determinism 177, 182–3, 188–90
dialectic 49–50, 54
Digby, Sir Kenelm 44
Dinet, Pierre (Father Dinet) 280
Dioptrics, see *Optics*
Discourse on the Method 31, 39, 42, 161 n.,
  162, 163, 167, 170, 278 n., 291
dishonesty 126
disputationes 56–7, 58, 59–60
distinct perception(s), *see* clarity and
  distinctness
distinction, real, *see* real distinction
divine veracity 115
doubt:
  and demolition of knowledge 159–60,
    163, 164, 165, 175–6
  and God's existence 92

and the intellect 125, 126, 128–9, 130,
134–5, 142, 168, 253
as a means of acquiring knowledge 90,
100, 101, 112, 130, 161, 164, 165,
171, 209
and Method 94–103
and perfect knowledge 100, 101
as a quasi-religious imperative 58
rational 92
and the will 168, 169, 170
dualism, mind and body 58, 273,
274–300 *passim*

effect(s) proved/explained from causes
(reasoning *a posteriori*) 138
efficient cause 89, 119, 125, 234 n.
Elizabeth, Princess (of Bohemia) 39, 183,
184, 185, 189, 190, 278 n., 279 n.,
283 n., 299
Elzevier, Lodewijk 289 n.
empiricism vs. rationalism 43
English Channel 43
Epicurus 33–4
error(s):
cause of 135
and ideas 240
and order of reason 141–55
and sensation 267–8
and truth 236–8
and the will 174, 175
see also falsity
erudition, treatise against 39
Essays 32–33
Geometry 48, 52, 54, 163 n.
Meteorology/Meteors 52, 163 n.
Optics 52, 163 n., 213, 214, 216, 217,
218, 219, 221, 222, 232, 252 n., 256,
257 n., 258 n., 261, 265
eternal truths 116, 127, 128, 237
ethics/morals 42
Euclid 48
Eustachius a Sancto Paulo 37
evil 143, 150, 152, 153, 154
evil/malicious demon 90, 95, 124, 127,
134, 142, 164, 165, 166, 168, 170,
171, 172, 173, 174, 175
see also deceiving God hypothesis
'exist in' (phase in Descartes) 75
experiments/observations 36, 43, 52–3
glass sphere filled with water
(refraction) 52–3
with prism (refraction) 53
on refraction of light 52–3

extension, *see* body
external world/reality 112, 114, 115,
116–17, 123
correspondence with what actually
is 111–39 *passim*

faith, religious 144
and God's immutability 115
and natural reason/cognition 143
falsity 143, 145, 146, 148, 149, 151, 152,
155
and truth 236–38
see also error
'father of modern philosophy', *see*
Descartes
Faulhaber, Johannes 51
fictitious entities, *see* chimeras
Fifth Set of Objections to the *Meditations*
(by Gassendi) 74, 79 n., 81 n., 98,
187, 248 n., 279 n., 300
final cause 119
first principles 112–13, 127
First Set of Objections to the *Meditations*
(by Caterus) 234, 235
Flèche, La, *see* Jesuits
Fonseca, Pedro de 47, 56
formal reality 233–4, 259–65
formal vs. material falsity 238–48
passim
formally (vs. eminently) 234
Fourth Set of Objections to the
Meditations (by Arnauld) 65, 156–7,
173 n., 239–40, 241, 259, 262–3,
265 n., 276, 280, 281 n., 289 n.
France 111
free decision 179
free will, *see* will, the
freedom:
Descartes's doctrine of 191–206
of the mind/soul 168
of the will 236–7
Frege, Gottlob 22, 24
French:
preface to the *Principles of
Philosophy* 31, 40, 41, 42
translation of the *Meditations* 144,
147–8, 191–206
Friesland 111 n.
Froidmont, Libert 33–4, 44

Galileo Galilei 44
Gassendi, Pierre 30, 44, 149

Gassendi, Pierre (*cont.*):
  Fifth Set of Objections to the
    Meditations (by Gassendi) 74, 79 n.,
    81 n., 98, 187, 248 n., 279 n., 300
geography 38
geometric properties 251
geometrical truths 119, 130
Geometry 48, 52, 54, 163 n.
Gibieuf, Guillaume 173 n., 181
God:
  attributes of 93, 106–9, 118–19, 121
  as author of our being 138
  as author of our ideas 113
  as author of our nature 135
  as author of all things 119
  causal argument 91, 92
  causal power of 70
  and causality 89–110, 119, 183
  concurrence of 64, 66, 68–9, 118,
    184, 187
  conservation of creation of 115
  cosmological argument 92
  not a deceiver 118–19
  doubt about 93
  as efficient and total cause 119
  existence of 37, 74, 92, 128, 134, 136,
    138, 142, 143, 173
  and free actions/will 184, 190
  as giver of faculty of knowing 124, 175
  as giver of natural light 139
  giving yourself perfection(s) of 77, 106,
    107, 149–50
  hypothesis of deceiving, 70, 74, 80–1,
    134–5
  idea of 89–109 *passim*
  immutability of 115, 118
  incomprehensibility of 118
  infinitely perfect 135
  infinitude of 118
  perfect knowledge 93–109 *passim*
  as a primary substance 64, 70
  rationalistic proof of His existence 92,
    93, 100, 107–9
  not a sensible entity 210
  is truthful 135
  understanding of 106–7
  is universal cause/creator 184, 189
good(s) 143

habit 168, 175
hand (analogy with substance) 65–6
Harvey, William 44
heart, movement of 34–5

heaviness, as a real quality 260
Hegelian 26
history 39
  of ideas 19–20
  of philosophy 19–21, 22
Hobbes, Thomas 30, 149
  Third Set of Objections to the
    Meditations 165 n., 180, 190, 230 n.,
    231 n.
Hogeland, Cornelis van 39
human being(s):
  as composite entities 41, 178
  and freedom 160–76
  nature of 159–79
  and reason 159–76
  and will 159–76
human-Aristotelian approach 47
Husserl, Edmund 231
hylomorphism 282–5
Hyperaspistes 68–9, 139 n., 298
hypothesis of deceiving God 70, 74,
    80–1, 134–5
hypothetical knowledge 138, 139

idea(s):
  cause of 89–90
  clarity and distinctness 103–4, 105,
    112, 235, 238, 242
  contradictory 247
  and error 240
  of God 92–3, 99
  history of 19–20
  and images 100, 209–28 *passim*, 232
  of infinity and finitude 92, 94, 104
  materially false 93
  meanings of 'idea' 230–2
  objective reality of 89–90
  obscure/confused 241–2
  of perfection and imperfection 92, 94,
    96–103
  representation of 258–65
  resemble external objects 211–12
  of sensible objects 169
identity, numerical, of humans, *see*
  personal identity
imagination 171
  vs. sense-perception 224
impact of bodies 115–16
imperfection(s), human and perfection of
  God 77, 106, 107, 149–50
Impressionism (analogy with history of
  ideas/philosophy) 20
impressions, and memory 174

independence:
 causal 69
 object 69
indifference:
 and freedom 181–2, 189–90, 193–6
 Jesuits and 'indifference' 181, 182,
  189, 195, 196
 liberty of 126
infinite:
 and God 97
 incomprehensibility of 104
 vs. indefinite/indeterminate 97
innateness of mathematical truths
  117–18
intellect:
 and doubt 125, 126, 128–9, 130,
  134–5, 142, 168, 253
 see also understanding
interaction between the body and the
  soul/mind, see mind, and body
intuition 38, 117, 132–3
 definition of 'intuition' 115
 intuitus 115

Jesuits (Society of Jesus) 54
 colleges: La Flèche 23, 29, 59, 285;
  Collegio Romano 56
 as commentators on Aristotle 56, 60
 and 'indifference' 181, 182, 189, 195,
  196
Jews 50

Kantian synthesis 44
knowledge:
 absolute 112, 113, 114, 117, 120, 127,
  128, 136, 137, 139
 demolition of 159–60, 163, 164, 165,
  175–6
 doubt as a means of acquiring 90, 100,
  101, 112, 130, 161, 164, 165, 171,
  209
 hypothetical 138, 139
 perfect 94–6, 100, 101, 103, 106
 rationalistic conception of 92
 'sources' of 164

Lambert of Auxerre 50
language(s) 32
 universal 50–1
Lateran Council 55, 56
laws of nature 116, 188
Leibniz, Gottfried Wilhelm 30, 44, 84, 274
 and Descartes's concept of
  substance 73

*New Essays concerning Human
 Understanding* 79 n.
libertarianism 177, 182–3, 188–90
liberty of indifference 126
 see also indifference
light 224
 natural, see natural light
 refraction of 52–3
 theory of 58
Light, Treatise on, see *World, The*
Locke, John 30, 84 n., 244
logical truths 119, 122–3, 125, 130, 139
Loyola, Ignatius of 57
Lull, Raymond 50, 51, 54
lumen naturale, see natural light
Luynes, duc de 148, 191, 197
 see also French translation of the
  Meditations

Malebranche, Nicolas 220
malicious demon, see evil/malicious
 demon
man 273–305
Man, Treatise on, see *Treatise on Man*
Manichaean doctrine 150, 153
Mas, Diego 56 n.
'material falsity' of ideas 104, 235, 236,
  237, 238–48
mathematics, eternal truths 111, 117–18
matter and motion 116
maxims, see axioms
measure, as primitive notion 116
mechanical explanation(s):
 of motion in material things 211
 of nature 161
medicine 41
Meditations on First Philosophy:
 dedication to the Sorbonne 151
 French translation of 144, 147–8,
  191–206
 Synopsis of 81, 82, 141–55, 166, 168,
  253
memory:
 and clear and distinct perceptions 174
 impressions of 174
Mersenne, Marin:
 letter(s) to 37, 51, 111, 115, 117–20,
  122, 125, 130, 141, 181 n.
 Second Set of Objections to the
  Meditations 65 n., 70, 75, 77, 78, 85–
  6, 124, 127, 133, 139, 144, 145 n.,
  150 n., 154, 166, 179, 186, 230 n.,
  233, 235, 286

Mersenne, Marin (*cont.*):
  Sixth Set of Objections to the
    Meditations 121 n., 181, 182, 185,
    186, 189, 216, 243, 279 n., 286
Mesland, Denis 67, 82, 126 n., 173 n.,
    178, 180, 181, 182, 185, 193–4, 195,
    201, 202, 203, 205, 282
metaphysics, deductive demonstration
    in 47–60
meteorology 35
Meteorology/Meteors 52, 163 n.
Method of Doubt 94–103
mind(s):
  autonomy of 185
  and body (dualism) 58, 273, 274,
    275–300 *passim*
  and death of body 85–6
  detached from the body 63
  have no parts 82–3
  immortality of 85–6
  joined to the body 63, 178
  and knowledge 118, 119
  nature of 70, 71
  pure and attentive 115
  really distinct from body 266
  not a sensible entity 210
  union with the body 65, 66, 67, 70, 71,
    210, 211, 219, 242–3, 247, 264 n.,
    266–7, 273–305
  and the will 185–6
  see also soul(s)
Monde, Le, see *World, The*
Montaigne, Michel de 22
Morin, Jean-Baptiste 32–3, 116–17
motion:
  definition of 'motion' 116
  conception of 94
  and matter 116
  as simple nature 122
  and sound 223, 224
Muslims 50

natural light 93, 112, 113, 114–15, 122,
    124–7, 129–32, 134, 135, 136, 139,
    146, 150, 151, 152, 153
  contrasted with intellect 125
  vs. faith 143
natural philosophy 15, 47–60, 120,
    139 n., 153
nature:
  intuitions of 188
  principle/laws of nature 116, 188
natures, *see* simple natures

necessary truths 119–20, 125, 139
Nietzche, Friedrich 21, 23
Nifo, Agostino 55
non-sciences 42
nothingness lacks attributes 71–2
number 97, 98, 99, 108
  as a primitive notion 116

Objections and Replies, *see* First, Second,
    . . ., Seventh Set of Objections
objective reality 89–90, 103–4, 219–20,
    232–4, 235, 239, 259–65
  principle of 259–65
observation(s)/experiment(s) 58
ontology 177
Optics 52, 163 n., 213, 214, 216, 217,
    218, 219, 221, 222, 232, 252 n., 256,
    257 n., 258 n., 261, 265
Oratory 181
order:
  of reason 52, 58, 141–55
  of subject-matter vs. reasoning 52,
    58

Padua, University of 55
pain, sensation/feeling of 223 n., 224–5
Panthéon 22
Pappus of Alexandria 49
Paris 22, 84 n.
passions 41, 179
  explanation of 188
  their seat 179
  and the will 185
Passions of the Soul 32, 41, 162 n., 178,
    179, 180, 184, 185, 186, 187, 188,
    279 n.
passivity and activity 160, 161, 167, 168,
    169, 170, 174, 175, 186
Peirce, Charles Sanders 22
per se 163, 166, 171
  and *per aliud* 163
perception(s):
  as an action or passion 187–8
  clarity and distinctness of 112–13,
    114–15, 122, 123, 124–7, 144–5, 146,
    147, 148, 150–1, 155, 163, 174, 175,
    182, 186–7, 251–2, 254, 266, 267
  and the will 185–6
perfect knowledge:
  absolute 95–6, 98, 104
  attributive 95–6, 108
  and material falsity 103–6
  and the Method of Doubt 94–103

perfection(s):
  as degrees of reality 95
  epistemic 96
  four senses of 95
  of God, *see* God, attributes of
  of humans, 96, 175
  knowledge of 95
  plural sense 95
personal identity 84
Peter of Spain 50
physical things themselves 210
piece of wax 67, 79 n., 91, 224, 242
Plato 31, 38, 277
  Cratylus 275
  Theatetus 275
  Timaeus 275
Platonic 55, 247
  dualism 273–300 *passim*
  perfection 99
Platonism:
  Extreme 274, 292–300
  Moderate 273, 274, 275–7
  Scholastic 274, 277–92
Plempius (Vopiscus Fortunatus Plemp) 33
Plotinus 154
poetry 42
Pomponazzi, Pietro 55
preconceived opinions 168
'primary' vs. 'secondary'
  qualities 244, 251–72
primitive notions/ideas, number as 116
principle(s):
  causal reality principle 89–109 *passim*,
    125, 183, 234 n., 259–65
  first 112–13, 127
  of nature 116, 188
Principles of Philosophy:
  French version of 31
  Part I 63–75
  as textbook 57
problem-solving 53
psychology:
  human 123, 132–3
  of judgement 148
  of knowledge 128
Pythagoras 33

quality/qualities 64, 66, 68
  'primary' vs. 'secondary' 244,
    251–72

rainbow 52–3
ratio 124

rationalism vs. empiricism 43
rationalistic:
  conception of knowledge 92
  proof of God's existence 92, 93, 100,
    107–9
real distinction:
  between thinking and extended
    substances 65, 161
  between two substances 64–5
reality:
  causal principle 89–109 *passim*, 125,
    183, 234 n., 259–65
  degrees of 89–90, 93, 94
  eminent 104, 105
  formal 89–90, 104, 105
  objective 89–90, 103–4, 219–20,
    232–4, 235, 239, 259–65
reason:
  as basis for science 38
  order of 141–55
  true use of 91, 170
refraction of light 53
Regius (Henry le Roy) 99, 100, 128, 136,
    137 n., 160, 170, 276, 277, 278, 280,
    281, 282, 283, 284–5, 295, 296, 298
religion 153
  and doubt 58
remembering certainties 129
res cogitans 74, 161–2, 170, 171, 172, 173,
    175
res extensa 161–2, 224, 226 n.
'resemblance' 209–28, 236–7
rest, conception of 94
rhetoric 42
Rosicrucianism 51, 60
Rousseau, Jean-Jacques 22
rule, general 131–2, 133–4, 135
*Rules for the Direction of our Native
  Intelligence* 38, 49, 50, 114–15, 122,
    161 n., 163 n., 205, 275

scepticism 58, 91, 125–6, 127, 131, 133,
    164
  see also doubt
scholastic philosophy 240
  and intentional forms 232
  and perception 253, 255
  and reality 89
  and substance 64
  and the will 180
science(s) 159, 174, 251–2, 253, 267
  Baconian idea of 41
  and history 38

science(s) (*cont.*):
and human benefit 41
of all sciences (rhetoric) 54
structure of 40–1
scientia 136, 137
derivation of '*scientia*' 136 n.
search after truth 265–71
Search for Truth 38, 162 n.
Second Set of Objections to the
Meditations (by Mersenne) 65 n., 70,
75, 77, 78, 85–6, 124, 127, 133, 139,
144, 145 n., 150 n., 154, 166, 179,
186, 230 n., 233, 235, 286
'secondary' vs. 'primary'
qualities 244, 251–72
semel in vita 163
sensation:
as confused perceptions 210–11,
224–6
and error 267–8
and images 219, 222
protect the mind-body union 267
and representation in the *Optics* 255–8
senses, uncertainity of 209–10
sensory awareness/sense-perception 175
confused/opaque 238–48
as a faculty of the soul/mind 211
as a mode of thinking
and passivity of intellect 167, 168, 169,
170, 174, 175, 186
Seventh Set of Objections to the
Meditations (by Bourdin) 164
simple natures/notions 122–3, 260
sin 143, 144, 152, 153
Sixth Set of Objections to the *Meditations*
(compiled by Mersenne) 121 n.,
181, 182, 185, 186, 189, 216, 243,
279 n., 286
Society of Jesus, *see* Jesuits
Sorbonne, dedication to *Meditations*
to 151
soul(s):
activity and passivity of 160, 161, 167,
168, 169, 170, 174, 175, 186
and body (dualism) 58, 273, 274,
275–300 passim
complete/incomplete 65
immortality of 55, 56
and the understanding 160–1
union with the body 65, 66, 67, 70, 71,
210, 211, 219, 242–3, 247, 264 n.,
266–7, 273–305
and the will 160–1

see also mind(s)
sound, as vibration of air 223, 224
space 97, 99, 100, 101, 102, 108
Spinoza, Benedictus de (Baruch) 30,
84 n., 243
Ethics 236, 237
Principles of Cartesian Philosophy 248 n.
spontaneity, and freedom 180–1, 182,
188–90
Stoicism 41
stone, as substance 65, 77
Suárez, Francisco 37, 56, 145, 240, 285
substance:
and accidents 70–1
the body as a 64
concept of 63–87
destruction of 84–6
distinction between 181
meaning of 'substance' 67–9
and mode(s) 70–1
nature and essence 70–1
the soul as a 65
substantial union of the mind/soul and
the body, *see* union of the soul/mind
and the body
sun, idea of 91–2, 226 n., 233, 237, 261
syllogism 50
and the Cogito 166 n., 171
Synopsis of the *Meditations* 81, 82,
141–55, 166, 168, 253

theodicy 143, 144, 148, 149, 150, 151,
152, 153, 154
theology 139, 149, 153, 154
thing, concept of 66
thinking thing/substance/nature
Third Set of Objections to the *Meditations*
(by Hobbes) 165 n., 180, 190,
230 n., 231 n.
time 102, 108, 122, 128, 274
discontinuity of 117
Toletus (Francisco Toledo) 285
total cause 89, 119, 125
Treatise on Light or *The World*, 111,
115–20, 138, 222, 223, 232 n.
Treatise on Man 252 n., 275, 299,
300
tree, analogy with 42
triangle, idea/conception of 130, 131,
132, 134
Trismegistus, Hermes 51
true philosophy 51
truth 143

assent, commanded by 124–6, 127–8, 129–30, 131, 144 n., 160, 182, 186–7, 200
criterion of 114, 182
and error 141–55
eternal 116, 127, 128, 237
and falsity 236–8
geometrical 119, 130
logical 119, 122–3, 125, 130, 139
mathematical 119–20, 125, 127, 128, 130, 139, 267
necessary 119–20, 125, 139
and the order of reason 141–55
rules of 125, 130
and self-evidence 124

understanding:
clarity and distinctness 112–13, 114–15, 122, 123, 124–7, 144–5, 146, 147, 148, 150–1, 155, 163, 174, 175, 182, 186–7, 251–2, 254, 266, 267
as the passivity of the mind/soul 160, 161, 167, 168, 169, 170, 174, 175, 186
union of the soul/mind and the body 65, 66, 67, 70, 71, 210, 211, 219, 242–3, 247, 264 n., 266–7, 273–305
United Provinces 111
universe 67
Utrecht:
controversy 291
University of 277

vacuum 34
impossibility of 84–5
Valéry, Paul 172 n.

vapours 35
Vatier, Antoine 57
veil-of-perception theory 213, 214, 215, 216, 218, 219, 220, 227–8
'virtual knowledge' 137, 138, 139
void, *see* vacuum
volition:
as an action/activity of the soul/mind 160, 161, 169, 170, 174, 175, 186
and cause 184–5, 188–9
two types of, *see* will, the
volo ergo sum 170
voluntariness, and freedom 180

wax, piece of 67, 79 n., 91, 224, 242
weight as primitive notion 116
White, Thomas 44
will, the:
and activity 160, 161, 167, 170, 174, 175, 186
and doubt 168, 169, 170
and error 174, 175
freedom of 236–7
infinity of 148
and the intellect/understanding 236–7
willing:
as the activity of the mind/soul 160, 161, 169, 170, 174, 175, 186
and understanding 124
world:
correspondence with what actually is 111–39 *passim*
external 112, 114, 115, 116–17, 123
World, The or *Treatise on Light* 111, 115–20, 138, 222, 223, 232 n.

Zúñiga, Diego 56 n.

Printed in the United Kingdom
by Lightning Source UK Ltd.
110032UKS00001B/18